TECHNOLOGICAL INNOVATION AND SUSTAINABILITY FOR BUSINESS COMPETITIVE ADVANTAGE

Series Editors: Allam Hamdan and Reem Khamis

Innovation and sustainability are broad terms that describe many interdisciplinary sciences—business success and competitiveness may not be separated from social and cultural aspects that interfere with any future development prospects. Research in across areas would provide a better understanding of international experiences, bridging the gap between developing and developed nations. This series promotes new visions for business research prospects that work in favor of innovation and sustainability in terms of governance, environment, and ethics.

Technological Innovation and Sustainability for Business Competitive Advantage highlights business problems faced by institutions in a scientific way, finding possible practical solutions. Contributing to setting and improving business theories and practices and encouraging scientific research in technological innovation and sustainability, volumes activate dialog between academics, practitioners, and individuals and provide recommendations to improve institutions.

Previous Volumes

Technological Innovations for Business, Education and Sustainability
Edited by Allam Hamdan

Technological Horizons: Technological Skills and Knowledge for Practitioners within Business Environment
Edited by Hashem Alshurafat and Claire Beattie

Technological Horizons: Insights for Accounting, Auditing and Internal Control in Emerging Markets
Edited by Hashem Alshurafat and Claire Beattie

From Digital Disruption to Dominance: Leveraging FinTech Applications for Sustainable Growth
Edited by Maha Shehadeh and Khaled Hussainey

The Role of Artificial Intelligence Applications in Business
Edited by Ra'ed Masa'deh

Ethical Standards for Technological and Business Education Sustainability
Edited by Esra AlDhaen, David Gallear, Vishanth Weerakkody, and Weifeng Chen

Digital Dialogues

Sustainability in Light of Governance and Artificial Intelligence Applications
Edited by Bahaa Subhi Awwad

Comprehensive Insights in Technological Sustainability, Education and Business
Edited by Allam Hamdan

Can Peace Journalism Flourish or Fade in Digital Media? Evidence from the Middle East
Edited by Zainab Abdul-Nabi

How Social Media Shapes Culture and Identity Among Youth: Empirical Insights from the Gulf Region
Edited by Zainab Abdul-Nabi and Mohamed Alawainati

Innovative Horizons: Insights for Technology, Sustainability and Education in the Digital Era
Edited by Hashem Alshurafat

Forthcoming Volumes

The Tech-Driven Future: Navigating Sustainability in the Digital Age
Edited by Jaheer Muthkar K.P., Berenika Byczek, Felix Claudio Julca-Guerrero, and Roger Pedro Norabuena-Figueroa

AI in Accounting: Revolutionizing the Profession. Leveraging Artificial Intelligence to Transform Accounting Practices
Edited by Hala Zaidan, Yaser Allozi, and Ra'ed Masa'deh

How ESG Drives Green Innovation and Growth: Inventing tomorrow
Edited by Husam Ananzeh

Intelligent Enterprise: The Fusion of Business Administration and Artificial Intelligence
By Ahmad Arieqat

Empowering Businesses Through Innovation, Education, and Sustainability – Volume 1
Edited by Allam Hamdan and Saad Laraqui

Empowering Businesses Through Innovation, Education, and Sustainability – Volume 2
Edited by Allam Hamdan and Saad Laraqui

Digital Dialogues: Exploring Media, Identity, and Society in the Arab World

EDITED BY

IMAD ASSALI
Ahlia University, Bahrain

AND

ABDULSADEK HASSAN
Ahlia University, Bahrain

emerald PUBLISHING

United Kingdom – North America – Japan – India – Malaysia – China

Emerald Publishing Limited
Emerald Publishing, Floor 5, Northspring, 21-23 Wellington Street, Leeds LS1 4DL

First edition 2026

British Library Cataloguing in Publication Data
A catalogue record for this book is available from the British Library

ISBN: 978-1-83708-687-0 (Print)
ISBN: 978-1-83708-686-3 (Online)
ISBN: 978-1-83708-688-7 (Epub)

Printed and bound by CPI Group (UK) Ltd, Croydon, CR0 4YY

Contents

About the Contributors

Maha Hameed Alanezi, Bahraini, is a researcher in the field of media and communication technology. She is interested in technological and smart applications and programs. She has published several research papers in various fields and works as a Learning Resources Specialist at the Ministry of Education in the Kingdom of Bahrain. She holds a Bachelor's degree in Computer Science and a Master's degree in Information Technology and Computer Science.

Maznah Khalifa Aldhahrani is an accomplished Assistant Director with over 15 years of expertise in educational leadership. Specializing in fostering stimulating learning environments and enhancing the performance of both teachers and students, she possesses strong skills in academic supervision, strategic educational planning, and human resource management. Her professional focus is on building successful, inspiring educational settings through effective student support, parental engagement, and community partnerships. Currently, she is furthering her academic credentials as a Doctorate candidate in Digital Media at Ahlia University, complementing her Master's in Human Resources and advanced diplomas in School Leadership and Social Counseling, underscoring her commitment to educational innovation and excellence.

Hessa Mahmoud Al-Dowei is a dynamic and versatile media professional with foundational experience gained at Bahrain's Information Affairs Authority. Through roles across News, Television, Radio, and Graphics departments, she has developed a comprehensive understanding of media production—from writing and editing news content to supporting broadcast and visual design. Skilled in research, communication, and teamwork, Hessa has contributed to national media projects, honing her ability to deliver timely and engaging content. Passionate about journalism and digital storytelling, she brings creativity, technical proficiency, and a strong editorial sense to every project, positioning her as an emerging voice ready to shape the future of media in Bahrain.

Abdullah Ahmed Aljighaiman is an accomplished professional in strategic communication, with diverse experience across PR, event management, and client strategy. Starting his career in the nonprofit sector, he progressed to key leadership roles at TRACCS, quickly proving his ability to manage high-profile projects and accounts. His academic credentials include a Master's in Strategic Communication (with distinction) and extensive training in areas like crisis communication, digital marketing, and leadership. He has worked on major initiatives, including strategic plans for entities such as Ministry of Tourism, PIF, Aramco and Riyadh Development Company. Abdullah played a pivotal role in organizing notable events like the Arab-Chinese Business Conference, LEAP Summit, and others under esteemed national entities. He has also led impactful PR campaigns, contributed to nonprofit fundraising goals, and received recognition for his communication excellence. His combination of academic knowledge, professional training, and hands-on expertise makes him a leader in his field.

Sh. Maryam Mubarak Alkhalifa is a PhD student in Digital Media and Communication Technology, Faculty of Arts and Sciences, Ahlia University, Manama, Bahrain.

Seeroz Almahadeen is a Bahraini researcher, who holds a Bachelor's degree in Media and Graphic Design from the University of Bahrain, and a Master's degree in International Media and Public strategy from the same university. He has worked in various fields of media such as digital design, media production, and PR since 2006, and currently works in the PR Department at the University of Bahrain. He is currently preparing for a PhD in Digital Media from Ahlia University in the Kingdom of Bahrain.

Abduljalil Mohsen AlMahari is a Bahraini Media and Communication Specialist and a PhD candidate in Digital Media and Communication Technology at Ahlia University. He holds a Master's degree in Media and PR from Ahlia University (2011) and has completed professional training in digital skills, ICT, information security, and journalism, including programs at BIBF (2024) and Fortinet Mon Consultancy, Kuwait (2022). AlMahari has extensive experience as a Media Specialist in PR at the Ministry of Education and as a journalist with The World Press Publishing Institution and *Al Ayam* newspaper. He has earned multiple certifications in digital literacy, web applications, and technology-enhanced teaching, demonstrating expertise in media management, digital communication, journalism, and ICT integration. His work emphasizes professional development, educational technology, and effective use of digital platforms in communication.

Fatema Waleed Al.Merbati is an Assistant Principal at a secondary school in the Kingdom of Bahrain. She holds a Bachelor's degree in Physical Education, along with a Higher Diploma in School Leadership, and a Master's degree in Human Resource Management. With over 18 years of experience in education and leadership, she is well-equipped to handle the various challenges that arise in the educational process. She is interested in integrating research related to technology and digital media into the educational process, which helps improve the learning experience for female students and enhances their skills. She strives to incorporate innovation in education, which strengthens students' critical thinking and problem-solving abilities. Additionally, she places great importance on providing an inclusive learning environment that fosters creativity and collaboration among students to meet their needs.

Afaf Ayesh Ali Al-Muhaysin is an accomplished Senior Announcer with the Saudi Broadcasting Authority and a pioneering media professional. With a multifaceted career spanning television, radio, and digital production, she excels as a presenter, program developer, and drama performer. Currently advancing her expertise as a Doctoral researcher in Digital Media, her work is recognized with prestigious accolades, including the Saudi Broadcasting Authority's Content Development Award and a Gold Medal at the Gulf Radio and Television Festival. Afaf seamlessly blends her on-air charisma with strategic event management and institutional training, positioning her as a dynamic leader shaping the future of broadcasting in the Kingdom and beyond.

Kaltham Alnamlaiti is a dedicated Senior Specialized Nursing Specialist at Bahrain's Government hospitals and a forward-thinking Doctoral candidate in Digital Media & Communication Technology at Ahlia University. She brings a unique, interdisciplinary perspective to her research, leveraging over a decade of clinical experience from her frontline role at the Military Hospital, Ministry of Health and recently at Government hospitals. She is having interest in health media and communication plus digital health and looking forward to learning about artificial intelligence uses in health sector. This practical expertise is complemented by a Master's in Human Resource Management from DePaul University. Kaltham is poised to innovatively bridge healthcare, strategic communication, and digital technology, aiming to enhance public health outcomes and redefine patient and community engagement through modern media channels.

Mohamed Alqahtani is Manager of Corporate Communications and PR at Southern Province Cement Company. He specializes in PR, media relations, and strategic communication, with extensive experience enhancing organizational reputation and strengthening stakeholder engagement. He has a strong ability to craft compelling narratives, handle crisis communication effectively, and build and maintain key relationships. He holds a master's degree in strategic communication and has a solid academic background in mass communication. Mohamed is a collaborative leader with excellent team management skills and is committed to continuous learning and staying current with industry trends. He also holds professional certifications in emotional intelligence, research, and quality management.

Mohammed Muflih Mohammad AlQahtani is a Strategic Internal Communication and PR leader with over 12 years of experience shaping corporate identity and fostering positive organizational culture. As a Manager of Corporate Communications and PR at Southern Province Cement Company, he builds departments from the ground up, designs impactful internal strategies, and forges strategic partnerships. A PhD researcher in Digital Media, he is also an active opinion columnist and lecturer. Recognized with national CSR awards, Mohammed has launched large-scale sustainability initiatives like "The Green Stamp" and delivered significant cost savings by developing internal frameworks, showcasing his blend of strategic vision and practical execution.

champion digital transformation, shape strategic communication, and develop next-generation storytelling models, positioning her at the forefront of the evolving media landscape in Bahrain and beyond.

Mona Mohamed Daabis is a Bahraini professional currently serving as the Head of the Business Process Reengineering Group at the Ministry of Finance and National Economy. She has over 16 years of experience in the government sector, specializing in Mass Communication and Business Administration. Mona is currently pursuing a PhD in Digital Media and Communication Technology at Ahlia University, Bahrain. She holds a Master's degree in Media with Excellent First-Class Honors from the University of Bahrain, as well as a Bachelor's degree in PR and Business Administration from the University of Bahrain.

Hani Hamza Ali Ebrahim is a PhD student in Digital Media and Communication Technology at Ahlia University. He holds a professional diploma in accounting from the Association of Accounting Technicians (2009), a Bachelor of Business Administration in Systems from the Arab Open University (2016), and an MBA with a GPA of 3.62 (2021). Hani has participated in numerous seminars, exhibitions, and conferences, including GCC entrepreneurship and customer service excellence programs, and served as the President of the Student Council at the Arab Open University. Professionally, he has experience in accounting, foreign exchange trading, business training, and leadership. He has held roles such as the team leader at the Central Information Authority, the Chair of the Innovation Conferences Organization Company, the General Manager at Brain Master Training Center (2018–2023), and currently serves as the Director of an accounting firm. His expertise encompasses digital media, business management, and leadership development.

Nadeya Mohamed Mahmood Ghuloom Ali is a distinguished Social Specialist at the Royal Humanitarian Foundation and a PhD candidate in Digital Media and Communication Technology at Ahlia University, Bahrain. With 25 years of exemplary service in humanitarian and social work, she is a highly dedicated professional and researcher. Her academic foundation includes a Bachelor's in Social Work from University of Bahrain, followed by a Master's in Media and PR from Ahlia University. Her pivotal Master's thesis: "The Mental Image of the Bahraini Personality in Local Television Drama and Its Role in Shaping Youth Attitudes." A recipient of "The Prince Salman bin Hamad Medal for Medical Merit," she secured four research publication acceptances in prestigious international journals in December 2024. Her research explores virtual reality's impact on children's behavioral disorders and digital media's role in risk awareness. She holds international certifications in leadership, creative problem-solving, and professional ethics within Bahrain.

Layla Abdarasool Hussain is a Specialist at the Ministry of Education, Bachelor of Physical Education from the University of Bahrain, Master of Media and PR from Ahlia University, and a PhD student at Ahlia University in the Kingdom of Bahrain.

Mohamed Naser Louri, currently serving as the Head of the Councils Affairs Department at the Ministry of Finance and National Economy, has been a weekly columnist for *Al-Watan* newspaper since 2005 and is the author of six published books. He also holds the position of the Vice President of the Bahrain HistoricaL & Archeological Society, overseeing the association's cultural season, in addition to managing the editorial direction of "Dilmun" refereed magazine. This publication is considered a cultural and literary reference, through which he strives to enhance scientific research on the history of Bahrain and the region. His professional biography weaves together leadership in the governmental sector with active participation in cultural and literary life, underscoring his prominent role in preserving heritage and fostering cultural and scholarly dialogue.

Menna Massod is a seasoned media professional and a specialized broadcaster, admired for her exceptional skills in crafting dialogues and preparing interviews. Her expertise in television presentation and hosting has captivated audiences and solidified her reputation in the field. Currently pursuing a PhD in Digital Media at Ahlia University starting January 2024, Menna is committed to achieving innovation and excellence in her academic and professional endeavors. She serves as the Head of the Media Committee at the Arab Center for Electronic Media in Bahrain, an organization affiliated with the Arab League. With a Master's in Quality Management from the Royal College of Surgeons in Ireland and a Certificate in English for Journalism Professionals from the US Embassy, she is also an active member of the Bahrain Management Society and Rotary Seef Bahrain. Menna's vision extends beyond her career, encompassing active participation in social and volunteer activities to make a positive societal impact. Her technical skills include public speaking, television presentation, and mastering the art of being an MC.

Menatalla Massod is a dynamic media professional and a doctoral researcher specializing in Digital Media at Ahlia University. With a proven track record in television presentation and PR, she excels at crafting compelling dialogues and preparing impactful interviews. As a driven communications professional with extensive expertise in media strategy, she was awarded a Medal of Excellence in recognition of her contributions to the field. Menatalla leverages her practical experience and academic research to innovate within the media landscape. Committed to societal impact, she actively contributes to her community through volunteer work with organizations like Rotary Seef Bahrain, driven by a vision to merge media excellence with positive social influence.

Ghazi Abdul Mohsen Ali is a Seasoned Media and Communication Specialist with a distinguished career spanning parliamentary affairs, PR, and broadcasting. Currently a Doctoral researcher in Digital Media, he leverages his extensive on-air experience as a former newsreader and program host with strategic expertise gained from key roles at Bahrain's Council of Representatives. Ghazi has led community communication initiatives and managed media relations for over a decade, complemented by international training and participation in global parliamentary conferences. A skilled lecturer in parliamentary and economic media, he uniquely bridges traditional media, strategic communication, and digital innovation to shape public discourse and advance the media landscape.

Nadia Ismail Moosa, is public figure, media and PR advisor in social media content with more than 20 years' experience in project management, quality coordinator, auditor, certified trainer, business continuity management systems coordinator and digital marketing. She holds a PhD in Digital Media and Communication Technology, with a master's degree in business administration from Ahlia University, and international master's in business sustainability from Bradford University in UK, Nadia's an accomplished writer and researcher in the fields of digital economy, artificial intelligence, innovation, and sustainability, publishing in both local and international newspapers and online platform. She awards medal of International Woman 2024 from the Global Universal Innovation (GOIDI), and one of the parliament election candidates in 2022. She's a board member in Bahrain Intellectual Property Society and member in The Arab Union for the Protection of Intellectual Property Rights with participation in social and volunteer in national and international activities.

Abdulrahman Seyadi is a Bahraini Media and PR Specialist with expertise in digital communication, traffic awareness, and strategic PR. He holds a Master's degree in Media and PR and is a PhD candidate in Digital Media and Communication Technology at Ahlia University. Seyadi has served in key government roles, including the Head of the Traffic Training Section at the General Directorate of Traffic, Ministry of Interior, contributing to Bahrain's traffic awareness curriculum and earning a Gold Stevie Award in 2021. He has also worked with the Ministry of Justice and Ministry of Education. A published researcher and international conference presenter, Seyadi has completed certifications in leadership, social media marketing, and innovation. His core skills—strategic communication, social media management, and public engagement—establish him as an expert in media, PR, and digital communication.

Zainab Mohsen Zain Aldeen is an accomplished economist with more than 13 years of in quality improvement and finance. She has worked as a Senior Economist, an Internal Auditor, and a Quality Coordinator, playing a focal role in economic analysis, budgeting, and project coordination. Zainab holds a PhD degree in Executive Management from Nevada University, awarded in January 2023, and a Master's degree in Business Administration. Her scholarly contributions include several publications focusing on women's empowerment, the impacts of artificial intelligence in education, and risk management practices. She is dedicated to enhancing women's participation in governance and public life. In addition to her professional accomplishments, Zainab is passionate about community engagement and lifelong learning. She is committed to fostering economic growth in Bahrain and empowering others through research and education which made her a respected leader and advocate in her field, inspiring those around her to strive for excellence.

Chapter 1

Cultural Identity Frameworks in Radio Bahrain Traditional and Digital Broadcasting: Comparative Study

Ghazi Abdul Mohsen Ali

Independent Researcher, Bahrain

Abstract

This study aims to identify the key topics covered by cultural programs on Radio Bahrain, both in traditional and digital broadcasting formats. It also aims to highlight the elements of cultural identity reflected in these radio programs from 1990 to 2024, including aspects such as language, traditional and folk arts, music, and more.

The study also emphasizes the role of both traditional and digital broadcasting in shaping the cultural identity of listeners across different age groups. Undoubtedly, the youth demographic stands at the forefront of cultural content creators' intellectual focus, as it has a significant impact on the young radio audience.

Another key objective of this study is to examine the nature of audience participating in those programs and their scientific and cultural classification, and the researcher has taken in this study for himself a line aimed at clarifying the extent of the commitment of Radio Bahrain to emphasize the producers and presenters of cultural programs to adopt the classical Arabic language during the dialogues they conduct within their programs, especially with the keenness of the Constitution of the Kingdom of Bahrain in its second article to indicate the official language of the country, where that article clarified that (the religion of the state is the Islam and Islamic Sharia is major source for legislation and its official language is Arabic) and whether the presenters and producers of programs adopted a culture of opinion and other opinion and promoted culture of democracy among the audience of radio listeners in Bahrain.

Digital Dialogues, 1–9

Published under exclusive licence by Emerald Publishing Limited
doi:10.1108/978-1-83708-686-320261001

where shared history is the cornerstone of identity construction (Anderson, 1983).

- *Religious framework:* relates to religion and spiritual beliefs that influence values and behaviors in society (Geertz, 1973).
- *Political framework:* includes policies and laws that regulate cultural life, such as official language and education (Huntington, 1996).
- *Economic framework:* focuses on the role of economic resources and modes of production in shaping cultural identities (Inglehart & Baker, 2000).

Types of Cultural Identity

Cultural identity is of many types according to the different frameworks that define its features. The types include the following:

- *Individual identity:* It expresses the cultural specificity of each individual based on his or her personal experience (Hofstede, 2011).
- *Collective identity:* It refers to belonging to a social group such as a family or tribe, where the common values of these groups are determined (Triandis, 1995).
- *National identity:* It is linked to belonging to the homeland through language, tradition, and shared history (Smith, 2000).
- *Ethnic identity:* It refers to belonging to an ethnic group that shares cultural or ethnic characteristics, such as language or religion (Anderson, 1983).
- *Religious identity:* It is associated with religious beliefs and values that determine the behaviors of individuals and groups (Geertz, 1973).
- *Global identity:* It arises as a result of globalization and cultural interaction between peoples, forming common values and cultures (Huntington, 1996).
- *Professional identity:* It relates to an individual's belonging to a particular profession and its influence on shaping their values and behaviors (Inglehart & Baker, 2000).

Previous Studies

- Al-Qarni (2020) explored the role of the Arabic language in preserving cultural identity. The research focused on the significance of language in general, and Arabic in particular, in safeguarding cultural heritage. Using an analytical approach, Al-Qarni examined the relationship between language and culture, emphasizing that language plays a crucial role in shaping civilizations, preserving their history, and maintaining knowledge. He described language as a twin of culture, as it aids in its preservation and transmission over time. Al-Qarni also referenced Ibn Khaldun's definition of language and explored it idiomatically, incorporating Dr. Jaber Asfour's definition, which views language as "the individual's sense of himself, his individuality, and his ability to preserve his integration, values, behaviors, and ideas across different contexts." Cultural identity, as defined by Al-Qarni, is "what provides people with a sense of belonging, security, communication, and interaction, equipping them with common values and aspirations and enabling them to predict the behavior of others... It is the final refuge to which nations, peoples, and communities turn in times of crisis." Al-Qarni outlined the functions of language, including its personal, moral, national, exploratory, imaginative, media, economic, historical, and symbolic functions. He also analyzed the components of identity, which include religious beliefs, mother tongue, values, and historical and urban heritage. Furthermore, Al-Qarni discussed the importance of the Arabic language in preserving Islamic heritage and highlighted several challenges to its preservation, including translation issues, colonialism, the rise of colloquialism, foreign education, and globalization.

- In her 2020 study, Bacchus explained that community radio is a powerful tool for communication and social change, yet it has struggled to create a platform for addressing "voice poverty" among marginalized groups due to structural and legislative constraints. However, community radio has proven effective in enhancing self-confidence and fostering a sense of identity, particularly among female listeners. Despite the study's limited geographical scope, the findings highlight significant potential for future research on the impact of community radio on identity. The study's main conclusion was that community radio has played a key role in empowering women, providing them with a platform to express their identities within the community.
- The third study, conducted by Saida and Prakashi (2021), examines the role of local radio stations in addressing societal problems, particularly issues such as unemployment and illegal immigration. The researchers explored how radio has provided solutions to these challenges and concluded that radio plays an essential role in raising awareness of these issues. Most participants in the study indicated that the radio is a vital part of society. The researchers based their study on the premise that "local radio can contribute to solving social problems." This research is significant because, despite the rise of other media, radio remains the most accessible form of communication for many people and thus has a crucial role in addressing social issues. The study applied developmental theory, which focuses on the media's role in the development of third-world countries, as well as functional theory, uses and gratification theory, and media dependency theory. The study involved a sample of 50 participants, consisting of 30 males and 20 females, using a questionnaire method. The results showed that 40% of respondents believe the radio station helped establish social values, 70% felt it contributed to reducing illegal immigration, and 72% believed it played a role in mitigating unemployment. The study also found that the morning broadcast period was the most popular among listeners.
- In his study, Akkad (2021) highlights the interest of Saudi youth in the context of the research, focusing on their importance as the future of the nation and the extent to which they are influenced by digital broadcasts. The study also examined the relationship between university students' reliance on digital broadcasts and their awareness of the social values targeted at them. It explored how these broadcasts impact the social values that prevail in their society.

- A study by Wahyuengtias et al. (2021), which aimed to identify cultural programs that could increase the number of listeners in four cultural radio stations in Indonesia and to find out the reasons why listeners prefer local cultural programs on each radio, showed the method of collecting data online, through Facebook and WhatsApp, but this study conducted few interviews with participants representing radio management, cultural figures and loyal listeners, although the results showed that each radio has listeners. Loyal to it, they follow its distinguished cultural programs with a strong appeal to maintain their loyalty, and the four radio stations hired cultural experts to design these cultural programs.
- In a study, conducted in Rajasthan, India, on the role of community radio stations in preserving indigenous culture through 250 radio stations, those community stations in Rajasthan were selected for this study. The study concluded that most of these stations played an important role in preserving and promoting folk arts and culture in the state (Sharma, Ruthuri and Shankar Sharma, 2021)
- As for the study of Laqmash (2022), which looks at the impact of cultural globalization, which has become a threat to the security and safety of countries, the study examined the problem of the communication revolution and the risks and damages it has produced on various peoples and nations. The study examined the local radio station Skikda in Algeria, where the study used the descriptive approach; while the study tool was the interview, as for the study population, it is the total community of cultural programs on Radio Skikda, where the deliberate sample was used.
- The study highlighted the effective ways to enhance community identity, which is to try to produce content, but the researcher believes that the method of promoting community identity is an insufficiently studied topic in community media studies and has not received sufficient attention from scholars, and the research concluded that community radio stations that broadcast within the geographical area adopt different strategies in expressing their community identity and go far in focusing on the so-called local, that is, talking about issues of concern to the local population.
- A study concluded that radio stations in Nigeria can effectively enhance their role as promoters of culture by engaging adolescents in recognizing and celebrating Nigeria's rich cultural heritage, as data were collected from 384 participants to learn about the types of cultural content broadcast by Nigerian radio stations, the habits and preferences of adolescents in consuming cultural content, and the extent to which they realize the importance of radio in promoting cultural awareness. The results showed a variety of cultural content of Nigerian radio stations and one of the most popular cultural content is music. Nigerian teenagers have been shown to have a strong preference for traditional platforms despite the existence of other competing media platforms.
- The 10th study shows in (Bin Swaydan, 2024) study the importance of digital broadcasting and how the services of this radio broadcasting, such as podcasts, have developed through the demand of Saudi youth for it and the

statement of the effects of listening to such applications, which leads us through this study to know the characteristics of the audience of young people interacting with it.

Conclusion

In Al-Qarni's study, the researcher focused on the theoretical aspects but did not explore the practical relationship between language and cultural identity. This oversight impacted the study's credibility, as Al-Qarni did not present sufficient challenges or difficulties to substantiate the theories and relationships he proposed.

Saida and Prakashi's study had its limitations, as it only focused on the local radio station Guelma in Algeria and specifically examined its role in addressing unemployment and illegal immigration. The narrow scope of the research is reflected in the small sample size, which consisted of just 50 participants. Additionally, while the researchers interviewed radio station officials to understand the basis for selecting characters and programs and the methods used to engage the audience, they did not conduct a direct, in-depth content analysis. Such an analysis could have offered a more impartial view of the radio's impact.

Qamsh's study primarily relied on interviews with those in charge of the program it focused on, without exploring the opinions of the program's audience. One positive aspect of this study is its broad approach to cultural identity, examining various facets such as societal crises like unemployment and migration, as well as topics such as religion, language, and heritage.

In Akkad's study, the researcher examined the relationship between university youth's reliance on digital radio stations and their awareness of the social values directed at them. This relationship was the core of the study, and the researcher's focus on it can be considered a strength, as it provides valuable insight into how digital media influences social values.

In the study by Wahyungtias and colleagues, the researchers sought to identify cultural programs that increase listener engagement with cultural radio stations. While we disagree with the limited number of interviews conducted to analyze the content, the results showed that loyal listeners to these stations exist, which in itself is a success for the study.

Sharma et al.'s study highlighted the strong attachment of the Indian public in Rajasthan to their local cultural beliefs, particularly the appreciation of folk arts. This study demonstrated that radio stations play a significant role in promoting local culture and heritage in the region.

Bacchus' study aligns with Sharma et al.'s in its focus on producing local content, with both studies addressing issues that are pertinent to the local populations they examine.

Finally, the study by Sanusi and Ogyumi stands out for its extensive use of a large sample size (384 participants), which provided diverse insights into the cultural content of Nigerian radio stations. One of the key findings was the

Chapter 2

The Relationship of Bahraini University Youth's Exposure to Foreign Films in Digital Platforms on Their Perception of Cultural Identity in Light of the Challenges of Globalization: An Applied Study

Nadeya Mohamed Mahmood Ghuloom Ali

Royal Humanitarian Foundation, Bahrain

Abstract

Globalization is one of the most prominent phenomena affecting modern societies. Its impacts extend beyond economic and political dimensions to encompass cultural aspects, particularly cultural identity. With the emergence of digital platforms such as Netflix, Amazon Prime, and others, university students are increasingly exposed to foreign films that present diverse cultures and values. This cultural openness has led to changes in thinking and behavior among youth, significantly affecting their local cultural identity.

In this context, the importance of studying the relationship between Bahraini youth's exposure to foreign films and changes in cultural identity becomes evident. Foreign films, along with the concepts of Western culture and globalization they convey, are among the most influential media components on the cultural identity of youth. This is particularly relevant as young people are in a life stage where their opinions are formed, and they test the social and cultural values acquired during their childhood and adolescence. Youth are also among the most active demographic groups in consuming foreign films.

This study is significant in highlighting the profound cultural impact of digital media on Bahraini youth, which is crucial for understanding how to enhance Bahraini cultural identity. This study aims to determine the effect

Digital Dialogues, 11–20

doi:10.1108/978-1-83708-686-320261002

of exposure to foreign films on the cultural values of Bahraini youth, understand the nature of the relationship between foreign entertainment content and cultural transformations among youth, and provide recommendations to address the challenges posed by cultural globalization.

Keywords: University youth; foreign films; digital platforms; cultural identity; globalization

Globalization is one of the most prominent phenomena that have affected modern societies, as its effects were not limited to economic and political dimensions, but extended to include cultural aspects, especially cultural identity, and with the emergence of digital platforms such as Netflix, Amazon Prime, and others, university youth have become more vulnerable to the content of foreign films, which present diverse cultures and values.

The problem of globalization and cultural identity occupies a major place in our time, especially at this severe stage, which is witnessing a different global historical situation, based on polarization, hegemony, and unilateralism, aimed at excluding civilizational identities and cultural specificities. This single civilizational domination, which is one of the features of our time, arose in light of scientific and technological globalization, which led to the comprehensive cultural domination of the other.

Foreign films and the concepts of Western culture and globalization are among the most influential components of the media on the cultural identity of young people, given that they are in a stage of life in which their opinions are formed and the social and cultural values that they derived from their socialization in childhood and adolescence are tested, and since young people are among the most follow-up groups in society to foreign films on digital platforms.

Digital platforms have become of wide interest to young people in various fields, as they have become the most influential and effective space to follow what they love from dramas, especially foreign films, due to the advantages of these platforms that are not available in others, as electronic platforms have their own audience, most of whom are young people, and they are characterized by boldness in their dramatic topics that they display through films.

From this standpoint, the importance of this study is highlighted in shedding light on the profound cultural impact that digital media has on Bahraini youth, which is crucial to understand how to enhance Bahraini cultural identity, as this study seeks to determine the impact of exposure to foreign films on digital platforms on the cultural values of Bahraini youth, understand the nature of the relationship between foreign entertainment content and cultural transformations among young people, and provide recommendations to address the challenges posed by cultural globalization.

Theoretical Framework of the Study

The study was based on the theory of cultural and media globalization (Cultural and media globalization theory) Ronald Robertson, where the researcher found that it is the closest to the current study, and some studies similar to the current study used it as a theory and the following is a definition of this theory and why it was adopted in the current study.

First: Definition of the Theory of Cultural and Media Globalization

It is a theory formulated by Roland Robertson by tracing the historical dimension of time that brought us to the current situation characterized by a high degree of cosmic density, complexity, and thus globalization reflected according to the theory the forces of global blocs, the new transformations resulting from technological innovation, and the forms of consumption developed such as cultural consumption of the dominant culture, where the availability of Robertson's theory is a comprehensive and flexible framework for understanding the interaction between local culture and global culture (Hassan, 2023).

It is clear to the researcher that Robertson focuses on the influence of the forces of global blocs that indicate the emergence of international institutions and agreements that enhance economic and cultural cooperation, as the theory of cultural and media globalization through this definition is an important theory from the researcher's point of view to understand the relationship between local culture and global culture in light of the rapid global changes that the world is currently witnessing.

Second: Stages of Cultural and Media Globalization Theory

The model presented by the theory of cultural and media globalization is divided into five stages (Haris, 2008; Homs & Obeid, 2023):

(1) Germinal Stage
(2) Emergence Stage
(3) Launch Stage
(4) Struggle for Hegemony Stage
(5) Uncertainty Stage

Through analyzing these five stages of cultural and media globalization theory, the researcher observes that each stage is characterized by distinct features that differentiate it from the others. The germinal stage is marked by the emergence of national communities,

1. University Youth: They are those segments of society who pursue their educational attainment after obtaining a secondary or preparatory certificate and who are between the ages of 18 and 35 years (Al-Eid, 2020).
   University youth are defined procedurally in the current study as Bahraini university youth who pursue their educational attainment in Bahraini universities after obtaining their secondary certificate and who are between the ages of 18 and 35 years.
2. Digital Platforms: Digital platforms are multi-party networks based on a technical infrastructure that enables interaction between multiple user groups (Arrigo, 2022).
   Digital platforms are procedurally known as the current study of the Netflix network, during which Bahraini university youth are exposed to foreign films.
3. Cultural Identity: Cultural identity is defined as the constant interaction between the subjective identity of individuals and the culture with which they interact, which determines the sense of belonging and discrimination within society (Taylor & Kachanoff, 2015).
   Cultural identity is defined procedurally in the current study as a dynamic process in which university youth reshape their cultural affiliations based on social and political influences.

- Globalization: Globalization is a complex web of economic, cultural, political, and social interactions that connect societies around the world, leading to profound shifts in national identities and global challenges (Robertson, 2011).
  Globalization is defined procedurally by the current study to the degree to which the respondent to globalization approved in the present study obtains.

4. Foreign Films
   Foreign films are films that are shown in any language other than Arabic, whether English, French, Hindi, or others.

Foreign films are procedurally known as the current study of films that Bahraini university youth are exposed to through the Netflix platform, which are shown in any language other than Arabic, whether English, French, Hindi, or others.

The First Axis: Digital Platforms

Definition of Digital Platforms

Kaplan and Haenlein (2010) define digital platforms as "a set of internet-based applications that build on ideological and technical foundations, and enable content to be created and shared by users."

Abdullah (2021) defines digital platforms as a set of technological applications and tools that allow users to produce, distribute, and interact with digital content online, contributing to the creation of a virtual interactive society.

When analyzing these definitions comprehensively, it becomes clear that digital platforms are understood in different ways depending on the angle from which the researcher looks at: Kaplan and Haenlein (2010) focused on applications and ideology, while Al-Rahmawi (2022) highlighted instant interaction, Abdullah (2021) focused on creativity and content production, and Culotta et al. (2024) technical aspect and infrastructure.

Digital Platforms for Movies

Digital film platforms have several characteristics that distinguish them from traditional means of presentation, such as cinemas or television, the most prominent of which are (Abdullah, 2021; Culotta et al., 2024):

- Instant and continuous access: Users can access the movie library anytime, anywhere, using smart devices, such as mobile phones and smart TVs.
- Personalized interaction: Platforms provide personalized recommendations for each user based on AI algorithms that track viewing habits and content preferences.
- Subscription and payment models: These platforms rely on monthly subscription or pay-per-view systems, giving users the flexibility to choose between different subscription plans.
- Online streaming: Online streaming is one of the most important characteristics, as the user can watch the movie in real time without the need for pre-downloading, which reduces the consumption of local storage of devices.

The foreign film industry has witnessed remarkable development in recent years, both in content and technical aspects, thanks to digital platforms.

As these films have increased on digital platforms, their viewership rates have increased dramatically (Khalaf, 2023).

It is clear from the above that foreign films, through digital platforms, are characterized by displaying diverse behaviors and knowledge, which contribute to shaping values and attitudes among viewers. Thanks to its exciting and beautiful scenes and situations, the viewer is able to interact emotionally and integrate with its events, which increases its ability to attract young people in particular. With this deep engagement, it can lead to changes in intellectual lifestyles, behaviors, and social values.

The Second Axis: Cultural Identity

Cultural identity is a complex term and multiple aspects and connotations, as each individual has a cultural identity, which is directly related to the cultural framework that they carry within them, where cultural identity works at the individual and collective levels, depending on a number of factors (Radwan, 2022).

Definition of Cultural Identity

Researchers have provided many definitions of this term, including Kim's (2007), who defined cultural identity as an evolving subjective experience in which individuals define themselves based on the cultural relationships they have with their original groups or with other cultures.

Taylor & Kachanoff (2015) defined cultural identity as a common framework of social meanings and values that groups individuals and determines their patterns of behavior and social identities.

The Role of Films in Shaping the Cultural Identity of Young People

Foreign films are one of the most prominent tools of cultural influence on young people, due to the elements of suspense and excitement they contain, as foreign films are often transmitted, which leads to a gradual change in their attitudes and behaviors, and may even reshape the features of their cultural identity (Fathi, 2020).

It is clear to the researcher that foreign films on digital platforms are able to reshape cultural identity, as young people begin to adopt Western lifestyles. Therefore, awareness of these risks is an urgent necessity.

Foreign films are one of the influential means of shaping the cultural identity of young people, due to the messages and ideas they sometimes carry that call for social liberation and openness to Western values and behaviors in their real lives (Bahauddin, 2023; Evans, 2016).

The researcher believes that the impact of these films is due to the ability of foreign films to arouse the feelings of viewers through elaborate cinematography, which reflects an attractive ideal image that makes young people feel a desire to emulate the heroes of the films. Over time, this repetition may contribute to the establishment of new values that contradict the original cultural values of society, leading to a "cultural invasion," in which local cultural elements are replaced by alien symbols and values.

Foreign films are also one of the most prominent factors that contribute to the distortion of the cultural identity of young people, as they lead to a fascination with Western cultures, and some may feel that their local culture is less attractive or "old-fashioned", which weakens their sense of belonging to their community of origin (Salem, 2023).

Thus, the researcher believes that these films contribute to imposing Western patterns of behavior on young people, such as promoting absolute autonomy and encouraging freedom from traditional values, values that may contradict the prevailing cultural principles in conservative societies.

The Third Axis: Globalization

Definition of Globalization

Giddens (2013) defines globalization as a process that reflects the increasing integration of countries and economies through trade, investment, technology, and cultural communication, leading to the shrinking of geographical and cultural boundaries.

According to Held and McGraw, globalization is the accelerated movement of goods, ideas, information, and services across national borders.

These definitions clearly show the complex nature of globalization, and cultural globalization, supported by media and digital technologies, is affecting cultural identities.

The impact of globalization on the cultural identity of young people

It is clear from the above that the problem of globalization and its effects on cultural identity has become one of the central issues in the modern era. Today, which is witnessing radical transformations in political and social systems, globalization is embodied as a major driver of changing the cultural identity of peoples, especially in light of scientific and technological globalization that has strengthened Western cultural hegemony. According to the researcher, this hegemony emerges in attempts to exclude local civilizational identities and impose a unified global culture.

The issue of the relationship between globalization and the cultural identity of young people has been raised on more than one level and continues to be raised because it is the most important, most difficult and complex issue, and its material consequences have penetrated all areas of life at the cultural, political, media, and social levels (Khion & Atshan, 2024).

It imposes on university youth Western models and philosophies through the production, distribution, and consumption of media and advertising content, which enhances the influence of foreign values and concepts on their lives and attitudes (Al-Eid, 2020).

References

Abdullah, M. (2021). Streaming platforms and the transformation of the film industry. *Media Innovation Quarterly*, *8*(2), 22–40.

Al-Eid, W. (2020). The cultural dimension of globalization and its impact on the cultural identity of Arab youth: Algerian university youth as a model. *Jeel Journal of Humanities and Social Sciences*, *2*, 9–25.

Al-Rahmawi, A. H. H. (2022). The role of digital media platforms in crisis management. *Arab Journal of Social Sciences*, *21*(3), 66–86.

Arrigo, E. (2022). Digital platforms in fashion rental: A business model analysis. *Journal of Fashion Marketing and Management: An International Journal*, *26*(1), 1–20.

Keywords: Infographic; editorial policies; visual communication; newspaper content analysis; Bahraini journalism

Introduction

The press is one of the most important media outlets that provide the public with news and information, and plays a major role in influencing public opinion. The press witnessed tremendous development in the 20th century as a result of the advances on technology, and with the impact of technology on newspaper production and the issuance process in general, the press witnessed a huge development that had a clear impact on media and journalistic performance, which occupied an important part of the interest of editorial policies in handling media content, and in the way of presenting and styling of journalistic content. With technology controlling media and journalistic production methods, the press did not delay in investing in the technical and artistic developments provided by modern technology, and in order for newspapers to keep pace with the movement of change that the world is witnessing in the field of communication and information revolution. The speed of information access and transmission to the public had a clear impact on the editorial policies of newspapers in the fields of editing, design, and production in order to achieve the greatest possible impact on attracting readers and increasing their interest in the media content of the press.

It is worthy to note that since the increase of the use of infographics, or what is known as data journalism, the role of newspapers in facilitating access to information has increased, and newspapers have begun to occupy a larger space of public interest and cultural, economic, and societal elites. Many specialists believe that newspapers' interest in new editorial methods, including the use of infographics in various sections of newspapers, has given them added momentum to face the challenges at the current stage. This study seeks to answer many urgent questions related to newspaper editorial policies and their relationship to the use of infographics in light of the communication and information revolution that human society is witnessing on the one hand and the size of the challenges facing journalism, which have begun to threaten its future and sustainability, on the other hand, after new media and social media have reached advanced stages of public interest.

Literature Review

Studies related to the topic of infographics in the press have addressed multiple aspects, including the study by Shatnawi (2024), which examined the treatment of infographics of economic content in the Jordanian electronic press by identifying the extent of interest of the Jordanian press in publishing economic infographics, the economic issues addressed by the infographics published in it, and explaining the reasons for focusing on them.

The study of Rafeeq (2024) sought to explore the infographics of the two Emirati newspapers, Gulf News and Al Bayan, in search of how these infographic publications are used in terms of their prevailing topics and their contribution to the narrative structure and editorial content, in addition to their frequency, complexity, and location.

The study of Muhammad et al. (2023) aimed to identify the use of infographics in addressing health crises on some websites.

Abdel-ATI's study (2023) aimed to identify the uses of Al Arabiya and BBC websites for infographics and motion graphics as a tool to enhance digital content and attract more viewers to follow the two websites, as well as to identify the most important issues that these media focus on in news bulletins, in addition to the persuasive uses that both infographics and motion graphics rely on to attract attention.

The study of Zinderen (2021) reviewed the principles of infographic design in the news to obtain an easy-to-understand and effective news presentation.

The study of Al-Khawli (2020) aimed to know the role of infographics in increasing the ease of reading media content on Egyptian and international newspaper websites.

Abdullah's study (2020) was dedicated to elaborate on Okaz newspaper's use of infographics in editorial forms, the type of issues it covers, and the elements of explanation used in its design.

Abu Al-Ala's study (2020) dealt with monitoring and analyzing the use of infographics on the website of the Bahraini Prime Minister's Media Center and its official Facebook page and identifying the role it plays as an advanced means of communication and as a mechanism to confront rumors.

While the study by Eldem Anar (2020) addressed increasing academic awareness about infographic journalism, whether through its contribution to the field of journalism or through its interactive features.

A study by Markus Beiler et al. (2020) sought to provide a representative quantitative overview of data journalism activities, content, and evaluations in Germany.

In the editorial policies section, the study of Sooknanan and Rojas (2024) focused on investigating the editorial policies related to organizing and monitoring citizen content published by the Trinidad Express newspaper.

The study of Othman (January 2023) addressed the impact of editorial policy on the standards of selecting a newspaper photo in Egyptian newspapers, and on the issues covered by the newspaper photo.

Gitau et al. (2023) examined the effects of editorial policies on the news coverage in print and social media in Kenya.

Jamal's study (2020) focused on monitoring the most important features of the work environment within press organizations and the relationship between communicators and editorial policy in each organization, in addition to monitoring the skills available in communicators working on different platforms and comparing them.

The study of Muskhanova et al. (2020) aimed to determine the details of covering online protest actions.

Observations on Literature Review

The review of literature shows that previous studies on the topic dealt with identifying infographics and their fields of use. The literature also explained the importance of infographics in print journalism. Most previous studies also focused on the volume of infographic reading in newspapers. Some studies addressed infographics' treatment of content in journalism and ways to employ infographics in websites, especially in highlighting content. In addition to identifying editorial policies and their impact on electronic and print news websites and the most influential factors in editorial policy on the communicator. It is noted that previous studies were similar to the current study in their approach to the study methodology, type of study, and sample. The current study was similar to the study of Shatnawi (2024), the study of Muhammad et al. (2023), the study of Abdel-Ati (2023 January), the study of Othman (January 2023), the study of Gitau et al. (2023), the study of Aslihan Zendirin (2021), the study of Afif (September 2020), the study of Eldem Anar (2020), and the study of Muskhanova et al. (2020) in terms of the type of study, as they are descriptive studies, and the method used is the descriptive method and the data collection tool is content analysis. The current study was also similar to these studies in terms of the study sample used, which is a simple random sample. The current study was similar to the study of Abdullah (2020) in the objective of the study, which is to know the use of Okaz journalism for infographics in analytical forms, and the type of issues it addresses. The current study was similar to the study of Jamal (2020) and the study of (Gitau et al., 2023) in the theory used, which is the gatekeeper theory; while the current study differed from the study of (Sooknanan & Rojas, 2024), the study of Rafeeq (2024), the study of Jamal (2020), the study of Khouli (2020), the study of Abu Al-Ala (2020), and the study of (Beiler et al., 2020) in terms of the methodology used, which varied between the survey, comparison, interview, and experimental methods.

The Extent of Benefit From Previous Studies

Previous studies benefited the researcher in determining the theoretical framework of the study, in crystallizing the study problem, in addition to determining the study sample and study community, and in trying to delve deeper and benefit from studies that addressed related topics in infographics and editorial policies, and in identifying the nature of the methodological procedures used in these studies and their uses, and in identifying the positives and negatives of the methods used in previous studies. Previous studies also helped in obtaining new sources of data, formulating scientific standards for the study and the way researchers deal with them, and learning more about the appropriate tools for the current study, in addition to identifying the results of previous studies and the possibility of making a comparison between them and the results of the current study that the researcher will reach and interpret them more clearly and deeply, and also addressing the recommendations of researchers in previous studies.

Study Results and Recommendations

Study Results

The study concluded with the following results:

- Al-Ayyam newspaperwas the newspaper that published the most infographics, then Al-Watan newspaper, then Al-Bilad newspaper, and Akhbar Al-Khaleej newspaper came in last place.
- The most pages where infographics were published were the inside pages, then the first page, and the most infographics included only one logo, and their number exceeded half the number of infographics, then infographics that included two logos, then infographics that included three logos or more.
- The newspapers focused primarily on publishing infographics that included objective images, and the majority of infographics published in the newspapers of the study sample were colored, as it was shown that there was a convergence in the number of infographics published in the longitudinal/vertical display method and the number of infographics published in the horizontal/landscape display method. While colored backgrounds were the most commonly used backgrounds in infographics published in the newspapers of the study sample, then infographics with white backgrounds.
- The majority of infographics were published in the newspapers of the study sample in Arabic, and a small section was published in both Arabic and English, and there were very few infographics published in English. The most topics covered by infographics in the study sample newspapers were health topics, then economic topics, then marketing topics. It was found that correspondents and government sources were the primary sources of infographics.
- The most important function that infographics in the study sample newspapers focused on was the illustrative function, then the advisory function, as well as the news function. Infographics in the study sample newspapers focused on the educational function and the entertainment function to a small degree.
- The majority of infographics in the study sample newspapers were in the local scope, then the infographics that were in the global scope, and there were a small number of infographics that were in the regional scope, while the Arab scope did not receive any infographics.
- The most important determinants of editorial policy in infographics published in the study sample newspapers were the community interests criterion, then the economic criterion, then the security criterion, and then the political criterion. The vast majority of infographics published in the study sample newspapers had a known source, while there was a small number of infographics with an unknown source.
- The editorial policy trend toward the infographics published in the newspapers of the study sample was between supportive and neutral, without the presence of an opposing editorial policy trend. The accuracy of the content of

- The necessity of diversifying the forms of infographics published in Bahraini newspapers, and not focusing on a specific form over another, especially increasing interest in infographics that take the form of a hierarchy, in addition to infographics that include maps, since newspapers' interest in them was little.
- Increasing interest in Bahraini newspapers in infographics that address Arab and regional topics, since these areas did not receive sufficient attention from those in charge of infographics in Bahraini newspapers.
- Paying attention to the design of infographics so that they are attractive to the reader, simple, and free of complexity by increasing attention to the elements that make up the infographic and ensuring the accuracy and precision of the numbers and information it contains.
- Establishing a clear and specific editorial policy related to infographics published in Bahraini newspapers.
- Conducting more studies and research on the editorial policies of local newspapers in the Kingdom of Bahrain.
- Benefiting from the experiences of editorial policies of some Arab and foreign newspapers, especially those related to the use of infographics.
- Creating a balance between editorial policy determinants and focusing on all different aspects and issues, not just the criterion of community interests.

References

Abdel-Ati, A. M. (2023, January). Displaying information using infographics and motion graphics technology in news bulletins television. *Scientific Journal of Radio and Television Research, 2023*(25), 621–673.

Afif, A. (2020, September). Saudi newspapers' use of infographics to highlight content, A descriptive and analytical study of Okaz newspaper. *Research Journal, 36*, 45–60.

Al-Khawli, S. (2020, July). The role of infographics in increasing the audience's readability of media content on Egyptian and international newspaper websites (an analytical and field study). *Journal of Media Research, 54*. Part Three, 1449–1534.

Ali, J. (2020, January). Editorial policy of multi-platform media institutions, A field study on communicators, published master's thesis. *Scientific Journal of Journalism Research, 2020*(19), 489–507.

Beiler, M., Irmer, F., & Breda, A. (2020). Data journalism at German newspapers and public broadcasters: A quantitative survey of structures, contents and perceptions. *Journalism Studies, 21*(11), 1571–1589. https://doi.org/10.1080/1461670X.2020.1772855

Eldem Anar, Ü. İ. (2020). Verinin işlenmesi sürecinde infografik ve interaktif haberciIik. *Kocaeli Üniversitesi İletişim Fakültesi Araştırma Dergisi, 16*, 133–160.

Gitau, A., Mwendwa, K. D., & Njoroge, K. P. (2023). Effects of editorial policies on demand for comprehensive research on news coverage in print and social media channels in Kenya. *African Journal of Empirical Research, 4*(1), 60–68.

Jamal, A. (2020). *Editorial policy of multi-platform media institutions: A field study on communicators* (Master's thesis). Scientific Journal of Journalism Research.

Muhammad, A.-G., Wahbi, S., & Mazid, W. (2023, December). Employing infographics in addressing health issues on websites. *Sohag Journal for Young Researchers*, *3*(1).

Muskhanova, I. V., Matveeva, E. S., Kolomiychenko, L. V., Skutelnik, O. A., Gadaborsheva, Z. I., Yakhyaeva, A. K., & Gabarova, K. V. (2020). Editorial policy problems on internet in transforming society. *EurAsian Journal of Bio-Sciences*, *14*(2), 3321–3327.

Othman, M. (2023, January). The impact of editorial policy on the criteria for choosing a press photo for publication in Egyptian newspapers. *Scientific Journal of Journalism Research*, *2023*(25).

Rafeeq, A. (2024). Infographics as a storytelling tool in UAE newspapers: A comparative study of Gulf news and Al Bayan. *Cogent Arts & Humanities*, *11*(1). https://doi.org/10.1080/23311983.2024.2406090

Salwa Abu Al-Ela. (2020, July). Using infographics on official websites to respond to rumors (the media center of the presidency of the council of ministers as a model). *Journal of Media Research*, *54*(54–1), 9–80.

Shatnawi, S. M. K. (2024). Infographic Treatment of Economic Content in Jordanian Electronic Journalism. *Scientific Journal of Journalism Research*, *8*(29), 175–196.

Sooknanan, P., & Rojas, K. (2024). *Citizen journalism and editorial policies: A case study of the Trinidad Express newspaper*. Authorea Preprints.

Zinderen, A. (2021). Veri gazeteciliğinde görsel hikâye anlatımı: Haberde görselleştirme ve İnfografik tasarım Üzerine bir göz İzleme çalışması. *Manas Sosyal Araştırmalar Dergisi*, *10*(3), 1861–1877.

Chapter 4

The Utilization of Digital Platforms in Promoting Youth Empowerment Initiatives and Their Attitudes Toward Them: A Case Study of Government Initiative Pages on Instagram

Abdulrahman Seyadi

Ahlia University, Bahrain

Abstract

This study specifically focuses on discovering the main threads of research in the utilization of digital platforms, especially social media, as the main platforms for performing the aims of the youth empowerment programs of the government. It makes a survey of a wide array of Arabic and international studies that used different tools, methods, and sample selections, showing that digital platforms are used by government for communication, community awareness, digital entrepreneurship support, and youth engagement. The survey indicated that the potential of these platforms was not fully exploited, especially in terms of interactive and dialogic communication. Moreover, the lack of unified policies and unclear regulatory frameworks do not help the effectiveness of communication and do not provide opportunities for empowerment. Also, the findings highlight that those youngsters with better digital skills are the ones who have more economic, social, and political opportunities thanks to digital platforms. Nevertheless, the accessibility for some groups is still restricted, as they are either unaware or they do not have the digital infrastructure available to them. The study recommends government-led training and providing incentives for institutions and professionals running digital content as the best means to achieve this. It also stresses that creating policies that are completely inclusive for everyone, including people with disabilities and the underprivileged, is also crucial.

Digital Dialogues, 31–41

Published under exclusive licence by Emerald Publishing Limited
doi:10.1108/978-1-83708-686-320261004

and the absence of engagement with people in certain countries. The paper suggested improving social media use for interactivity and transparency, creating comprehensive digital policies, and training personnel in effective digital content management. The report concluded that leveraging social media to foster relationships between governments and the public and address digital governance issues is the best solution.

El-Sherif's (2023) study analyzed the impact of digital platforms, particularly Facebook, on marketing and youth perceptions in Egypt. The research used a descriptive-analytical methodology, using qualitative content analysis and focus groups to collect data from official event pages and national conferences. The study found that Facebook pages improved user interaction and youth participation in events. Participants who were previously involved in such events had a higher tendency to integrate into digital platforms. The study highlighted the importance of creative and engaging content in managing digital platforms and the need for media teams to effectively utilize social media. The study provides a practical model for improving national event marketing strategies and engaging youth through digital platforms, ultimately enhancing youth engagement.

The study by Hakim and Jayanti (2022) evaluated the effectiveness of the South Tangerang City Government's official Instagram account in presenting credible and interesting information to its followers. A survey methodology was applied with 100 Instagram followers aged 18 to 44. The results showed that the account answered 48.3% of users' questions correctly and had a strong positive relationship with the provision of relevant information by the government. Instagram is seen as the favorite platform among followers due to its high-quality visual and interactive content. However, the study suggested the need to increase interactive content and provide incentives for users to avoid switching to other channels for information. It recommended developing more engaging visual content, conducting regular user needs surveys, and implementing awareness campaigns to communicate information to the masses and establish the account as an authority. The study concludes that Instagram is a crucial social media platform for strengthening government communication and engaging media.

Ahmed's (2022) study examined the ministry's communication strategies to enhance social health programs and public knowledge. The research focused on the topics of published material, dissemination intentions, and methods used on the Ministry's official website from January 1 to December 31, 2021. The study used a descriptive-analytical methodology, analyzing content analysis for relevant posts. The Ministry primarily used informational strategies (71.33%) and persuasion and explanation techniques (65.60%). Conversations were primarily one-way, with dialogic strategies (1.15%) and consensus-building approaches (2.75%) being less used. The study highlighted the inefficiency of using social media for authentic engagement. It suggested creating communication strategies that incorporate two-way interactions, consensus-building, and multimedia content to engage readers and increase participation. The study also suggested training digital content management teams for the smooth execution of social media communication.

Fajriyah et al. (2020) conducted a study on the role of social media in e-government, focusing on the municipal government of Prabumulih, Indonesia. The study examined the impact of technological factors, interaction, and social media variables on improving government communication. A sample of 200 participants from the Prabumulih government's Facebook page was used for the generalization. The results showed that instructional technology was highly reliable in affecting government communication. Online tools proved helpful in disseminating information and engaging the public, despite the current usage often being limited to technology and interaction. The study also highlighted the importance of bidirectional engagement strategies between the government and the public. It suggested improving technological know-how, improving the quality of government websites, and enhancing direct interaction with the public. Participants were instructed to train government personnel on effective social media management. The study demonstrated the potential of a functional model for improving communication and creating more transparent governance through digital media, reinforcing the role of social media as a vital tool for democratically governed people.

Second Theme: Youth Empowerment Initiatives

The study by Crispus and Sophie (2024) explores the impact of social media on the empowerment of youth in Kampala, Uganda. The research, which involved 400 young individuals aged 18–35, found that social media is a major driver for economic empowerment by providing access to new opportunities. The study also found that digital skills are crucial for youth to utilize the economic opportunities offered by these platforms. Education and income levels significantly impacted the youth who engaged in social and political activities through social media. Internet access was identified as the primary enabler, as it allowed better engagement and connectivity in sociopolitical activities and information provision. However, the study also highlighted challenges such as a lack of digital literacy, inequalities in digital device availability and reliable internet services, and the distribution of misinformation and cyberbullying. Despite these challenges, the study suggests that social media can be a valuable tool for youth empowerment if they have the necessary tools and knowledge to effectively use these platforms.

Kumar et al.'s study on social media platforms like Instagram, TikTok, and YouTube highlights the impact of these platforms on youth creativity development. The research highlights the benefits of these platforms, such as exposure to a wide audience, feedback, collaboration, and educational resources. However, it also highlights the disadvantages, such as unrealistic content pressure, cyberbullying, excessive online communication, time management issues, and the addictive nature of these platforms. The study suggests that digital education should be a more effective tool for learning responsible social media involvement, including copyright and time management. It also emphasizes the need for a balanced mix of online and offline creative activities and mental health care, as these interventions are crucial for young people in digital interactions and the pressures they face.

Goedhuys et al. (2024) developed an index to measure youth empowerment in Tunisia, based on a 2017 household survey. The index identified four main aspects of empowerment: future control, access to resources, leadership, and personal freedom. The composite index, based on the Women's Empowerment in Agriculture Index (WEAI), revealed a significant skill imbalance among Tunisian youth in economic sectors, particularly in employment, personal assets, and bank credits. The study also found gender differences in empowerment, with women being the weaker sex in terms of economic participation. However, leadership and personal freedom were the most prevalent forms of empowerment among the youth. The index could be used to assess the impact of youth-targeting policies on their social and economic participation.

The study by Victoria and Nicholas (2024) examined the impact of government programs on youth empowerment in Tirinyi County, Eastern Uganda. A survey of 200 young individuals aged 18–30 showed that the project improved their economic situations by teaching financial management, saving, and investment skills. The study also explored the effects of skills training programs, entrepreneurial grants, employment services, and leadership mentoring on youth engagement in local governance and employability skills. However, the study identified several main issues that led to the failure of various government projects, including insufficient promotion of opportunities, limited funding, a lack of collective voice among implementing bodies, and a lost sense of program continuation after the initial phase. The study emphasized the need for a comprehensive youth plan to facilitate collaboration among youth-related government departments, ensuring effective and lasting programs.

Geetha et al.'s (2024) study explores the impact of social media on youth empowerment in career development. The research uses social capital theory and social cognitive theory to analyze how platforms like LinkedIn and YouTube provide job opportunities, professional networking, and personal branding. Social media also facilitates youth connecting with mentors and accessing necessary teaching materials. However, challenges such as privacy issues, digital footprint management, cyberbullying, and the digital divide persist. Despite these challenges, social media has enabled young individuals to build personal brands, showcase their achievements, and connect with potential employers. The study recommends that school leaders enhance digital education by organizing workshops on digital skills and social responsibility, raising awareness about privacy protection and online safety, and addressing the digital divide through technology and educational resources. The study also emphasizes the importance of mentoring and online educational resources for youth to acquire knowledge and skills for professional development.

Tafuh and Priyadi's (2024) study examined the link between youth empowerment and national development in Buea Municipality, Southwest Region of Cameroon. The research involved 60 young people and found that the government's empowerment policy was ineffective, with policy documents like the 2006

National Youth Policy, the Three-Year Youth Plan, and the 2010 Growth and Empowerment Strategy Document often not being known to the public. Key barriers faced by the youth included a lack of vocational training, limited jobs, prejudices of elderly people, and a lack of openness from local authorities. The study also noted a gap in national business mentorships for empowering young people in entrepreneurship. However, young citizens participated in local initiatives and remained hopeful with great prospects if the right opportunities were available. The report recommended promoting education and vocational courses, ensuring accountability and transparency in local governance, and credited successful government and civil society partnerships for youth empowerment.

Udeh et al.'s (2023) study examined models of youth empowerment in Africa and their potential for fostering development in the United States. The research highlighted the importance of youth empowerment in African sustainable development, as two-thirds of the population are young. The study highlighted successful African programs such as the "Integrated Youth Initiative" in Nigeria, the DREAMS program in Uganda, and community volunteer programs in Zimbabwe. The study suggests that the findings can be applied to the United States by establishing African youth empowerment projects through surveys targeting at-risk groups and delivering vocational education and entrepreneurship activities. Challenges faced by these programs include minimal funding, corruption, and lack of youth participation. However, these issues can be resolved through effective partnerships between governments and communities. The study suggests that US politicians should adopt similar strategies to build strong youth-worker partnerships between African and US regions. Programs should be culturally and geographically inclusive, using technology and vocational training to ensure sustainability.

Abdul Kader's (2019) study analyzed the perception of youth empowerment and sustainable human development in societies. The research used anthropological methods, including participant observation and in-depth interviews with university students from Alexandria University. The study used theoretical frameworks such as Maslow's hierarchy of needs, human and social capital theory, and symbolic interactionism. It found that youth empowerment is connected to social and cultural needs and evolves slowly, requiring collaboration between families, government institutions, and civil society organizations. The study emphasized the role of young people in sustainable development, specifically in capacity-building, expanding opportunities, and nurturing talents. However, the study found that ongoing initiatives and practices are not enough to meet young people's expectations, with obstacles such as limited financial and human resources causing mistrust of executive institutions. Young participants emphasized the importance of active inclusion and self-realization in the empowerment process. The study suggested developing policies that involve youth in innovation processes, fostering trust between institutions and individuals, and establishing a knowledge management and innovation society. It also highlighted the importance of integrating younger development into the national development agenda.

- Global Reach: Facilitates access to audiences worldwide.
- Feedback: Provides insights into audience preferences and opinions.
- Two-Way Communication: Establishes a bilateral communication channel between the organization and its relevant audiences.

Concept of Digital Communication Strategies

These are long-term plans and practices that organizations rely on to use digital communication tools such as the internet, social media, mobile applications, and websites.

Importance of Communication Strategies

The importance of having a communication strategy in an organization's policy lies in ensuring the success of communication within the institution; a suitable communication strategy or plan must be developed.

- The Motivating Users: It has become clear to most institutional managers today that without motivating users, they cannot develop their institutions. Motivation cannot be imposed on individuals; the organization must create the conditions.
- Coordinating Actions: No institution can achieve its strategic goals without being able to coordinate its actions and initiatives. A lack of information at the general level may lead to inconsistency.
- Changing Behaviors and Institutions: Organizations today face a set of internal and external changes that require continuous adaptation to ensure survival and competitiveness. Such changes include alterations in the scope of activity, the emergence of fierce competition, and advancements in technology and investments. Although the necessary tools for development and facing these changes may be available, many institutions may still experience significant failures due to resistance to change. Here, the communication strategy helps confront this rigidity in positions and provides the necessary responses.
- Improving Productivity: The fourth goal that the institution seeks to achieve is improving productivity and competitiveness within the organization. Communication helps achieve this goal by disseminating information and familiarizing everyone with the steps, procedures, rules, and knowledge. The importance of communication strategy within the institution also lies in building bridges of trust.

Challenges Facing Digital Communications

Digital communications face numerous challenges due to the novelty of the digital tools activated. These challenges necessitate that traditional communications practitioners receive additional training and education to adapt and utilize these tools effectively.

- Challenges Related to Organizational Management: The reluctance or unpreparedness of senior management to adopt and implement technological innovations that hinders the ability to leverage these advancements.
- Challenges Related to Technological Systems: Barriers in the exchange of information between the organization and its audiences.
- Challenges Related to Digital Content: Digital content created for public relations is often subject to criticism.
- Challenges Related to Practitioners: The age of public relations practitioners can pose challenges. As Panopoulos points out, organizations may struggle to develop the technical skills of older practitioners.
- Challenges Related to Information: The overwhelming abundance of information within the organization and the spread of misinformation provided by other organizations.

The researcher believes that one of the most significant challenges facing digital communications is developmental planning. This refers to the organization's ability to transition from traditional communication practices to digitally driven strategies while maintaining strategic coherence and institutional stability.

Strategies Based on How Audiences Respond to Persuasion in Digital Communication Strategies: While persuasion might seem straightforward, it poses a significant challenge for planners and designers of communication programs in public relations.

The Hierarchy of Effects

This model is significant for explaining how individuals respond to communication messages. It assumes that messages go through several stages between being broadcast and triggering a behavioral response. It reflects a symmetrical view of public relations, as follows:

- Exposure: Ensuring the audience is exposed to the campaign's message.
- Attention: The message must capture the audience's attention.
- Engagement: The audience becomes interested in the message content and discusses it.
- Understanding: Audience attention and interest indicate they have comprehended the message as intended.
- Skill Acquisition: Providing the audience with the skills to respond effectively to the message.
- Persuasion: Altering attitudes is essential but insufficient.
- Memory Retention: Associating the message with a well-known event or social context aids memory retention.

The researcher notes that this model faces criticism, particularly regarding its assumption that individuals are entirely rational in their thinking.

The Elaboration Likelihood

This model emphasizes individual differences in their engagement with a given issue. It provides a useful framework for digital communications programs, recognizing that audiences interact with messages in varying ways based on the following:

- Central Route: Focused on logical arguments and careful consideration by the audience.
- Peripheral Route: Emphasizes emotional appeals and the source's attributes.

The Diffusion of Innovations

This model provides a framework for campaign planners in public relations to encourage audiences to adopt new ideas and products. Sociologists and communication researchers have identified stages in the adoption process.

- Awareness: Individuals become aware of a concept or practice.
- Interest: The audience develops interest.
- Evaluation: Individuals assess the idea based on personal attitudes.
- Trial: The audience engages in practical experimentation.
- Adoption: The audience confirms the idea's value.

Researcher's Perspective: Communication strategies in public relations vary based on the organization's size and scope. The organizational structure under senior management is a critical pillar for implementing strategies effectively.

Communication strategies encompass traditional tools—such as audio, visual, and written methods—and modern technological tools like multimedia, social networks, websites, and other new media platforms. These tools and strategies rely heavily on the role of digital content creators.

Stages of Developing Digital Communication Strategies

The strategic plan goes through several stages, from defining goals to implementation.

Defining Goals

- This refers to the manager's attempt to identify and confirm the collective acceptance of the general goals of the communication strategy. The determination of these Defining Specific Goals: This requires involving everyone in the management team. This stage relies on several activities, including planning methodology and integrating management within the overall strategy.

- Studying the Organization's Social and Cultural Environment: In this phase, the organization searches for its identity and image. The identity is defined by its structures, systems, and history.

Ruler's Communication Strategies Model

The Ruler Model (2004) is based on the basic assumption that it is difficult to use a single communication strategy in public relations, and there is no optimal strategy. Instead, the most suitable strategy can be used for each specific communication situation. Ruler developed his model, which he called the "Situational Model of Communication Strategies," where a specific strategy can be applied to a particular situation.

- Information Strategy: Communication in this strategy is one-way (Asymmetrical), and the communication content expresses the organization's views, carrying singular meanings and implications (Denotative). The strategy involves providing information to key audiences to assist them in forming opinions and making decisions.
- Persuasion Strategy: This strategy combines one-way communication with content that expresses both the organization's and the audience's views, carrying implications that reflect both sides' perspectives (Connotative). Persuasion is the fundamental strategy used in advertising and public relations. It is used in organizational communications when the goal is to establish strategic relationships with key audiences. Through this strategy, the organization aims to intentionally change the knowledge.
- Building Consensus: This strategy combines two-way communication (Symmetrical) with content that expresses the organization's views (Denotative). It is used to build strategic relationships between the organization and its external environment or between the organization and its employees. It is typically applied when there is a conflict of interest between parties that depend on each other for existence. For example, organizations rely on key external audiences, and there is often a conflict between the organization's interests.
- Dialogue Strategy: The Dialogue Strategy combines two-way communication with content that expresses both the organization's and the audience's views, carrying implications that reflect both perspectives. This strategy involves consulting the audience on the organization's policies and considering their opinions on various issues. The audience is involved in the decision-making process. This is known as the facilitating strategy, where the organization facilitates audience participation and engagement in shaping its policies.

Sally, S. G. (2011). *An analytical study of the views of workers in the public and private tourism sector towards E-Government services* Master's Thesis, unpublished. Ain Shams University: Faculty of Girls, Department of Sociology, Media Section.

Shaima Abdel-Aty Said. (2015). *The use of social media by public relations practitioners in multinational companies operating in Egypt and its impact on their professional performance*. PhD Dissertation, unpublished. South Valley University: Faculty of Media, Public Relations and Advertising Department.

Sinha, A. K., Kumar, R., Sengupta, P. P., & Bandhopadhyay, G. (2017). Impact of organization's culture on employees' commitment: Evidence from five homogeneous units under a group of company operating in different states in India. *Journal of Business Studies Quarterly*, *8*(3), 89–105.

Sriramesh, K., Rivera-Sanchez, M., & Soriano, C. (2013). Websites for stakeholder relations by corporations and non-profits: A time-lag study in Singapore. *Journal of Communication Management*, *17*(2).

Tarigan, Z. (2017). The influence of corporate management commitment in building organizational culture and cross-functional integration to improve company business performance: The mediating role of employee organizational commitment. *International Journal of Education, Business, Management, and Learning*, *7* (3).

Zainab Saleh Abdel-Fadeel. (2018). *Communication and organizational culture and their relationship to shaping identity: An applied study on Egyptian telecommunication companies*. PhD Dissertation, unpublished. Al-Azhar University: Faculty of Media, Public Relations and Advertising Department.

Zoghloul, S. (2021). Digital public relations communication strategies and their role in enhancing organizational culture in multinational companies: An applied study. *Egyptian Journal of Mass Communication Research*, *2*.

Chapter 6

Employing Digital Technology of the Instagram Platform in Empowering Bahraini Women Politically, Economically, and Socially in Light of Sustainable Development Goals (SDGs) 2030

Zainab Mohsen Zain Aldeen

Ahlia University, Bahrain

Abstract

This study aims to identify the political, economic, and social dimensions of women's empowerment by utilizing digital technology of Instagram in light of the Sustainable Development Goals (SDGs) 2030. The study connects three key variables: the increasing direct impact of decision-making through social media, particularly Instagram, SDGs, and women empowerment. The study analyzes the significant participation of Bahraini women on Instagram and examines how the platform addresses women's issues. Additionally, it explores the cognitive and emotional effects of Instagram on its audience to empower Bahraini women and explores data and statistics that illustrate how Bahraini women rely on Instagram as a tool to empower them for achieving the SDGs 2030 through the supporting parties. The study used a theoretical framework based on three theories: feminist theory, media richness theory (MRT), and dependency theory. The study compared findings from Instagram pages of organizations that support women's empowerment in Bahrain, including the Supreme Council for Women, the Ministry of Social Development, the Council of Representatives, the Council of Senates, and the Tamkeen Institute, to secure in-depth understanding with regard to utilizing Instagram platform to support women's initiatives.

Digital Dialogues, 53–62

Published under exclusive licence by Emerald Publishing Limited
doi:10.1108/978-1-83708-686-320261006

Keywords: Digital technology; Instagram; women empowering issues; woman empowering; Bahraini woman empowering; empowering woman politically economically and socially; sustainable development goals

Introduction

The use of social media has become one of the most effective tools of mutual impact by communicating information and ideas. Social media networks have emerged as a critical component for millions globally, facilitating communication and interaction in the present era. The aspects of using social media have expanded, with Instagram being one of the most significant platforms. It has become an impactful and effective tool for shaping public opinion, influencing general decisions, and expanding freedom of speech regarding economic, political, and social issues. Instagram possesses several audience-attracting characteristics through artificial intelligence features that enhance user interaction with provided content.

Social media, specifically Instagram, has provided ample space for freedom of participation. It empowers individuals and communities to work toward positive change. Since women are primary partners alongside men, they contribute actively and progressively to advancing society through their capacity as cognitively and practically active agents. At the Arab level, many countries have taken important steps to support women's rights in alignment with their developmental goals. However, the outcomes have often not met expectations, as highlighted in the Arab Development Report of 2005 (Regional Office for Arab States, 2006).

On the national level, the Kingdom of Bahrain has approved numerous constitutional principles that support the political, economic, civil, and social rights of Bahraini women. According to The Constitution of Bahrain, "the country guarantees alignment between the duties of women towards their families and their roles in the community, ensuring equality with men in political, social, cultural, and economic aspects" (Legislative and Legal Opinion Authority, 2002). Therefore, the Bahraini government has worked diligently through various policies and agreements to empower women. One of the most significant initiatives was the establishment of the Supreme Council for Women, which aims to empower women, particularly in economic, political, and social spheres.

Despite these national efforts in public and private arenas, indicators of women's empowerment have not yet reached the targeted levels set in the Kingdom of Bahrain's Development Goals 2030, particularly in political and economic realms. This situation necessitates the use of all legislative tools to showcase the issues surrounding Bahraini women's empowerment, especially through social media platforms such as Instagram, the most widely used and interactive platform in Bahrain. This study aims to provide evidence derived from previous research work with regard to the role of Instagram in the political, economic, and social empowerment of Bahraini women. This study focuses on identifying the dimensions of employing the Instagram platform to empower Bahraini women and its role in addressing empowerment issues in alignment with the Sustainable Development Goals (SDGs) 2030 through the accounts of women empowerment-supportive parties. The study question is, "How is the Instagram platform being utilized through the accounts of Bahraini women-supporting parties politically, economically, and socially within the SDGs 2030?"

Literature Review

First: Theories Utilized to Explain the Study

The researcher relied on three key theories in this study: feminist theory, dependency theory, and media richness theory (MRT). These theories were employed to evaluate the utilization of the Instagram platform for Bahraini women in political and economic issues, aligning with the SDGs 2030.

Feminist Theory

Feminist theory assists in understanding how women interact with social media and how this interaction helps them build their Bahraini identity. It examines how social media represents the stereotypes of Bahraini women and explains the impact of social media content on public perception regarding women's issues to increase support for feminist topics in the Kingdom of Bahrain. Feminist theory also provides insights into the psychological effects and societal acceptance of social content among Bahraini women through affecting their capacity to engage in the development initiatives within the Kingdom. The theory enables an understanding of the dynamics of interaction between Bahraini women and the Instagram platform, identifying various interaction styles between women and their communities. Moreover, it facilitates an exploration of Bahraini women's experiences with Instagram, considering their diverse cultural, social, political, and economic backgrounds. This theory enhances research efforts by leveraging media tools to develop effective strategies that support the empowerment of Bahraini women within the framework of SDGs 2030.

Dependency Theory

Dependency theory assists in understanding the cognitive, behavioral, and emotional effects resulting from the interaction between Bahraini women and the Instagram platform. This theory explores how social media impacts Bahraini women regarding their empowerment in political, economic, and social spheres, all in alignment with the SDGs 2030. It also examines the reasons behind Bahraini audiences' reliance on the Instagram platform and their acceptance of the emotional, cognitive, and behavioral influences that arise from it.

Media Richness Theory

MRT helps measure the increase in information resulting from the utilization of the Instagram platform to achieve empowerment goals among Bahraini women. It emphasizes the need for women to acquire new knowledge and identify specific directions for their empowerment across various dimensions. MRT focuses on the nature of interaction between the audience and the message sender, particularly regarding parties concerned with enabling Bahraini women. It evaluates how effectively the platform's content facilitates understanding and engagement in line with the SDGs 2030. MRT assists in measuring feedback through the Instagram platform, highlighting its richness as a communication tool. As the most widely used social media platform in Bahrain, Instagram allows women to select messages based on their richness, enabling interaction between women and social media. This selection process helps identify the benefits received from utilizing social media in achieving the targeted empowering of Bahraini women.

Second: Relevant Studies

First Domain: Studies Relevant to Social Media Platforms

- A study by Zainaldeen & Alhalwachi (2024) examined the impact of digital social media on empowering women, particularly Bahraini women, across various levels and fields. The findings emphasize the effectiveness of the Bahraini government's initiatives in achieving SDGs related to women's empowerment, aligning with the Kingdom's Vision 2030. Key results indicate that digital media has significantly advanced women's participation in multiple fields, with Bahraini women achieving foundational digital skills through various transformation programs. The study suggests that Bahraini women are driven to lead in modern technology, actively participating in all areas of life.
- A study by Gamal El-Din & Mohammed (2023) aimed to identify the role of social media platforms in empowering Egyptian women, focusing on how these platforms influence their social identity through the Media Richness framework. The findings revealed that increased exposure to social media positively correlates with issues of women's empowerment, particularly in social aspects, highlighting the platforms' significant role in fostering empowerment among Egyptian women.
- A study by Al-Maimani (2021) aimed to determine whether female Twitter users in Arab countries believe that the religious and cultural restrictions imposed by their governments are overcome by the internet and how this perception affects them in real life. The findings revealed that the concept of empowerment is a multidimensional and interdisciplinary process. Additionally, the use of the internet by Arab women has supported education, healthcare, governance, and economic policies.
- A study by Kadeswaran et al. (2020) analyzed women's perspectives on the role of social media in their empowerment using semistructured interviews

with 23 users of women-only cafes. Key findings revealed that the majority of participants use social media for entertainment and information gathering. Additionally, social media networks often present stereotypical images of women, reinforce traditional roles, and highlight issues of violence against women.

- A study by Abu Snah (2020) focused on assessing the extent to which Saudi women rely on social media networks to enhance their knowledge of entrepreneurship in light of Saudi Arabia Vision (2030) and the empowerment of Saudi women. Key findings indicated that 68.33% of Saudi women consistently rely on social media to develop their knowledge of entrepreneurship-related topics. Additionally, 94.08% of participants perceived the role of social media as positive regarding entrepreneurship.
- A study by Sharfa (2018) aimed to explore the role of social media in economically and socially empowering Palestinian women in Tulkarem Governorate. The researcher relied on in-depth face-to-face interviews with 10 women who run marketing businesses through social media platforms. The study was grounded in social role theory, feminist theory, needs theory, and uses and gratifications theory. The findings revealed that social media served as a primary tool for self-empowerment, social empowerment, economic growth, and knowledge enhancement for Palestinian women.

Second Domain: Studies Relevant to Women's Empowering Issues

- A study by Abdel Tawab (2024) aimed to identify the extent to which Egyptian women benefit from digital platforms. The study examines their ability to interact freely on these platforms to achieve social, economic, political, cultural, and educational benefits. The results indicate that the level of connectivity among Egyptian women is a crucial factor in achieving women's empowerment. Furthermore, the findings suggest that Egyptian women require additional efforts to provide equal communication opportunities through digital platforms to enhance their economic, social, and political participation.
- A study by Kamel et al. (2024) aimed to identify the key concepts of women's social empowerment by reviewing the theoretical issues surrounding women's empowerment through empowerment theory and feminist theory. The findings highlight significant concepts related to women's social empowerment, including self-confidence, reliance on self, and the ability to establish social relationships and new friendships, as well as developmental concepts aimed at increasing women's awareness of their social rights.
- A study by Jalambo & Akroush (2024) aimed to explore the role of social workers in empowering abused women within social institutions in Amman. The study is based on feminist theory and structural functionalism, employing a descriptive analytical approach through a questionnaire that included a sample of 160 abused women in Amman. The findings revealed that social workers play a significant role in informing Jordanian abused women about

their rights, legal procedures, and the penalties related to the abuse of women according to Jordanian judicial legislation.

- A study by Abdal (2024) aimed to uncover the efforts to politically empower Kuwaiti women through statistics indicating their participation in public life, decision-making positions, and the challenges and obstacles limiting their empowerment. The results indicated that the majority of respondents believe that the statements regarding the political participation of Kuwaiti women have been achieved, while they rated the statements regarding the obstacles to women's empowerment in Kuwait as moderate. The study concluded that official entities need to coordinate more broadly with civil society organizations to support the political empowerment of Kuwaiti women.
- A study by Hussein Saleh (2022) aimed to explain the relationship between civil society organizations and the political empowerment of Egyptian women. The theoretical framework of the study employs feminist theory. One of the key findings indicates that the Egyptian Center for Women's Rights lacks a clear policy regarding the political empowerment of Egyptian women; all its initiatives are still in the developmental stage and lack specialized administrative support and programs that align with the political, economic, and social changes in the Arab Republic of Egypt.
- A study by Omar (2020) seeks to explore the attitudes toward the economic empowerment of Saudi women and the obstacles to this empowerment concerning principles, mechanisms, levels, and indicators. The results revealed that one of the essential principles needed by Saudi women is the development of their personal capabilities for economic success, which depends on their self-efficiency in light of the current laws that provide greater opportunities for women in the economic field. Saudi women still require further achievement of legal and economic equality and economic decision-making.
- A study by Abu Al-Khair (2019) indicated a persistent male social dominance over most of the sample, particularly from first-degree relatives such as fathers, husbands, and brothers, which has delayed the engagement of Emirati women in social activities more than expected. The findings show that the political empowerment of Emirati women by official institutions in the UAE is progressing more rapidly than their social empowerment, primarily due to social constraints based on traditional norms that delayed the development and social progress of Emirati women.

Third Domain: Studies Relevant to Sustainable Development

- A study by Al-Askari (2024) aimed to address the feminist societies' pages on platforms to highlight the roles that women should play in rural communities and identify the social challenges that hinder sustainable development plans for empowering rural women. The study found that Facebook platforms predominantly use images and text to engage the audience (71.79%), showcasing the achievements of Egyptian women in society. Additionally, it noted that the content shared on the primary center's page comprised 44.87% of the available public material, indicating that feminist association pages on Facebook effectively present content supportive of women's empowerment.

- A study by El Tarabishi & Hassan (2023) aimed to explore the role of social media in empowering women within the framework of the fifth SDG. The research findings highlighted that social media has become the most successful medium for empowering women, facilitating direct and easy interaction between women in need of development and the organizations focused on women's growth. Moreover, the study found that social media has overcome various social, economic, and political barriers.
- A study by Salama (2022) focused on the empowerment of Saudi women and its impact on their attitudes toward sustainable development plans. Utilizing MRT to construct variables and interpret results, the research findings revealed that Twitter is the most utilized platform among Saudi women due to its interactive features. The study highlighted Twitter's role in shaping women's attitudes and providing a realistic perspective on sustainable development in the Kingdom, enhancing acceptance of sustainable development plans and strategies.
- A study by Sharaf (2021) aimed to reveal the empowerment of Egyptian women across media, economic, social, and political dimensions through the significant role of social media in sustainable development plans. The findings established a correlation between social media use and reliance on information related to SDGs for empowerment. Additionally, the study concluded that respondents expressed confidence in the content of social media regarding women's empowerment.

Conclusion

Most previous studies employed feminist theory as a framework to explain the impact of social media platforms on audience awareness regarding women's issues, thereby increasing support and advocacy for feminist issues. Other studies utilized MRT, focusing significantly on the interactions between the audience (Al-Askari, 2024; Gamal El-Din & Mohammed, 2023; Salama, 2022; Sharaf, 2021), while Abu Snah (2020) and Sharaf (2021) relied on social media theory.

Most previous studies were descriptive and employed screening as an approach. Approximately half of these studies utilized questionnaires, while the other half relied on interviews, though in-depth interviews, semistructured interviews, or direct field interviews were less common.

The studies revealed a significant role for various social media platforms in empowering women and supporting women's issues. These platforms have become primary sources for women's participation across all aspects of social life, extending to decision-making levels and achieving high gains on national, political, economic, and social aspects. Other studies indicated that the content of digital media platforms serves as a crucial information reference, enabling women from different regions to identify the developmental procedures necessary in their lives. Social media platforms foster diverse opinions and support for women's empowerment in an incremental overall approach. Social media platforms support women's issues and serve as a landmark in amplifying women's voices while providing opportunities for greater participation in social life. Additionally, these studies highlighted significant efforts by formal institutions and civil society organizations to support women's issues. There is a consensus that empowering women within the frameworks of SDGs has led to unprecedented advancements at the political, social, and economic levels through the utilization of social media.

References

Abdal, Y. (2024). Political empowerment of women in the State of Kuwait. *Journal of the Faculty of Arts (JFA)*, *84*(3–3), 389–423. https://jfa.cu.edu.eg/cgi/viewcontent.cgi?article=1609&context=journal

Abdel tawab, N. M. (2024). Mu'alajat mawsaat Al-Raqmiyah Li Qadayaa Tamkeen Al-Mar'ah Wa 'Alaqatuh Bi Mustawa Al-Hudur Al-Ittisali Li Mustakhdimiha [digital platforms address women's empowerment issues and their relationship to the level of contact presence of its users]. *Scientific Journal of Research on Women, Media, and Society Studies*, *2*(1), 338–363. https://doi.org/10.21608/jwms.2024.290260.1011

Abu Al-Khair, O. (2019). Mushkilat Al-Mar'ah Al-Imaratiyah Bayn Al-Tamkeen Al-Siyasi Wal-Tamkeen Al-Mujtama'i: Dirasat Halat Imarat. [Emirati women's problems between political and societal empowerment: A case study of the Emirates]. *Al-Adab Journal*, *128*, 429–472. https://doi.org/10.31973/aj.v0i128.403

Abu Snah, N. H. M. (2020). I'timad Al-Fatat Al-Saudiyah Ala Shabakat Al-Tawasul Al-Ijtima'i Fi Tanmiyat Ma'arifaha Nawh Ri'adat Al-A'mal Fi Dhaw Al-Ru'yah (2030) Wa Tamkeen Al-Mar'ah Al-Saudiyah [Saudi Girls' Dependence on Social Media Networks in Developing Their Knowledge Towards Entrepreneurship in Light of Vision 2030 and the Empowerment of Saudi Women]. *Journal of Media Research*, *55*(2), 751–800. https://doi.org/10.21608/jsb.2020.117969

Al-Askari, H. R. (2024). Mu'alajat Safahat Al-Jam'iyat Al-Naswiyah Ala Mawaqi' Al-Tawasul Al-Ijtima'i Li Qadayaa Al-Mar'ah Al-Rifiyah Fi Itar Khutat Al-Tanmiya Al-Mustadamah Fi Misr: Dirasah Tahliliyah [The Treatment of Women's Issues by Women's Associations on Social Media in the Framework of Sustainable Development Plans in Egypt: An Analytical Study]. *Egyptian Journal of Media Research*, *89*, 597–648. https://doi.org/10.21608/ejsc.2024.390355

Al-Maimani, H. A. J. (2021). Online versus offline world: A thematic analysis of Arab women's empowerment via social media. *Athens Journal of Mass Media and Communications*, *7*(3), 165–182. https://doi.org/10.30958/ajmmc.7-3-2

El Tarabishi, M., & Hassan, R. H. (2023). The role of social media campaigns in supporting the SDG of women's empowerment. *The Arab Journal of Media and Communication Research (AJMCR)*, *41*, 2–26. https://jkom.journals.ekb.eg/article_315823_c9a0c3ce43c5d98d732b0a5d451e9843.pdf?lang=en#:~:text=Social media has proven to,in the past few decades

Gamal El-Din, S. A. H., & Mohammed, R. A. M. (2023). Dawr Mawaqi' Al-Tawasul Al-Ijtima'i Fi Tamkeen Al-Mar'ah Wa Madha In'ikasaha Ala Huwiyatiha Al-Thaqafiyah [The Role of Social Media in Empowering Women and Its

Reflection on Their Cultural Identity]. *Journal of Media Research*, *66*(1), 333–370. https://doi.org/10.21608/jsb.2023.201472.1576

Hussein Saleh, A. M. A. (2022). Dawr munazzamat Al-Mujtama' Al-Madani Fi Al-Tamkeen Al-Siyasi Lil-Mar'ah Al-Misriyah [The Role of Civil Society Organizations in the Political Empowerment of Egyptian Women "An Empirical Study on the Egyptian Center for Women's Rights.". *Egyptian Journal of Social and Behavioral Sciences*, *6*(6), 22–55. https://doi.org/10.21608/ejsbs.2022.138229.1007

Jalambo, D. J. R. A., & Akroush, L. J. (2024). The role of the social worker at social institutions in empowering battered women: A study from Amman. *Dirasat: Human and Social Sciences*, *51*(4), 112–128. https://doi.org/10.35516/hum.v51i4.4084

Kadeswaran, S., Brindha, D., & Jayaseelan, R. (2020). Social media as a gateway for accelerating women empowerment. *Parishodh Journal*, *9*(3), 4876–4885. https://www.academia.edu/42314005/Social_Media_as_a_Gateway_for_Accelerating_Women_Empowerment

Kamel, S. M., Lotfi, T., & Madbouli, G. (2024). Al-Tamkeen Al-Ijtima'i Lil-Mar'ah: Al-Mafhum Wal-Mu'ashirat [Social Empowerment of Women: Concept and Indicators]. *Journal of the Faculty of Arts, Beni Suef University*, *8*(72), 323–342. https://doi.org/10.21608/jfabsu.2024.286203.1334

Legislative and Legal Opinion Authority. (2002). *Dustur mamlakat Al-Bahrain Al-Mu'addal Al-Ma'ada Al-Khamisah [the amended constitution of the kingdom of Bahrain, Article] 5*. https://www.lloc.gov.bh/page/دستور مملكة البحرين

Omar, A. A.-A. M. (2020). Al-Tamkeen Al-Iqtisadi Lil-Mar'ah Al-Saudiyah: Al-Ab'ad Wal-Mu'awwiqat [Economic Empowerment of Saudi Women: Dimensions and Obstacles]. *Umm Al-Qura University Journal of Social Sciences*, *12*(2), 1–41. https://drive.uqu.edu.sa/_/jss/files/12/2/5.pdf

Regional Office for Arab States. (2006). *Taqrir Al-Tanmiya Al-Inسانiyah Al-Arabiyah Lil-Aam 2005 – Nahw Nuhud Al-Mar'ah Fi Al-Alam Al-Arabi, Barnamaj Al-Umam Al-Muttahida Al-Tanmi, Al-Sunduq Al-Arabi Lil-Inma' Al-Iqtisadi Wal-Ijtima'i,* Barnamaj Al-Khalij Al-Arabi Lid'am Munazzamat Al-Umam Al-Muttahida Al-Tanmiya, Al-Matba'a Al-Wataniyah [Arab Human Development Report 2005 – Towards the Advancement of Women in the Arab World,United Nations Development Programme, Arab Fund for Economic and Social Development, Gulf Cooperation Council Programme to Support UN Development Organizations]. https://www.un.org/ar/esa/ahdr/pdf/ahdr05/intro-ar.pdf

Salama, M. W. (2022). Dawr Mawaqi' Al-Tawasul Al-Ijtima'i Twitter Fi Tashkeel Ittijahat Al-Mar'ah Al-Saudiyah Nawh Idrak Khutat Al-Tanmiya Al-Mustadamah [The Role of Twitter in Shaping Saudi Women's Attitudes Towards Understanding Sustainable Development Plans]. *Arab Universities Union Journal for Media Research and Communication Technology*, *9*, 69–109. https://doi.org/10.21608/jcts.2022.269818

Sharaf, J. (2021). I'timad Al-Mar'ah Al-Misriyah Ala Mawaqi' Al-Tawasul Al-Ijtima'i Wa 'Alaqatuh Bi Tamkeenha Fi Dhaw Khutat Al-Tanmiya Al-Mustadamah [The Dependence of Egyptian Women on Social Media and Its Relationship to Their Empowerment in Light of Sustainable Development Plans]. *Egyptian Journal of Public Opinion Research*, *20*(4), 149–193. https://doi.org/10.21608/joa.2021.214930

Sharfa, L. H. K. (2018). *Dawr Mawaqi' Al-Tawasul Al-Ijtima'i Fi Tamkeen Al-Mar'ah Al-Filastiniyah Iqtisadiyan Wa Ijtima'iyan Fi Muhafazat Tulkarem - Facebook Anmuthajan [The Role of Social Media in Economically and Socially Empowering Palestinian Women in Tulkarem Governorate - A Case Study of Facebook].* [An-Najah National University]. https://hdl.handle.net/20.500.11888/15816

Zainaldeen, Z., & Alhalwachi, L. (2024). The impacts of digital media on the empowerment of Bahraini women in the light of SDGS 2030. In *Business development via AI and digitalization* (Vol. 538, pp. 259–269). Springer. https://doi.org/10.1007/978-3-031-62102-4_21

Chapter 7

The Effect of Perceived Innovativeness and Social Media Channels on Entrepreneurship Intentions

Fatema Waleed AlMerbati

Ahlia University, Bahrain

Abstract

This study aims to investigate the impact of social media channels on individual innovation, focusing on the mediating role of self-efficacy among employees in the telecommunications sector in Bahrain. The study reviewed a wide range of previous research studies, varying in methodologies, tools, and samples. The results showed that the positive use of social media channels contributes to enhancing individual innovation by expanding the interaction circle, knowledge exchange, and providing social support.

The survey revealed a crucial role of self-efficacy in enhancing this effect; personal confidence enables individuals to try new experiences and adopt creative ideas, which positively impacts their performance and innovation. The results also indicated that the correct use of social media channels increases opportunities for resource and information exchange and boosts individual motivation. However, some organizational and skill-related factors may limit the full benefit from these platforms.

The study recommends intensifying institutional training and awareness for employees on how to effectively utilize social media channels in the workplace, with a focus on developing their self-efficacy through targeted workshops and training courses, thereby fostering a spirit of innovation and initiative. It also calls for clear policies to regulate the use of these platforms while safeguarding information privacy and creating an organizational climate that encourages the exchange of ideas and constructive dialogues, allowing individuals an appropriate space to develop their innovative capabilities.

Digital Dialogues, 63–71

Published under exclusive licence by Emerald Publishing Limited
doi:10.1108/978-1-83708-686-320261007

Keywords: Social media channels; self-efficacy; individual innovation; job innovation; telecommunications sector

Introduction

Employee innovation is considered one of the most important sources of competitive advantage and success for businesses. Previous studies have shown that employees with innovative ideas are crucial for the performance and productivity of organizations (Kaveski & Beuren, 2020). Studies also indicate that employees with innovative ideas possess a high level of self-confidence (Bormann, 2020) and those characterized by innovation are always engaged in social networks (Sigala & Chalkiti, 2015). Additionally, employees with innovative ideas consistently bring change to the organization and are adept at solving complex problems (Qahir et al., 2022).

The new idea depends on the context in which it is evaluated as good or bad, and an idea is considered innovative if it is unique and useful (Asghar et al., 2022). Innovation is defined as the emergence of original and creative ideas within organizations, related to products, services, practices, or technologies. Innovation thus plays a pivotal role in the sustainability and performance of organizations (Sun et al., 2020).

Specifically, social media channels are one of the main applications of digital technology in work and life (Ramdani et al., 2022). They are defined as "a group of online applications based on the ideological and technological foundations of Web 2.0, allowing the creation and exchange of user-generated content" (Kaplan & Haenlein, 2010). The use of social media in organizations reflects significant changes in organizational life (Leonardi & Vaast, 2017).

In this regard, literature suggests that the use of social media impacts individuals' self-efficacy, meaning that an individual's behavior may vary depending on their self-efficacy levels when using social media platforms (Choi & Noh, 2023). The use of social media enhances certain cognitive abilities, allowing individuals to gain better self-value or self-efficacy and achieve superior life outcomes (Mohammed et al., 2021).

Therefore, this study aims to examine the impact of social media usage on individual innovation, with self-efficacy as a mediating role, focusing on employees in the telecommunications sector in Bahrain.

Previous Studies

This section of the research addresses the previous studies reviewed, which have been categorized into three groups: studies that addressed social media channels and individual innovation, studies that addressed social media channels and self-efficacy, and, finally, studies that addressed self-efficacy and individual innovation.

Previous Studies Addressing Social Media Channels and Individual Innovation

The study by Pitafi and Xie (2024) aimed to measure the impact of social media usage on employee innovation in the context of the mediating role of basic psychological needs (perceived relatedness, autonomy, and competence) among employees in technology companies in China. The study applied a descriptive-analytical method using a survey distributed to 415 of these employees. The results showed a statistically significant positive impact of social media usage on the innovation of these employees. The study concluded that using social media improved employee innovation by enhancing perceived relatedness between them and their colleagues, as well as their perceived competence, since they were able to provide valuable information to their colleagues. The study recommended that managers distribute responsibilities among employees properly and provide them with the ability to determine their own destiny, which could help them develop new ideas. It also recommended that managers assign work tasks based on employees' competencies whenever possible.

The study by Zhang and Mao (2023) aimed to examine the effect of social media usage on individual innovation among students in a university and employees in a national bank in China. The study applied a descriptive-analytical method using a survey distributed to 64 university students and 493 pairs of employees and their direct supervisors in a national bank in China. The results showed a statistically significant positive impact of social media usage on the innovation of students and employees. The study concluded that social media usage helps individuals develop reciprocal relationships with others, which encourages risk-taking and enhances the learning culture in the workplace, increasing their innovation, specifically because the learning culture satisfies their psychological needs and increases their motivation, making them more active at work and dedicated and ultimately improving their innovation level. The study recommended that users should be proficient in utilizing the knowledge and social resources of social media channels while minimizing the loss of material and mental resources resulting from social media through mindful job design, which would increase their capacity for innovation.

The study by Wang et al. (2022) investigated the impact of social media usage (for work and social purposes) on employee innovation in the context of the mediating roles of performance-related and expressive-related links among employees in various commercial companies in China. The study applied a descriptive-analytical method using a survey distributed to 325 of these employees. The results revealed a statistically significant positive correlation between social media usage (for work and social purposes) and employee innovation. Additionally, the study found that the use of social media for both work and social purposes led to performance and expressive links among employees, which in turn enhanced their innovation. The study concluded that using social media increases opportunities for knowledge exchange between individuals, and this exchange helps form a contextual trait to meet individuals' needs for autonomy and competence, thus allowing them access to the necessary resources to generate innovative ideas. The study recommended that employees take steps to enhance their interaction with colleagues.

The study by Gulzar et al. (2022) aimed to measure the impact of social media usage on student innovation and academic participation in the context of the mediating role of intrinsic motivation among students in various universities in Hefei, Anhui Province, China. The study applied a descriptive-analytical method using a survey distributed to 267 university and graduate students enrolled in these universities. The results showed a statistically significant positive correlation between social media usage and innovation among these students. The results also revealed a statistically significant positive impact of social media usage on these students' innovation. The study concluded that students' use of social media acted as a key driver for innovation and participation in academic activities, as it facilitates the development of reciprocal relationships with others, which in turn encourages risk-taking and enhances the learning culture, leading to increased innovation, particularly because the learning culture satisfies their psychological needs and increases their motivation, making them more active and more dedicated to their work, thus improving their innovation level. The study recommended that educational institutions, teachers, students, and parents should recognize the positive application of social media in academic environments, and students should be encouraged to benefit from social media platforms such as ResearchGate, Scribd, LinkedIn, Academia.edu, and others.

Studies Addressing Social Media Channels and Self-Efficacy

In this context, the study by Choi and Noh (2023) aimed to investigate the mediating role of self-efficacy in the relationship between social media channels and preventive behavior during the COVID-19 outbreak in South Korea. The study applied a descriptive-analytical method using a survey distributed to 1,500 South Korean adults. The results showed a statistically significant positive correlation between social media channels and self-efficacy among these adults. The results also revealed a statistically significant positive impact of social media channels on the self-efficacy of these adults. The study concluded that social media channels increased the limits of personal interaction on social platforms and enhanced the level of social support received by users, which encouraged users to engage in learning and benefit from this social support. The study recommended paying more attention to social media channels, as they can help develop useful strategies for healthy communication and risk reduction for the public in future public health crises.

Similarly, the study by Wasike (2023) aimed to investigate the mediating role of self-efficacy in the relationship between social media influencers and the social interaction of social media users in the United States. The study applied a descriptive-analytical method using a survey distributed to 834 social media users in the United States. The results showed a statistically significant positive correlation between social media channels and self-efficacy among these users. The results also revealed a statistically significant positive impact of social media channels on the self-efficacy of these users. The study concluded that following social media influencers has an empowering effect on followers, as it not only increases their self-efficacy but also enhances their knowledge acquisition.

In the same regard, the study by Mohammed et al. (2021) aimed to investigate the mediating role of self-efficacy in the relationship between social media usage and the academic performance of students in several higher education institutions in Malaysia. The study applied a descriptive-analytical method using a survey distributed to 644 Malaysian students from higher education institutions. The results showed a statistically significant positive correlation between social media channels and self-efficacy among these students. The results also revealed a statistically significant positive impact of social media channels on the self-efficacy of these students. The study concluded that the correct usage of social media channels for academic purposes enhances students' self-efficacy and academic performance, especially since self-efficacy enables students to acquire more information. The study recommended that faculty members observe the extensive use of social media channels among their students and recommended that students help their peers manage the use of social media channels.

Studies Addressing Self-Efficacy and Individual Innovation

The study by Fadhilah (2024) aimed to measure the impact of self-efficacy on the innovation of students at Fatimawati Sukarno State Islamic University in Bengkulu, Indonesia. The research applied a descriptive-analytical methodology, distributing a survey to 74 students at the university. The results revealed a statistically significant positive impact of self-efficacy on the innovation of these students. The study concluded that students exhibiting high levels of self-efficacy were able to contribute numerous ideas by combining various ideas and approaches to solving problems. The study recommended that, in order to enhance innovation among students, they should focus on strengthening their self-confidence in their abilities. Additionally, the study recommended that university decision-makers take the necessary steps to build and improve the self-confidence of students, as this could lead to an increased level of innovative thinking and behavior.

Similarly, the study by Huang et al. (2024) sought to investigate the impact of self-efficacy on the innovation of English as a Foreign Language (EFL) teachers in China. The study applied a descriptive-analytical method, utilizing a survey distributed to 542 teachers. The results indicated a statistically significant positive correlation between self-efficacy and the innovation of these teachers. The research concluded that self-confidence, which is central to self-efficacy, serves as a psychological asset that helps individuals perform various tasks with greater ease. The authors recommended that educational authorities make more use of the novel ideas and creative solutions proposed by these teachers to design professional development programs that focus on enhancing self-efficacy. The study also emphasized the importance of giving teachers a higher degree of autonomy when designing and implementing curricula to create an environment conducive to higher levels of innovation.

Another study by Qahir et al. (2022) aimed to explore the mediating role of self-efficacy in the relationship between emotional intelligence and employee innovation in primary healthcare centers in Pakistan. This study applied a descriptive-analytical approach, distributing surveys to 94 employees working in primary healthcare settings. The results demonstrated a statistically significant positive relationship between self-efficacy and employee innovation. Moreover, the study found that self-efficacy had a statistically significant positive impact on the innovation of employees. The research concluded that employees with high levels of self-confidence are more likely to embrace challenging tasks without fear of failure or uncertainty. The study further revealed that employees who possess high emotional intelligence are more adept at generating innovative ideas and applying them to their daily and formal work activities. These employees use their emotional intelligence to navigate challenges in ways that foster innovation in the workplace. The study concluded that a strong sense of self-efficacy creates a powerful combination that enables employees to bring new ideas and improvements to the organization. The authors recommended that organizations review their policies and practices to promote and strengthen self-confidence among their employees.

Commentary on Previous Studies

Based on the reviewed literature, which examined the key variables of the study—social media channels, self-efficacy, and individual innovation—there is a significant diversity in the studies, primarily due to the different environments in which they were conducted, such as China, South Korea, the United States, Malaysia, Indonesia, and Pakistan. Although these studies utilized the descriptive-analytical methodology, they varied in their research objectives, study populations, and sample sizes. As a result, the findings differ significantly from one study to another. Below is a detailed commentary on the previous studies:

Impact of Social Media Usage on Individual Innovation (Job Innovation or Employee Innovation)

Studies investigating the relationship between social media usage and individual innovation consistently show a statistically significant positive impact on innovation (Gulzar et al., 2022; Pitafi & Xie, 2024; Wang et al., 2022; Zhang & Mao, 2023). Several studies attribute this positive impact to the enhancement of employees' perceived connection with their colleagues, which helps them perceive themselves as competent by providing valuable information to others. This connection also enables employees to achieve a higher level of control over their tasks, which satisfies their need for autonomy, thus fostering their creativity and innovation (Pitafi & Xie, 2024).

Other studies highlight how social media allows individuals to develop reciprocal relationships, which promote risk-taking and foster a learning culture within the workplace. This learning culture not only satisfies individuals' psychological needs but also increases their intrinsic motivation. Consequently, individuals become more engaged, ultimately improving their level of innovation (Zhang & Mao, 2023).

A number of studies also emphasize the role of social media in enhancing knowledge sharing among employees, which helps them address their need for autonomy and competence. Through frequent knowledge exchange, individuals gain access to the necessary resources that enable them to generate innovative ideas. Both types of social media usage—whether in professional interactions or knowledge-sharing contexts—are critical for fostering innovation among employees (Wang et al., 2022). Moreover, another study specifically focusing on students found that social media usage was a key driver of innovation and participation in academic activities. As a result, students work with greater dedication, thereby improving their level of innovation (Gulzar et al., 2022).

Impact of Social Media on Self-Efficacy

Studies examining the impact of social media on self-efficacy found a statistically significant positive effect (Choi & Noh, 2023; Mohammed et al., 2021; Wasike, 2023). One study explains this effect by stating that social media expands the boundaries of personal interaction, increases users' social support, and promotes learning. As a result, users engage in knowledge exchange through social platforms, which in turn helps them build group identities within social networks (Choi & Noh, 2023).

Another study highlights how social media enables users to follow influencers, which increases social interactions and promotes knowledge acquisition. This improved knowledge sharing helps boost self-efficacy by encouraging individuals to apply what they learn (Wasike, 2023).

Furthermore, another study examining students' use of social media for academic purposes found that it significantly enhances self-efficacy and academic performance. The study argues that when students use social media for educational reasons, it helps them acquire more information, which ultimately improves their self-efficacy and academic outcomes (Mohammed et al., 2021).

Impact of Self-Efficacy on Individual Innovation

The relationship between self-efficacy and individual innovation was also widely studied, and the results show a statistically significant positive effect (Fadhilah, 2024; Huang et al., 2024; Qahir et al., 2022). One study highlighted that students with higher levels of self-efficacy are more capable of generating numerous innovative ideas by integrating various concepts to form creative solutions. The behaviors observed among students who cultivate innovation include a strong curiosity, a willingness to experiment, and an eagerness to receive new stimuli. These behaviors demonstrate their inclination toward innovation and their desire to create (Fadhilah, 2024).

Another study argued that self-efficacy, particularly self-confidence, is a crucial psychological asset that enhances employees' ability to perform tasks and increases their intrinsic motivation to overcome challenges. When employees possess high self-confidence, they are more likely to engage in innovative behaviors because they feel empowered to face obstacles in their work environment (Huang et al., 2024).

Similarly, a study on healthcare workers in Pakistan pointed out that self-efficacy enables employees to take on difficult tasks without fear of failure (Qahir et al., 2022).

Conclusion

The findings underscore the importance of effectively integrating social media channels with organizational efforts aimed at boosting self-efficacy. This integration is vital in driving innovation and development. At the same time, these results urge decision-makers, managers, and educational institutions to prioritize creating supportive environments—whether through developing policies or implementing field activities—that raise awareness about the positive use of social media and direct it toward achieving creative goals.

In conclusion, this study suggests that the key to an institution's success today lies in developing its human capital through fostering self-confidence and innovation. This requires focused efforts to enhance self-efficacy among employees and students, ensuring progress in innovation and institutional performance.

References

Asghar, F., Mahmood, S., Iqbal Khan, K., Gohar Qureshi, M., & Fakhri, M. (2022). Eminence of leader humility for follower creativity during COVID-19: The role of self-efficacy and proactive personality. *Frontiers in Psychology*, *12*, 1–10.

Bormann, K. (2020). Turning daily time pressure into a creative day: The interactionist roles of employee neuroticism and time pressure dispersion. *Applied Psychology*, *69*(3), 589–615.

Choi, D., & Noh, G. (2023). The impact of social media on preventive behavior during the COVID-19 outbreak in South Korea: The roles of social norms and self-efficacy. *Sage Open*, *13*(3), 1–15.

Fadhilah, F. (2024). Exploration of the influence: Self action, self efficacy on student creativity in general biology. *Journal of Academic Biology and Biology Education*, *1* (1), 19–27.

Gulzar, M., Ahmad, M., Hassan, M., & Rasheed, M. (2022). How social media use is related to student engagement and creativity: Investigating through the lens of intrinsic motivation. *Behaviour & Information Technology*, *41*(11), 2283–2293.

Huang, M., Zhang, M., & Greenier, V. (2024). Modeling the contribution of self-efficacy, collective efficacy, and autonomy to professional creativity of Chinese EFL teachers. *International Journal of Applied Linguistics*, 1–21. https://doi.org/10.1111/ijal.12626

Kaplan, A., & Haenlein, M. (2010). Users of the world, unite! The challenges and opportunities of social media. *Business Horizons*, *53*(1), 59–68.

Kaveski, I., & Beuren, I. (2020). Influence of management control systems and creativity on job performance. *Cadernos Ebape. Br*, *18*(3), 543–556.

Leonardi, P., & Vaast, E. (2017). Social media and their affordances for organizing: A review and agenda for research. *The Academy of Management Annals*, *11*(1), 150–188.

Mohammed, M., Ibrahim, F., & Yunus, N. (2021). Exploring the relationship of social media usage and multitasking of social media on self-efficacy and academic performance. *Jurnal Komunikasi: Malaysian Journal of Communication*, *37*(1), 227–243.

Pitafi, A., & Xie, W. (2024). Exploring how enterprise social media usage affects employee creativity: Based on self-determination theory. *Heliyon*, *10*(5), 1–10.

Qahir, A., Karim, J., & Kakar, A. (2022). The mediating role of self-efficacy between emotional intelligence and employees' creativity. *Pakistan Social Sciences Review*, *6*(2), 209–220.

Ramdani, B., Raja, S., & Kayumova, M. (2022). Digital innovation in SMEs: A systematic review, synthesis and research agenda. *Information Technology for Development*, *28*(1), 56–80.

Sigala, M., & Chalkiti, K. (2015). Knowledge management, social media and employee creativity. *International Journal of Hospitality Management*, *45*, 44–58.

Sun, Y., Wang, C., & Jeyaraj, A. (2020). Enterprise social media affordances as enablers of knowledge transfer and creative performance: An empirical study. *Telematics and Informatics*, *51*, 1–10.

Wang, Z., Hangeldiyeva, M., Ali, A., & Guo, M. (2022). Effect of enterprise social media on employee creativity: Social exchange theory perspective. *Frontiers in Psychology*, *12*, 812490.

Wasike, B. (2023). The influencer sent me! Examining how social media influencers affect social media engagement, social self-efficacy, knowledge acquisition, and social interaction. *Telematics and Informatics Reports*, *10*, 1–10.

Zhang, G., & Mao, S. (2023). A double-edged sword: Social media use and creativity. *Information Technology & People*, 1–26. https://doi.org/10.1108/ITP-09-2022-0682

Chapter 8

Professional and Ethical Standards Related to the Use of Artificial Intelligence Applications by Public Relations Practitioners in Bahraini Government Institutions

Fatema Abdulwahed Alseddeqi

Media Advisor, Bahrain

Abstract

Public relations (PR) serve as a cornerstone in shaping organizational reputation and managing behavioral and communication challenges across diverse contexts. As technological innovation transforms media and communication landscapes, PR practitioners must adapt to new ethical and professional realities shaped by artificial intelligence (AI). This study explores the implications of AI integration in PR practice, emphasizing the ethical and professional standards required to ensure transparency, accountability, and public trust.

The deployment of AI-driven tools in PR facilitates strategic communication, crisis management, and data-driven decision-making while enhancing efficiency and productivity. However, these advances also generate ethical dilemmas related to privacy, misinformation, and the potential dehumanization of communication processes. The relationship between PR practitioners and intelligent technologies must therefore be framed as a collaborative partnership rather than a competitive dynamic, where human judgment and ethical reasoning remain central to practice.

The study underscores the importance of establishing robust ethical frameworks and institutional policies to guide AI applications in PR, ensuring responsible innovation aligned with societal values and communication ethics. Ultimately, strengthening professional ethics in the era of

Digital Dialogues, 73–81

Published under exclusive licence by Emerald Publishing Limited
doi:10.1108/978-1-83708-686-320261008

intelligent technologies enhances the credibility, legitimacy, and sustainability of organizational communication.

Keywords: Professional ethics in public relations; artificial intelligence in public relations; communication ethics; digital media responsibility; ethical communication governance

Introduction

Public relations (PR) plays a clear role in promoting effective communication, which is an essential element in the strategy of communication, which contributes to building trust and enhancing the reputation between the institution and its audience in order to provide the best services and provide information to its audience objectively and seek to attract customers and investors by improving the institution's image. PR also plays a vital role in crisis management and dealing with any crisis in a professional manner with the aim of reducing damage. PR also uses a set of tools as a means that contribute to communication between institutions and their audience, in addition to benefiting from available technologies in practicing PR with full professionalism. Artificial intelligence (AI) is one of the significant modern tools that contribute to performing tasks with the full use of technology through AI applications, which include data, press conferences, newsletters, writing articles, marketing about the institution, and many others. In light of the use of AI applications in the field of PR, it is necessary to point out the importance of highlighting the professional and ethical standards of PR practitioners when using AI in various institutions as well as the positive and negative effects that these smart applications carry through the practice of legal controls in addition to ethical and professional rules when used, especially for PR practitioners—this directly and indirectly affects the institution's audience. Communication behaviors among PR practitioners must be characterized by professionalism and ethics; therefore, institutions seek to enhance the standards of professionalism and ethics when using AI applications and be aware when employing these applications while practicing PR and communicating with the public.

The use of technology has become very important and is of utmost significant in its application in various fields. Rather, people have become indispensable in benefiting from smart applications. Technology, including AI, has become an integral part of programs and projects. The keenness to benefit from smart applications is not only on the individual or personal level but also on the level of governmental and private institutions. The use of AI applications has become increasingly common because it contributes to improving production efficiency due to the importance of technological development in performing more effective and accurate tasks that are comparable to human intelligence—and exceed it by great strides. Therefore, this technology can be used in all fields in medicine, industry, education, marketing, and many vital fields due to the ability of these smart applications to provide multiple services simultaneously, including analyzing data in large numbers that contribute to predicting future expectations, which benefits various sectors and creates innovation in products and services, including in the field of PR, since PR plays a major role in the success of governmental and private institutions as well as organizations. There are governments that have succeeded in managing their PR effectively, such as Singapore, the United Arab Emirates, and Australia. PR has been used effectively to enhance communication and achieve transparency and trust with citizens and the international community.

The current study seeks to identify the ethical and professional standards when PR practitioners use AI applications.

Professional Ethics of PR

Definition of Professional Ethics in PR

Ethics in PR are principles and standards practiced in PR, and it is an approach which ensures honesty, transparency, and justice in dealing with the public through responsible dealing that requires integrity, professionalism, and respect in all situations and at all times. In return, this approach helps maintain confidentiality and avoids conflicts of interest. Therefore, PR practitioners contribute to building trust and credibility in both the work environment and with the institution's audience (Al- et al., 2024). The *Dictionary of Journalism and Media* defines ethics as a set of rules and foundations related to the behavior of practitioners of the profession; a collection of ethics, morals, and duties that complement legislation and its applications by the judiciary (Al-Anzi, 2020). The need for ethical standards has emerged to keep pace with new media and electronic platforms as well as ensure its standardization in a manner consistent with other definitions so that they are adopted by international organizations related to human rights (Bouchoucha, 2021).

Professional ethics is defined as "a set of rules and principles that must be adhered to by professionals in order to maintain the level of their profession and raise its status. It is sometimes called work ethics or job ethics, and its essence is to do the work without negligence" (Al-Salmi, 2019a). It also means a set of ethical rules and values that characterize the behavior of the individual and the group for actions that may be correct or incorrect, contributing to determining the necessary standards for the behavior of the individual or the group and their actions (Austin & Toth, 2011). PR ethics can also be defined as a set of principles stemming from the approach of the Holy Quran and the Sunnah of the Prophet, peace be upon him, which regulates the behavior of individuals and categorizes them as permissible, forbidden, disliked, or desirable. The practice of PR has ethical considerations that must not conflict with these general rules, principles, and standards (Al-Moussawi, 2021a).

PR Ethics

Ethics of PR practitioners are considered one of the basic elements that contribute to building trust and credibility between the institution and its audience.

Previous studies in this regard have highlighted that the PR profession in the Arab world requires additional controls for ethical standards in PR. The study outlined that the lack of financial allocations, work pressures, and the work of non-specialists in the field of PR are among the reasons that push PR practitioners disregard professional ethics (Al- et al., 2018). This showcases that ethical standards in PR are complex and differ from one country to another due to various intellectual perspectives relating to ethics, especially in institutions with multiple cultures. The researcher, Giampietro Becciato, indicated that "ethics refers to something greater than mere compliance and respect for the law and considers it as daily behavior capable of not harming others but also taking into account their needs and expectations" (Mokhtari, , 2022). It is imperative to highlight the ethical values of PR practitioners, including the ethics of practitioners toward themselves and their respect for their work in order to serve society. Additionally, the overall message conveyed from PR should be based on good conscience, whereby practitioners should appreciate the work and believe in the outcomes. Honesty, justice, truthfulness, and mastery in work, as well as the ability to innovate and be professional in work, are essential in PR (Al-Moussawi, 2021b).

Characteristics of Professional Ethics in PR and Influencing Factors

Professional ethics are categorized based on basic characteristics which are considered principles and values that an individual must adhere to in the work environment. These ethics are not limited to a specific field but rather concern all fields on individual and collective levels, as they constitute explicit controls in work and human relations. These ethics can be improved and developed to serve the work environment, as they perform an extremely important function in controlling behavior, with the aim of improving and developing work, reducing errors, and avoiding the waste of human and material energy (Peaceful, 2019).

Professional ethics is affected by several factors which can form a work environment that determines the extent to which its members adhere to professional ethics. Among these factors is the failure of officials in the institution to adhere to ethical standards, which encourages employees follow suit, and, in turn, this leads to unethical practices at work. Additionally, the ethics of a society acts as a mirror reflecting the ethics of its members—this can be translated to the way employees mirror their institutions. Among the factors affecting professional ethics are financial needs, which in turn may affect adherence to ethical standards. Furthermore, the failure of PR specialists to work leads to a failure to understand the most important ethical and professional standards in the institution, whereby practical pressures may affect PR practitioners in the institution to underestimate adherence to ethical standards (Al-Salmi, 2019b).

The Importance of Professional Ethics in PR

Professional ethics are one of the basic elements of the work environment and holds great importance to the organization and its employees. Its significance is encapsulated in enhancing trust between senior management and employees, improving the organization's reputation, encouraging productivity to achieve sustainable goals, in addition to avoiding legal risks and protecting the rights of employees and customers.

Professional ethics are among the most crucial topics that concern human societies, as they differentiate between right and wrong, which governs the behavioral choices of individuals that consider the controls of the public interest. They are "a set of rules and standards that the individual adheres to and maintains himself without being forced to do so by any external factors." (Khalil, 2015a).

Behavioral controls regulate multiple relationships, as divine legislations have urged high morals since they represent a pillar for preserving rights and ensuring their progress. The importance of individuals' commitment to ethical standards in the field of work enhances the mental image and reputation of the institution. This enables the best results to be achieved and global certification to be obtained due to ethical professionalism in the workplace. Conversely, if an institution does not adhere to ethical standards, it may result in embarrassing situations that increases costs on the institution when facing lawsuits in court (Al-Jaid and Walaa, 2024). There are also patterns that PR practitioners must adhere to in order to reflect the ethical dimension at work; this includes the adherence to laws and the rights of others, in addition to the continuous aspiration to achieve the public interest and the ethical principles that govern the policymaking process of the institution (Al-Moussawi, 2021c).

Professional Ethics and Effective PR Performance

There is a close and interconnected relationship between professional ethics and the effectiveness of PR performance, as ethics greatly affects how PR strategies are implemented and their success, whereby enhancing the confidence of the institution's audience and the feeling of comfort when such audience seeks ethical and professional standards at work. This contributes to building a positive image of the institution and strengthening relations with various target groups for the role it plays in shaping relationships through communication based on high ethical standards. Moreover, commitment to ethical standards in work contributes to the sustainability of businesses as they enjoy great support from society, in addition to helping in managing crises with great effectiveness, which leads to the least amount of damage.

Adherence to ethical standards in institutions is a basic requirement for achieving effective organizational performance in PR. PR is the link between the institution and its audience. Therefore, practitioners in this field must adhere to professional standards due to their impact on the interests of the institution. The failure of the institution to adhere to ethical standards results in the public's lack of confidence, which certainly leads to lawsuits being filed against the institution, which violated the rights of its customers. From this standpoint, ethical commitment is a requirement that gives the institution an opportunity to continue, in line with the public's aspirations, toward a level of ethical and professional standards. This path is extremely important to achieve the audience's commitment, which requires more effort and cooperation from the institution (Khalil, 2015b).

Using Artificial Intelligence in PR

The Concept of Artificial Intelligence in the Field of PR

The term artificial intelligence refers to systems and devices that simulate human intelligence in order to perform human tasks according to the information provided to perform tasks with complete proficiency, whereby it uses superior thinking and data analysis. Robots or digital devices can be controlled through computers, and AI technologies have developed and have become extremely similar to human intelligence in various fields (Ali, 2022a).

Studying AI in PR is essential to employ AI applications in the field of PR. AI is a branch of computer science that simulates the method of human intelligence and is able to perform the tasks assigned to it instead of humans. It aims to understand human intelligence to solve complex issues or make decisions through inferential processes that have been fed into various programs by humans (Al- et al., 2023). AI in its content is electronic and cloud-based, as well as integrated and consistent with other technologies such as algorithms, chatbots, and augmented reality. It works at a level similar to human intelligence in interpretation, comprehension, and adaptation (Qandouz, 2023). There are certainly several concepts of AI, whereby AI is a group of advanced technologies characterized by many features. These machines are capable of understanding, learning, acting, sensing, and thinking—they can perform their tasks exactly like humans through the use of programs and algorithms (Taha, 2023).

Using Artificial Intelligence Technologies in the Field of PR

AI adds value to PR, as it keeps pace with the increasing developments in improving efficiency and communication with the public through the many uses in data management and responding to tweets, inquiries, and complaints on social media. PR has a great need for AI in their work, as influencers' messages and audience interaction with them can be analyzed, content can be created, and the content marketing strategy can be aligned with AI in collecting data and searching for customers. AI also allows measuring the extent to which the organization's audience feels about the service, brand or product, or campaign performance, in addition to the decision-making mechanism, as well as predicting sales and future market trends. As for advertising, PR practitioners can benefit from AI in advertising better by collecting and analyzing data (I am sick Virgin, 2024a). AI can generate ideas and inspiration that can be used in PR work, such as creating videos and films by converting text into video, and monitoring fake videos that can harm the reputation of the institution's brand (Ben et al., 2024).

Many studies have shown the significance of PR practitioners to comprehend the role of AI in developing PR practice and building brand awareness, the impact of using AI in developing marketing and its effectiveness, and the impact of AI on e-commerce (Nasser, 2023), as well as understanding the most important problems that the institution's audience is exposed in a time-effective manner. This is crucial to provide various services, as well as involving the audience in important events that affect PR such as informing its audience of the latest news and developments (Ali, 2022b).

Advantages and Importance of Using Artificial Intelligence in the Field of PR

The use of AI in the field of PR has become vital and extremely important. AI can contribute significantly to improving the quality and effectiveness of PR efforts, leading to better results and increased customer satisfaction. Many researchers have confirmed that with technological progress, societies have become in need of innovation in the media and communication industry, which requires high-tech skills (Ali, 2022c).

Some aspects of the importance of AI can be pointed out, as AI contributes to preserving and transferring human accumulated experiences, and it also plays an important role in alleviating psychological risks and pressures, and AI helps in diagnosing diseases and provides interactive education (Aiwaj, 2024). As for the advantages of AI and benefiting from it in PR, they are many, including monitoring social media and analyzing the audience of these sites in terms of comments, posts, interests, and knowing the trends that can then form a clear picture for the institution. This can be utilized with the aim of enhancing the institution's reputation with the client and promotes positive interactions. AI can also aid in improving communication by analyzing linguistic data, immediate responses, and customizing messages and content based on the client's personal information and interests. As for self-support, AI can be used to apply chatbot technologies to answer common inquiries and problems, in addition to providing advice and guidance, as well as making decisions based on clear facts (I am sick Virgin, 2024b).

Characteristics of Smart PR

Digital PR tools have several features that make them effective in communicating with the public, through smart searches for knowledge or purchases to obtain quick results, as well as visual search, where the shopper can search for what he needs visually, saving effort and time. Moreover, voice assistance can be interacted with more widely instead of using the writing feature, and the chat robot is a considered a milestone in simulating dialogs and answering some inquiries received from the institution's audience (Ali, 2022d).

It is noteworthy that the aforementioned characteristics of AI optimizes the use of PR through immediate effective interaction with the target audience very quickly and aids in knowing the audience's preferences. This increases the effectiveness of cooperation and interaction through measurement tools, which contributes to improving the performance of the institution's PR practitioners and enables unique and diverse content through images, videos, and podcasts. It also contributes to building strong relationships between the institution and the target audience groups, especially during a crisis, all of which can be accomplished at the lowest costs compared to traditional methods, thus making PR a powerful contemporary tool.

Artificial Intelligence Applications in PR: Government Institutions

Each institution has its own strategy for dealing with AI, its uses in PR, and the methods of reaping the benefits from smart applications by adopting technologies and employing them in the workplace.

The United Arab Emirates has developed a special strategy to benefit from AI in government institutions through several smart applications. This includes robots performing public services such as the robotic police to detect the movement of objects, recognize specific signals, and interact with and respond to people's inquiries in different languages. The United Arab Emirates has also placed a robot lifeguard on public beaches in Dubai and launched a robot to serve customers where it can complete ID card renewal requests and update data. The robot has become a cleaner in the Dubai metro station, as well as a smart assistant for living in Dubai to answer user inquiries about procedures, documents, and requirements necessary for their transactions, in addition to assistance in issuing permits, visas, passports, and more (Thabet, , 2023).

AI applications in PR for government institutions are very diverse and can be widely used in the field of PR. There are applications for image recognition, applications for understanding consumer needs, social media monitoring applications, and automation applications. Furthermore, the uses also include automated interactions in social media using AI, sales prediction and recommendation applications as insights for the institution, speech-to-text conversion applications, and personalization applications, i.e., creating customized messages for a group of audiences. As a whole, this leads to more interactivity with the institution (Taha, 2023).

References

Aiwaj, V. (2024). *Previous reference* (p. 155).

Al-Anzi, K. (2020). *Media legislation and professional ethics, Syrian virtual university, Syria* (1st ed., p. 22).

Al-Dulaimi, A.-R. (2024). Public relations ethics and practice: An original theoretical research. *Journal of Digital Media Research, Suez University*, 105–128.

Al-Issawi, N. (2018). Ethics of public relations practitioners in Arab universities: A survey study on a sample of public relations practitioners in Arab universities. *International Journal of Social Communication, Abdelhamid Ben Badis University, Algeria*, 5(3), 241.

Al-Jaid, Walaa. (2024). The role of school leadership in promoting professional ethics among secondary school teachers in the city of Taif from their point of view. *Educational Journal, South Valley University, Saudi Arabia*, 669–670.

Al-Moussawi, K. (2021a). *Ethics of public relations workers in the Iraqi press: A field study of workers in Al-Sabah, Al-Adala, and Al-Mada* (p. 11). AlBahith Alalami Issue 8, University of Baghdad.

Al-Moussawi, K. (2021b). *Previous reference* (p. 13).

Al-Moussawi, K. (2021c). *Previous reference* (p. 11).

Al-Salmi, M. (2019a). Public relations practitioners' attitudes towards professional ethics and their relationship to the level of performance: A comparative study between the public and private sectors. *Journal of Humanities and Social Sciences*, *3*(3), 3.

Al-Salmi, M. (2019b). *Previous reference* (pp. 3–4).

Al-Tayeb, I., & Ziad, S. (2023). *Previous reference* (pp. 89–90).

Ali, M. (2022a). *Previous reference* (p. 458).

Ali, M. (2022b). *Previous reference* (p. 459).

Ali, M. (2022c). *Previous reference* (p. 455).

Ali, M. (2022d). *Previous reference* (pp. 462–463).

Austin, L., & Toth, E. (2011). Exploring ethics education in global public relations curricula: Analysis of international curricula descriptions and interviews with public relations educators. *Public Relations Review*, *37*(5), 506.

Ben, L. Y., & Belghithia, S. (2024). Emerging trends and technologies in public relations practice. *Emirates Journal of Digital Arts and Media*, *2*(1), 36.

Bouchoucha, H. (2021). Media work ethics: An analytical study of media laws in Algeria. *Scientific Horizons Journal, University of Constantine, Algeria*, *13*, 149–167.

I am sick Virgin. (2024a). *The magazine scientific for research relationships general advertisement* (Vol. 7, pp. 15–16).

I am sick Virgin. (2024b). *Previous reference* (pp. 15–17).

Khalil, A. (2015a). *The awareness of the specialized university student of the ethics of professional practice of public relations: A field study* (p. 378). University of Sharjah.

Khalil, A. (2015b). *Previous reference* (p. 377).

Mokhtari, F. (2022). *op. cit.*

Nasser, N. (2023). Modern trends in research and studies on the uses of artificial intelligence in public relations: A second-level analytical study. *Journal of the Association of Arab Universities for Media and Communication Technology Research*, *11*(1), 191.

Peaceful, M. (2019). *Previous reference* (p. 3).

Qandouz, T. (2023). The impact of artificial intelligence on integrated marketing communications: A theoretical study. *Iraqi Journal of Economic Sciences*, *79*, 98.

Taha, F. Al-Z. (2023a). The future of public relations in light of the transformation to artificial intelligence technologies: A foresight vision. *Egyptian Journal of Media Research*, *83*(3), 583.

Taha, F. Al-Z. (2023b). *Previous reference* (pp. 585–586).

Thabet, G. (2023). Modern trends in the use of public relations in managing government services using artificial intelligence tools. *Egyptian Journal of Media Research, Cairo University*, *82*, 662–663.

Chapter 9

The Relationship Between the Institutions' Use of Interactive Dialogical Communication Strategies and Digital Reputation Management Among the Audience

Maha Hameed Alanezi

Ministry of Education, Bahrain

Abstract

The world is experiencing a rapid digital transformation, making interactive dialogical communication across social media platforms a fundamental pillar in developing digital public relations and in managing the digital reputation of institutions. This study aims to explore dialogical communication strategies that focus on two-way interaction between institutions and their audience.

The study highlights the role of dialogical communication in achieving credibility in building sustainable relationships with the public by applying digital reputation management strategies within the changing digital environment. Using a literature review approach, the study analyzed the theoretical frameworks, methodologies, and data collection tools used in the reviewed studies.

The findings showed that digital reputation is a crucial element that supports the private and public institutional position socially and commercially and emphasized the importance of integrating communication elements to improve interactivity, thereby increasing the audience's satisfaction level.

The study confirmed that applying dialogical communication strategies is no longer an option, but has become a prerequisite to achieve excellence, competitiveness, and ensuring the sustainability of institutional success. The

Digital Dialogues, 83–92

doi:10.1108/978-1-83708-686-320261009

study concluded that building a strong institutional reputation requires performance excellence, information delivery transparency, and consistency between the organization's messages and its actual actions, which reinforces a positive and sustainable image among the audience.

Keywords: Strategy; communication; communication environment; dialog; dialogical communication; digital reputation; digital reputation management; digital public relations

Introduction

The concept of communication has changed dramatically due to the hasty innovations in digital technology, which has become an integral part of our daily lives. Interactive dialogic communication has expanded to include social media, smart applications, and digital platforms. Many organizations have established official accounts on social media platforms. These platforms are fed with the organization information, news, and events in an attempt to activate interactive communication with their audiences and engage them positively in expressing their opinions. In 1998, Kent and Taylor developed a guide for researchers and practitioners in public relations titled "Dialogic Communication Principles" to assist public relations professionals in building positive, interactive, and dialogic relationships with their audiences. Dialogic communication strategies have been employed in many studies to evaluate social media platforms of organizations from a dialogic perspective. A set of principles, indicators, and metrics has been developed to suit the nature of these social media platforms for those institutions (Al-Otaibi, 2023). By employing interactive dialogic communication strategies, organizations can better understand how to improve their operations effectiveness in achieving their desired goals amid ongoing societal changes. Digital reputation represents a fundamental pillar for the success of organizations, serving as a sustainable competitive advantage. A positive reputation enhances the institution's media, while a negative reputation can adversely affect customer loyalty and audience engagement (Ghalab & Nawari, 2021). Managing digital reputation is a primary goal of the communication and public relations departments within any organization. This goal involves interactive communication that aims to shape a positive image of the organization among the largest possible audience (Aslan & Abu Arqoub, 2023), which requires the development of strategic plans that capitalize on strengths and opportunities to meet its goals and overcome its weaknesses. Therefore, it is crucial for organizations to be present on social media platforms and to leverage the advantages of digital media (Al-Yubi et al., 2024).

Organizations can utilize applications and social media to gather feedback on the provided services, activities, and information (Zayed, 2024). The use of Instagram by public and private institutions contributes to establishing and building a favorable reputation for the institution among their audience. The interactive communication facilitated by Instagram helps reinforcing the institution's position to meet the needs and ambitions of the audience that interacts with its posts.

In this context, this study aims to explore the relationship between the institutions' use of interactive dialogic communication strategies through Instagram and the management of their digital reputation. Communication is a process of exchanging information, ideas, and emotions between individuals or groups to achieve mutual understanding, coordinate activities, and influence behaviors (Jerab, 2024).

Elements of Communication

Communication is an interactive process of transmitting ideas and information between parties using codes derived from a shared culture to achieve specific goals (Belkhiri & Al Jabri, 2020). The communication process relies on essential elements including the **sender**, which is the primary source of the message, aiming to convey it to the receiver. The second element is the **receiver**, which represents the entity that receives the message, analyzes its codes, and understands its content. The third element is the **message**, which is the content conveyed from the sender to the recipient. The fourth element is the **medium**, or the channel that transmits the message from the sender to the receiver. The fifth element is **noise**, which refers to obstacles that may affect the clarity of the message during transmission. The sixth element is **feedback**, which is the response that the receiver shows in response to the message. The seventh element is **impact,** which is the final outcome of the communication process, manifested through changes in the recipient's behavior, thoughts, or feelings. The success of communication is measured by its influence on the audience (Belkhiri & Al Jabri, 2020). The success of the communication process depends on the cohesion of these elements and their freedom from any obstacles to achieve the desired objectives. The elements of communication are combined in an interactive environment known as the "communication environment," which is the general framework in which the communication process takes place. The environment includes the surrounding social, political, and economic conditions (Zaki, 2016).

Communication Strategies for Public Relations through Online Platforms

Strategy is defined as the art of leading and organizing actions to achieve the major goals of the organization through a set of decisions that determine the overall direction of the organization (Abdul Aal, 2024). Communication strategies in the field of public relations are linked to Roller's model, which theorizes that each situation has its own specific communication strategy (Zatili, 2024). Communicative messages vary according to the parties involved in the communication process. Based on these domains, Roller proposes four main strategies for practicing public relations, which were discussed in Ahmad's study (Ahmed, 2023). They include **media strategy, persuasion strategy, consensus-building strategy, and**

dialog strategy. In the present study, the researcher selected the dialog strategy as a primary approach. This strategy aims to achieve two-way communication, facilitating the exchange of opinions and ideas in a comprehensive manner.

Dialog

Dialog is an interactive communication process that goes beyond transmitting information between two parties. Dialog is considered a tool capable of building lasting relationships, as it enhances mutual understanding, cooperation, and trust (Hussein, 2023). Dialog is characterized by its ability to serve the interests of both the organization and the public through a participatory approach in public relations. However, many public relations practitioners lack the necessary skills to implement dialog in their practices (Braktia & Sawaliha, 2022). Some public relations practitioners pretend to engage in dialogic roles online, while still adhering to the perspective of public relations.

Dialogic communication is implemented as an official and purposive expression by the organization, where the organization communicates through the use of various means to facilitate its internal operations and create a public image that reflects the organizational personality (Jum'a, 2024). It is a form of interaction that emphasizes the importance of mutual understanding, open exchange, and cooperation among participants. This approach fosters a culture where individuals can share ideas and viewpoints while actively listening and responding to one another, creating an inclusive and transformative discussion. It is considered an ethical practice aims to improve societal relationships and the relationships between the organization and the audience, enabling organizations to fulfill their social responsibilities. The functional model dominated education and research in public relations (such as excellence theory, public relations theory, and contingency theory) and has been widely applied in public relations (Taylor & Kent, 2014). To advance ethical and transparent practice, dialogic communication practitioners need to treat the public as partners in a process.

Significance of Dialogic Communication in Digital Public Relations

The significance of dialogic communication can be described in several aspects. First, **enhancing trust and building long-term relationships**. Dialogic communication contributes to creating mutual trust between the organization and its audience, as the audience feels that the organization listens to them and cares about their needs and opinions. (Khalil, 2019). Second, **increasing interaction and meeting audience needs**. Audience interaction with the organization increases when it provides effective dialogic channels, especially through social media (Taha & Musa, 2022). Third, **improving the organization's public image**. Dialogic communication helps build a positive image of the organization which enhances the organization's reputation and increases its credibility (Abdel Latif, 2021). Fourth, **providing reliable and accessible information.** Providing reliable and accessible information enhances the organization's credibility and makes it a trusted source for the audience (Khalil, 2019). Fifth, **increasing audience satisfaction and loyalty**. Dialogic communication contributes to increasing audience satisfaction. Over time, this satisfaction evolves into loyalty and ongoing support for the organization (Abdel Latif, 2021).

Digital Reputation

Digital reputation involves the continuous search and analysis of information related to an individual's, professional, industrial, or commercial reputation online. Managing digital reputation presents a valuable opportunity for organizations, enabling them to control their public image. However, this reputation can be jeopardized by the spread of rumors and wrong information that could negatively impact their image (Ghalab & Nawari, 2022). Studies, especially in the United States, focused on the relationship between reputation, innovation, social responsibility, and talent attraction, demonstrating its positive impact on organizational financial performance. With technological advancements and the spread of social media, digital reputation has become a key element in valuing organizations. Its influence extends to governments and small and medium-sized enterprises, especially in service sectors. The concept of online reputation management (ORM) emerged to protect and enhance brands, relying on audience evaluations and the role of websites in shaping the organization's image. The term "e-reputation" was first used in 2000 to refer to the role of vision and mission in highlighting organizations' status online (Qaboor & Salem, 2023).

The process of managing digital reputation aims at continuous monitoring and analysis of information related to the personal or professional reputation of organizations online. This is achieved through monitoring the content published across various digital media and is defined as an attempt to control what is said about the organization online, using monitoring tools that keep it informed about what is published about it, allowing timely intervention to improve its relationship with its audience (Ghalab & Nawari, 2022). Operationally, it is defined as the process of researching and investigating digital content to reduce the negative impact of content that may harm the organization (Satataha & Qarnani, 2023).

Goals of Digital Reputation Management for Organizations

Digital reputation is considered the element that enhances the value of the organization and strengthens its position. Organizational value depends on various behaviors of stakeholder groups. Reputation management aims to achieve shared interests with stakeholders and requires a clear connection with the organization's strategy, as building and protecting reputation is an essential part of leadership responsibilities and helps in shaping a shared vision (Ghalab & Nawari, 2022).

Importance of Digital Reputation Management for Organizations

Digital reputation management is one of the most important topics adopted by many companies and governments. Arab countries still need more awareness of the importance of this management. It is essential for business owners and managers to be fully aware of their organizations' image in the vast space of the internet. The mental image of an organization, regardless of its size, significantly affects its status; a positive digital reputation leaves a good impression, contributing to increased sales and enhancing the organization's media value. Conversely, a negative reputation not only harms sales but also affects other investment aspects. Any internet browsing person can be influenced by that reputation, potentially posing a serious threat to the company and leading to decreased revenue and the avoidance of talented job applicants. A study by Suleiman et al. (2024) highlighted the importance of digital reputation management for organizations by increasing customer satisfaction, enhancing the image of the brand, improving the efficiency of public relations, conducting periodic and rapid monitoring, providing digital monitoring tools, helping organizations discover gaps and deficiencies, adapting to technological developments, and overcoming challenges that hinder communication processes.

Elements of Digital Reputation Management

A study by Satataha and Qarnani (2023) identified that the process of managing digital reputation consists of six main operations:

(1) **Building:** Forming a council for managing digital reputation within the organization.
(2) **Monitoring:** Verifying the consistency of the content displayed online about the organization.
(3) **Analysis:** Quantitatively and qualitatively analyzing and classifying digital content.
(4) **Evaluation:** Highlighting priorities and necessary actions to activate that content and improve the overall digital image of the organization.
(5) **Actions:** Steps in managing online reputation include improving search engine optimization (SEO) to achieve high rankings, enhancing social media optimization (SMO) with distinctive content, producing effective content for customer interaction.
(6) **Auditing:** Establishing systems for periodic review and analyzing results, ensuring the implementation of action plans, and monitoring progress.

Characteristics of Organizational Reputation

Reputation reflects impressions and ideas that form in individuals' perspectives, reputation is dynamic, reputation embodies the way the organization presents its products and services, reputation undergoes continuous planning, and organizational reputation can be measured using contemporary methods based on scientific research (Omar, 2023).

Factors Affecting Reputation Management

Excellence: A strong reputation is achieved when the organization establishes a unique and distinguished position in the minds of its audience, which depends on its ongoing efforts to achieve excellence and success. This is closely linked to the organization's credibility with stakeholders and its ability to meet the needs of its community and environment while transparently and reliably fulfilling its responsibilities.

(1) **Trust in the Organization:** Trust is the cornerstone of the organization's success.
(2) **Transparency and Clarity:** Transparency is a key factor in the development of the organization's reputation, necessitating the provision of accurate and truthful information.
(3) **Consistency and Cohesion:** The organization's reputation grows significantly when its actions and communications are consistent and harmonious.

In the context of reputation management, there is a strong interconnection between the organization's identity, image, brand, and culture, as these elements intertwine to form a positive and distinctive reputation that contributes to enhancing its standing (Nasser, 2023).

Digital Public Relations

Digital public relations include websites, digital games, and text messaging services to convey information online. It also involves integrating texts, graphics, images, and videos. Some define it as the use of modern communication technologies by public relations departments to support their activities and contribute to achieving their goals (Al-Yubi et al., 2024). The importance of dialogic communication includes **enhancing transparency and credibility** thereby enhancing its positive image (Saleh, 2020), **managing digital crises through** (Ghalab & Nawari, 2021), and **building sustainable relationships** (Zayed, 2024).

Conclusion

This study emphasizes the importance of dialogic communication strategies in enhancing digital reputation management. The results showed that effective dialog with the audience enhances trust and credibility, positively reflecting on the organization's digital image. Communication is no longer merely a means of transmitting information; it has become a fundamental cornerstone for managing digital public relations and enhancing institutional reputation. By employing interactive dialogic communication strategies, organizations can establish two-way communication that enables them to respond promptly to audience concerns, provide tailored content, and manage crises effectively. This study recommends that organizations adopt communication strategies based on active listening and quick responses to interact with the audience through digital platforms. It also stresses the need for continued research in this area to explore new techniques and measure their impact in different environments. Therefore, digital reputation is no longer just a promotional tool; it has become an essential part of institutional identity that requires sustainable and wise management to ensure success and continuity in the digital era.

References

Abdel Latif, M. M. (2021). The use of electronic platforms in Egyptian universities to manage dialogue with their audiences. *Middle East Journal of Public Relations Research, 32*, 237–288.

Abdul Aal, R. N. A. (2024). *Istratijiyāt al-Ittiṣāl fī Hay'at al-Tawjīh al-Siyāsī wa-al-Waṭanī wa-Dawruhā fī Taʿzīz al-Huwiyya al-Waṭaniyya ladā ṭāliba al-Jāmiʿāt al-Filasṭīniyya. [Communication Strategies in the Political and National Guidance Authority and Their Role in Enhancing National Identity Among Palestinian University Students].* Arab American University. http://repository.aaup.edu/jspui/handle/123456789/2067

Ahmed, N. M. A. (2023). Al-Istratijiyāt al-Ittiṣāliyya li-Rasā'il al-Muʾassasāt al-Duwalīyya wa-al-Iqlīmiyya ʿabra Mawqiʿ al-Tawṣul al-Ijtimāʿī Twitter. [Communication strategies for messages from international and regional organizations via the social networking site Twitter]. *Egyptian Journal of Media Research, 2023* (86), 619–667. https://doi.org/10.21608/ejsc.2023.323860

Al-Otaibi, M. S. A. (2023). Tawẓīf Mawāqiʿ al-Muʾassasāt al-Ḥukūmiyya al-Kuwaitiyya li-Mabādiʾ al-Ittiṣāl al-Ḥiwārī fī Bināʾ al-ʿAlāqa maʿa al-Jumhūr. [Utilization of Kuwaiti Government Institutions' Websites for Dialogue Communication Principles in Building Relationships with the Public]. *Annals of Arts Ain Shams, 51*(2), 191–217. https://doi.org/10.21608/aafu.2023.295869

Al-Yubi, A. W. M., Al-Sulami, N., & bin, A. M. (2024). Idārat al-Sum'a fī al-Manṣāt al-Raqmiyya li-Muʾassasāt al-Taʿlīm al-ʿĀlī fī al-Mamlakah al-ʿArabiyyah al-Suʿūdiyyah: D study Mīdāniyya ʿalā ṭāliba Jāmiʿat King Abdulaziz. [Reputation Management in Digital Platforms of Higher Education Institutions in Saudi Arabia: A Field Study on Students of King Abdulaziz University]. *Arab Research in Quality Education, 36*(1), 131–162. https://doi.org/10.21608/raes.2024.383915

Aslan, R., & Abu Arqoub, O. (2023). Idārat al-Nukhba al-Siyāsiyya al-Filasṭīniyya li-Sum'itahā al-Raqmiyya ʿabra Manṣat Facebook. [The Palestinian political elite manages its digital reputation through the Facebook platform]. *Scientific Journal of Public Relations and Advertising Research, 2023*(26), 403–445. https://doi.org/10.21608/sjocs.2023.337098

Belkhiri, R., & Al Jabri, S. (2020). *Istratijiyāt al-Ittiṣāl wa-al-ʿAlāqāt al-ʿĀmma. [Communication and public relations strategies].* University Book House, United Arab Emirates.

Braktia, S., & Sawaliha, Z. (2022). Istikhdām Mumārisi al-ʿAlāqāt al-ʿĀmma Mahārat al-Ḥiwār fī Tathmīn al-Mas'ūlīyya al-Ijtimāʿiyya lil-Muʾassasa. [Public relations practitioners use the skill of dialogue to value the social responsibility of the organization]. *Al-Risalah Journal for Media Studies*, *6*(2), 631–644.

Ghalab, N., & Nawari, A. (2021). Al-Ittiṣāl al-Raqmī wa-Sum'it al-Muʾassasa: Al-furṣ wa-al-Thahdīdāt. Digital communication and enterprise reputation: Opportunities and threats. *Journal of Humanities Sciences*, *21*(2), 172–191.

Ghalab, N., & Nawari, A. (2022). Idārat al-Sum'a al-Raqmiyya lil-Munazzama ʿabra Shabakat al-Tawāṣul al-Ijtimāʿī bayna al-Ta'thīr wa-Mutalabbas Idāratihā. [Managing the organization's digital reputation via social media networks: Between the impact and the requirements for its management]. *Journal of Studies and Research*, *14*(2), 723–733.

Hussein, K. A. (2023). Mafhūm al-Ḥiwār wa-Ahmiyyatuhu wa-Ahdāfuh wa-Ādābuh: D study Waṣfiyya. [The concept of dialogue, its importance, goals, and etiquette: A descriptive study]. *Al-Mustansiriya Journal of Arts*, *47*(102), 143–163.

Jerab, D. (2024). The impact of communication on organizational performance: A comprehensive analysis. https://doi.org/10.2139/ssrn.4809789.

Jum'a, F. (2024). *āʿiliyyat Tawẓīf Naẓariyyat al-Ittiṣāl al-Ḥiwārī fī Ansheta al-ʿAlāqāt al-ʿĀmma fī al-Munazzamāt Ghayr al-Ḥukūmiyya fī Muḥāfaẓat Nāblus: Derast Ḥāla. [Effectiveness of Using Dialogue Communication Theory in Public Relations Activities in Non-Governmental Organizations in Nablus Governorate: A Case Study].* An-Najah National University.

Khalil, E. M. A. S. (2019). Tawẓīf Mabādiʾ Idārat al-ʿAlāqāt al-Ḥiwāriyya ʿalā al-Manṣāt al-Iliktrūniyya lil-Jāmiʿāt al-Miṣriyya. [Utilizing Principles of Dialogic Management on the Electronic Platforms of Egyptian Universities]. *Egyptian Journal of Public Opinion Research*, *18*(4), 483–557. https://doi.org/10.21608/joa.2019.92475

Nasser, N. A.-S. A. N. (2023). Tawẓīf Mumārisi al-ʿAlāqāt al-ʿĀmma li-Tatbīqāt al-Iʿlām al-Jadīd fī Idārat al-Sum'a al-Iliktrūniyya: D study Mīdāniyya Muqārana ʿalā al-Munazzamāt al-ʿĀmila fī al-Qitāʿ al-Ḥukūmī wa-al-Khāṣ bi-al-Mamlakah al-ʿArabiyyah al-Suʿūdiyyah. [Employing public relations practitioners for new media applications in electronic reputation management - a comparative field study on organizations operating in the governmental and private sectors in the Kingdom of Saudi Arabia]. *Journal of Media Research*, *65*(2), 679–742. https://doi.org/10.21608/jsb.2023.127751.1439

Omar, Y. A.-S. (2023). *Al-Sum'a al-Muʾassasiyya wa-Dawruhā fī Bināʾ al-ʿAlāma al-Tijārīyya. [Institutional reputation and its role in building the brand].* Qatar University Publishing House.

Qaboor, H., & Salem, A. (2023). Al-Ta'sīl al-Nazari li-Sum'it al-Raqmiyya fī al-Muʾassasa al-Iqtiṣādiyya. [Theoretical Foundation for Digital Reputation in Economic Institutions]. *Digitization Journal of Media and Communication Studies*, *3*(1), 10–30.

Saleh, H. F. (2020). Dawr al-Shafāfiyya fī Daʿm Maṣdāqiyyat al-Muʾassasāt al-Ṣaḥafiyya ladā al-Jumhūr: Deras Mīdāniyya. [The Role of Transparency in Supporting the Credibility of Press Institutions with the Public: A Field Study]. *Egyptian Journal of Media Research*, *2020*(71), 1–83. https://doi.org/10.21608/ejsc.2020.126771

Satataha, S., & Qarnani, Y. (2023). Al-Yaqẓa al-Tiknūlūjiyya wa-Idārat al-Sum'a al-Iliktrūniyya fī al-Mu'assasa al-Jazā'iriyya: Derasa Mīdāniyya bi-Mu'assasat Ittiṣālāt al-Jazā'ir. [Technological vigilance and electronic reputation management in the Algerian institution - a field study at the Algeria Telecom Corporationu]. *Al-Muqaddimah Journal for Humanities and Social Studies*, *8*(2), 239–264.

Suleiman, A. S. A., Abdel Maboud, A. A.-S., Qawra, O. A.-S., & Reda, A. (2024). Dawr Manṣāt al-Tawāṣul al-Ijtimā'ī fī Idārat al-Sum'a al-Raqmiyya lil-Fanādq fī Miṣr. [The role of social media platforms in managing the digital reputation of hotels in Egypt (Facebook as an example)]. *Journal of the Higher Institute for Qualitative Studies*, *4*(7), 2503–2538. https://doi.org/10.21608/hiss.2024.277560.1318

Taha, M. A. A.-T., & Musa, A. A.-K. A.-Z. B. (2022). Fā'iliyyat Wasā'il al-Tawāṣul al-Ijtimā'ī fī Barāmij wa-Ansheta al-'Alāqāt al-'Āmma: Derast Ḥāla li-Wazārat al-Thaqāfa wa-al-I'lām al-Ittihādiyya, 2020-2021. [The effectiveness of social media in public relations programs and activities (a case study of the Federal Ministry of Culture and Information, 2020-2021)]. *Humanitarian and Natural Sciences Journal*, *3*(12). https://doi.org/10.53796/hnsj31228

Taylor, M., & Kent, M. L. (2014). Dialogic engagement: Clarifying foundational concepts. *Journal of Public Relations Research*, *26*(5), 384–398. https://doi.org/10.1080/1062726X.2014.956106

Zaki, I. A. A. H. (2016). *Naẓariyyāt al-Ittiṣāl wa-al-I'lām li-Kul Yawm Naḥyāh. Jeddah, Saudi Arabia: Dār Khwarizm al-'Ilmiyya li-l-Nashr. [Communication and Media Theories for Every Day We Live]*. Al-Khwarizmi Scientific Publishing House, Jeddah, Saudi Arabia.

Zatili, R. (2024). Mumārasa al-Ittiṣāl al-Ḥiwārī fī al-'Alāqāt al-'Āmma 'abra al-Mawqi' al-Iliktrūnī lil-Mu'assasa: Derast 'Analītī li-l-Mawq'ayn al-Rasmiyyayn li-Mu'assasat Sevetal. [Practicing Dialogue Communication in Public Relations Through the Institution's Website: An Analytical Study of the Official Websites of Sevetal]. *Journal of Media and Communication Studies*, *6*(1), 123–139.

Zayed, L. H. (2024). Istratijiyāt al-Ittiṣāl al-Ḥiwārī al-Tafā'ulī lil-Munazzamāt al-Khidmiyya 'abra Mawāqi'ihā al-Raqmiyya wa-Dawruhā fī Idārat Sum'itahā al-Raqmiyya. [Interactive dialogic communication strategies for service organizations through their digital websites and their role in managing their digital reputation]. *Scientific Journal of Public Relations and Advertising Research*, *2024* (27), 223–262. https://doi.org/10.21608/sjocs.2024.349928

Chapter 10

The Use of Digital Public Relations Strategies in Addressing Unemployment Issues in KSA

Tareq hamed Alshabanat

The Embassy of the Kingdom of Saudi Arabia, Bahrain

Abstract

This study investigates the use of digital public relations (PR) strategies to address unemployment issues in the Kingdom of Saudi Arabia (KSA). Digital PR is an evolving field leveraging internet-based tools and modern communication technologies to enhance organizational communication and engagement. This research explores how digital platforms, including social media, online advertisements, and interactive forums, facilitate job opportunities by connecting employers with job seekers. The study highlights the role of digital PR in raising awareness of unemployment-related issues, promoting necessary skill development, and bridging the gap between labor market demands and available workforce capabilities.

The research findings emphasize that digital PR strategies can improve communication channels, enhance the visibility of job opportunities, and create sustainable networks that support employment growth. By incorporating these strategies, organizations and governments can address challenges associated with high unemployment rates, foster transparency, and encourage innovation in addressing labor market demands. The study illustrates the significance of continuous adaptation of digital PR practices to align with technological advancements and evolving economic conditions, thereby contributing to long-term economic and social development in KSA.

Keywords: Digital public relations; strategies; unemployment issues; KSA; research

Digital Dialogues, 93–101

doi:10.1108/978-1-83708-686-320261010

Introduction

Public relations (PR) is a modern concept that has only been significantly utilized in this century. However, as a human activity, its roots extend back to the very history of humanity. Humans are social beings who rely on interaction with others in their daily lives, which has led to the formation of relationships within communities. These relationships began within the family and gradually expanded to include clans and tribes as social units grew larger. Consequently, PR evolved from simplicity to complexity (Bazza, 2019).

According to Darwish et al. (2024), PR is a distinct managerial function that contributes to building effective communication, mutual understanding, shared attitudes, and collaborative efforts between an organization and its internal and external audiences. It plays a key role in addressing challenges faced by management, proposing appropriate solutions, and ensuring the smooth flow of information and data, which enables it to stay engaged with public opinion.

Al-Thubaity (2024) pointed out that PR often aims to present individuals, institutions, or ministries in the best possible light. PR contributes significantly to the success of various organizations by enhancing their opportunities for growth and expansion across different fields.

PR, in general, refers to the strategic communication process undertaken by organizations to engage with the public to build or enhance their image or address public issues and related discussions. PR serves as a vital tool that enables organizations to effectively convey their messages, respond to public needs, and foster mutual trust.

Introduction to PR

The Concept of PR

The concepts of PR vary and differ depending on researchers and specialists, as each definition reflects a perspective that focuses on a specific aspect while potentially overlooking others. It is widely agreed that PR aims to assist organizations in meeting individuals' needs in the best possible way. Serving individuals and ensuring their well-being is considered the fundamental path to the survival of any organization, regardless of its type or purpose. Achieving this is only possible through understanding individuals' desires and recognizing their requirements (Abdullah & Al-Rousan, 2024).

Wynne (2021) indicated that PR is a strategic communication process aimed at influencing the audience and persuading them to adopt a particular idea, support a specific position, purchase a product, or appreciate the organization's achievements. PR seeks to build mutually beneficial relationships between organizations and their audiences through effective communication that enhances understanding and mutual trust.

In general, PR, as viewed by the researcher, is a strategic communication process aimed at building mutually beneficial relationships between organizations and their audiences. This is achieved by enhancing effective communication to understand individuals' needs and meet their requirements, which contributes to improving the organization's image and achieving its goals.

The Objectives of PR

Every department within organizations and institutions aims to achieve specific objectives, and PR management plays a pivotal role in achieving these goals by enhancing its administrative role. PR focuses on building mutual understanding between the organization and its audience, in addition to establishing a positive image and a distinguished reputation. It ensures continuous and effective communication with various target groups, which contributes to supporting the organization's good reputation and enhancing its standing (Medani & Derbali, 2024).

According to Radi and Al-Azzawi (2024), PR, as an effective communication and administrative function, seeks to address the challenges faced by the organization and society, regardless of the type of activity it is associated with, using its effective tools.

However, Hayes (2024) emphasized that one of the goals of PR is to focus on highlighting a distinctive and positive image of an individual or organization, making it a crucial element for the success of institutions. It provides a high level of trust with the public. Unlike advertising, PR aims to present the targeted entity in a natural way that seeks to build a positive image and enhance interaction that serves the interests of the public.

The researcher concludes from the above that PR plays a crucial role in enhancing the position of organizations by building a positive image and establishing trust with the public. This is achieved through effective internal and external communication, providing counsel, and implementing interactive strategies that strengthen relationships with the community. Additionally, PR contributes to sustainable development through social initiatives, which support the organization's continuity and success in facing challenges.

Digitization

The Concept of Digitization

Digitalization refers to the integration of digital technology into all areas of business, leading to a fundamental change in how an organization operates and delivers value to customers (Xue et al., 2022). Jafari-Sadeghi et al. (2023) defined digitalization as the change in how an organization uses digital technologies to develop a new digital business model that helps create greater value for the organization and its alignment. In other words, digital transformation is crucial for organizations to gain a competitive advantage and remain successful in both national and global markets.

According to Ghazi (2023), digitalization is defined as the use of technology to improve performance or access to institutions, primarily utilizing digital advancements such as analytics, mobility, social media, and embedded smart devices, while enhancing the use of traditional technologies like enterprise resource planning and transforming customer relationships and internal processes.

The researcher believes that digitalization is the process of converting information and data from traditional forms into digital formats using modern technologies. Its goal is to improve efficiency, speed up processes, and enhance access to information in a more accessible and flexible manner. Digitalization is seen as the foundation for digital transformation across various sectors such as education, industry, and services.

The Objectives of Digitization

Digitalization aims to improve the quality of life by enhancing living conditions and offering electronic services. It seeks to transform institutions into digitally connected organizations, ensuring efficiency through integrated systems. Additionally, it promotes transparency, accountability, innovation, and digital inclusion, empowering institutions and fostering collaboration (Ibrahim, 2023).

The researcher concludes that digitalization aims to improve the quality of life by offering innovative and advanced services, creating digital interconnection between systems and institutions to enhance efficiency. It also seeks to foster transparency and accountability, encourage innovation, and increase customer satisfaction through improved processes and productivity, contributing to outstanding and sustainable organizational performance.

Obstacles to the Implementation of Digitization

The reasons hindering the implementation of digitalization in organizations vary, including the lack of a broad understanding of administrative processes and business operations by IT leaders. Leaders responsible for IT departments are often purely technical professionals who focus more on technology than on customer needs. Additionally, the lack of knowledge and experience in technology and information systems among senior leadership can also be a barrier (Fari, 2021).

Al-Murji and Al-Rashidi (2022) identified several barriers to digitalization in organizations, including digital disruption caused by technological advancements, business and technology transformation driven by innovation and digital marketing, the challenges of managing big data due to its growing volume and speed, and regulatory pressures focusing on privacy, cybersecurity, and resilience, which complicate business operations across industries. The primary response to these challenges is adjusting the organizational approach.

The researcher concludes that barriers to digitalization include a lack of understanding among IT leaders of administrative processes, limited technological knowledge in senior leadership, unclear vision, organizational rigidity, employee resistance to change, and insufficient managerial support, all of which complicate the digitalization process.

Digital PR

PR and Digitization

PR has evolved with globalization and digital technologies, enhancing its multifaceted nature. The key challenge is understanding its role, highlighting the clear connection between digital technologies and PR. This emphasizes the need to align PR practices with digital strategies to address technological challenges (Wiencierz & Röttger, 2017). Digital technologies have transformed how the public interacts with PR, as individuals are increasingly becoming "producers" and "creators" of information, shaping their own content and leaving a digital footprint in the global information space. This creates new meanings, symbols, and images. "The new public relations have generated an active audience that directly participates in shaping, broadcasting, and sharing media content" (Mantulenko, 2020).

Al-Rahmi et al. (2020) showed that digital PR has become increasingly important, as it has become an integral part of people's lives in the current era. The general significance of digital PR lies in its ability and speed in transmitting information, enhancing communication, and effectively and rapidly covering events and issues.

Given the recent digital transformation and widespread adoption of modern technology across various segments of society, institutions and organizations of all sizes and fields must leverage digitalization to enhance operations and engage diverse audiences. They must also train staff across departments to effectively utilize digital tools, meeting organizational needs and achieving goals (Al-Salhi, 2021).

The researcher concludes that PR has evolved due to globalization and digital technology, becoming more diverse and specialized. It highlights a strong link between digital technologies and PR practices, emphasizing the need for integrating digital strategies to address technological challenges. Digital PR has become essential, offering swift information dissemination and effective communication.

The Concept of Digital PR

Digital relations are a key contemporary concept that has rapidly evolved in recent years, aligning communication efforts with current dynamics. By leveraging advanced tools, technologies, and methodologies, organizational communication processes have been enhanced, advancing PR practice in sync with the current era's technical advancements (Farhat et al., 2024).

Al-Thobyty (2024) showed that digital PR involves leveraging various internet-based media channels to reach and engage target audiences through digital media. Mubarak and Mahmudi (2022) define digital media as a comprehensive suite of modern technologies designed to access, process, store, transmit, and reuse information in various forms, including text, images, audio, and video.

Rodsevich (2024) defines digital PR as a promotional tactic used by marketers and PR specialists to increase brand or individual online presence.

The researcher concluded that digital PR involves utilizing modern media and communication technologies to convey information and enhance public engagement, providing rapid and effective issue management and event response through electronic and digital means.

The Importance of Digital PR

The digital media has significantly enhanced the importance of PR, as it has facilitated digital connectivity between countries around the world. This has made it essential for PR to update its systems and adopt the latest technological methods. As a result, organizations are now in direct and more effective communication with their audiences (Haroun & Lagbash, 2021). Therefore, organizing PR activities is closely linked to defining its objectives and strategy, with careful and clear planning in light of the social structure within which the organization operates. In turn, this allows the organization to create goals that benefit the institution, making RP activities more effective (Haroun & Lagbash, 2021).

Although digitalization provides innovative opportunities for marketers to implement PR functions, further studies are needed to explore the effectiveness, importance, and power of utilizing digital media and other tools offered by the internet for PR. The emergence of the internet in all areas of life has benefited from ongoing developments and has become an integral part of the media and communication fields in all their aspects and forms (Ziyada, 2023).

According to Allagui and Breslow (2016), modern and digital tools have significant potential in enhancing organizational reputation awareness and serving individuals. These tools enable organizations to carry out PR activities more efficiently and effectively by increasing interaction with customers, thereby fostering long-term relationships.

Qadim (2022) summarized the importance of digital PR by highlighting its ability to foster closer connections between organizations and their target audiences through constant interaction. It enables PR professionals to quickly share detailed information about the organization and engage the public while also enhancing the ability to monitor media and online mentions in real time. This allows organizations to respond swiftly to rumors or criticisms, preventing potential crises.

The researcher concluded that digital media enhances PR by enabling instant communication and direct interaction, improving reputation and efficiency. However, further studies are needed to assess its effectiveness, particularly in providing accurate information, monitoring coverage, and engaging with the public to prevent crises.

Digital PR Strategies in Addressing Unemployment Issues

High unemployment is one of the key social and economic challenges facing many developing countries, making it a major concern for policymakers and relevant authorities. The media, including television, radio, music, and the internet, plays a significant role in influencing individuals and communities, helping to find solutions to this issue (Okande, 2015).

Digital PR strategies are an effective tool for addressing unemployment issues by enhancing communication between job seekers and employers through digital platforms. Social media and online advertisements can be used to provide accurate information about available jobs, making it easier for job seekers to access suitable opportunities quickly and efficiently.

In general, digital PR contributes to building virtual networks that connect employers with job seekers, creating an interactive environment that enhances collaboration and employment opportunities. These networks provide platforms for discussion, knowledge-sharing, and the exchange of information, which support the workforce and help reduce unemployment rates sustainably.

Conclusion

The current theoretical framework addresses the topic of digital PR strategies and their role in addressing unemployment issues. Studies have shown that digital media has become a key tool in disseminating information and guiding young people toward suitable job opportunities, particularly in light of the current economic challenges. These strategies help bridge the gap between job seekers and employers, providing a platform for effective communication and fostering opportunities for employment in a rapidly changing job market.

Through the analysis of the reviewed literature and studies, it became evident that digital PR significantly contributes to raising awareness about unemployment-related issues and motivating individuals to acquire the skills required by the labor market. The findings also showed that implementing these strategies enhances interaction between the public and organizations, which in turn increases the effectiveness of government policies in reducing unemployment rates.

In conclusion, digital PR strategies are essential tools that governments and companies should leverage to address the challenges of unemployment. As digital technologies continue to evolve, it is crucial to continuously improve and update these strategies to align with the future needs of the labor market.

References

Abdullah, N. R., & Al-Rousan, L. M. (2024). The impact of work environment on the performance of public relations practitioners in Jordanian universities: A field study. *Scientific Journal of Public Relations and Advertising Research*, *1*(28), 103–144.

Al-Sheikh, S. N. (2021). *A short article on unemployment*. Accessed on December 10, 2024 https://mawdoo3.com/

Al-Kou, M. F., & Asbitaan, T. F. (2022). The Palestinian center for anti-normalization's use of persuasion techniques on Facebook: An analytical study. *Al-Risala Journal of Media Studies*, *6*(2), 194–219.

Al-Murji, M., & Al-Rashidi, M. (2022). The impact of digital transformation on the quality of internal auditing. *Arab Journal of Management*, *43*(1).

Al-Rahmi, W. M., Alzahrani, A. I., Yahaya, N., Alalwan, N., & Kamin, Y. B. (2020). Digital communication: Information and communication technology (ICT) usage for education sustainability. *Sustainability*, *12*(12), 5052.

Al-Salhi, H. A. (2021). Digital public relations: A theoretical review. *Al-Hikma Journal of Media and Communication Studies*, *9*(2), 47–75.

Al-Thaibiti, A. M. (2024). The impact of digital public relations on raising public awareness of the housing program at the Ministry of Municipal and rural affairs and housing in Saudi Arabia. *Arab Journal of Media and Communication Research*, *47*(1), 310–351.

Allagui, I., & Breslow, H. (2016). Social media for public relations: Lessons from four effective cases. *Public Relations Review*, *42*(1), 20–30.

Bazzi, K. (2019). *The use of public relations in developing the tourism sector in Algeria* Ma thesis. University of Oum El Bouaghi.

Ben Abd El Hafidh, M., & Jomai, H. (2024). *The role of electronic public relations in building the reputation of economic institutions: A case study* Ma thesis. Biskra University.

Darwish, K. A., Al-Samari, H. O., & Mohamed, A. N. (2024). Quality of work life in public relations departments of sports clubs: An analytical study. *Journal of Physical Education and Sports Sciences*, *3*(105), 211–250.

Farhat, M. S., Ajwa, A., & Ateran, M. (2024). Digital public relations and interactive communication through electronic platforms. *Scientific Journal of Public Relations and Advertising Research*, *2*(29), 67–89.

Fari, L. S. (2021). An analytical study of the determinants of successful digital transformation in companies. *Algerian Journal of Economics and Finance, IEEE*, *8*(1), 33–45.

Ghazi, A. M. (2023). Identifying the needs of university youth in light of digital transformation. *Journal of the Faculty of Social Work for Social Studies and Research*, *30*(2), 189–246.

Haroun, Z., & Lagbash, I. (2021). *The role of digital public relations in improving the performance of service institutions: A field study* Ma Thesis. University of Tebessa.

Hassanien, H. A. (2021). Digital public relations and its impact on marketing hotel services in Egyptian hotels. *Journal of the Faculty of Tourism and Hotels*, *1*(10), 1–53.

Hayes, A. (2025). *Public relations (PR): Meaning, types, and practical examples.* https://www.investopedia.com/terms/p/public-relations-pr.asp?utm_source=chatgpt.com. Updated August 04, 2025.

Ibrahim, D. I. (2023). Requirements for achieving digital transformation in the social protection sector in light of Egypt's Vision 2030. *Journal of Future Social Sciences*, *1*(12), 125–131.

Jafari-Sadeghi, V., Mahdiraji, H. A., Alam, G. M., & Mazzoleni, A. (2023). Entrepreneurs as strategic transformation managers: Exploring micro-foundations of digital transformation in small and medium internationalisers. *Journal of Business Research*, *154*(1), 113287.

Khadir, M. (2019). *The concept of public relations.* Accessed on December 10, 2024 https://mawdoo3.com/.

Kiyosh, K. K. (2024). Public relations activities in the light of artificial intelligence technologies. *Al-Mustansiriya Journal of Arts*, *48*(106), 362–391.

Lordan, E. J. (1999). Guidelines for implementing new technology in public relations. *Public Relations Quarterly*, *44*(3), 15.

Mantulenko, V. (2020). Essential characteristics and types of digital media in the educational context. *Journal of Physics: Conference Series*. IOP Publishing.

Medani, S., & Derbali, F. (2024). *The role of public relations in managing organizational conflict in institutions: A field study* Ma Thesis. University of Biskra.

Misbah, A., & Tahirin, B. (2024). *The impact of oil price fluctuations on unemployment: A case study* Ma Thesis. University of Ouargla.

Mubarak, Z., & Mohammed, A. (2022). How media and communication technology contributed to the spread of cyber deviance among adolescents and youth. *Journal of Studies in the Psychology of Deviance*, *7*(3), 251–265.

Nasir, D. M. (2024). The role of modern communication technology and its relation to the performance of public relations practitioners: A field study. *Egyptian Journal of Media Research*, *1*(88), 693–722.

Okande, J. O. (2015). *The influence of media in creating awareness of job opportunities for the youth in Kenya: A case study of the Uwezo fund initiative* Ma Thesis. University of Nairobi.

Qadam, J. (2022). Digital public relations and building the mental image of modern organizations: An analytical reading. *Media and Society Journal*, *6*(1), 146–167.

Radi, D. T., & Al-Azzawi, S. J. (2024). The role of public relations in building the mental image of airlines: A survey study. *Lark Journal of Philosophy, Linguistics, and Social Sciences*, *16*(4), 556–572.

Rikrouk, K., & Aissaoui, T. (2021). The digital communication system as an investigative mechanism for sustainable health development: Mechanisms of control and follow-up. *Journal of Integration in Social and Sports Research*, *5*(1).

Rodsevich, M. (2024). *What is digital PR [and how to do it step by step]*. Accessed on December 10, 2024 https://prlab.co/.

Valentini, C., & Sriramesh, K. (2024). Forms and strategies of personal influence in "public" relations practices: Evidence from Italy. *Corporate Communications: An International Journa*l, *29*(7), 39–57.

Walker, D. (2023). *Why is digital transformation important for business growth*? Accessed on December 10, 2024 https://www.itpro.com/.

Wiencierz, C., & Röttger, U. (2017). The use of big data in corporate communication. *Corporate Communications: An International Journal*, *22*(3), 258–272.

Wynne, R. (2021). *Five things everyone should know about public relations*. Accessed on December 10, 2024 https://www.forbes.com/.

Xue, L., Zhang, Q., Zhang, X., & Li, C. (2022). Can digital transformation promote green technology innovation? *Sustainability*, *14*(12), 7497.

Ziyada, N. (2023). *Digital public relations and building the mental image of service institutions: A descriptive study* Doctoral dissertation. University of Algiers 3.

Chapter 11

Cybercrime Through Social Media Platforms[1]

Abduljalil Mohsen AlMahari

Ahlia University, Bahrain

Abstract

Cybercrimes have emerged as a significant threat in the digital age, targeting software on internet-connected devices. These offenses are particularly concerning due to their covert nature and the advanced skills required for their execution. Often conducted by highly skilled professionals using innovative technology, cybercrimes present unique challenges that demand a comprehensive understanding and response. This research focused on the relationship between cybercrimes on social media platforms and their impact on the psychological security of Bahraini women. It explored the frequency of their exposure, reasons for engagement, levels of interaction with such crimes, and perceptions of their effects on others compared to themselves. Additionally, it investigated attitudes toward restricting cybercrime-related content and the role of demographic variables in influencing psychological security. The research was organized into four sections. The first section provided a theoretical framework, introducing cybercrimes and their psychological impact. The second section examined cybercrimes in Bahrain, detailing their definitions, origins, objectives, risks, motivations, and the legal measures in place to combat them. The third section discussed the evolution, advantages, and disadvantages of social media platforms, highlighting their role in facilitating cybercrimes. The fourth section delved into the concept of psychological security, analyzing its definitions, manifestations, and the psychological effects of cybercrimes on social media users. This research underscored the urgent need to

[1]A scientific paper extracted from the PhD thesis proposal in Digital Media and Communication Technology, College of Arts and Sciences, Ahlia University.

Digital Dialogues, 103–112

doi:10.1108/978-1-83708-686-320261011

understand and address the effects of cybercrimes, particularly on vulnerable populations such as Bahraini women, emphasizing the importance of effective preventative measures and awareness campaigns.

Keywords: Cybercrimes; Bahraini women; psychological security; social media platforms; internet

Introduction

Technological advancements in media and communication, particularly the internet revolution, have significantly influenced various aspects of life. Social media platforms, as a major development, have created a virtual reality that facilitates social interaction. While these platforms offer numerous benefits, they are also exploited for cybercrimes, including accessing personal information and targeting individuals, especially women. Such crimes threaten psychological security—a critical psychological state that ensures mental well-being. Psychological security, particularly for women, is vital for achieving inner peace and fulfilling other basic human needs (Najadat, 2024). Arab women increasingly face cybercrimes that impact their personal and professional lives, as social media accounts have become targets for cybercriminals. Despite efforts to address these crimes, current measures remain inadequate in effectively reducing them (Al-Ajmi, 2024). In this context, the concept of psychological security becomes essential, as cybercrimes can lead to psychological disturbances and conflicts, undermining women's mental well-being. This research explores the impact of cybercrimes on social media platforms and their effects on the psychological security of Bahraini women. It aims to emphasize the importance of combating cybercrimes, protecting society from their consequences, and promoting awareness through continuous education, particularly for Bahraini women, to prevent victimization (WHO, 2021).

First Theme: Cybercrimes

The Emergence of Cybercrimes

The emergence of these crimes can be traced back to the increasing use of information technologies and the internet, which opened the door for hackers and intruders to take advantage of vulnerabilities in systems and software for illegal purposes. Over time, cybercrimes have continued to diversify and evolve, making their prevention and control a significant challenge (Najat, 2017). Accordingly, the concept of cybercrimes evolves over time with advancements in technology and its applications. This evolution can be categorized into distinct stages (Aqeili, 2017):

- The first stage of computer crime development occurred during the 1960s and 1970s, coinciding with the growing use of computers and the emergence of networks. This period saw the rise of new forms of computer crimes, such as data manipulation, system destruction, and cyber espionage, which were widely discussed in newspapers. Initial debates centered on whether these acts were isolated incidents or represented a new criminal phenomenon. There were also questions about whether these actions should be classified as crimes or merely considered unethical behaviors within the realm of information technology. While they were initially viewed as ethical breaches rather than legal offenses, the 1970s marked a shift, with expanding research and discussions recognizing these acts as a distinct criminal phenomenon that required specific legal frame works (Murad, 2016).

- The 1980s marked a significant shift in how researchers and stakeholders addressed the phenomenon of cybercrimes. The increasing number of cases involving the misuse of technology, particularly as media attention on such issues intensified, began to raise global societal concerns. Issues such as hacking, software piracy, manipulation of electronic payment systems, and the spread of harmful viruses became prominent during this period.
- During the 1990s and early 2000s, cybercrime surged significantly, driven by the rapid evolution of the internet from a limited academic network (Kurbalija, 2005) into a global platform for business, investment, and communication. This transformation facilitated system breaches, unauthorized access to information networks, and the rise of diverse cybercrimes (Mohammed, 1999). Despite the internet's expansion, information security was largely overlooked, with priorities centered on improving connectivity and accessibility. This oversight led to an increase in cybercrimes and their associated consequences, highlighting the urgent need for robust security standards to protect online systems (Al-Alfi, 2009). In this era, computers became primary targets for cybercriminals, with attacks on stored data, unauthorized system control, and intellectual property theft. Additionally, computers were used for illegal activities, including unauthorized financial transactions, distributing pirated software, and disseminating illegal content (Al-Shawaa, 1993).

The Concept of Cybercrimes

Cybercrime is commonly defined as unlawful acts committed using computers and networks, including mobile phones (Abad, 2016). The term "Cybercrime" itself comprises two components: "crime" and "cyber." The term "cyber" refers to concepts related to computer components or the information age (Marai, 2018).

Crimes committed over the internet are considered one of the negative outcomes of global technological advancement, making this criminal phenomenon a central topic of research aimed at defining its concept. These efforts have led to the development of various terms to describe it, including "cybercrimes" (Al-Kurdi, 2018).

Fourth: Objectives of Cybercrimes

The objectives of cybercrimes can be summarized into some key points. They include unauthorized access to information, such as stealing or modifying data to achieve the perpetrator's goals (Abdullah, 2007). Additionally, cybercrimes involve infiltrating servers through networks and disrupting their operations. Perpetrators also aim to obtain confidential information from entities that rely on technology, such as companies, banks, government institutions, and individuals, and use that information for extortion. Another major objective is to achieve unlawful financial or political gains through information technologies, including hacking, disrupting websites, credit card fraud, and stealing banking accounts, among other activities (Hilali, 2011).

Motivations Behind Cybercrimes

Cybercrimes are driven by various motivations, which can be broadly categorized into personal and external motivations. Personal motivations often stem from individual desires and behaviors. These include acts of revenge or threats directed at employers, whether individuals or companies. Some perpetrators commit cybercrimes to demonstrate their superiority in the field of hacking, while others are driven by a competitive nature and a desire to challenge their peers. Additionally, cybercrimes may be committed for entertainment or amusement purposes, showcasing the diverse personal reasons behind such activities (Bassiouni, 2013).

On the other hand, external motivations are influenced by broader economic, political, and strategic factors (Hafsi, 2015). Economic motives often involve the need for financial gain, with cybercriminals seeking to amass substantial wealth through illicit means. Politically, cybercrimes may serve as tools for blackmail, defamation, damaging reputations, or spreading false information and data (Lutfi, 2019). Strategic motivations, meanwhile, are frequently associated with government-level operations, such as hacking and stealing sensitive data. These activities may also involve leveraging technological advancements in economic and military fields, sabotaging and infiltrating competitors' systems for specific goals, conducting espionage across sensitive domains, undermining rival governments' capabilities, or even assessing the effectiveness of newly developed programs. These external drivers highlight the complex and multifaceted nature of cybercrime motivations (Al-Radaydah, 2013).

Types of Cybercrimes

- *Hacking:* It involves illegal activities targeting data processing systems with the intent to manipulate or destroy electronic documents. Hackers may use custom-written code or readily available software. The motivations (Ahmed, 2019) and objectives behind hacking are often complex and vary greatly (Ismail, 2014).

- *Exploitation of Children:* This crime involves using young children and adolescents in pornographic content, including images or films depicting sexual abuse. These acts are considered criminal offenses under the laws of most countries worldwide, which address them with strict penalties (Al-Afifi, 2018).
- *Cyberstalking:* Cyberstalking involves the use of the internet and electronic communication tools to harass individuals through public embarrassment, personal harassment, or financial fraud. Stalkers often gather personal information about their victims, such as names, family details, phone numbers, residences, and workplaces, using social media and other platforms. These actions threaten individuals' privacy and safety, causing significant fear and distress (Mousa, 2009).
- *Computer Viruses:* Computer viruses are programs designed to damage systems or devices by corrupting data, taking control, or stealing sensitive information. Viruses are characterized by their ability to replicate and spread. They attach themselves to host programs and are transmitted through storage media and email messages.
- *Piracy Software:* This involves illegally copying operating systems and programs, which are often distributed on websites for free or for a fee. Such software aims to infiltrate systems and cause harm (Al-Dairibi, 2012).
- *Internet Fraud:* Internet fraud exploits users by stealing their money through tactics such as stealing credit card numbers, convincing them to make financial transfers, or issuing checks for personal gain. These activities may also involve espionage, identity theft, or accessing sensitive accounts and locations (Yacoub, 2014).

The Importance of Combating Cybercrimes: The significance of combating cybercrimes lies in several critical aspects. First, it involves raising awareness about the dangers of cybercrimes and their strategies, which helps reduce their prevalence by educating individuals about the risks and preventive measures (Awad, 2004). Second, establishing strict laws to combat these crimes and informing the public about such regulations can effectively limit their recurrence. Third, enforcing these laws rigorously and educating the public about the severe penalties associated with cybercrimes are essential. Finally, developing an efficient electronic monitoring system that allows for early detection can significantly minimize losses.

Methods for Preventing Cybercrimes: As reliance on the digital world continues to grow across various aspects of life, the threat of cybercrimes increases daily. In response, nations have implemented mechanisms and regulations to protect data and combat these crimes proactively (Al-Masri, 2013). Preventive measures include raising awareness about the dangers of cybercrimes and their impact on families and communities, aiming to prevent their occurrence. Specialized training programs are also essential, which can be facilitated by establishing dedicated departments in universities (Ibrahim, 2007). Additionally, harmonizing laws and fostering international cooperation play a crucial role in streamlining collaborative efforts in cyber protection (Khairallah, 2012). Enacting specific laws and regulations targeting cybercrime prevention further strengthens these measures, while coordinating the efforts of authorities and relevant stakeholders ensures a comprehensive and effective approach to tackling these threats.

Second Theme: Social Media Platforms

The Concept of Social Media Platforms: Social media platforms are defined as electronic tools that enable individuals to create personal accounts and build relationships with other users on the same platform. Examples include websites such as Facebook, WhatsApp, YouTube, and other modern platforms (Al-Raddoud, 2012).

Classification of Social Media Platforms by Chronological Emergence

- *Blogs:* Emerging in the late 1990s, blogs are websites featuring posts arranged chronologically, with the most recent entries displayed first. Blogging platforms allow users to engage through comments and links, fostering interaction and discussion.
- *LinkedIn:* Established in 2002, LinkedIn is the largest professional networking platform globally. It serves as an effective tool for individual connections, knowledge exchange, idea sharing, and showcasing user profiles with verified credentials. Large companies utilize LinkedIn to post job opportunities and connect with professionals across diverse fields (Suhail, 2023).
- *Facebook:* Launched in 2004, Facebook is among the largest social media companies worldwide (Youssef & Mazari, 2022). It enables users to share various media, including videos, posts, and updates, while staying connected through news, chats, games, and live streams. By the end of 2018, Facebook had approximately 2.32 billion active monthly users and continues to grow and evolve (Al-Nazeeli, 2013).
- *YouTube:* Founded in 2005, YouTube is a platform for sharing a wide range of videos across multiple domains. It offers users the opportunity to stream live and is one of the top content creation platforms. Users can create free accounts and upload videos, provided they adhere to the platform's ethical guidelines (Al-Dehey, 2015).
- *Twitter (X):* Launched in 2006, Twitter allows individuals to interact via short posts known as "tweets" (limited to 280 characters). It also supports direct messages and video sharing. Official accounts for major global companies and influential personalities are prominently active on the platform (Tawfeek, 2018).
- *WhatsApp:* Introduced in 2009, WhatsApp began as a small startup and rapidly grew to serve 250,000 users within a few months. Acquired by Facebook in 2014, the app has experienced continuous growth, reaching one billion users by July 2017. Today, it is used by over a billion people across more than 180 countries, making it the largest free online messaging application globally (Ismail, 2021).

- *Instagram:* Established in 2010 by Facebook, Instagram is a social media platform specializing in photo and video sharing. Users can edit and share their content after creating an account, and anyone with an Instagram account can view and interact with posts. Recently, the platform added features such as text and voice messaging to enhance communication (Youssef & Mazari, 2022).
- *Snapchat:* Launched in 2011, Snapchat is a messaging app for sharing photos and videos. Users can view shared content for a limited time before it disappears entirely, as the platform automatically hides the content after a set duration. However, users can take screenshots to save what has been sent (Kraus, 2022).

The Role of Social Media Platforms in the Spread of Cybercrimes

Social media platforms have become a medium through which various forms of cybercrimes are perpetrated, especially against women. These crimes include personal account theft, emotional blackmail, manipulation, defamation, and the dissemination of inappropriate materials or images of victims. Additionally, they encompass fabricating and distributing indecent images on social platforms, sexual extortion, financial fraud, and the misuse of technology by cybercriminals. Cybercrimes are often the result of the ingenuity and creativity of the perpetrators, who exploit the capabilities of these platforms to commit offenses (Abdul Latif, 2022).

Key Advantages of Social Media Platforms

Social media platforms offer numerous benefits that positively impact individuals and communities. They enable users to stay connected with family and friends, regardless of geographical boundaries or distances, and allow users to follow important events through news sites. These platforms contribute to spreading diverse cultures, fostering a better understanding of the world around us, promoting acceptance of others, and deepening communication between nations.

Additionally, social media provides access to scientific research, enhancing knowledge and general cultural awareness. It also creates employment opportunities by enabling users to design pages that generate a steady income and support e-commerce. Furthermore, these platforms play a role in promoting religious coexistence and bridging differences between religions by creating dedicated pages for this purpose (Rohrs, 2014).

Key Disadvantages of Social Media Platforms

Social media platforms come with several negative impacts that can affect individuals and society. They often lead to addiction as users spend excessive amounts of time browsing, which can result in neglect of other aspects of life. These platforms also violate privacy by sharing personal information without consent. Moreover, they contribute to social isolation by disconnecting individuals from real-world social interactions.

Another concern is their role in exposing children to inappropriate or unethical content, as well as providing a marketplace for fraudulent transactions that can result in financial losses. Additionally, social media is a breeding ground for fake news and rumors, creating confusion and misinformation. Privacy violations, including account hacking and the dissemination of personal information, are also prevalent. These platforms further contribute to the spread of violence, destructive ideologies among teenagers, and the promotion of negative thoughts. Lastly, they often distribute misleading information, distorting facts, ideas, and historical narratives (Awaj, 2012).

Conclusion

The use of the internet is one of the hallmarks of modern technology, significantly enhancing opportunities for communication and connections through virtual relationships. Social media platforms, as a prominent part of this phenomenon, enjoy widespread popularity across all segments of society. This research aimed to explore the impact of cybercrimes occurring through social media platforms on the psychological security of Bahraini women in the Kingdom of Bahrain. A review of previous research reveals that such crimes play a critical role in deteriorating women's mental well-being, affecting their sense of safety and self-confidence. Examples of these crimes include online harassment, privacy violations, and digital violence, which can have varying degrees of negative effects on mental health. The research highlights the negative use of social media platforms and its repercussions, identifying cybercrimes as one of the most prominent and dangerous consequences. These crimes profoundly impact social and psychological aspects, potentially leading to the fragmentation and weakening of communities. Therefore, concerted efforts are essential to address this serious issue.

References

Abad, A. K. (2016). Cybercrime. *National Journal of Legal and Judicial Sciences*, *35*.

Abdul Latif, S. (2022). Risks of cybercrimes faced by women and ways to confront them: A sociological study on a sample of social media users. *Journal of Social Research and Development*, *4*(4), 165.

Abdullah, A. (2007). *Cybercrimes and the internet* (1st ed.). Al-Hali Legal Publications.

Ahmed, E. M. (2019). *Electronic extortion crime: A comparative study* [Master's thesis] (pp. 34–37). Amman Al-Ahlia University, Faculty of Law.

Al-Afifi, A. (2018). *Electronic theft and its ruling in Islam* (2nd ed.). Wadi Ay Kotub.

Al-Ajmi, M. (2024). Cybercrimes committed against Kuwaiti women and mechanisms to reduce them: A field study. *Journal of the Gulf and Arabian Peninsula Studies*, *50*(193), 121–163.

Al-Alfi, M. (2009). *Electronic publishing crimes* (Vol. 49). Center for Performance Development and Training.

Al-Dairibi, A. (2012). *Cybercrimes*. National Center for Legal Publications.
Al-Dehey, M. (2015). *The impact of social media networks on media audience perceptions*. Dar Al-Wafaa Legal Library for Publishing and Distribution.
Al-Kurdi, Z. (2018). *Cyberterrorism crimes* (1st ed.). Al-Halabi Legal Publications.
Al-Masri, H. (2013). *The coming threat of internet crimes*. Dar Al-Sharaf, Amman.
Al-Nazeeli, S. A. (2013). *Learn and master Facebook*. Modern Scientific Library.
Al-Radaydah, A. (2013). *Emerging crimes and strategies to confront them*. Dar Al-Hamed for Publishing and Distribution.
Al-Raddoud, A. (2012). *The role of social media in political change in Tunisia and Egypt from the perspective of Jordanian journalists* (p. 30). Master's thesis. Middle East University, Faculty of Media.
Al-Shawaa, S. (1993). Informational fraud as an emerging criminal phenomenon [Conference paper]. In *Conference of the Egyptian society for criminal law, October 25–28* (p. 516).
Aqeili, F. (2017). Cybercrime and measures to confront it through Algerian legislation [Conference paper]. In *Proceedings of the 14th international conference, Tripoli* (pp. 24–25).
Awad, E. (2004). *Crime in a changing society*. The Egyptian Library.
Awaj, S. (2012). New media and social networking sites. *Al-Mi'yar Journal*, *15*(30), 13.
Bassiouni, A. H. (2013). *Internet programming* (1st ed.). Dar Al-Kotub Alelmiyya.
Hafsi, A. (2015). *Cyber forgery crimes: A comparative study* (p. 106). Doctoral dissertation. University of Oran.
Hilali, A. A. (2011). *The general theory of evidence in criminal matters* (p. 46). Dar Al-Nahda Al-Arabiya.
Ibrahim, H. (2007). *Methods to combat cybercrime* (1st ed.). Dar Al-Rahab.
Ismail, A. A. (2021). The role of WhatsApp in enhancing social relationships during the Corona pandemic: A field study on Arab citizens. *Algerian Journal of Communication*, *20*(2), 116–150.
Khairallah, S. (2012). *The internet and information security* (1st ed.). Dar Esmat for Publishing.
Kraus, S. (2022). Facebook and the creation of the metaverse: Radical business model innovation or incremental transformation. *International Journal of Entrepreneurial Behavior & Research*, *28*(9), 52–77.
Kurbalija, J. (2005). *Governance de internet: Enjoins, auteurs et fractures*. Published by DiploFoundation and Global Knowledge Partnership.
Lutfi, K. H. (2019). *Computer data and information*. Dar Al-Fikr Al-Jamei, Faculty of Law.
Marai, E. G. (2018). Cybercrimes: Objectives, causes, crime methods, and solutions. *Media Studies Journal, Arab Democratic Center*, *1*, 424.
Mohammed, R. H. (1999). *Emerging computer crimes* (1st ed., p. 110). Dar Al-Kutub Al-Qanuniya.
Mousa, M. (2009). *Criminal investigation in cybercrimes*. Police Press.
Murad, A. (2016). *The role of computers in committing cybercrimes*. Egyptian Book and Documentation House.
Najadat, A. (2024). Cyber extortion through social media and its social risks for Jordanian women: A field study. *Journal of Humanities and Social Sciences*, *51*(4), 302–324.

Najat, B. M. (2017). *Criminal policy to combat information crimes*. Al-Khaldounia Publications.

Rohrs, J. (2014). *Audience: Marketing in the age of subscribers, fans & followers* (p. 195). Wiley.

Suhail, S. (2023). LinkedIn: Origins, features, and a comparative analysis. *International Journal of Social Communication*, *10*(2), 217–241.

Tawfeek, M. M. A. (2018). Social media networks: Origins and development. *Journal of the Faculty of Education*, *24*, 228–229.

World Health Organization (WHO). (2021). *Devastating prevalence of violence against women: Report on global, regional, and national estimates of violence against women*. https://www.who.int/ar/news/item. Accessed on November 14, 2024.

Yacoub, A. (2014). *New media and crime* (p. 222). Dar Al-Alamiya for Publishing, King Faisal University.

Youssef, B., & Mazari, F. (2022). Uses of social media – Facebook and Instagram – and their impact on youth relationships: A field study. *Al-Siraj Journal for Education and Society Issues*, *6*(2), 102–121.

Chapter 12

The Impact of Digital Transformation in the Media Environment on Intellectual Property Rights and Digital Works

Sh. Maryam Mubarak Alkhalifa

Ahlia University, Bahrain

Abstract

This current study seeks to identify the perspectives of media and academic elites regarding the effects of digital transformation in Bahrain's media environment on intellectual property rights and digital works. The research problem revolves around the following central question: What are the perspectives of media and academic elites regarding the effects of digital transformation in Bahrain's media environment on intellectual property rights and digital works? To address this question, the researcher distributed a questionnaire among the study sample, comprising media and academic elites in Bahrain. The questionnaire was structured into various sections, including demographic data, attitudes of elites, digital transformation in Bahrain's media environment, and intellectual property rights concerning digital works. Statistical data were analyzed using SPSS to derive the study's findings, which were subsequently discussed and interpreted. The study adopted the Media Richness Theory and concluded with several recommendations, most notably the need for stricter legal protections for digital works to safeguard intellectual property rights.

Keywords: Digital transformation; media environment; intellectual property rights; digital works; legal protection

Digital Dialogues, 113–119

doi:10.1108/978-1-83708-686-320261012

Introduction

Since ancient times, humans have recognized the necessity of recording and preserving information. Early civilizations depicted and engraved images of animals on cave walls using the tools available to them. The Stone Age has left behind numerous such engravings, representing the pinnacle of development at that time. Subsequently, writing was invented, assigning symbols to phonetic syllables. The earliest recorded script is the cuneiform writing used for the Akkadian language around 3000 BCE. Assyrian and Babylonian civilizations utilized clay tablets for writing and engraving information, driven by the need to archive their sciences and histories. However, this method was not practical for the easy transmission of information.

The use of inscriptions on tree bark, bones, and stones coincided with the ancient Egyptians' invention of papyrus. Writing evolved to introduce the alphabet, enabling the documentation of texts that were previously impossible to inscribe, thus conveying sciences, emotions, news, and arts. Documentation, publishing, and preservation became more precise, necessitating more practical writing materials. This advancement occurred in the first century CE with the invention of paper in China. The craft of papermaking underwent significant developments, especially through Islamic conquests, gradually spreading from China to Europe during the Middle Ages. The primary materials used in papermaking changed considerably during this period. The global eagerness for paper was further fueled by the invention of the printing press in the 15th century, followed by the typewriter in the 18th century, which greatly facilitated the dissemination of printed materials and books and streamlined documentation processes.

In the 19th century, writing in Bahrain was influenced by the British presence. Journalism and media began to emerge modestly during this period, utilizing both Arabic and English in newspapers and magazines. In 1936, the first newspaper, "Akhbar Al Bahrain" ("Bahrain News"), was published, featuring news and reports on local and international affairs. In recent decades, the Kingdom of Bahrain has experienced a surge in the development of journalistic and media writing, leading to the proliferation of local newspapers such as "Al-Waqt," "Al-Ayam," and "Al-Bilad," as well as the publication of numerous magazines and books reflecting Bahrain's political, social, and cultural landscape.

Bahrain has consistently kept pace with developments in documentation, writing, and journalism—from inscriptions on stone to the digital realm. In the era of digital transformation and the widespread adoption of technology and electronic publishing platforms, including blogs and various digital media, the speed of publishing and distribution has increased globally. Electronic writing facilitates the creation of multimedia content—texts, images, audio, and video—allowing for secure storage and easy access. However, this accessibility introduces significant challenges, notably the difficulty in determining and tracking intellectual property rights for published content. Protecting digital works has become more complex, as unauthorized copying and distribution have become easier. Anyone in Bahrain or elsewhere can access digital content via the internet and reproduce or republish it without the creator's or rights holder's permission. Although the Kingdom of Bahrain has enacted laws to protect intellectual property, enforcing these regulations and monitoring compliance is challenging amid the vast expansion of the internet and digital media. The rapid dissemination of digital content complicates the prevention of intellectual property rights violations and the effective prosecution of offenders.

This study aims to explore the perspectives of media and academic elites regarding the impact of digital transformation within Bahrain's media environment on intellectual property rights and digital work.

Literature Review

Abdullah (2024): This study aimed to examine the attitudes of media and academic elites toward interactive forms of data journalism in promoting Saudi Vision 2030. A sample of 155 respondents was analyzed, revealing significant interest in updates related to Vision 2030, particularly in economic and social content. Respondents favored narrative and data-supported reports across platforms. The richness of data journalism in Saudi electronic newspapers was rated moderately, emphasizing diverse use of interactive multimedia.

Mohamed (2023): This research explored the attitudes of media and academic elites toward employing artificial intelligence (AI) applications in journalism, using a purposive sample of 112 respondents. The study found a moderate positive correlation between attitudes toward AI and the factors of expected performance and social influence. Significant differences were noted in perceptions between media and academic elites regarding AI's implications based on experience and institutional ownership.

Ismail et al. (2023): The study assessed academic elites' evaluations of digital media ethics and social responsibility in reporting violent crimes among youth, based on a purposive sample of 100 respondents. The study concluded that social media platforms were the most followed outlets. While digital media's positive aspects (e.g., multimedia usage and immediacy) were highlighted, its negatives, such as the spread of rumors, were also noted.

Fizi (2024): This study analyzed the impact of technological transformations in the digital media environment on journalism, based on a purposive sample of 293 respondents. Key findings included how such transformations influence journalists' roles and empower them through new tools like data analysis, which improve journalistic skills and create new professions such as content creators.

Atabiqa (2023): This research provided a foresight on the future of digital transformation in media departments at Arab universities from 2023 to 2033. A random sample of 112 respondents indicated an optimistic outlook. The study emphasized the importance of qualified personnel and highlighted academic performance improvement among faculty members as a key positive aspect of digital transformation.

Sulaiman (2023): This comparative study examined the effects of digital transformation on authors' rights and fair use of intellectual production under Egyptian, Moroccan, and Emirati laws. Using content analysis, the study highlighted the dual effects of digital transformation, including economic gains and challenges like unauthorized reproduction and knowledge monopolization.

Shukri (2022): Investigating journalism students' attitudes toward digital transformation in Egyptian media, this study identified positive trends in utilizing digital applications for journalism. However, issues like limited internet access and outdated curricula in governmental universities hindered the quality of digital education.

Akrami (2024): This research explored the impact of digital media on intellectual property rights and examined the challenges of copyright infringement in cyberspace. The descriptive-analytical approach revealed that digital media has revolutionized information dissemination, complicating the detection of intellectual property violations.

Hamamah et al. (2024): The study investigated the impact of social media on intellectual property law using normative research methods. The results underscored the need for raising legal awareness and adapting intellectual property law to the digital age.

Al-Mutairi et al. (2023): This historical and analytical study traced the evolution of intellectual property rights in the digital era, focusing on the types of protected digital works and legal frameworks. It highlighted the significance of recognizing intellectual property rights and the institutions responsible for their protection.

Adams (2023): The study analyzed the evolution of intellectual property rights in the digital age, addressing challenges like digital piracy and the need for new enforcement mechanisms. The findings revealed a gap in contextual and methodological approaches to adapting intellectual property frameworks.

Mir and Rao (2023): Focusing on India, this study examined the challenges of protecting intellectual property rights in the era of social media. Recommendations included registering intellectual property with government bodies and employing digital tools like watermarks and digital rights management.

Al-Jarraf (2021): This research examined the awareness and commitment of university faculty and students to intellectual property rights in Saudi Arabia, particularly regarding digital educational materials. The findings highlighted a lack of awareness among students and recommended implementing policies to enhance protection for digital works.

Bin Ali Bernat and F Khalil (2021): This study evaluated the role of media in promoting intellectual property rights and the influence of modern communication technologies. Using a snowball sample of 52 journalists, the study found that intellectual property is deeply rooted in cultural values and that the media plays a crucial role in reinforcing these concepts.

Hammoudi (2020): This study explored the realities of intellectual property rights in Iraq, focusing on digital content creators. It revealed significant gaps in legislative frameworks, leading to weak adherence to intellectual property standards and subsequently poor-quality digital content.

Conclusion

This study concludes that, akin to other modern societies, the Bahraini community is experiencing significant transformations in the media landscape due to rapid digitalization. Opinions among media and academic elites regarding this digital shift and its impact on intellectual property rights and digital works vary, reflecting their distinct professional and intellectual interests.

Media professionals in Bahrain emphasize the necessity of updating media legislation to keep pace with swift digital advancements. They advocate for the adoption of new media platforms and the enhancement of digital media tools, acknowledging the substantial challenges in preserving and protecting intellectual property rights. Notably, existing copyright laws require amendments to address modern technologies such as online sharing, digital copying, and editing, which complicate content tracking and protection. Ensuring public access to digital content without infringing upon authors' and producers' rights has become increasingly difficult.

Academic elites focus on the imperative of developing legal frameworks for intellectual property rights that align with the rapid changes in digital media. They stress the importance of educating students and media professionals about digital rights and training them to navigate laws related to intellectual property. Universities play a pivotal role in advancing research on safeguarding digital works in the digital era, whether through reviewing local legal systems or engaging at the international level.

In conclusion, the perspectives of Bahrain's media and academic elites converge on the need to adapt to digital transformation, underscoring the importance of evolving legal frameworks to protect intellectual property rights and digital works. There is also a call to balance digital innovation with rights protection, prompting Bahraini society—including policymakers and creators—to develop legal and technical solutions that shield digital works from infringements while leveraging digital advancements in the media sector.

Bahrain has demonstrated a commitment to protecting intellectual property rights through its legal frameworks and initiatives. The Kingdom has implemented robust IP legal frameworks and support mechanisms to protect and promote the rights of creators, inventors, and innovators. Additionally, Bahrain has launched the "Technology Transfer" program, aiming to increase patents and transform inventions into projects that contribute to job creation for citizens.

Furthermore, Bahrain's digital economy strategy emphasizes the development of a comprehensive regulatory framework, including personal data protection and transaction laws, to support digital transformation at the national level. This approach has positioned Bahrain as a leading country in the region in financial technology (FinTech) and reflects its commitment to fostering a sustainable, inclusive digital landscape that empowers communities and drives economic growth.

These efforts underscore Bahrain's proactive stance in balancing digital innovation with the protection of intellectual property rights, ensuring that the benefits of digital transformation are realized while safeguarding the interests of creators and innovators.

References

Abdullah, L. A. (2024). Trends of the media and academic elite towards interactive forms in data journalism to introduce the Kingdom's Vision 2030. *Scientific Journal of Journalism Research*, *2023*(26), 615–640.

Adams, R. (2023). The evolution of intellectual property rights in the digital age. *Journal of Modern Law and Policy*, *3*(2), 52–63. https://doi.org/10.47941/jmlp.1554

Akrami, K. (2024). The digital media and intellectual property. *News Science Quarterly*, *13*(3). https://doi.org/10.22034/lrsi.2024.339753.1085

Al-Jarraf, R. (2021). Intellectual property rights in the environment of e-learning and distance education in Saudi universities. *ResearchGate*, (16), 68–93. https://www.researchgate.net/publication/280565428_hqwq_almlkyt_alfkryt_fy_byyt_altlym_alalktrwny_waltlym_n_bd_fy_aljamat_alswdyt/references

Al-Mutairi, A. R., Abdul-Jawad, S. Z., & Al-Laithi, H. A.-B. (2023). Intellectual property in the digital age. *Benha Journal of Humanities*, *2*(3), 15–34.

Atabiqa, A. M. A. (2023, November 21–22). A future vision for digital transformation in media departments and faculties in Arab universities "A prospective study for the period from 2023 to 2033" [Submitted research]. The First International Scientific Conference of the Faculty of Media at the University of Ez-Zitouna, Tunisia. *Journal of Communication Research*, *2023*, 185–210.

Bin Ali Bernat, H., & Khalil, S. F. (2021). Role of media promoting art intellectual property (A survey study on a sample of Saudi journalists). *International Journal of Learning Management Systems*, *9*(1), 32–49. https://doi.org/10.18576/ijlms/090202

Fizi, H. M. B. (2024). The impact of technological transformations in the digital media environment on the reality of the journalism industry and its relationship to journalists' perception of their jobs and roles. *Journal of the Faculty of Arts*, *72*(72), 577–616.

Hamamah, F., Munaji, M., Erna, E., Sukama, S., & Marhendi, M. (2024). The impact of social media on intellectual property law. *Al-Mustashfa: Jurnal Penelitian Hukum Ekonomi Syariah*, *9*(1), 123–140.

Hamoudi, S. H. (2020). Intellectual property rights in Iraqi digital content - A study on a sample of students of the college of media at the University of Baghdad. *Al-Farahidi Journal of Literature*, *12*(43), 330–352.

Ismail, M. S. I., Qansouh, F. M. E. E.-D., Kamel, N. A. I., Abdel Malek, S. M. A., & Abu Talib, A. E.-S. M. (2023). Academic elite evaluation of the ethics of digital media coverage of violent crimes among youth. *Arab Journal of Communication and Digital Media Research*, *2*(4), 303–335.

Mir, A. A., & Rao, A. N. (2023). Intellectual property rights in the age of social media: Challenges and strategies for India. *Education and Society*, *47*.

Mohamed, S. A. H. (2023). Trends of the media and academic elite towards employing artificial intelligence applications in journalistic work. *Egyptian Journal of Media Research*, *2023*(84), 911–963.

Shukri, G. (2022). Trends of journalism students towards digital transformation in the Egyptian media environment and its relationship to academic qualification within media colleges and institutes. A study within the framework of comprehensive quality. *Egyptian Journal of Public Opinion Research*, *21*(3), 267–309.

Sulaiman, M. D. (2023). The impact of digital transformation on copyright protection. *Scientific Journal of Intellectual Property and Innovation Management*, (6), 109–128.

Chapter 13

Misleading Advertising on Social Media and the Bahraini Public's Awareness of Its Risks: An Applied Study on Real Estate Advertising

Hani Hamza Ali Ebrahim

Ahlia University, Bahrain

Abstract

This study addresses the concerns of Bahraini society regarding misleading information and its effects, with a particular focus on misleading advertising strategies in the real estate sector. The aim of this study is to analyze the ethical implications of consumer protection in the digital age. Ideally, advertisers should adhere to honesty and integrity, presenting their offers accurately in accordance with marketing standards and legal frameworks. However, the reality often differs from this principle, as misleading advertisements have become prevalent, exploiting consumers' lack of expertise and knowledge.

The primary goal of this research is to explore the prevalence of fraud and misleading information in social media advertisements related to the real estate sector. The research examines the identification and analysis of common deceptive practices in these advertisements, emphasizing the urgent need for stricter monitoring and regulation of their content.

Furthermore, the research seeks to underline the necessity of legal frameworks that address fraudulent activities. In conclusion, the researcher aims to contribute to the promotion of more transparent and reliable advertising practices in the real estate sector, protect consumer interests, and enhance ethical standards in marketing.

Keywords: Misleading advertising strategies; social media; transparency in advertising; real state sector; real state fraud; misinformation

Digital Dialogues, 121–128

Published under exclusive licence by Emerald Publishing Limited
doi:10.1108/978-1-83708-686-320261013

Introduction

Modern media are dominant in the traditional media of the last century, such as terrestrial television stations, radio, and newspapers. This positive shift has forced traditional media to adapt to technological developments in the field of communications and information. Television stations had begun to create satellite copies, radio had Internet broadcasting services, and every printed newspaper had an electronic version. This progress reflects a different lifestyle, where information is made available faster and easier. In this era, restrictions on information can no longer be imposed, making efforts to resist misinformation more difficult. The speed and abundance of access to information enhances the media's ability to influence public opinion, thereby increasing opportunities for misinformation. Enhancing media education also requires how we deal with media to address these challenges (Al-Shamimri, 2013).

Media is at the core of the cultural communication process, playing a vital role in the transfer of information and knowledge to the recipient. The media contributes to shaping individuals' awareness and building societies and their progress toward modern times, making them an essential tool in everyday life. As media evolves as a profession, it has principles and rules governing its function and objectives, focusing on the moral and human dimension, highlighting the importance of being committed to them.

Media methods determine the type of impact they can have on the cultural level. Adherence to ethical standards helps promote unity and harmony, promotes cooperation in problem-solving, and reduces tensions. This commitment also encourages good in all spheres of life, contributing to scientific and practical progress. However, modern media sometimes play a negative role, as they can contribute to widespread division and raise doubts among individuals. When the media contribute to creating inaccurate awareness, they promote stereotypes that may harm society's interests in general.

First, the Reality of Misinformation

Definitions of misinformation are multiple, helping to understand its consequences and dimensions. Media misinformation is defined as the deliberate dissemination of false information aimed at manipulating and controlling consciousness. Al-Murr (2019) also explains that there is a growing awareness of the advertising deception pattern in the public, reflecting how these methods can influence purchasing decisions.

Media disinformation is a planned action by known or unknown entities, aimed at deceiving recipients and manipulating public opinion. This includes creating a misleading reality through the use of mass media and the latest propaganda arts. Hamoud (2018) also emphasizes the role of visual deception in promoting misleading messages and how to use design arts to achieve this.

Second: The Effectiveness of Misinformation

The effectiveness of disinformation is a phenomenon that requires an accurate understanding of the nature of the means used in it. No misinformation activity can be effective unless it is without the misinformation of the misleading party, and there is credibility or acceptance of the person performing it. This acceptance requires the ability of oneself and the community in general, and particularly misleading, to fall into disinformation.

When the media exploits people and deceives them with lies, presenting falsehood as truth and vice versa, it achieves the goals set for it, such as sowing discord and fueling conflict. These goals lead to easier penetration of communities and increased division among their members. Al-Fadl studies (2019) have pointed to real estate marketing strategies that can be used as a means of visual misinformation.

A quick look at what some media outlets publish, both traditional and modern, shows how provocative material can go so far as to ignite discord and destroy values. Such materials not only contribute to the creation of false awareness but also promote the spread of disinformation. In this context, Al-Khoja (2017) highlights the importance of clarifying how information is marketed and its impact on community awareness.

The media of our time is characterized by the spread of space broadcasting, which includes diverse and competitive channels. We have also seen an increase in electronic news sites, reflecting a significant shift in how news is consumed. These modern media have overwhelmed traditional media, forcing them to adapt to changes in the world. In this competition, it becomes easier for misguided actors to exploit these spaces to promote misinformation.

It is therefore essential that we have effective mechanisms in place to address these challenges. Public awareness of how to analyze information objectively and consciously should be enhanced; this contributes to building a society more capable of distinguishing between facts and imagination.

Third: The Challenges of Modern Media

Is the content provided by modern media innocent, impartial, and absolutely willing to disseminate the truth? Today's media is considered a double-edged weapon; it has become, in part, a programmed tool for misinformation, making millions of recipients victims of it. There are many reasons for this, including the nature of the actors responsible for each media outlet, their funding, as well as the increasing competition between them.

Frustration with the loss of control over the flow of information also plays an important role, as many suffer from an inability to manage this constant flow. To minimize this risk, media ownership should be strengthened and guided by clear societal visions and beliefs.

Modern media is characterized by its skillful deception in concealment and camouflage, making it difficult to detect disinformation. Digital media and the internet offer freedom of choice, but relying on these freedoms can be misleading, as competitive factors determine the recipient's exposure to a particular set of information. Research suggests that the rates of information consumption via social media are not without bias, promoting a nonobjective information lifestyle, and this bias can be the result of business policies that aim to increase consumption and channel messages, increasing the negative impact (Yasmin & Hussainia, 2023).

The ability of the recipient to resist misinformation remains limited, especially in the presence of media outlets that master the art of "media makeup." Studies indicate that these media outlets are active in deliberate sensationalism and stimulation, which increases the weaknesses in the recipient's awareness (Mohammed, 2019). Therefore, it is necessary to promote media literacy and empower individuals to consciously analyze information, which contributes to building a society that is better able to distinguish between fact and fiction.

Ultimately, there is an urgent need to develop recipients' critical thinking skills, enabling them to scrutinize the choices and messages offered by the media. To enhance these skills, individuals should receive appropriate training, contributing to the production of media content that is more accurate and less susceptible to misinformation, and media education is one of the key solutions to modern-day challenges (Al-Shamimri, 2013).

Concepts and Definitions

- *Misleading strategies in the Declaration*: A study (Al-Fadl, 2019, p. 218) are tactics used by advertisers to provide information about a product or service in a way that intentionally deceives or misleads consumers. In the real estate context, this includes overstatement of benefits, concealment of restrictions, visual and engineering deception, or the provision of false information.
- *Social media*: Al-Khoja, (2017, p. 75) defines social media as platforms such as Facebook, Instagram, Twitter, and LinkedIn that are used to entertain and promote products and services. This type of advertising takes advantage of the wide reach and targeted advertising capabilities of these platforms to engage potential customers.
- *Transparency in advertising* (Abdul Latif et al., 2019) refers to the practice of providing clear, honest, and complete information in advertisements to enable consumers to make informed decisions. Transparency ensures that all relevant facts about the product or service are communicated without omission or misrepresentation such as including accurate descriptions of property features, explicitly mentioning any restrictions or limitations, and providing real photographs rather than digitally enhanced images.
- *The real estate sector*: A study (Al-Murr, 2019, p. 24) refers to it as the industry concerned with the purchase, sale, and development of land and buildings. This sector includes residential, commercial, industrial, and agricultural real estate and includes residential real estate (houses, apartments), commercial real estate (office buildings, retail space), and industrial real estate (factories, warehouses).

- *Real estate fraud*: A study (Mohammed, 2019) refers to it as illegal acts or deceptive practices in the real estate sector aimed at achieving unfair or illegal gains. This can involve false representation, concealment of important information, or deliberate misrepresentations about property such as selling real estate without proper title, or falsifying ownership documents.

Dimension of Media Disinformation Study

First: Characteristics of Studies in Disinformation

- *Incomplete comparison*
  This phenomenon suggests that one element is considered to be superior to another in an inaccurate manner, raising questions about the criteria for comparison. Advertisers often fail to determine the basis for comparison, whether in terms of price, size, or quality. Phrases such as "best" are meaningless without specifying what to compare with. For example, the ad "Our cold medicine is better" can claim that it is better than not eating anything, which loses its true meaning. The use of the phrase "better than the leading brand" without clarifying standards or statistics makes it unreliable.
- *Inconsistent comparison*
  This comparison involves focusing on the positive features of one drug compared to another, which conveys the false impression that it is the best among all available options. This method is used to suggest that the drug in question generally excels, while the comparison may be unfair and subjective.
- *Misleading illustrations*
  Illustrations showing components that are not present in the drug in question are one of the most prominent methods of deception. Although there are legal requirements regarding the disclaimer, the customer's inattention to these notes may lead to the assumption that all items offered are available for purchase. This type of advertising contributes to the creation of unrealistic expectations among consumers, which necessitates the need to strengthen the media culture and raise awareness about these misleading methods (Mohammed, 2019).
- *Fake colorization*
  Some advertisers rely on the use of deceptive colors to make a product appear more attractive or healthier than it actually is. This strategy can influence the purchase decision, as consumers buy items based on misleading visual impressions, creating a gap between reality and expectations. Studies indicate that this type of deception can lead to a loss of trust between consumers and products, and calls for the need to correct the promoted information and adhere to transparency in advertising (Al-Fadl, 2019).

Second: The Benefits of Research in Disinformation

- Raising awareness: Studies help raise awareness about how misinformation is spreading and its impact on society. Badani (2019) also notes the importance of enhancing media awareness to address the challenges associated with misinformation.

- Developing counter strategies: Studies can contribute to the development of effective anti-misinformation strategies, such as the use of artificial intelligence to analyze and monitor fake news.
- Promoting critical thinking: These studies encourage individuals to think critically and help them distinguish between real and fake news.
- Improved policies: Studies can lead to improved digital policies and legislation to ensure a more transparent and credible media environment.

Third: Challenges Associated With Studies on Disinformation

Complexity and cost: Disinformation studies require significant resources in terms of time and money, as well as the need for advanced data analysis techniques. As Badani (2019) points out in "A Guide to Verifying Disinformation and Media Manipulation," these studies require significant investments to ensure their accuracy and effectiveness.

Technical Challenges: Studies face technical challenges in monitoring and analyzing the vast amount of information flowing online. According to Al-Murr (2019), the public's perception of advertising deception reflects the need for advanced analytical tools to address these challenges.

Social and political resistance: Anti-disinformation efforts may face resistance from some beneficiaries of the spread of misinformation. He also addresses Al-Shamimri (2013) in his book "*Media Education: How We Approach Media*," the importance of media awareness in the face of this resistance.

Limited impact: Despite efforts, the actual impact of these studies may be limited by the rapid spread of misinformation and the difficulty of fully controlling it. Research suggests that there is an urgent need to develop effective strategies to counter this phenomenon, as described in Yasmin & Hussainia (2023) about the influence of influencers in shaping young people's trends toward fake advertising.

Fourth: Types of Disinformation

The following types of misinformation were based on the concepts and ideas addressed in Al-Shamimri's book (2013), which reviews how media is handled and its effects on the public:

- Misleading selectivity that selects some words, facts, ambiguity, and sources and ignores others, focuses on one fact and ignores another associated reality.
- Misleading by manipulating information and arranging facts to give a certain meaning and impression and interpret it in a particular way that is contrary to reality.
- Misleading ignoring the background of events which makes them incomplete and distorted, and the recipient cannot understand and interpret them.
- Misleading the confusion, overlap, and nondiscrimination between the news on the one hand and opinion, analysis, and comment on the other, so that the

recipient does not know whether this is part of the news or the journalist's opinion and view.

- Misleading irrelevant information at the expense of important facts.
- Misleading headlines and news presentations based on exaggeration, intimidation, ambiguity, and incomplete information that sometimes do not correspond to the content of the news or the journalistic content of the material.
- Distortion through the use of certain vocabulary that leads to condemnation of attitudes, individuals, groups, or states, or to a favorable or negative view.
- Misleading sources and information through deception and fraud, and providing misleading information from their sources in incomprehensible terms, namely false information and news.
- To mislead by claiming a formal balance between only two opinions and two options, while deliberately ignoring other views and ignoring multiple possibilities, opinions, and solutions.
- Misleading by selecting false issues and problems and avoiding other issues of public interest that contribute to shaping the right consciousness.
- Misleading the public with unnecessary information, the so-called waste of information.
- Misleading the recipient with a very large amount of information that he or she cannot relate to or interpret, making him or her negative and feeling helpless in the face of the flow of information.
- Misinformation by diverting attention from a particular issue by emphasizing it—misinformation through coverage, camouflage, erasure, and disregard—it is a problem, event, or issue that makes it out of public consciousness.
- Misleading by exaggerating a cause, event, or problem with the aim of creating a false impression of its size in society.
- To mislead by downplaying and diminishing the issue, despite its importance to the public and its connection with their interests and concerns.
- Confusion through fragmentation, disaggregation, and limiting the discussion to specific details, cutting it off from the general framework, its natural context, and the big picture.
- Misunderstandings, turning the picture over, to the point of portraying the perpetrator as the victim and the victim as the criminal aggressor.
- Misleading through fabricated artificial terminology that builds and solidifies a particular concept that corresponds to the interests of the creator of the term he has created and promoted with the aim of concealing facts and falsifying awareness.

Conclusion

Media deception has not been born of high values and noble morals. It will not be a means of progress and progress for humanity. It has become an obedient instrument in the hands of power-bearers and conspirators. Deception has played a role in changing beliefs and misrepresenting facts, inviting us all to have a greater responsibility in distinguishing truth from falsehood.

When we listen carefully to the facts and sense the dimensions of the news, we realize that this information is not just passing data, it is tools that target our society. So, we have to be vigilant and adopt a critical attitude toward what we're offered.

Moving toward the future, guided by truth, requires all of us to be part of the solution. Misinformation can influence public opinion and undermine democratic processes, making the need for reliable platforms more urgent than ever. Maintaining truth and accuracy is very important.

We must also recognize the challenges associated with tracking and analyzing misinformation, as this requires collective efforts and detection of influence networks and hidden stories in a wide sea of information. Our responsibility as individuals and society is to promote awareness and build a future based on facts by following developments in media monitoring and contributing to the creation of real and reliable information, thereby protecting our society from the dangers of misinformation.

References

Abdul Latif, T., Abu Donia, S., & Farmawi, E. (2019). Visual dazzle in the design of advertising displays. *Journal of Architecture, Arts and Humanities*, (18).

Al-Fadl, M. (2019). Real estate marketing strategies in achieving rational development (A quantitative approach applied to public housing projects in Amman, Jordan). *Journal of North African Economics*, (6).

Al-Khoja, S. (2017). Marketing in a real estate organization. *Journal of Humanities*, *A*(47), 75–88.

Al-Murr, A. M. A. (2019). The Egyptian audience's perception of advertising deception methods for commercial products on television and its impact on their purchase decisions. *Journal of Media Research*, *51*(51).

Al-Shamimri, F. (2013). *Media education how to deal with media.* https://www.noor-book.com/en/ebook-التربيه-الاعلامي-كيف-نتعامل-مع-الوسائل-الاعلاميه-pdfnoor-book+1

Badani, R. (2019). A guide to verifying disinformation and media manipulation. *Journal of Journalism*. https://institute.aljazeera.net/en/node/1256

Hamoud, M. H. (2018). The visual deception of the art of Ego Morphosis and its role in enriching the advertising idea. *International Design Journal*, (18).

Mohammed, T. E. (2019). Innovative e-marketing methods with augmented reality and their impact on product design. *Journal of Architecture, Arts and Humanities*, (17).

Yasmin, A., & Hussainia, B. R. (2023). *The role of influencers in shaping young people's attitudes towards fake advertisements through social media: A field study on a sample of young people using Instagram.* Master's thesis. University of Constantine 3, Saleh Boubnaider, Faculty of Media, Communication and Audiovisual Sciences.

Chapter 14

Employing Artificial Intelligence Applications in Internal Communication in the Kingdom of Bahrain's Institutions and Their Relationship to the Effectiveness of the Organizational Performance of Public Relations Practitioners

Hessa Mahmoud Al-Dowei

Ministry of Information, Bahrain

Abstract

The field of artificial intelligence (AI) has witnessed significant advancements and transformative developments, leading to a wide range of applications in public relations (PR) practices. These advancements are expected to have a positive future impact on institutional and organizational operations. Numerous studies and scientific research have extensively explored this area in recent years due to the growing role of AI applications. Additionally, the increasing reliance on AI-driven technologies in PR-related functions has significantly enhanced organizational performance, particularly in terms of engaging with target audiences—whether internal or external—by identifying suitable messaging strategies and optimizing relevant services and applications. Furthermore, the latest developments in PR, driven by AI applications, have positively influenced the overall performance of organizations and institutions, given their direct and effective engagement with audiences. AI has reached unprecedented levels of human-like capabilities, raising both excitement and concern. Scholars have expressed apprehensions about the potential negative consequences of complete reliance on AI applications, particularly regarding rising unemployment rates, especially in developing countries.

Digital Dialogues, 129–139

Published under exclusive licence by Emerald Publishing Limited
doi:10.1108/978-1-83708-686-320261014

Keywords: Artificial intelligence; digital public relations; organizational performance; audience engagement; automation

Introduction

Artificial intelligence (AI) has become an essential tool in the practice of public relations (PR) across various institutions worldwide. The traditional functions of PR are no longer sufficient, as AI-driven technologies have introduced new dimensions to the field. Organizations have increasingly leveraged AI applications to enhance customer service, streamline various operational processes, and strengthen relationships with stakeholders. These technologies have facilitated more efficient communication between organizations and their audiences while optimizing service delivery. This study explores the different roles AI plays in PR, with a particular focus on its implications for organizational performance.

First: Definition of AI

AI is a branch of computer science and a fundamental pillar of modern technological advancements. Artificial intelligence, commonly abbreviated as AI, refers to the ability of machines and digital systems to perform tasks that mimic human intelligence, such as reasoning, learning from past experiences, and executing cognitive functions.

The primary goal of AI is to develop intelligent systems that can comprehend, learn, and behave similarly to humans, thereby offering various interactive services, including education, guidance, and problem-solving. AI-driven systems are designed to assist users by providing personalized recommendations and engaging in human-like interactions.

John McCarthy, widely regarded as the "father of artificial intelligence," defined AI as the science of engineering intelligent machines, particularly computer programs, that replicate human cognitive processes and behavior. AI is essentially the simulation of human intelligence through computer systems, enabling machines to analyze human behavior, learn from observed reactions, and replicate decision-making patterns.

In his work, Copeland (2019) describes AI as an attempt to mimic human reasoning and behavior through complex computational models, allowing machines to understand and respond to various situations in a human-like manner. This continuous evolution of AI technologies has played a pivotal role in transforming the landscape of PR and corporate communication.

Second: History and Evolution of AI

The origins of AI can be traced back to the 1940s when computer scientists began designing systems capable of reasoning, using artificial neural networks instead of relying solely on fixed relationships between symbols and responses. During this period, significant research efforts emerged, particularly in the late 1940s.

Scientists Warren McCulloch and Walter Pitts developed rudimentary electronic networks that mimicked neural cells, enabling logical calculations using Boolean algebra as a method for expressing mathematical concepts in a logical form (Al-Ajmi, 2022).

The development of AI as a formal discipline dates back to the first half of the 20th century when researchers started exploring ways to represent human knowledge and cognitive processes within computational systems. In 1956, a landmark conference was held at Dartmouth College in the United States, where the concept of AI was officially defined, and research goals were established to guide its future development. Since then, AI technologies have evolved significantly, leading to the emergence of various models and techniques used across multiple applications. Scholars have identified distinct waves in the evolution of AI, as outlined by Zouinar (2020):

- *First Wave (1950–1980):* This phase was characterized by rule-based systems, control mechanisms, input-output programming, and fixed software. It marked the initial experiments with AI, with one of the most prominent applications being computer chess programs.
- *Second Wave (1980–2010):* AI in this era shifted toward machine learning applications, deep learning algorithms, and artificial neural networks. Some of the most notable advancements during this period included machine learning, natural language processing (NLP), and robotics.
- *Third Wave (2010–Present):* This wave focuses on solving complex problems that require a combination of machine learning techniques, NLP, and robotics. AI applications in this era have expanded significantly, encompassing deep learning-based voice and image recognition, speech-to-text conversion, and AI-driven solutions in healthcare, autonomous vehicles, smartphones, and e-commerce (Artabaz, 2022).

Third: Applications of AI in Social and Human Sciences

Since its emergence, AI has played a pivotal role in revolutionizing various fields, including the social and human sciences. AI has facilitated the integration of multiple disciplines, significantly advancing research methodologies, data analysis, and the understanding of complex human phenomena.

One of the most prominent applications of AI in the humanities and social sciences is text, image, and video analysis. With its advanced capabilities, AI can efficiently analyze texts, articles, books, and documents, extracting key information and insights. This has greatly assisted researchers in comprehending ideas, perspectives, and concepts related to social and human sciences.

Furthermore, AI's ability to analyze images and videos has enabled a deeper understanding of visual content by interpreting facial expressions, emotions, movements, and behavioral patterns. This has contributed to enhanced research on human behavior and social interactions, offering new dimensions in disciplines such as psychology, sociology, and media studies (Seminar, 2023).

Fourth: Challenges and Considerations Facing AI

Despite the vast opportunities that AI offers to the social and human sciences, it also presents several challenges that must be carefully addressed:

- *Ethical Considerations:* The use of AI applications raises significant ethical concerns, particularly regarding privacy, algorithmic bias, and the responsible handling of sensitive personal data. Striking a balance between technological advancement and ethical considerations is essential to ensure the fair and responsible deployment of AI (Manyika, 2011).
- *Interpretation and Transparency:* Some AI algorithms, particularly black-box models, pose challenges in terms of understanding and interpreting their decision-making processes. This lack of transparency can hinder accountability and reliability. Therefore, researchers must work toward developing more transparent AI models that allow for clearer explanations of how decisions are made, ensuring both trust and efficacy (Simonite, 2018).
- *Interdisciplinary Collaboration:* Successfully integrating AI into the humanities and social sciences requires collaboration between technology specialists and domain experts. Establishing interdisciplinary research teams is crucial to unlocking AI's full potential in these fields and ensuring that technological advancements align with academic and societal needs.

AI continues to play an increasingly transformative role in research, analysis, and innovation within the social and human sciences. As AI processes and applications become further embedded in these disciplines, it is imperative to address ethical considerations, enhance transparency, and foster interdisciplinary cooperation to fully harness the capabilities of this groundbreaking technology (Doshi-Velez & Kim, 2017).

Public Relations

One of the simplest definitions of PR is establishing and managing positive relationships between an organization and its audience to ensure satisfaction, mutual understanding, and trust. Organizations strive to gain public support and confidence, as this is a fundamental responsibility of management and a key indicator of success (Ferjani, 2018).

In media terminology, PR is defined as:

> planned, continuous, and goal-oriented administrative efforts aimed at building strong and effective relationships based on interaction, persuasion, and mutual communication between an organization and its audience. These efforts seek to achieve the interests of all parties involved and establish harmony through internal activities, such as self-assessment and corrective actions, as well as external activities that leverage all available media channels to disseminate information, ideas, and explanations through specialized personnel. (Hijab, 2002)

Additionally, PR can be seen as an activity that fosters trust and mutual understanding between two parties—such as the government and the people, a leader and their followers, or an institution and its audience. It applies to organizations of all types, whether governmental, commercial, political, religious, or sports-related, and their engagement with relevant audiences, including employees, consumers, shareholders, and the broader community.

Digital PR

PR is a dynamic and evolving field that continuously adapts to technological advancements. The advent of the internet and digital networks has opened new opportunities for creativity and efficiency in PR, making it a critical tool for organizations to achieve their communication and strategic objectives.

The definitions and practices of digital or electronic PR vary, but the fundamental concept revolves around integrating new communication technologies into traditional PR efforts. Digital PR emerged as a logical extension of traditional PR practices for several key reasons:

- Keeping pace with societal changes driven by advancements in communication technologies.
- Optimizing these technologies to enhance PR operations and achieve organizational goals (Al-Khayyat, 2015).

In the digital era, PR functions have become faster, more precise, and highly targeted. Digital PR has revolutionized how institutions promote their activities and engage with audiences through various media channels. It enables the use of professional and social media platforms, blogs, and interactive comments, not only for disseminating news but also for fostering dialogue and engagement.

Al-Khayyat (2015) defines digital PR as "the practice of PR departments utilizing modern communication technologies to execute their activities and contribute to the achievement of their objectives."

The term "internet public relations" or "electronic public relations" is relatively newer compared to digital PR. It often involves the strategic planning of digital tools and new media technologies to facilitate two-way communication between an organization and its audience. Moreover, digital PR plays a crucial role in crisis management through online platforms, ensuring an organization's reputation is maintained in an increasingly interconnected world (Faris, 2017).

According to the International Public Relations Association (IPRA) and the British Institute of Public Relations, digital PR is defined as "the process through which public relations departments utilize and harness modern communication technologies and digital media channels to execute their activities, contributing to the organization's engagement with the public and society at large" (Hadadi, 2018).

PR in the Era of AI

The history of AI traces back to John McCarthy, a pioneering computer scientist who first coined the term in 1956. He defined AI as "the science and engineering of making intelligent machines" during his tenure at the Massachusetts Institute of Technology (MIT) in 1958. McCarthy, along with his colleague Marvin Minsky, who later co-won the Turing Award, launched the AI research initiative, delving into multiple fields, including robotics, computational theory, commonsense logic, and human–computer interaction.

Minsky also invented LISP (LIST Processor), which became the widely preferred programming language for AI research and education—a status it maintains to this day. Notably, LISP is the second-oldest programming language after Fortran.

During the 1960s and 1970s, AI research increasingly focused on knowledge-based systems, which remained a dominant approach into the 1980s. The Japanese Fifth-Generation Computing Project in the early 1980s marked a significant milestone, triggering a major leap in AI research. Today, AI applications span across general-purpose cognitive tasks, such as perception and logical reasoning, as well as domain-specific applications, including chess-playing algorithms and medical diagnostics. Scientists and experts leverage AI to preserve and apply their lifetime knowledge and expertise, solidifying AI's role as a globally adaptable field that transcends industry boundaries (Al-Hadi, 2005).

The Relationship Between PR and AI

PR has been constantly reshaped since the rise of globalization and digital technologies, expanding its multidisciplinary nature. PR is an integral part of every organization, but as technology advances, practitioners must continuously adapt and redefine their roles.

Recent academic literature highlights a growing relationship between AI and PR, emphasizing the need for innovation in PR practices. The convergence of AI and PR is crucial for tackling technological challenges and optimizing decision-making within organizations.

Although the proactive role of PR is not new, its transformation has been ongoing since the 1970s. PR evolved into a strategic function aimed at preventing conflicts, monitoring external environments, and responding to societal changes. With AI's systematic, predictive, and technological capabilities, PR professionals can now analyze trends, anticipate risks, and engage with audiences more effectively.

One of AI's fundamental contributions to PR lies in its ability to deliver the right information to the right people at the right time, enhancing strategic decision-making and providing a competitive edge for PR in the future (Millar Porter, 1985).

Types of AI Applications and Tools in PR

AI has introduced numerous practical applications and tools that have transformed PR. Some of the most notable AI-driven tools include the following (Al-Din, 2023):

- *Automated Journalism:* AI-powered agents continuously monitor local and global news outlets, extracting essential information and generating media reports with high efficiency.
- *Exploratory Services:* AI provides automatic discovery and crisis monitoring tools, enabling PR professionals to analyze past crises, examine the measures taken to address them, and learn from previous experiences.
- *Analytical Services:* AI systems can process and analyze massive volumes of data related to an organization and its external environment, allowing PR teams to predict crises before they occur and develop proactive strategies.
- *Influencer and Media Engagement:* PR professionals often struggle to directly reach and engage with their target audiences or media outlets. AI analyzes audience behavior and characteristics, helping PR teams craft and distribute effective communication messages. AI also identifies the most interactive and influential audience segments, providing precise data-driven insights into the effectiveness of PR campaigns and initiatives.
- *Future Trend Prediction:* Given the rapidly changing global landscape, AI has become a vital tool for predicting future market trends. It helps organizations anticipate digital marketing trends with minimal cost, effort, and time.
- *Smart Cities:* AI and the Internet of Things (IoT) are integrated to enhance urban efficiency and sustainability, improving the quality of life for city residents through automated infrastructure and intelligent systems.
- *Digital Robots:* AI-powered physical robots use reinforcement learning and sensory perception to interact with the surrounding environment, assisting in various industrial and commercial applications.
- *Guidance and Advisory Services:* Certain AI applications can provide expert advice in specific fields, such as medical diagnosis, where AI analyzes symptoms to suggest potential illnesses and treatments.
- *Digital Content Creation:* AI plays a major role in digital content production, including the automated generation of text-based content. However, it also presents ethical concerns, as AI can be used to create fake news or manipulate video and image content, making it appear as though politicians and celebrities have said or done things they never actually did.
- *Visual System Interaction:* AI is capable of detecting image manipulations, recognizing handwritten text, interpreting various languages, and analyzing inputs within visual media.

Organizational Performance

Achieving high organizational performance is a primary objective for institutions, including educational organizations. One of the most effective strategies for enhancing performance is managerial empowerment, which enables organizations to adapt to administrative changes and maintain competitive efficiency. Many institutions continuously seek innovative approaches to retain employees and enhance their engagement, leading to higher productivity and improved performance.

Senior management prioritizes employee retention and empowerment, recognizing that human resources are a vital asset. By embracing empowerment, organizations foster initiative, creativity, and job stability, which are essential for achieving long-term organizational success.

Entrepreneurs and business leaders have extensively discussed organizational performance, emphasizing that no organization—whether large or small—can sustain high productivity in the long run without a motivated and engaged workforce. Effective organizational performance serves as the cornerstone of an institution's progress, sustainability, and continued excellence. Consequently, organizations must invest in employee satisfaction, a supportive work environment, and a culture that instills pride in working for the institution (Al-Zeyadi, 2020).

Key Performance Indicators for Organizational Performance

Organizational performance is evaluated based on several key indicators (Al-Mansi & Abduh, 2020):

- *Productivity:* The quantity and quality of work completed within a specified timeframe.
- *Quality:* The standard of work performed, and the quality of products or services delivered.
- *Efficiency:* The optimal utilization of resources to maximize output with minimal waste.
- *Satisfaction:* The level of employee and customer satisfaction within the organization.
- *Profitability:* The ability to generate financial profits and maintain economic sustainability.

By focusing on these indicators, organizations can assess their performance, identify areas for improvement, and implement strategies to enhance overall efficiency and effectiveness.

Factors Influencing Organizational Performance

Several factors significantly impact organizational performance, including (Al-Ma'bqi, 2020):

- *Leadership:* Effective leadership plays a crucial role in planning, guiding, motivating, and inspiring employees to achieve organizational goals.

- *Human Resources:* The competence and efficiency of employees are among the most critical factors contributing to an organization's success.
- *Organizational Structure:* A well-designed structure with clear roles, responsibilities, and workflow organization enhances efficiency.
- *External Environment:* Factors such as market changes, competition, economic fluctuations, and political developments influence an organization's performance.
- *Organizational Culture:* The values and beliefs prevalent within an organization shape employee behavior and workplace dynamics.
- *Technology:* Leveraging modern technological tools and innovations is essential for improving performance and ensuring competitiveness.

Criteria for Evaluating Organizational Performance

Numerous studies highlight the importance of behavioral and performance-based criteria in evaluating organizational effectiveness. Researchers suggest that organizational performance, particularly concerning human resources, can be classified into three key areas:

(1) *Job Satisfaction:* Managers emphasize the significance of assessing organizational performance through employee-related metrics, as job satisfaction is a key indicator of organizational effectiveness. Job satisfaction refers to the emotional state an employee experiences toward their job, which can be either positive or negative (Abu Ziyada, 2011). Job satisfaction is influenced by five main factors:

    - *Individual Factors:* Education level, personality traits, age, and personal abilities.
    - *Social Factors:* Relationships with colleagues within the organization and informal social networks outside of work (Abutayeh et al., 2012).

(2) *Organizational Commitment:* Organizational commitment is a critical area of interest for many institutions due to its direct link to employee behavior, attendance, and productivity. A strong sense of commitment positively affects an organization's overall performance and its relationship with external stakeholders (Al-Kharshoum, 2011).

References

Abu Ziyada, Z. (2011). The impact of applying the concept of total quality management on organizational performance: An applied study on a sample of Palestinian commercial banks (Unpublished). *An-Najah Research Journal*, *52*(4), 889.

Abutayeh, B. K., Al-Hiyari, K., & Al-Qatawana, M. I. (2012). The relationship between organizational climate and job satisfaction in some Jordanian business organizations (Unpublished). *The Islamic University Journal for Economic and Administrative Studies*, 168.

Al-Ajmi, H. (2022). The role of artificial intelligence applications in facilitating communication in effective organizations. *Saudi Journal of Educational and Psychological Studies*, *3*(1), 81–90.

Al-Din, Y. A. T. H. (2023). *Uses of artificial intelligence in public relations: A case study of Reblack Foundation*. Published master's thesis. Mohamed Boudiaf University of M'sila.

Al-Hadi, M. M. (2005). *E-learning over the internet*. Egyptian Lebanese Publishing House.

Al-Kharshoum, M. M. (2011). The impact of climate on organizational commitment: A field study on employees in cultural institutes affiliated with Aleppo University (Unpublished). *Damascus Journal of Economic and Legal Sciences*, *3*, 371–471.

Al-Khayyat, A. B. S. (2015). Digital public relations: Concepts, roles, and challenges. In *A research paper presented at the third forum of the Saudi association for public relations and advertising, April 8-9, Riyadh.*

Al-Ma'bqi, F. A. (2020). *The impact of the four-way alignment on organizational performance: A field study in banks operating in the Republic of Yemen*. Doctoral dissertation. University of Science and Technology.

Al-Mansi, M. A., & Abduh, H. S. (2020). The relationship between intellectual capital and organizational performance: The mediating role of entrepreneurial orientation. An applied study on small and medium enterprises in Tabuk, Saudi Arabia. *Journal of Commercial Research*, *42*(3), 55–98.

Al-Zeyadi, B. A. (2020). The impact of job tenure on supporting organizational reputation: A field study. *Arab Journal of Administration*, *40*(4), 71–114.

Artobaz, S. (2022). The impact of using artificial intelligence applications on improving institutional performance. *Journal of Humanities at Oum El Bouaghi University*, *9*(3), 1249–1270.

Copeland, B. J. (2019). *Artificial intelligence*. Britannica. https://mawdoo3.com. Accessed on October 7, 2019.

Doshi-Velez, F., & Kim, B. (2017). *Towards a rigorous science of interpretable machine learning*. https://doi.org/10.48550/arXiv.1702.08608

Faris, W. (2017). Electronic public relations in the Arab world: Reality and challenges. *Journal of Social Sciences, Laghouat University*, *7*(30).

Farjani, A. (2018). *Public relations and communication strategies* (1st ed., p. 18). Amjad Publishing and Distribution House, Jordan.

Hadadi, W. (2018). Electronic public relations in the Arab world: Reality and challenges. *Journal of Social Sciences, Laghouat University*, *7*(30).

Hijab, M. M. (2002). *Media Dictionary* (p. 462). Dar Al-Fajr Publishing and Distribution.

Manyika, J., Chui, M., Brown, B., Bughin, J., Dobbs, R., Roxburgh, C., & Byers, A. H. (2011). *Big data: The next frontier for innovation, competition, and productivity*. McKinsey Global Institute.

Millar Porter, M. (1985). How information gives you competitive advantage. *Harvard Business Review*, *63*(4), 50–561.

Seminar. (2023). *The first peer-reviewed scientific journal in multimedia technology* (Vol. 1(2), p. 18). Faculty of Arts, Girls' College of Science and Education, Ain Shams University.

Simonite, T. (2018). The unreasonable effectiveness of the algorithm in social science. *Wired*. https://www.wired.com/story/the-unreasonable-effectiveness-of-the-algorithm-in-social-science

Zouinar, M. (2020). Évolutions de l'Intelligence Artificielle: Quels enjeux pour l'activité humaine et la relation Humain-Machine au travail? *Activités [En ligne]*, *17*(1). http://journals.openedition.org/activites/4941. https://doi.org/10.4000/activites.4941

Chapter 15

Communication Strategies for Digital Diplomacy and Its Role in Building the Image of the Kingdom of Bahrain in Coexistence and Peacebuilding

Fawaz Bubashait

Ahlia University, Bahrain

Abstract

This study aims to highlight digital diplomacy as a modern and effective tool to achieve foreign policy goals, promote the values of coexistence and peace, and build a positive mental image of countries. The theoretical framework shows that digital diplomacy depends on the use of social media and digital platforms to communicate with local and international audiences, which contributes to the dissemination and clarification of foreign policies; in addition to enhancing digital public relations and organizing international events, he also pointed to successful international experiences, such as the British experience for strengthening soft power and preserving cultural heritage, and the role of the European Union in activating external communication through strategic units; however, digital diplomacy faces challenges related to accuracy and reliability in disseminating information, which requires tight strategic guidance to ensure the effective use of these tools.

Keywords: communication strategies; digital diplomacy; image; Kingdom of Bahrain; coexistence; peace

Introduction

Technological development, especially in the field of communications, has led to a radical change in the form of diplomatic work, which allowed the emergence of

Digital Dialogues, 141–150

doi:10.1108/978-1-83708-686-320261015

the concept of "digital diplomacy." This diplomacy reflects how social media has become an effective tool to achieve diplomatic goals, as countries can use it to deliver information to people and gain the support of world public opinion (Al-Qarar Center for Media Studies, 2024a).

First: The Concept of Digital Diplomacy

Digital diplomacy is a modern form of communication resulting from the development of communication technology. Issawi (2022, p. 76) defined it as "the use of digital communication tools (social media) by diplomats to communicate with others and the public and focuses on digital and network technologies, including the internet, mobile devices, and social media channels."

Al-Arabi and Zain al-Din (2021, p. 8) defined digital diplomacy as "a key tool used by the state to achieve foreign policy goals and influence states and groups to co-opt them and gain their support, which is the science and art of negotiations."

Hazrat (2016, p. 23) defined digital diplomacy as "the art of practicing diplomacy using the Internet, and digital diplomacy promotes direct communication with society through social media."

Mirza (2018, p. 329) defined digital diplomacy as "one of the areas of public diplomacy that aims to serve the interests and foreign policies of the state, by communicating with, informing and persuading the masses, with a focus on effective dialogue using multiple means."

Second: Objectives of Digital Diplomacy

Digital diplomacy significantly accelerates the dissemination of information, especially during various crises. This acceleration reflects its fundamental objective, which is to promote immediate and effective communication between states and the public.

The transformation in the field of diplomacy, especially digital diplomacy, helps to strengthen international relations through partnerships and renewed strategies that keep pace with global developments (Al-Issawi, 2022, p. 76). Digital diplomacy works to achieve several key objectives through the exploitation of digital platforms, as explained by Mohammed (2017, p. 56) in the following:

- It aims to increase mutual perception between states, thus improving international relations.
- It illuminates countries' foreign policies and interpretations for users of these networks, helping to provide a deeper understanding of their goals and purposes. Digital diplomacy also enables foreign policy by communicating messages to external audiences, explaining their contexts and backgrounds.

- In this context, each country seeks through its digital diplomacy to promote its vision and strengthen its positions on disputed issues while trying to weaken competing visions.

Third: The History of Digital Diplomacy

Since man was created, the need to communicate and interact with others has driven the development of diplomacy, which aims to expand horizons, understand cultures, and protect interests. The Treaty of Westphalia in 1648 marked a key point in diplomacy, establishing the modern state and legal frameworks for state relations. Over time, the system of permanent missions evolved, culminating in the 1961 Vienna Convention on Diplomatic Relations, which remains the foundation of modern diplomacy (Al-Ghannam and Abdullah, 2023, p. 540).

The 21st century's rapid advancements in information and communication technology have significantly impacted all areas of life, including diplomacy. The digital revolution has expanded diplomacy from state-to-state relations to include interactions between states and people. Social media platforms have played a key role in this shift, enabling direct communication, instant interaction, and greater public involvement in international issues, making diplomacy more transparent and accessible (Bouachiba Waifi, 2019, p. 23).

Fourth: The Role of Digital Media in Promoting Digital Diplomacy

With the development of technology and increasing reliance on the internet, the field of public relations has undergone a significant change, especially with the emergence of modern web applications (Ben Donia, 2022, p. 131). Accordingly, digital media is vital in promoting digital diplomacy through several aspects. It can be highlighted through the following:

- Digital media enables the rapid and immediate dissemination of news and information, helping countries deliver official messages and react to current events.
- Digital media, such as social media, enable governments to communicate directly with the public, promoting dialogue and popular participation on diplomatic issues.
- By disseminating information and data, digital media enhance the transparency of diplomatic work, contributing to building trust between states and the public.
- Digital media influence public opinion and promote issues of concern to countries, helping to form positive attitudes toward their policies.
- Digital media provide tools to analyze trends and public opinions, enabling states to understand public reactions and adjust their strategies accordingly.

Fifth: The Concept of Digital Diplomatic Communication Strategies

The idea of "communication strategies for digital diplomacy" is one of the modern concepts that has raised differences in definitions between researchers and fields. The following are the definitions contained in Arab and foreign literature:

Mirza (2018, p. 327) defined digital diplomatic communication strategies as "a set of important decisions about the communication goals that must be reached and the means applied to achieve them, and this strategy achieves the objectives of digital public diplomacy."

Al-Qarar Center for Saudi Media Studies (2024) defined digital diplomatic communication strategies as "employing modern communication technology and social networks to achieve foreign policy goals and public diplomacy practices."

Oloo (2024, p. 1) also defined digital diplomacy as "an element of public diplomacy that requires diplomats to use various digital platforms, such as Twitter, Facebook, WhatsApp, blogs, Weibo, WeChat, and websites, to connect with a foreign digital audience."

Communication strategies for digital diplomacy can be defined as "a set of plans and tactics used by states and diplomatic organizations to exploit digital means, such as social media and websites."

Sixth: The Concept of Coexistence

The term "coexistence" has recently emerged as one of the concepts that are receiving increasing attention and wide circulation, which makes it important to clarify its meaning and present the concepts that have been put forward about this concept as follows:

Al-Otaibi (2019, p. 2554) defined coexistence as "the coexistence of Muslims with other religions, whether within the Islamic state and others, by Islamic guidance and what is required by the interests of all parties in matters of life, pension, and common citizenship."

As Elkhosht (2019, p. 413) defines coexistence as "a continuous interaction between man and the other to ensure the integrity of life. In light of the pluralism and diversity in the composition of the national and religious society, it becomes necessary to lay the foundations for this interaction, which is known as coexistence."

Jalawi (2020, p. 822) defined coexistence as "a set of pillars that are the basis for achieving coexistence between human beings, where agreement occurs between people, and the organization of life relations among them to get out of the circle of chaos and randomness to order."

Al-Jamali (2020, p. 82) defined coexistence as "accepting the other and resolving all controversial issues by peaceful means in a way that contributes to strengthening security and peace and achieving development and prosperity."

Finally, coexistence can be defined as "the ability to live in peace and harmony between different individuals or groups while respecting cultural, religious, and social diversity." Coexistence expresses acceptance of the other and positive interaction with them.

Seventh: The Concept of Peacebuilding

Domli (2014, p. 12) defined peacebuilding as "a science that has its foundations and needs mechanisms, components, studies, and plans based on the needs of the parties responsible for achieving peace and meeting the necessary needs of conflict communities that have been damaged as a result of conflict."

The United Nations Development Programme (2017, p. 29) defined peacebuilding as "actions that will consolidate healthy relations, support political, social, economic and cultural institutions capable of addressing conflict and strengthen mechanisms that will either create or support the conditions necessary for sustainable peace."

Bousaha (2018, p. 17) defined peacebuilding as "a long-term commitment to address the root causes of inherent conflicts, which must begin in all cases with building and strengthening government and civil society institutions. If the root causes are not addressed, violence is more likely to recur."

Khreisan (2018, p. 140) defined peacebuilding as "creating a structure for peace based on justice, equity, and cooperation, and then addressing the underlying causes of violent conflict so that they become less likely in the future."

Peacebuilding is defined as "referring to the comprehensive process aimed at promoting social and political stability in societies suffering from conflict or tensions. Peacebuilding goes beyond the cessation of armed conflict to achieve social justice, human rights, equality, and sustainable development."

Eighth: The Concept of the Ministry of Foreign Affairs

The Saudi Ministry of Foreign Affairs (2024) defined the Ministry as "formulating and implementing foreign policy to protect and promote national interests, care for citizens, and contribute to maintaining security, stability, and prosperity through qualified human competencies, specialized technical and information systems, and effective diplomatic programs."

The Ministry of Foreign Affairs of the United Arab Emirates (2024) defined the Ministry of Foreign Affairs "as the voice of the state in Arab, Islamic and international forums and in terms of its tasks and by which it looks forward to carrying out many tasks related to the foreign policy of the state and supervising its implementation in coordination with the concerned state agencies."

The Omani Ministry of Foreign Affairs (2024) also defined the Ministry of Foreign Affairs as "the body responsible for developing the Sultanate's diplomatic relations and managing all its foreign affairs."

Therefore, the Ministry of Foreign Affairs can be defined as "the governmental body responsible for managing diplomatic relations and international communication of the State. The functions of the Ministry are to represent the State in international forums, regulate foreign affairs, and promote bilateral and multilateral cooperation in various fields."

Ninth: The Role of Media Strategies During Crises

Social media is an essential part of contemporary life, as it has changed the ways of communication and interaction between individuals, especially in times of crisis. These means play a crucial role in the response of government institutions and business organizations during crises, risks and natural disasters. They help promote awareness of the current situation and provide the necessary information to mitigate the effects of crises (Salem, 2016, p. 375).

The Mediterranean Center for Strategic Studies (2024) reveals the media's role and importance, especially in times of crisis and war. The media becomes the main source for followers wishing to know the details of events and their developments.

Abu Saree (2017, p. 338) pointed out that social media should be essential to organizations' strategic management. Its integration into daily activities enables more effective communication, broader audience engagement, and enhanced diplomatic outreach. Environmental and social media should be integrated into the organization's policies to ensure effective crisis management.

Tenth: The Role of Social Networking Sites in Building a Mental Image of the State

Social networks are used to communicate effectively and enhance their public image in society. Social media also plays a vital role in shaping the mental image of the country, as it contributes to changing the language of communication among young people and expanding the scope of dialogue from the local context to the regional and global (Al-Qarar Center for Media Studies, 2024b).

These means contribute to a deeper and more interactive understanding of social and political issues, enhancing the public's image of the state (Abadneh, 2017, p. 695). This enhances the public's understanding of the country's culture and increases the level of public information about it (Asiri, 2022, p. 19).

With the emergence of social media such as Twitter and Facebook, government officials can reach a wider audience and interact directly; this shift has given a new dimension to foreign policy (Bouachiba & Waifi, 2019, p. 22).

Eleventh: International Experiences in the Field of Digital Diplomacy

International experiences in the field of digital diplomacy can be shown as follows:

(1) British Experience

The United Kingdom uses digital diplomacy to amplify its soft power and showcase its cultural contributions to music, art, and education. By addressing global issues such as climate change and public health, the UK's strategic campaign is working to show it as a responsible country (Oloo, 2024, p. 2).

The United Kingdom has also used its digital diplomacy to stay on the global stage, manage its international relations, and maintain its share with strategic partners post-Brexit and post-COVID (Fakuade, 2024, p. 77).

The official document "Digital Strategy" issued by the Foreign and Commonwealth Office has outlined the United Kingdom's approach to integrating digital technologies into diplomatic activities since 2012. This strategy emphasizes the transformative impact of digital tools on diplomatic communications and policy formulation (Frey, 2024, p. 112).

Muhia (2022) also pointed out that Britain is among the few countries that take digital diplomacy and policy seriously, especially in its creative industry and cultural sectors, as it recognizes the importance of digital capabilities in promoting and preserving its national cultural heritage, through several initiatives such as the following:

- The Government of Britain has established the National Archives of the United Kingdom, which preserves the United Kingdom's heritage in digital form to make it more accessible to people around the world online and spread British culture.
- The British Council is using the full potential of new media such as the internet to promote the richness of British arts and culture, as museum galleries have applied digital technologies to reach new audiences.
- The British Council has also developed many online programs and websites to provide access to UK creative and cultural products on a global scale.

(2) EU Experience

Digital diplomacy and external communication in general have been recognized by creating a dedicated unit within the European External Action Service, the Strategic Communications and Foresight Unit (Zaiotti, 2024, p. 460). In Europe, digital diplomacy has been adopted as a tool "to secure the EU global role in the digital world, protect its strategic interests and strengthen its dynamic human-centered regulatory framework for inclusive digital transformation, and the regional bloc has since proposed a set of priority actions that ensure a stronger and more effective EU policy and actions in global digital affairs" (IE University, 2024).

Council of the European Union (2022, p. 3) noted that the purpose of EU digital diplomacy is to:

- Strengthen the EU's global role in digital affairs, based on common geopolitical priorities, with particular attention to countries of strategic importance or with a high level of vulnerability.

- Actively promote universal human rights, fundamental freedoms, the rule of law, and democratic principles in the digital space and promote a human-centered and rights-based approach to digital technologies in relevant multilateral forums and other platforms.
- Promote an open, free, global, stable, and secure internet based on the multi-stakeholder model of internet governance.
  The US State Department has activated official accounts to convey its messages and clarify its policies. The United Kingdom has implemented a digital diplomacy strategy through online platforms to expand its outreach to local and international citizens and enhance its image in areas such as human rights. The government has taken serious steps to develop digital diplomacy in countries such as China.

References

Abadneh, M. A. (2017). The role of social media in building individuals' mental perceptions of Turkey's reputation: A field study of a sample of internet users in Algeria. *Al-Badr Magazine*, *9*(12), 695–710.

Abu, S., & Muhammad, E. (2017). The use of social media in crisis management. *Scientific Journal of Public Relations and Advertising Research*, (11), 305–358.

Al-Arabi, A., & Zain al-Din, S. M. (2021). *Digital diplomacy*. Unpublished Master's Thesis. Yahya Fares University.

Al-Ghannam, M. H., & Abdullah, M. A. I. (2023). Digital official diplomacy and its impact on international relations. *Journal of the Association of Arab Universities for Research in Higher Education*, *43*(1), 540–549.

Al-Issawi, N. A. K. A.-H. (2022). Communication strategies in Arab digital diplomacy: Employment and relevance. *Journal of the Association of Arab Universities for Research in Higher Education*, *42*(4), 1–23.

Al-Otaibi, A. A. R. (2019). Religious and social coexistence in Islam and its contemporary challenges: A jurisprudential advocacy study. *Journal of Arab Studies*, *39*(5), 2549–2578.

Al-Qarar Center for Media Studies. (2024a). *Communication strategies for Saudi digital diplomacy*. https://alqarar.sa/5509. Accessed on December 2, 2024.

Al-Qarar Center for Media Studies. (2024b). *The impact of social media on shaping cultural capital*. https://alqarar.sa/5425. Accessed on November 11, 2024.

Asiri, M. A. (2022). The impact of social networks on forming a mental image of European countries "Britain, Sweden, Norway" according to a sample of Saudi youth. *Arab Journal of Science and Research Publishing*, *8*(4), 19–38.

Ben Donia, F. K. (2022). The role of digital public relations in enhancing diplomatic work: A field study at the organization of Islamic Cooperation in Jeddah. *Arab Journal for Media and Communication Research*, *39*, 130–167.

Bouachaiba, A. (2019). Digital diplomacy and building mental images through social media: A study of some global experiences. *Algerian Journal of Humanities and Social Sciences*, *3*(29), 21–43.

Council of the European Union. (2022, July 18). *EU digital diplomacy: Council conclusions, foreign affairs council*. https://data.consilium.europa.eu/doc/document/ST-11406-2022-INIT/en/pdf

Domli, K. (2014). *Writings on peacebuilding and coexistence.*

Elkhosht, H. H. A. R. (2019). From the guidance of the Prophet's Sunnah in coexistence with the other. *Al-Raya*, (18), 409–495.

Fakuade, D. (2024). UK digital diplomacy. In *Digital diplomacy in the OSCE region: From theory to practice* (pp. 77–87). Springer.

Frey, C. (2024). Digital diplomacy: The impact of technology on modern diplomacy and foreign policy. Current realities and future prospects. *Romanian Journal of European Affairs*, *24*(1), 107–126.

Hazrat, F. K. (2016). *Digital diplomacy: Prospects and challenges.* Qatar National Bank.

Hegazy, N. F., & Salah El-Din, K. (2022). The role of social media in shaping the mental image of political leaders and institutions: A survey study on Egyptian youth. *Scientific Journal of Radio and Television Research*, *24*, 587–622.

IE University. (2024). *Digital diplomacy: Where tech meets international relations.* https://www.ie.edu/uncover-ie/digital-diplomacy-where-tech-meets-international-relations/

Issa, A. S. M., Awad, M. M. A. N., Shura, S. A. M., & Abu Taha, M. A. F. (2021). *Coexistence is practical images from the history of Muslims through the ages.* Egyptian General Organization for the National Library and Archives.

Issawi, H. (2024). *Digital communication strategies in educational institutions: A study of a sample of secondary schools in the Wilayat of Tebessa.* Unpublished Master's Thesis. University of the Martyr Sheikh Larbi Tebsi.

Jalawi, M. (2020). Human coexistence. *Arab Journal for Scientific Publishing*, (25), 820–832.

Jamali, A. A. A. (2020). Peaceful coexistence. *Journal of the National University*, (15), 77–102.

Meliani, K. A., Moghamesi, M. A., & Salma, M. S. (2024). The effectiveness of the communication activities of the digital diplomacy of the Saudi Ministry of Foreign Affairs in marketing the national identity. In *The 1st media innovation: Opportunities and challenges.* Emirates Scholar Research Centre.

Meliani, K. A., & Salem, D. F. (2021). Communication strategies for Saudi digital diplomacy via Twitter: A study within the framework of consolidating the Kingdom's position as a global logistics center. *King Abdulaziz University Journal: Arts and Humanities*, *29*(8), 189–261.

Ministry of Foreign Affairs, United Arab Emirates. (2024). *About the ministry.* https://www.mofa.gov.ae/The-Ministry. Accessed on December 1, 2024.

Mirza, H. (2018). Communication strategy for U.S. digital public diplomacy in Algeria via social media networks – An analytical study. *Abaad Magazine*, (7), 325–342.

Muhammad, W. K. A. (2017). Digital diplomacy in the official websites of the Egyptian and American Ministries of Foreign Affairs and its role in presenting the image of the state. *Scientific Journal of Public Relations and Advertising Research*, *11*(11), 55–104.

Muhammad, Z. F. (2024). *The role of social networking sites in shaping the mental image of politically empowered Iraqi women.* https://cdnx.uobabylon.edu.iq/undergrad_projs/zgb9d1kiwEu1x2DOys1Qqw.pdf. Accessed on December 1, 2024.

Muhia, E. (2022). *Digital diplomacy in the United Kingdom*. https://protocoltoday.nl/digital-diplomacy-in-the-united-kingdom/

Oloo, O. O. A. D. (2024). The implementation of the digital diplomacy of the United States, the UK, and China in Kenya. *Place Branding and Public Diplomacy*, *20*(2), 1–12.

Omani Ministry of Foreign Affairs. (2024). *The role of the ministry*. https://www.fm.gov.om/ministry-ar/about-us-ar/the-role-of-the-ministry-ar/?lang=ar. Accessed on November 11, 2024.

Organization of Islamic Cooperation. (2022). *Coexistence and acquaintance in Islam*. Organization of Islamic Cooperation.

Salem, S. A.-S. (2016). The role of social media in crisis and disaster communication management. *Egyptian Journal of Media Research*, (56), 313–386.

Saudi Ministry of Foreign Affairs. (2024). *The Ministry's Vision*. https://www.mofa.gov.sa/ar/ministry/Pages/ministryvision.aspx. Accessed on December 1, 2024.

United Nations Development Programme (UNDP). (2017). *Training manual in peacebuilding skills*. United Nations Development Programme.

Zaiotti, R. (2024). The European Union and digital diplomacy: Projecting global Europe in the social media era. In *The Oxford handbook of digital diplomacy*. https://doi.org/10.1093/oxfordhb/9780192859198.013.25

Chapter 16

Evaluating the Efficiency of Digital Institutional Transformation in Enhancing the Organization's Competitive Advantage in Saudi Institutions

Mohammed Muflih Mohammad AlQahtani

Southern Province Cement Company, Saudi Arabia

Abstract

This study aims to analyze the impact of digital institutional transformation on enhancing the competitive advantage of Saudi institutions. The study is based on understanding the role of digital technologies such as artificial intelligence, cloud computing, and data analytics in improving operational efficiency and fostering innovation, which contributes to strengthening the competitive ability of Saudi institutions in both local and global markets. By implementing these technologies, institutions aim to achieve the highest levels of performance efficiency and continuous innovation, which directly reflects on their ability to adapt to the rapid changes in the business environment.

The study was conducted by collecting data through surveys and interviews with officials from several Saudi institutions that have adopted digital transformation in order to explore their experiences and assess the impact of these transformations on various aspects of operations within the institutions. The results of the study showed that digital transformation enhances operational efficiency by automating processes, reducing costs, and increasing productivity. It also contributes to fostering innovation, allowing institutions to develop new products and services that align with the changing market needs. Moreover, digital transformation strengthens the ability of institutions to compete in the global market by enabling them to quickly adapt to changes.

Digital Dialogues, 151–160

Published under exclusive licence by Emerald Publishing Limited
doi:10.1108/978-1-83708-686-320261016

The study recommends accelerating the adoption of digital transformation in Saudi institutions, providing continuous training programs for employees, and updating digital infrastructure to meet the needs of digital transformation, thus contributing to enhancing the institutions' ability to compete and achieve sustainable growth in the global market.

Keywords: Digital institutional transformation; competitive advantage; artificial intelligence; cloud computing; digital transformation; competitiveness

Introduction

Saudi institutions strive to achieve significant digital advancement in an era marked by rapid technological evolution and increasing challenges. With continuous changes in the global business landscape, these institutions are adopting modern technologies and smart systems to enhance their competitive position and ensure their sustainability. Digital transformation in Saudi institutions reflects a strategic vision aimed at keeping pace with global developments and improving both internal and external performance efficiency. This requires the adoption of well-thought-out strategies to ensure continuous innovation and effective achievement of strategic objectives.

Digital institutional transformation involves the application of information and communication technologies across all aspects of organizational work, whether to improve internal processes, facilitate communication with customers, or provide more advanced and flexible services. Digital transformation is not limited to the use of technology but extends to the restructuring of organizational processes within institutions and changing organizational cultures to suit the new digital environment. The demand for this transformation is increasing among institutions aiming to enhance their operational efficiency in the face of global market pressures.

With the rapid advancement of technology in the digital revolution era, it has become essential to assess the effectiveness of digital transformation in achieving the organization's strategic objectives, particularly in enhancing its competitive advantage. Digital transformation can make a significant difference in an institution's ability to adapt to rapid market changes and outperform competitors. In the context of Saudi institutions striving to strengthen their position in global markets, competitive advantage emerges as a key goal, as it is tied to developing and improving productivity, reducing costs, and enhancing the quality of products and services provided to customers.

The competitive advantage of an institution depends on its ability to leverage digital technology to improve internal processes and enhance customer interaction, which strengthens loyalty and satisfaction. These processes help provide added value, whether through service improvement or offering innovative solutions that meet the changing needs of the market. To achieve this advantage, the role of strategic leadership in Saudi institutions is pivotal. Effective leadership and the institution's forward-looking vision are fundamental elements in turning challenges into opportunities. In light of these changes, institutions focus on measuring the extent to which digital transformation achieves the desired goals and evaluating tangible outcomes, such as improved productivity, cost reduction, and the provision of innovative solutions.

Theoretical Framework of the Study

Concept of Digital Organizational Transformation

According to Alam (2021), digital transformation is defined as the transition from a traditional system to a digital system based on information and communication technology in all areas of business. This transition involves a set of strategic, cultural, material, financial, human, security, and legislative requirements.

Meanwhile, Khamis (2021) defines digital transformation as a complex technical, organizational, and cultural process undertaken by organizations to meet the changing needs of their clients and adapt to the demands of their employees. This is achieved by leveraging digital capabilities to build business models, innovate new services, improve user experiences, and digitize operational processes, with the aim of enhancing performance, reducing risks, supporting competitive advantage, and ultimately creating added value for the organization.

As for Baitam (2021), he defines transformation in business or government as a radical change affecting the business model, procedures, and processes. This transformation may involve altering the product or the way services are delivered entirely, and it could be strategic, influencing all functions of the organization, from sales to supply, information technology, and the entire value chain.

Based on these definitions, digital organizational transformation encompasses the adoption of information and communication technologies not only to improve internal performance but also to create innovative business models and provide solutions that meet customer needs and adapt to market changes more effectively and efficiently.

Benefits of Digital Transformation

Digital transformation offers numerous and diverse benefits that impact individuals, both in material and intangible terms, as well as various sectors. It reduces costs and effort, improves operational efficiency, and organizes workflows. Moreover, it enhances the quality of services and simplifies the procedures for obtaining services provided to the public. It also creates opportunities to offer creative and innovative services, moving away from traditional methods of service delivery. This shift can foster a sense of satisfaction among the public regarding the services provided. Additionally, digital access enables institutions to expand and reach a broader audience, not just locally but also regionally and internationally through various digital channels.

The benefits of digital transformation can be summarized in the following points (Saqat, 2022):

- contributing to the establishment, management, and development of both governmental and private institutions;
- enhancing transparency and governance, which leads to reduced errors and expenditures;
- increasing productivity and improving products, thereby ensuring business and service continuity;
- leveraging modern technologies to improve performance, forecast trends, and plan for the future;
- enhancing the quality of services provided to beneficiaries in fields such as education, healthcare, security, and safety;
- increasing the competitiveness of industrial institutions while protecting resources like water, energy, and raw materials.

Dimensions of Digital Transformation

- Organizational Strategy: Strategy refers to "decisions that concern the relationship of the organization with its external environment." The conditions in which decisions are made are often marked by uncertainty or lack of knowledge. Therefore, the management is responsible for ensuring the organization's adaptation to environmental changes. Digital transformation is a complex and continuous task that can significantly disrupt a company's operations if not properly prepared for. It is crucial to clearly define responsibilities and strategies for the successful implementation of digital transformation. If the digital transformation strategy is approached passively, companies risk losing their scope and facing operational challenges. Thus, companies must ensure that the individual responsible for the operational aspect of the digital transformation strategy has sufficient expertise in transformational projects (Shadid, 2021).
- Organizational Culture: This refers to a set of shared beliefs among the top management of an organization, including how they manage themselves, their employees, and how they conduct the organization's operations. These beliefs are intangible to the senior management, but they have a profound impact on their thoughts and actions. Organizational culture can also be viewed as the comprehensive system of values, beliefs, and norms prevalent within an organization, which may either facilitate or hinder the effectiveness of its performance.
- Transformational Leadership: Transformational leadership refers to the process by which leaders transform individuals and organizations from a state of stagnation to a dynamic and evolving one, aiming to meet the demands of roles. It enhances the freedom of action for users while considering values, ethics, standards, goals, and objectives within systems and individuals (Al-Ma'aita and Al-Rousan, 2021).
- Human Resources: Human resources encompass all individuals working within the organization, both leaders and subordinates, employed to perform its functions and tasks. It also shapes the organizational culture by outlining,

unifying, and regulating behavioral patterns. Furthermore, human resources consist of plans, systems, policies, and procedures that organize the performance of tasks by employees, ensuring that their roles contribute to the organization's mission and goals (Shadid, 2021).

Objectives of Digital Transformation

Digital transformation aims to achieve several objectives, as highlighted by Al-Swat and Al-Harbi (2022), as follows:

- Objectives Related to Enhancing Performance: These include the ability to transfer information in detail, smooth communication between different departments, and ensure the accuracy of data, which increases the trust in the correctness of exchanged data. This also minimizes errors resulting from manual data entry.
- Streamlining Administrative Procedures: With the availability of information in digital form, paperwork is reduced, and the need to create copies of documents every time they are required is eliminated as long as they are available electronically.
- Optimal Utilization of Human Resources: When information is stored digitally, it becomes easier to move and reuse it electronically. This allows human resources to focus on more productive tasks, leading to better efficiency.
- Increasing Productivity and Reducing Costs: By using technology that relies on information networks, it is possible to find better ways to engage citizens in the execution process, ultimately improving performance and reducing costs.
- General Indirect Objectives: These are more challenging to interpret as tangible financial benefits but include reducing errors associated with human factors, aligning with other countries, especially developed ones, and enhancing the competitive advantage of organizations.

Determinants of Achieving Digital Transformation

According to a study by Al-Sayed (2018), the main determinants preventing the achievement of digital transformation are outlined as follows:

- Culture of Resistance to Change: Digital innovation can only succeed by fostering a culture of collaboration. Employees must be capable of working together, exploring new ideas, and crossing boundaries. However, the current reality indicates that most organizations are trapped in a culture that resists change—one built on individualism and hierarchical work structures. IT managers wishing to create a new digital culture should begin by clearly defining a digital mindset, forming a digital innovation team, collaborating with them, and protecting them from the rest of the organization to allow the development of a new work culture. Afterward, the synergy between digital

innovations and core teams can be strengthened to expand new ideas and spread the work culture.
- Limited Participation and Collaboration: The reluctance to participate and collaborate is not only a challenge at the inter-organizational level but also a significant issue within any organization. Issues of controlling processes, information, systems, and ownership make employees hesitant to share their knowledge and experiences. Often, digital innovation with teams involved in diverse tasks is entirely different from what employees are used to, in terms of roles and hierarchies. Therefore, resistance will naturally arise regarding participation and collaboration.
- Current Practices Do Not Support Talent: Having the right talent is crucial, but the right practices must be in place to allow that talent to work effectively. Highly structured, slow-moving traditional processes cannot support digital transformation. Moreover, there are no pretested, ready-to-implement business models. Instead, each organization must find the business practices that best suit its needs to support talent.

The Importance of Digital Transformation for Startups

Digital transformation can help startups streamline their operations, reduce costs, increase efficiency, access new markets, and communicate with customers online. Adopting modern technologies such as artificial intelligence (AI), Blockchain, and the Internet of Things (IoT) can also aid in developing new revenue streams and business models. Additionally, using Big Data technology for market research helps in understanding customer preferences, improving the customer experience, and entering new markets. Startups can better respond to market changes and evolving customer needs, gaining a competitive edge in their industries through digital transformation. However, adopting new technologies is only one part of the digital transformation journey; a shift toward a more innovative and flexible cultural mindset is also essential. Startups must be ready to experiment, iterate, and embrace failure as a vital step in the learning process.

Requirements for Digital Transformation

According to a study by Brees and Jaber (2021), there are several requirements that need to be met in organizations, especially in banks, for digital transformation. These requirements include:

- Administrative Requirements: The plans and methods defined for implementing digital management, including developing a digital business strategy and fostering a digital culture.
- Human Resources Requirements: The presence of qualified human resources is crucial, as digital management cannot be implemented without competent staff.

- Technical Requirements: These refer to the infrastructure necessary for digital management, as digital management is tied to all forms of digital technologies such as media, networks, tools, and advanced technologies.
- Communication Network Requirements: This includes the use of internet networks (intranet for the bank and extranet for interactions with external stakeholders, such as service providers or agents).
- Security Requirements: Ensuring the availability of technologies that protect client data confidentiality and store it digitally (Brees & Jaber, 2021).

The Relationship Between Digital Transformation and Enhancing Competitive Advantage

The relationship between digital transformation and competitive advantage is primarily driven by building a strategic plan for digital transformation. This plan involves creating a long-term strategy that has strong support from senior management. It includes making changes to the organizational structure, allocating financial resources, and ensuring the availability of qualified human resources. Additionally, the spread of a digital transformation culture is essential. This culture fosters organizational positivity and encourages the sharing of resources, knowledge, and learning. The dissemination of digital transformation culture can be achieved by continuously providing guidance to both customers and employees. Furthermore, human resource requirements, which include having qualified personnel trained to use digital technologies for data analysis and retrieval, play a critical role in supporting effective decision-making.

Competitive advantage is also discussed through several dimensions, such as reducing service costs. Organizations aiming for a competitive advantage focus on offering services at lower prices, allowing them to overcome competitors and capture a larger market share. The next dimension is the quality of service, which involves the organization's ability to meet customer needs by providing services that satisfy their expectations. Another key factor is service flexibility, which includes the ability to adapt to changing customer desires and expectations by offering multiple methods and alternatives for service delivery. Innovation in service performance is also vital, which depends on the efficiency and creativity of the workforce in developing new ways to deliver services in line with customer preferences and technological advancements. Finally, speed in service delivery is crucial, with the organization's ability to complete tasks quickly ensuring that services meet customer satisfaction and are delivered on time (Alam, 2021).

Conclusion

In recent years, Saudi institutions have witnessed significant transformations toward digital transformation. These institutions have sought to adopt modern technologies and smart systems in order to enhance their operational efficiency and expand their presence in both local and international markets. Amid a complex and rapidly changing economic environment, digital transformation has become a strategic necessity for organizations striving to keep up with continuous changes and gain a competitive edge. This transformation is no longer just about implementing new technologies in operations but has become an integral part of organizational culture. It requires the effective deployment of modern digital technologies to improve performance and provide innovative solutions that meet customer expectations and market demands.

Undoubtedly, digital transformation encompasses multiple aspects, ranging from improving operational efficiency and developing products and services to enhancing customer relationships and expanding the organization's reach into new markets. Therefore, digital transformation goes beyond updating technological systems; it extends to changing the organizational culture and enhancing human resource capabilities to engage with modern technology. All of this contributes to achieving a competitive advantage that enables Saudi institutions to excel in various fields by fostering innovation and increasing productivity.

On the other hand, digital transformation reflects the importance of strategic leadership in effectively implementing these changes. Strategic leadership is a crucial element in guiding the organization's efforts toward adopting modern technology. Leaders with a clear strategic vision for the organization's future understand the significance of digital transformation in achieving long-term goals and strive to integrate these technologies into daily business strategies. Effective leadership can also contribute to creating a flexible environment that encourages adaptation to changes and supports processes that enhance the organization's ability to innovate and outperform competitors.

References

Abdul, L., Muslih, M. A., & Adel, M. A. B. (2020). The impact of human resource development strategy on achieving sustainable institutional excellence in Yemeni banks. *The Journal of Social Studies*, *26*(4).

Al-Amin, D. (2021). *The importance of digital transformation in achieving effective strategic Insight for organizations: A field study at the 'Corara Timimoun' hotel in Algeria*. Master's Thesis. Ahmed Draya University of Adrar, Faculty of Economic, Commercial, and Management Sciences.

Al-Jbour, M. S. T. (2022). *The impact of digital transformation on organizational performance development: A case study of greater Amman municipality, Jordan*.

Allam, W. K. M. K. (2021). *Digital transformation and its impact on enhancing the competitive advantage of banking services from the perspective of customer service managers: A field study applied to banks in upper Egypt*.

Baitam, S. (2021). The impact of digital transformation on sovereignty and citizenship. In *Research paper presented at the digital transformation and its impact on sustainable development conference organized by madar company, 2021*.

Balooshia, N., Al-Harasi, N., & Al-Oufi, A. (2020). The reality of digital transformation in Omani organizations. *Published in QScience Journal*, *1*, 2020.

Bar, A. (2019). Digital transformation technologies. In *Paper presented at the Asbar Global forum*.

Berghaus, S., & Back, A. (2016). Stages in digital business transformation: Results of an empirical maturity study. In *Tenth Mediterranean Conference on Information Systems (p. MCIS 2016 proceedings. 22)*. aisel.aisnet.org. http://aisel.aisnet.org/mcis2016/22

Berghaus, S., Back, A., & Kaltenrieder, B. (2017). *Digital maturity and transformation report 2017*. Universität St.Gallen. https://office-roxx.de/wp-content/uploads/2019/01/digital-maturity-transformation-report-2017.pdf

Carvalho, A., Saraiva, P., & Sampaio, P. (2019). 35 years of organisational excellence, and perspectives ahead for excellence 4.0: A systematic literature review. *Total Quality Management and Business Excellence*, 1–10. https://doi.org/10.1080/14783363.2019.1691915

Chanias, S., Myers, M. D., & Hess, T. (2019). Digital transformation strategy making in pre-digital organizations: The case of a financial services provider. *The Journal of Strategic Information Systems*, *28*(1), 17–33. https://doi.org/10.1016/j.jsis.2018.11.003

Dimitrios, M., & Fotis, K. (2019). Digital transformation strategy: A literature review. *6th student conference of the Hellenic society for business research* (pp. 59–61). Xanthi: 6th Student Conference EEEE/28.2- 3.3. https://6eeeestudent.files.wordpress.com/2019/06/6eeeestudentproceedings-1.pdf

Facchini, F., Oleśków-Szłapka, J., Ranieri, L., & Urbinati, A. (2020). A maturity model for logistics 4.0: An empirical analysis and a roadmap for future research. *Sustainability*, *12*. no1, 86. https://doi.org/10.3390/su12010086

Faisal, M., Abdul, Z. K., & Mohammad, B. K. (2019). *Digital organizational transformation issues, challenges and impact: A systematic literature review of a decade. International Islamic University, Islamabad, Pakistan. Abasyn Journal of Social Sciences* –, *12*(2). https://doi.org/10.34091/AJSS.12.2.03

Golmohammadi, M., Ghorbani, A., & Feyzi, M. (2016). The effect of job attitudes and organisational identity in organisational excellence of employees (case study: Staff of department of natural resources and watershed of ardabil province). *International Journal of Humanities and Cultural Studies (IJHCS) ISSN 2356-5926*, *1*(1), 1281–1288.

Gomez-Trujillo, A. M., & Gonzalez-Perez, M. A. (2022). Digital transformation as a strategy to reach sustainability. *Smart and Sustainable Environment*, *11*(4), 1137–1162. https://doi.org/10.1108/SASBE-01-2021-0011

Hatamla, H., & Droucheh, N. (2019). Institutional performance and its role in improving the productivity of private universities in Northern Jordan: From the perspective of academic leaders. *Published in Journal of Educational Sciences Studies*, *46*(Issue 2), 2019.

Hosni, M. S. (2022). *Strategic intelligence as an approach to managing institutional excellence in organizations.*

Hossamuddin, M. H. B. (2022). *The role of digital transformation in achieving organizational excellence: A proposed model* (unpublished PhD dissertation). Helwan University.

Khames, A. (2021). The impact of digital transformation on the job performance of employees in Egyptian commercial banks, *Scientific Journal of Financial and Commercial Studies and Research, Article 30*, Vol. 2, Issue 2.

Mohamed, M. S. (2022). A proposed model for the relationship between Excellence management and organizational performance: A field Study. *Middle East Research Journal.*

Rabghi, R. (2022). Digital government in light of digital transformation programs and achieving the goals of Saudi Arabia's vision 2030: A case Study of the digital government authority. *Arab International Journal of Information and Data Technology*, *2*(Issue 2). April-June 2022.

Saqat, A. A. (2022). Digital transformation in government institutions according to vision 2030: A case Study of Al-Noor Hospital in Mecca for the period 2021-2022. *Journal of Economic, Administrative, and Legal Sciences*, *6*(Issue 25).

Shadid, M. (2021). The impact of digital transformation on the quality of services provided: A Study applied to employees of the general directorate of traffic in Cairo, *Journal of Economics and Political Science, Article 8*, Vol. 22, Issue 4.

Shahat, A. M. A. (2021). *Managing institutional excellence in Egyptian universities according to the European excellence model: EFQM - A field Study at Alexandria University* (unpublished PhD thesis). Alexandria University.

Teh, A. (2021). The impact of competency management on organizational performance: A field Study at Algeria's telecommunications Corporation. *Journal of Economic Development*, *6*(1), 2021.

Thanaa Maawad Ali Abu Shahta. (2021). The role of administrative reform in the relationship between toxic leadership and the application of the European model for organizational excellence: A field Study on the Egyptian Nile River transport authority. *Journal of Financial and Commercial Research, Faculty of Commerce, Port Said University*, *22*(Issue 4). Article 45.

Zghdoud, M. (2020). *The impact of digital transformation on education approaches: E-learning - A case study of the national office for distance education and training*, University of Algiers Journal, Change Management Research Laboratory,

Zidan, A. (2021). Digital transformation in higher education institutions, *Egyptian Journal of Media Research, Article 12*, Vol. 75, 2021.

Chapter 17

Employing Artificial Intelligence Technologies in Sports Content Creation: "A Case Study on Bahrain Sports Channel"

Mariam Isa Bukamal

Ministry of Information, Bahrain

Abstract

This study explored the role of artificial intelligence (AI) technologies in enhancing sports content creation for Bahrain Sports Channel by evaluating their impact on program quality and audience engagement. It focused on leveraging AI for sports data analysis, content development, and future forecasting to improve the channel's performance and competitiveness. Drawing on relevant prior research about AI applications in media, particularly sports media, the study employed theories like the Media Richness Theory, which highlights the importance of rich media in improving communication quality, and the Diffusion of Innovations Theory, which helps individual behaviors toward technological advancements. The findings suggest that AI can significantly improve media production processes, including automating news editing, analyzing data, and enhancing audience interaction. However, challenges such as limited infrastructure and insufficient professional training in Arab countries persist. The study posed research questions and specific objectives to demonstrate how AI technologies could drive a transformative shift in the programs of Bahrain Sports Channel.

Keywords: Artificial intelligence; sports media; Bahrain sports channel; content; algorithms; automation

Digital Dialogues, 161–170

doi:10.1108/978-1-83708-686-320261017

Introduction

In the contemporary world of sports media, creating compelling content for sports channels remains an ongoing challenge that demands constant renewal and innovation. Among the modern technologies increasingly shaping this field are artificial intelligence (AI) tools, which are designed to enable computer systems to replicate or simulate intelligent human behavior. This pivotal role arises from the ability of AI technologies to analyze data efficiently and extract relevant insights, thereby enhancing the quality of content delivered to viewers.

The Kingdom of Bahrain has made significant strides in digital transformation and the adoption of AI technologies, consistently striving to advance comprehensive digital development by upgrading systems and embracing cutting-edge technologies. These efforts aim to improve the quality of services provided, enhance operational efficiency, and boost competitiveness. The Kingdom has launched numerous initiatives focusing on improving governmental performance and increasing its effectiveness, reflecting Bahrain's steadfast commitment to keeping pace with global technological advancements.

Sports channels, including Bahrain Sports Channel, offer a wide array of programs and events to their sports audience. With the growing competition and demand for engaging and distinctive content, the use of AI technologies represents a crucial step in enhancing the viewing experience and attracting audiences.

This exploratory study aims to investigate how AI technologies can be utilized in sports content creation to enhance the programs of Bahrain Sports Channel and analyze the effectiveness of such technologies in improving content quality and increasing audience engagement. The study will address various aspects, including sports data analysis, examining the behavior of program developers, and enhancing program categorization and classification processes, among other related areas. Additionally, it will explore two key theories that help explain phenomena related to communication and technology. The first is the Media Richness Theory, which emphasizes the importance of employing media channels capable of conveying information clearly and effectively. The second theory is the Diffusion of Innovations Theory, which provides an analytical framework for understanding how individuals interact with new technological innovations, including factors influencing their adoption, such as perceived benefits, ease of use, and surrounding social influences.

Through this study, the researcher anticipates that the findings will provide a comprehensive and precise framework to assist Bahrain Sports Channel in effectively adopting AI technologies in program production. These technologies are expected to enhance the channel's ability to analyze sports data quickly and accurately. Moreover, AI offers opportunities to deliver personalized content tailored to the diverse preferences of the audience, thereby creating a unique viewing experience and increasing engagement and viewership rates.

Literature Review

First Theme: Studies Addressing the Use of AI in Media

- The study by Najib (2024) explored the use of AI in media as a transformative tool in the news industry, aiming to analyze the potential impacts of these technologies on media values and news quality. The study focused on AI techniques such as algorithms, natural language generation (NLG), and machine learning to enhance media production processes, including news writing, data analysis, and content management. The findings revealed that AI can significantly improve media efficiency by automating routine tasks and reducing costs. However, it also raised concerns about ethics, quality, and the loss of human creativity. The study emphasized the need to strike a balance between leveraging intelligent technologies and preserving the human values of media by enhancing the skills of media professionals to adapt to these advancements.
- A study by Abbas et al. (2023) focused on employing AI technologies in television content creation, aiming to analyze the mechanisms used in this field and understand their impact on media production. The study highlighted the potential of AI to enhance production speed and quality, including content translation, data analysis, and automation of editing and directing processes, thereby saving time and effort while improving production efficiency. The research utilized a questionnaire with a sample of 60 experts in digital media and television content production. The findings demonstrated that AI significantly contributes to advancing production methods, reducing time and effort, and enhancing content quality. However, the study also identified challenges related to the over-reliance on algorithms, a lack of qualified personnel, difficulties in integrating algorithms with human work, and concerns about trust among communication professionals, potentially leading to diminished innovation and creativity. The study recommended developing strategic plans to effectively integrate AI by training professionals and establishing robust databases to support technical systems, ensuring optimal results.
- The study by Ubaid (2023) explored the future of television production amidst the challenges posed by AI, examining its impact on the form and content of television messages and identifying areas for its application in media work through future development scenarios. The research adopted an exploratory methodology, utilizing in-depth interviews with a purposive sample of 30 experts, evenly split between 15 AI specialists and 15 media professionals. The findings highlighted AI's contributions to detecting fake news, writing news, analyzing data, and enhancing television broadcasting quality. However, challenges such as the need for specialized personnel, weak technical infrastructure, and difficulties in keeping up with rapid advancements remain. The study recommended increasing investment in training media professionals on AI technologies, improving the technical infrastructure of media institutions,

and advancing scientific research to better understand the influence of these technologies on media work.

- The study by Reda et al. (2023) analyzed the role of modern communication technologies in enhancing the performance of television channels, focusing on the impact of technological innovations on audiovisual production quality and the development of employee skills. Conducted on a purposive sample of 65 participants from television channels, including experts and specialists in editing, filming, and directing, the study selected participants based on demographic criteria such as educational and social levels and years of experience. The findings revealed that television channels possess advanced technological equipment, such as digital studios, filming tools, and digital processing systems, which contribute to improving media performance. However, the study also highlighted disparities in how these resources are utilized among employees. The results emphasized that modern technology enhances the speed of news processing and production quality, but the need for continuous employee training remains critical to keeping pace with technological advancements. Key recommendations included increasing investment in modern technological equipment and organizing ongoing training programs to enhance employee skills.
- The study by Al-Dulaimi (2023) explored the applications of AI and its significance in improving television news production and enhancing efficiency in the future. The research aimed to shed light on the future potential of AI in high-performance data analysis and media content creation. Using a theoretical and exploratory approach, the study examined the current practical applications of AI and their impact on media institutions without employing a field sample. The findings revealed that AI serves as a powerful catalyst for enhancing news production processes and contributes to delivering innovative and efficient media experiences. The study recommended that media institutions adopt AI technologies and focus on developing the skills of professionals in this field. Additionally, it emphasized the importance of integrating AI to improve media content quality and increase audience engagement with television news.
- The study by Al-Husseini and Farhat (2022) examined the impact of AI technologies on the content of media messages on foreign newspaper websites, focusing on how these technologies enhance the form and substance of media messages and their richness. The study selected The Washington Post, The Wall Street Journal, The New York Times, and The Guardian as its research sample, aiming to understand the effects of technologies such as virtual reality (VR), augmented reality (AR), and robot journalism on media content. Content analysis was employed as the primary tool for data examination. The findings revealed that foreign newspapers utilized a variety of technologies, including VR to enhance reader experiences, thermal imaging to track and document events, and robot journalism for generating editorial reports. Despite the advantages, full adoption of these technologies remains limited.
- The study by Abdel-Razek (2022) aimed to analyze the use of AI technologies in media by examining the adoption of these technologies in Egyptian and Arab

media institutions and forecasting future developments in the field. The study relied on an available sample of 451 participants, including 265 Egyptian media professionals and 186 Arab media professionals, selected from departments related to the digital environment. The findings revealed a high level of interest among media professionals in following AI technologies, reflecting increased awareness of their importance and their ability to mimic human behavior in performing media tasks. This highlights their significance in improving media performance. The most common applications were data journalism, machine translation, and the use of robots in editing. The most frequently employed AI technologies were in service journalism, such as weather forecasting, and economic journalism. The researchers recommended increased investment in technical infrastructure to effectively adopt AI technologies and enhanced media training to develop professionals' skills in using AI.

Second Theme: Studies Addressing AI Applications in Sports and Sports Media

- The study by Wang (2024) examined the impact of ChatGPT on the sports industry, focusing on how this technology enhances operations within the sector. The research highlighted ChatGPT's role in advancing data analysis, generating personalized content for audiences, and improving interactions between fans and sports teams. Utilizing secondary data from multiple sources, the study explored the technological, social, and economic implications of this AI application. The findings revealed that ChatGPT contributed to more efficient report generation, accurate and swift sports performance analysis, enhanced fan-team interactions through smart chat platforms, and precise player data analysis to support managerial and technical decisions. Additionally, it reduced operational costs by automating routine tasks. The study recommended expanding the use of AI technologies like ChatGPT for performance analysis, developing innovative interactive platforms for audiences, and emphasizing the ethical and privacy aspects of employing such technologies.
- The study by Schatteman (2024) focused on the current uses of AI, its future potential, and the ethical concerns surrounding its application. The exploratory research employed a qualitative methodology, conducting eight interviews with professionals in sports media from diverse roles such as digital video management and graphic design. The findings revealed that AI is utilized as a tool to enhance efficiency in tasks such as image and video processing, text content creation, and data analysis. However, participants raised ethical concerns about AI's impact on creativity and the potential reduction in demand for routine human jobs. The study recommended fostering integration between technology and human creativity to enhance media processes, emphasizing the importance of training professionals to effectively utilize advanced AI tools and preparing for their future applications.

- The study by Hashim Khan (2023) examined the integration of AI in the media industry, focusing on dimensions such as content production, workforce dynamics, marketing and advertising strategies, and ethical challenges. Utilizing a systematic literature review, the study analyzed how AI influences various components of the media industry. The findings revealed that AI enhances content production through automation and improved efficiency in processes like news editing and data analysis. It also facilitates personalized user experiences via recommendation systems, increasing engagement with media content. Additionally, AI-driven analytics support marketing and advertising strategies through precise and effective customer targeting. However, the study highlighted ethical challenges associated with AI, including algorithmic bias, privacy concerns, and transparency issues. The researchers recommended establishing stringent ethical standards for AI use in media, providing training programs to develop AI-related skills among professionals, and enhancing oversight mechanisms to ensure fair and responsible use of the technology.
- The study by Al Adwan et al. (2023) focused on the impact of AI applications on the media industry, analyzing their roles in transforming media operations and presenting future scenarios for these changes. The research aimed to understand the professional and occupational shifts brought about by AI applications and to explore the challenges of their use in global and Arab media contexts. The study employed a qualitative exploratory methodology, using interviews with academics specializing in media and AI from Arab and international universities, selected based on their expertise and specialization. The findings revealed that AI represents a "new media with new technology," contributing to the automation of media operations, the development of audience analysis algorithms, and the use of robots and drones for data collection. It also highlighted professional transformations affecting key components of communication, such as content, channels, and audiences. Challenges identified included high costs, inadequate professional training, lack of appropriate regulations, and limited public acceptance of the technology in some regions. The study recommended developing university curricula, enhancing scientific research on ethical and legal dimensions, and organizing training programs to prepare media professionals for AI advancements.
- The study by Mande et al. (2023) examined the impact of AI technologies on the media and communication industry in Nigeria, with a focus on AI's role in improving media operations and the challenges of its application. Data were collected using a questionnaire from a sample of 150 employees, with 123 responses (82%) from three major media companies: Vanguard, Guardian, and Punch. The findings showed that AI improved the efficiency of media operations by automating news editing, data collection, and audience analysis, resulting in enhanced media coverage quality and increased engagement. However, challenges included a lack of technical infrastructure, insufficient professional training, and ethical issues such as algorithmic bias and data privacy concerns. The study recommended addressing these challenges by

strengthening infrastructure, offering training programs to enhance journalists' technical skills, and raising awareness of AI's importance in media development through seminars and conferences.

- The study by Al-Meligy (2023) explored the role of AI in advancing the sports industry and enhancing athletic performance across various levels. It focused on AI applications such as player performance analysis, injury prediction, and the development of personalized training strategies using machine learning and data analysis algorithms. The research adopted an exploratory approach, providing examples from multiple sports, including football, basketball, and baseball. The findings highlighted AI's significant contributions to improving athletic performance, enabling strategic decision-making, and reducing costs. However, challenges such as algorithmic bias and inadequate technical infrastructure were also noted. The study recommended increasing AI use in sports through algorithm development and raising awareness of the technology's potential via training programs and workshops.
- The study by Aissani et al. (2023) examined the use of AI tools in media and journalism, focusing on their role in improving writing, editing, production, and the dissemination of specialized media content. The study analyzed AI tools employed by media organizations such as Associated Press and Reuters, which utilize applications like Wordsmith and Lynx Insight. The findings revealed that these tools enhance efficiency by automating routine tasks, supporting journalists in fact-checking and combating fake news, and delivering tailored content to specific audiences. However, significant challenges were identified, including the risks of deepfakes, biased outcomes from unbalanced data, job losses due to automation, and ethical concerns related to transparency and privacy. The study recommended establishing strict ethical standards for AI use in media, training journalists to use these tools effectively, and strengthening oversight mechanisms to prevent content manipulation or bias.

Third Theme: Discussion on Literature Review

This discussion synthesizes key findings, identifies commonalities and differences, and outlines gaps for further exploration.

- **AI Applications in Media:** AI has been widely adopted as a transformative tool in media production, as evidenced by studies such as those by Najib (2024) and Abbas et al. (2023). These works emphasize the ability of AI technologies, including machine learning and natural language processing, to automate tasks, optimize production processes, and improve content quality. Ubaid (2023) and Reda et al. (2023) further illustrate AI's potential to detect fake news, enhance audiovisual quality, and streamline operations. However, challenges like inadequate technical infrastructure and over-reliance on algorithms, as highlighted by Abbas et al. (2023), signal areas needing targeted intervention. The reviewed studies reveal a consensus on the necessity of training programs for media professionals to effectively integrate AI technologies. For instance, Abdel-Razek (2022) underscores the importance of skill development to overcome implementation barriers and maximize AI's potential.

- **AI in Sports Media:** The application of AI in sports and sports media demonstrates an equally transformative impact. Wang (2024) and Schatteman (2024) explore AI's role in enhancing operations and audience engagement through tools like ChatGPT and advanced data analysis. Similarly, studies like those by Al Adwan et al. (2023) showcase AI's utility in transforming sports journalism through automated content generation, personalized experiences, and spatiotemporal data analysis. A notable aspect of AI in sports media is its ability to foster innovation while addressing operational inefficiencies. Aissani et al. (2023) highlight tools like Wordsmith and Lynx Insight, which support journalists by automating routine tasks and fact-checking. However, ethical dilemmas, such as deepfakes and data privacy concerns, are prevalent, as identified in studies like Mande et al. (2023).
- **Recommendations for Future Research:** Future research should prioritize longitudinal studies to assess AI's evolving role in media and sports. Investigating the interplay between AI-driven efficiency and creativity could provide valuable insights into balancing technological advancements with human values. Additionally, exploring strategies to mitigate ethical risks and improve infrastructure readiness, particularly in underrepresented regions, remains critical.

Conclusion

This study concludes that AI represents a strategic tool capable of transforming the content of sports programs on Bahrain Sports Channel. By leveraging AI, the channel can enhance audience engagement, expand its viewership base, and strengthen its competitiveness with other sports networks. The reviewed literature highlights the critical importance of addressing technical and professional challenges by improving infrastructure, training the workforce, and adopting innovative strategies that integrate AI into media content production. Based on these findings, the study offers practical recommendations to optimize AI utilization in the channel's operations. These include fostering collaboration between media and technology organizations, developing comprehensive plans for AI integration, and organizing specialized training programs for Bahrain Sports Channel staff. Effective implementation of these strategies can drive a qualitative leap in sports programming, positioning the channel as a leading model in Arab sports media. The study emphasizes that the successful integration of AI in content production is not only a technological advancement but also a strategic opportunity to redefine media standards in the region. By overcoming existing challenges and embracing innovation, Bahrain Sports Channel can set a benchmark for excellence in sports media, paving the way for further developments in AI-driven broadcasting.

الدراسات العربية

عبد الحميد، م. (1992). بحوث الصحافة. القاهرة: عالم الكتب للطباعة والنشر والتوزيع.

عبد المجيد، ع. ع. م. (2021). مستقبل الصحافة المصرية في ظل تقنيات صحافة الذكاء الاصطناعي خلال العقد القادم (في الفترة من 2021 حتى 2030): دراسة استشرافية. مجلة البحوث الإعلامية، *58*(3)، 1485–1397.

عبد الرازق، م. (2022). تقنيات الذكاء الاصطناعي في الإعلام: الواقع والتطورات المستقبلية. المجلة المصرية لبحوث الإعلام، *18*(1)، 647–603.

الحسيني، ه. أ.، & فرحات، د. ه. (2022). تقنيات الذكاء الاصطناعي وانعكاساتها على محتوى الرسالة الإعلامية بمواقع الصحف الأجنبية. المجلة المصرية لبحوث الإعلام، *80*(2)، –1495، 1518.

الدليمي، ع. م. (2023). الذكاء الاصطناعي ومستقبل أخبار التلفزيون: بحث استشرافي تنظيري. مجلة علوم الإنسان والمجتمع، *21*(21)، 316–289.

الجادري، ع. ح. (2016). الأسس المنهجية والاستخدامات الإحصائية في بحوث العلوم التربوية والإنسانية (ط. *2*). إثراء للنشر والتوزيع.

رضا، م. ع. م. (2023). دور تكنولوجيا الاتصال الحديثة في تطوير أداء القنوات التلفزيونية. مجلة لارك للآداب، *50* (2)، 493-511.

رضا، م. ع. م. (2023). توظيف تقنيات الذكاء الاصطناعي في صناعة المحتوى التلفزيوني. مجلة آداب المستنصرية، العدد 102، 581-603.

رضا، أ. (2023). *(المنصات التلفزيونية التعارض والتكامل في الإعلام الرقمي.* مصر: العربي للنشر والتوزيع.

عبد العزيز، إ. ل. (2021). مستقبل استخدام تطبيقات الذكاء الاصطناعي في المؤسسات الإعلامية ودورها في تطوير المحتوى الإخباري.في المؤتمر العلمي الدولي السادس والعشرين: الإعلام الرقمي والإعلام التقليدي: مسارات للتكامل والمنافسة (ص ص. 603-647). جامعة القاهرة، كلية الإعلام.

عبيد، م. ح. (2023). مستقبل العمل التلفزيوني في ظل تحديات الذكاء الاصطناعي: دراسة استشرافية. مجلة الباحث الإعلامي، *15*(60)، 26–7.

العلاق، ب. (2011). نظريات الاتصال: مدخل متكامل. عمان، الأردن: دار اليازوري العلمية للنشر والتوزيع.

كامل، ن. (2024). الذكاء الاصطناعي في الإعلام: مفهوم جديد في صناعة الأخبار ومخاطر جديدة. المجلة الجزائرية للأبحاث والدراسات، *7*(3)، 106–92.

قطب، إ. (2018). نظرية ثراء الوسيلة. https://doi.org/10.13140/RG.2.2.25344.07687

لعياضي، ع.، & عشب، ل. (2021). نماذج عن تطبيق الذكاء الاصطناعي في علوم الرياضة. مجلة علوم الأداء الرياضي، *1*(3)، 89-104.

المشاقبة، ب. (2015). نظريات الاتصال. عمان، الأردن: دار أسامة للنشر والتوزيع.

لمليجي، م. إ. (2023). الذكاء الاصطناعي وصناعة الرياضة. المجلة العلمية لوزارة الشباب والرياضة - البحوث التطبيقية في المجال الرياضي، *3*(1).

References

Abbas, A., Hassan, R., & Saleh, M. (2023). Employing artificial intelligence technologies in television content creation. *Arab Journal of Media and Communication*, *15*(1), 77–102.

Abdel-Razek, M. (2022). Artificial intelligence technologies in media: Reality and future developments. *Egyptian Journal of Media Research*, *18*(1), 603–647.

Aissani, R., Abdallah, R. A., Taha, S., & Al Adwan, M. N. (2023). Artificial intelligence tools in media and journalism: Roles and concerns. *Conference Proceedings*, IEEE, 10185738. https://doi.org/10.1109/MCNA59361.2023.10185738

Al Adwan, M. N., Mahmoud, M. A. A., Abdallah, R., Abokhoza, R., & Taha, S. (2023). The impact of artificial intelligence applications on media industries: A prospective study. *Journal of Namibian Studies: History, Politics, Culture*, *33*, 721–734. https://doi.org/10.59670/jns.v33i.534

Al-Dulaimi, A. M. (2023). Artificial intelligence and the future of television news: A theoretical foresight study. *Journal of Human and Social Sciences*, *21*(2), 289–316.

Al-Husseini, H. A., & Farhat, D. H. (2022). Artificial intelligence technologies and their reflections on media message content on foreign newspaper websites. *Egyptian Journal of Media Research*, *80*(2), 1495–1518.

Al-Meligy, M. A. (2023). Artificial intelligence and the sports industry. *Scientific Journal of the Ministry of Youth and Sports*, *3*(1).

Ashava, D., Sharma, L., & Yadav, D. N. (2021). *Artificial intelligence and mass media: Roles and concerns*. IMS Law College, Meerut University.

Canavilhas, J. (2022). Artificial intelligence and journalism: Current situation and expectations in the Portuguese sports media. *Journalism and Media*. *3* (3). 510-520. https://doi.org/10.3390/journalmedia3030035

Khan, M. H. (2023). *The impact of AI on the media industry*. Uppsala University, Department of Informatics and Media. (Master's Thesis).

Mande, S., Taofeek, O. K., & Oko, F. A. (2023). *The impact of artificial intelligence technology in media and communication industry in Nigeria: Case of Vanguard, Guardian, and Punch media limited. Festschrift for Professor Ifeyinwa Nsude*.

Najib, A. (2024). Artificial intelligence in media: A transformative tool in the news industry. *Journal of Media Studies*, *18*(2), 45–62.

Reda, M. A. M., Hassan, S., & Youssef, A. (2023). The role of modern communication technologies in developing television channel performance. *LARK Journal for Arts*, *50*(2), 493–511.

Schatteman, H. (2024). *AI's influence in the sports media industry*. University of South Carolina. Senior Theses. https://scholarcommons.sc.edu/senior_theses/665

Ubaid, M. H. (2023). The future of television production in light of artificial intelligence challenges: A foresight study. *Al-Baheth Al-I'lami Journal*, *15*(60), 7–26.

Wang, Y. (2024). The impact of ChatGPT on the sports industry: Opportunities and challenges. *International Journal of Sports Technology and Innovation*, *6*(1), 1–15.

Zhiyu, L., Siyuan, L., & Jie, L. (2022). The main influencing factors of artificial intelligence big data sports news coverage. *Wireless Communications and Mobile Computing*, *2022*, 1-11 (7440337). https://doi.org/10.1155/2022/7440337

Chapter 18

Journalists' Attitudes Toward Digital Newspapers' Reliance on Artificial Intelligence Technologies in Producing Journalistic Content

Seeroz Almahadeen

University of Bahrain, Bahrain

Abstract

This study explores journalists' attitudes toward the use of artificial intelligence (AI) applications in producing journalistic content. It seeks to identify the extent and nature of AI adoption in news production, the most commonly used applications, their effectiveness, and differences in content quality compared with traditionally produced journalism. The study also examines the perceived advantages and challenges of AI integration, focusing on journalists' ease of use, professional acceptance of this emerging technology, and public response to AI-generated news content.

Using a literature review approach, the research synthesizes findings from studies conducted in both Arab countries—such as Egypt, Jordan, and Palestine—and Western contexts, including the United States and China. The review reveals a consensus on the growing significance of technological innovation in journalism and highlights AI as a transformative force in content creation and newsroom workflows. While acceptance levels vary across journalistic cultures, resistance is generally limited to implementation methods rather than outright rejection.

Findings further indicate that media institutions increasingly support AI integration, investing in advanced tools and staff training to enhance productivity and quality. Moreover, audiences show positive engagement with AI-assisted journalism, often perceiving it as more dynamic and accessible than content produced through traditional methods.

Digital Dialogues, 171–177

Published under exclusive licence by Emerald Publishing Limited
doi:10.1108/978-1-83708-686-320261018

Keywords: Artificial intelligence; digital journalism; technology acceptance model; media innovation; newsroom automation

Introduction

More than two decades ago, a new type of global technological development product began to be circulated, which is artificial intelligence (AI). Like any type of human creativity in the world of technology, the beginnings were somewhat secretive, and even what was leaked to the public was merely speculation about the nature of this new type of technological production. Little by little, this new technology began to be released, which was expected to be the ultimate creativity of the human mind in this field.

Intelligence can be defined as the science that attempts to create human intelligence in electronic systems, enabling these systems to collect and analyze data, make appropriate decisions, and act accordingly. (1)

Many developed countries, such as the United States, Japan, China, and Germany, have become heavily dependent on AI in many fields, starting from the industrial field, such as factories that contain production lines that are entirely managed by AI, to military systems that rely on AI in the programs that operate the weapons they produce. The beginning was with the employment of AI in specific tasks such as genetics, early detection of viruses and diseases, and completing surgeries without human intervention, and it developed to include all other aspects of life. (2)

What concerns us in this study is the media aspect of this modern technology, especially in the world of journalism, which has become clear in the world of electronic marketing, and was a reason for the orientation of press institutions to use artificial intelligence applications. Currently, many media and press institutions rely on AI applications in producing journalistic content. (3)

This leads to reshaping the relationship between the sender and the receiver and reshaping the receiving audience, as AI provides more advanced applications in producing journalistic content and marketing news and data of all kinds. (4)

Of course, any new technology that comes to traditional technologies is met with suspicion and caution until the benefits of this modern technology, its development, and the risks and challenges of these technologies and their avoidance become clear to some extent. Its emergence is also accompanied by the emergence of many questions that address the importance of the human factor considering artificial intelligence, which has been raised by many researchers and thinkers around the world and in various fields. This leads us to summarize the research problem in the following question: What is the reality and future of journalistic work relying on AI in producing journalistic content?

Therefore, we had to address those working in the field of journalism, including leaders of journalistic institutions and journalists, to learn about how to deal with artificial intelligence in journalistic work and to learn about the challenges facing this modern technology in this sensitive field, to learn about the impact of AI on the current world of journalism, both Arab and international, in addition to trying to anticipate the future of journalistic work in light of the use of artificial intelligence.

Review of Literature

Study (Sholola et al., 2024) (5): The expected impact of AI on journalism ethics among journalists in Kwara State

This study aimed to identify the significant impact of artificial intelligence on ethical journalism among journalists in Kwara State. The study used the survey methodology, applying it to 134 journalists from a population of 250, and used questionnaires as the data collection tool.

The study came to several results, including the positive feelings and a clear level of awareness of using artificial intelligence in journalism work.

Study (Abdul Basit, Naira, 2023) (6): The impact of the adoption of AI technology by journalistic institutions in editing journalistic texts

The study aimed to identify the impact of the adoption of AI technology by journalistic institutions in editing journalistic texts and to try to identify the extent to which the journalistic institutions in the study sample applied AI technology. The study also tried to identify the extent of the respondents' awareness and familiarity with AI tools and technology in journalistic institutions and the tools provided by AI technology in journalistic institutions and to monitor the most important proposals of journalists working in journalistic institutions to apply AI technology in serving journalistic work and developing the journalistic content provided. The study relied in its theoretical construction on the unified theory of accepting and using technology.

This study is considered a descriptive study that relied on the survey method. It applied to a sample of 150 individuals from journalists working in the press institutions of Egyptian newspapers, including Al-Ahram, Al-Youm Al-Sabea, and Al-Wafd. This study concluded with a number of results, the most important of which are: Egyptian press institutions apply AI technology to some extent at a rate of 83.33%, followed by 16.67%. The results also indicated the most concepts that the respondents see as clarifying the concept of artificial intelligence journalism technology. In first place came "new journalistic and media technology and tools", then "formulating more influential journalistic and media content" in second place, and third was "a type of preserving the diversity of efforts and meeting needs."

It also became clear that the Egyptian press institutions in the study sample adopt AI technologies in producing and editing journalistic texts to a very large extent.

Study (Haddad, Ismat, 2023) (7): Implementing AI techniques in Jordanian Press institutions and its impact on the professional practice of journalists

The study aimed to identify the extent of the employment of AI technologies in Jordanian press institutions and its reflection on the professional practice of journalists, the extent of the readiness of these institutions to employ AI technologies, the skills and requirements necessary for them, and the areas in which artificial intelligence can be employed in these institutions, in addition to the challenges that may face the future of traditional journalism. In this descriptive study, the descriptive and survey methods and mutual relations were used, and data were collected using the survey questionnaire tool. The study sample consisted of 300 individuals from journalists who are members of the Jordanian Journalists Syndicate, using the available sample method within the time limit from 7/31/2022 to January 9, 2022.

The study concluded with several results, the most important of which are that most journalists believe that Jordanian press institutions are somewhat ready to employ AI technologies, and the most important areas of employing these technologies from the journalists' point of view were in "collecting and editing journalistic material." The study also showed that "weak knowledge of algorithm keys" was one of the most important difficulties facing the employment of artificial intelligence technologies, and that the most prominent positive effects resulting from the employment of artificial intelligence technologies are that they work to "increase the speed of producing journalistic content." Journalists saw that there is an integrated relationship between AI and the nature of the work of Jordanian journalists, as it is based on journalists employing modern technologies to serve the profession of journalism.

The study recommended that Jordanian press institutions should focus on employing AI technologies and ensuring that the environment and capabilities necessary for their work are provided, in addition to working on training journalists and providing them with skills to deal with them, and creating new courses in Jordanian universities to teach these technologies.

Study (Al-Bahary, Sherine, 2022) (8): Attitudes of Egyptian journalists toward using the application of AI (Robot Journalism) in producing press content for Egyptian newspapers

The study aimed to identify the attitudes of Egyptian journalists toward the use of AI in the production of journalistic content in Egyptian newspapers. The study also attempted to identify the most prominent challenges facing the application of AI technologies in journalism. The study adopted the descriptive approach, and the data collection tool was a questionnaire with two axes: measuring the scale of Egyptian journalists' attitudes toward the use of modern technologies of AI technologies in journalism. To produce journalistic content in Egyptian newspapers, the second axis was to measure the challenges facing the application of AI in the production of journalistic content. A deliberate sample of 40 journalists was selected from the most prominent newspapers in the Arab Republic of Egypt, namely Al-Ahram Foundation, Akhbar Al-Youm, Al-Gomhuria, Al-Youm Al-Sabea, and Al-Masry Al-Youm. The study concluded that the scale of Egyptian journalists' attitudes toward the use of modern technologies and AI techniques in journalism increased to produce journalistic content in Egyptian newspapers. Additionally, the study found a rise in the scale of challenges facing the application of AI technologies in journalism and media in Egyptian newspapers. Based on these results, the study recommends generalizing the application of modern AI technologies in journalism to produce journalistic content in all

Egyptian newspapers and eliminate all obstacles that stand in the way of implementing this.

Study (Ismail, Fathi, 2022) (9): Journalists' attitudes toward the use of artificial intelligence In the development of journalistic content in Egyptian newspapers and websites Field Study of Al-Masry Al-Youm Sites, Masrawy, Cairo 24

The study aimed to reveal journalists' attitudes toward using AI in developing journalistic content in Egyptian newspapers and websites. It also aimed to identify the reality of employing AI applications in developing newspapers and websites. The study also aimed to determine the extent of success in employing AI applications in developing newspapers and websites, the effects of this employment, whether positive or negative, and whether there are specific skills required to work in newspapers and websites that use AI technologies. The study also tried to put forward proposals to enhance the use of AI techniques in Egyptian newspapers and websites, in addition to trying to monitor the challenges facing Egyptian newspapers and websites in the use of AI technologies. What are the features of the future of Egyptian newspapers and websites with the start of using artificial intelligence technologies, and finally analyzing the relationship between networks social communication and the role of artificial intelligence in developing the content provided in newspapers and websites.

The study yielded a set of results, including that 60% of the study sample believed that the use of artificial intelligence technologies helped in developing content in newspapers and websites, while 22% of the study sample saw the use of AI technologies in newspapers and websites as having a negative impact, leading to a decrease in the number of journalists working in the press institution.

The study also concluded that part of the challenges facing Egyptian newspapers and websites is the use of AI techniques from a technical and technological point of view is the increasing problems of information piracy. Among the most important effects expected to occur on the media role for Egyptian newspapers and websites – Considering the development of AI technologies- is the availability of a distinguished multi-skilled journalist. Almost half of the sample indicated that the most important expected impacts on the media role are for Egyptian newspapers and websites. Considering the increasing presence of AI technologies, it is important to use keywords to facilitate the process of browsing websites and rely on distinguished media content at both quantitative and qualitative levels.

Comment on Literature Review

After reviewing previous studies, it was clear that there is a consensus on the importance of the technological factor in journalistic work and that technological development, especially the use of AI in the field of producing journalistic content, is a matter of utmost importance. Through the results of previous studies conducted in many Arab countries, such as the Arab Republic of Egypt, the Hashemite Kingdom of Jordan, and the State of Palestine, and other Western countries, such as the United States of America and China, it is clear to us that technological development is not limited to a specific region but rather a source available to everyone to draw from. There may be a difference in the extent to which some journalistic communities accept the use of AI in journalistic work, but it was an objective difference such that there was no complete rejection of this new technology, but rather in the methods of implementation.

We also found through the recommendations included in many previous studies that many journalistic institutions encourage the use of AI and strive to provide the latest AI technologies. They also train workers in the journalistic sector to achieve the best results. In addition, the public accepts journalistic content prepared with the help of AI very positively and increases its interest in journalistic content compared to that prepared by traditional means.

Previous studies have provided an important cognitive framework for the importance of AI and its uses in the field of producing journalistic content in Arab and Western countries. They have helped in defining the research problem and choosing the appropriate theoretical and procedural frameworks to achieve the best and most accurate results by providing many examples of the suitable structure that can be followed in current studies, given that the topic is somewhat new and uses new theories and cognitive frameworks.

Among the methods and objectives mentioned in many previous studies were identifying the depth to which the current press uses AI tools in producing journalistic content, identifying the opinions of the elite in the world of journalism on the issue of using AI in journalistic work, and identifying the positives and negatives of using AI in producing journalistic content, which leads us to develop visions of what the future of journalistic work might look like in light of the increasing use of AI in journalistic work.

From the above, we can say that the current study will contribute to increasing awareness of the extent of the use of AI applications in the production of journalistic content. It will also contribute to providing more knowledge about the extent of acceptance of workers in the Bahraini press sector toward this modern practice and how they deal with it. Additionally, it aims to identify the challenges and difficulties they face using these applications and gather their opinions regarding the future of this type of journalistic production.

Conclusion

Finally, this study suggests that researchers who wish to elaborate on the topic of using AI technologies in producing journalistic content should address the main aspects of this sensitive and important issue. This includes the preparations taken by countries and institutions with the aim of developing these practices in the journalistic field, the steps taken by these institutions to prepare their staff and individuals to accept these new technologies, and the measures taken by these countries and institutions to develop their technical infrastructure to be ready to work on using AI technology and obtain the best possible results.

It is also possible to address concerns about AI applications replacing the human element, which affects the societal view of this modern technical practice.

In addition, reaching a satisfactory balance between the human and technical elements within the state's press institutions so that maximum benefit can be achieved from modern technology without harming the work safety of workers in these fields.

It is also important to discuss the steps taken by journalists to use AI applications in their field of work, which is the production of journalistic content in all its fields. This includes refining journalistic material or supplementing existing material with digital media elements such as videos, audio clips, or hologram clips. Many journalists, as we have seen in the literature mentioned in this study, have a real desire to develop in this field but do not know the appropriate channels that must be followed to achieve this goal. This is in comparison to the same segment in other countries, as seen in the literature of this study, where they have the appropriate means to develop but prefer to use a minimum of AI applications in producing their media content.

References

Abdul, B. S. E., & Naira. (2023). The impact of the adoption of artificial intelligence technology by journalistic institutions on editing journalistic texts. *Journal of Research of the Faculty of Arts. Menoufia University*, *35*(136.3), 603–640.

Al-Bahary, S. (2022). Egyptian journalists' attitudes towards using the application of artificial intelligence journalism (Robot Journalism) in producing journalistic content in Egyptian newspapers. *Scientific Journal of Journalism Research*, *2022* (24), 129–158. https://doi.org/10.21608/sjsj.2023.278367

Haddad, A. T., & Ismat, T. (2023). Employing artificial intelligence techniques in Jordanian press institutions and its reflection on the professional practice of journalists. *Scientific Journal of Journalism Research*, *2023*(25), 37–60.

Ismail, F. I. (2022). Journalists' attitudes towards using artificial intelligence in developing journalistic content in Egyptian newspapers and websites: A field study of Al-Masry Al-Youm - Masrawy - Cairo 24 websites. *Egyptian Journal of Public Opinion Research*, *21*(4), 31–86.

Sholola, Y. A., Banjo, Y. O., Saliu-Yusuf, M. J., Ogundeyi, T. S., & Ayantunji, K. A. (2024). Perceived effect of artificial intelligence on ethical journalism among journalists in Kwara state. *International Journal of Research and Innovation in Social Sciences*, *8*(2), 2051–2063.

Chapter 19

The Role of Artificial Intelligence Technologies in Enhancing News Content on Satellite Channel Websites

Basheer Hasan Al-Tarouty

Ahlia University, Bahrain

Abstract

With rapid technological advancements reshaping every aspect of life, the media sector stands out as one of the most profoundly transformed. Digitization and artificial intelligence (AI) have become essential pillars of modern media systems. In particular, the integration of AI into news production has become a key driver in enhancing the accuracy, speed, and interactivity of news content, offering audiences more dynamic and engaging visual experiences.

News channels have led this transformation, each seeking to harness AI technologies to strengthen their market position and meet the evolving expectations of today's audiences. These technologies support a range of functions, including data analysis, automated news editing, and advanced graphics generation, all contributing to more innovative and higher-quality content delivery.

This study examines and compares the strategies adopted by two leading Middle Eastern news channels in applying AI technologies. It explores how technologies influence the content presented and investigates the attitudes of media elites toward their use. In doing so, the study also addresses the ethical and professional challenges that accompany this technological shift.

The analysis highlights media values promoted by AI—such as transparency, speed, and accuracy—while also acknowledging emerging concerns around credibility and ethical standards in an increasingly automated environment.

Ultimately, this study moves beyond surface-level observations to explore critical questions about the future of traditional media in the age of

Digital Dialogues, 179–190

Published under exclusive licence by Emerald Publishing Limited
doi:10.1108/978-1-83708-686-320261019

AI: Can these technologies preserve core journalistic values? And to what extent can they be leveraged to meet the expectations of modern, digitally savvy audiences?

Keywords: Artificial intelligence; news websites; news channels; media digitization; middle east

Concepts and Terminology of the Study

Artificial Intelligence (AI) Technologies

Definition: AI technologies are computer systems designed to perform tasks requiring human intelligence. In journalism, they are used for data extraction, topic selection, news production, error correction, content enhancement, audience analysis, fake news detection, and even article writing (Al-Dalou et al., 2022, p. 65).

Function: This term refers to technologies that simulate human journalistic capabilities, particularly in editing and reporting, and includes the use of virtual studio environments.

News Content

Definition: AI helps news organizations automate routine tasks, analyze trends quickly, and frame narratives professionally. This enhances journalistic performance, reduces costs, boosts output, and supports competitiveness in a changing media landscape (Khattab, 2024, p. 525).

Function: Refers to journalistic material—whether written, visual, or audio—that is presented to the public through various media platforms to report on events and developments.

News Websites

Function: Digital platforms that deliver a variety of media content—including text, images, and videos—with the aim of conveying news and information to the public via the internet.

News Satellite Channels

Function: Television channels that rely on satellite broadcasting to transmit news and journalistic reports to both local and international audiences.

Media Elites

Function: Influential figures within the media industry—such as journalists, editors, managers, and experts—who play a significant role in shaping media policy and content production.

Study Variables

Independent Variables

Use of AI Technologies

Refers to the degree to which satellite news channels, such as Al Jazeera and Al Arabiya, integrate AI into news content development. This includes the use of automated news writing tools, AI-driven fact-checking technologies, and data analysis systems.

Technological Deployment Strategies

Relates to how news channels implement AI technologies in newsrooms and on their digital platforms.

Dependent Variables

News Content Quality

Encompasses the accuracy of information, depth of analysis, and innovation in content presentation, as measured through feedback from both audiences and media professionals.

Audience Engagement Level

Indicates audience engagement with AI-generated content, exemplified by metrics such as click-through rates, time spent interacting with the content, and frequency of content sharing.

Media Elites' Perspectives

Reflects the perspectives and attitudes of journalists and media professionals regarding the use of AI in news content development, which can be assessed through surveys and in-depth interviews.

The Historical Emergence of AI

AI began in the 20th century with efforts to mimic human intelligence, formally emerging at the 1956 Dartmouth Conference. It has since evolved into a key driver of the digital revolution (Al-Dalou et al., 2022; Santos & Cirone, 2022).

Types of AI

AI is typically classified into three main types:

Artificial Narrow Intelligence (ANI)

Specialized in specific tasks such as image recognition.

Artificial General Intelligence (AGI)

Capable of replicating human-like intelligence across a broad range of functions.

Artificial Superintelligence (ASI)

Surpasses human intelligence in all domains.

Studies indicate that the currently applied forms of AI are primarily focused on narrow AI, especially in news and media applications (Al-Zahrani, 2022; Attard et al., 2024).

Media Applications of AI

Al-Jadi (2021) and Fezzi (2024) explain that AI is being applied in various areas of the media industry, including:

- writing news articles and reports using AI-powered tools such as Generative Pre-trained Transformers (GPTs);
- detecting fake news through machine learning techniques;
- analyzing big data to identify media trends;
- enhancing the quality and credibility of news content;
- automating media-related processes.

Objectives of Using AI in News Production

- To generate faster and more accurate news content.
- To improve news coverage using journalistic robots.
- To strengthen news credibility via verification tools.
- To customize news content according to audience needs.

A study by Arguedas et al. (2024) found that while AI contributes to improved efficiency, it also raises concerns related to trust.

Notable AI Technologies

Zardaq (2023) outlines the following major AI technologies influencing the industry:

- machine learning;
- natural language processing (NLP);
- big data analysis;
- robot journalism.

Theories Utilized in the Study

The Integrative Approach

The concept of an integrative approach refers to the systematic linking of different branches of knowledge to achieve a unified understanding and remove barriers between them in the educational process. Many researchers have agreed upon this definition in various educational contexts (Al-Sawafi et al., 2024, p. 21).

Media Substitution Theory

Media substitution theory suggests that new communication technologies can partially or fully replace traditional media, with outcomes varying based on social and technological factors.

Application of the Theory in This Study

This study illustrates how new media platforms may replace traditional media in fulfilling audience needs and preferences. The theory is employed to explore the impact of digital news content on the production and relevance of traditional television news content in the following ways (El-Sayed, 2024, p. 33):

Replacement of Traditional Media

Digital platforms offer an alternative to traditional television, with audiences increasingly using smartphones and social media to access news content.

Interaction and Content Customization

Digital platforms allow for greater audience interaction compared to traditional television. Viewers can select content that aligns with their interests and share it through social media, influencing how news is disseminated and engaged with.

Targeted Advertising and Revenue Generation

Digital media platforms gather detailed data on viewer preferences, allowing for more precise ad targeting and subsequently boosting advertising revenues. This shift is reshaping the structure and monetization strategies of traditional television advertising.

Shifts in Importance

Audiences now prefer digital platforms for specialized news, shifting focus away from traditional TV. Media Substitution Theory explains how this trend impacts TV news in engagement, content priorities, and ad revenues (El-Sayed, 2024, p. 33).

Review of Previous Literature

Theme 1: The Use of AI in News Production

The study by Al-Shibini (2024) aligns with Al-Jadi (2021) in emphasizing the importance of regulating AI legally and ethically within the media sector. While Al-Shibini highlights the necessity of international laws and regulations to protect media content from misinformation, Al-Jadi underscores the effectiveness of monitoring technologies in combating fake news and enhancing news credibility.

On another front, the studies by Hajar and Nafisa (2023) and Abdulrazzaq (2023) emphasize the importance of AI technologies in news editing. The former points to the capabilities of algorithms in improving news collection and editing, whereas the latter explores the broader application of AI across fields such as marketing and media, reflecting a more expansive perspective.

Both Abdulhaleem (2024) and Al-Zahrani (2022) focus on the application of AI in covering service-related and economic news. However, they differ in the way they assess the impact of these technologies: Abdulhaleem investigates journalists' perceptions and their adoption levels of AI, while Al-Zahrani evaluates the extent of journalists' expertise in utilizing these technologies.

The studies by Zaater and Maghrebi (2023) and Za'anouf and Azeemi (2023) investigate the transformative impact of technology on media practices. Zaater and Maghrebi examine the integration of augmented reality and holographic technologies in delivering interactive news content, while Za'anouf and Azeemi explore how "robot journalism" is reshaping media production workflows and appealing to a new generation of technologically adept journalists.

Lastly, Al-Harbi (2022) and Ba'uthman (2024) demonstrate partial alignment in acknowledging the role of AI technologies in enhancing media production. However, Ba'uthman concentrates on the design of homepage layouts in Saudi Arabia and American electronic newspapers, while Al-Harbi addresses the cultural and regulatory challenges faced in television production.

Researcher's Commentary

The reviewed studies consistently highlight the significance of AI technologies in enhancing media efficiency and improving news content. They also emphasize the professional and ethical challenges associated with AI integration. The diversity in application areas and analytical approaches across the studies offers a comprehensive understanding of the opportunities and challenges facing the media industry in the AI era.

Trends in International Studies

The study by Tufel and Simon (2023) aligns with that of Arguedas et al. (2024) in analyzing the impact of AI on trust and credibility in news. Both studies indicate that news content generated solely by AI tends to be perceived as less credible by audiences. However, Arguedas et al. (2024) add a positive dimension, showing that news co-produced by journalists and AI systems tends to gain higher trust compared to content produced solely by AI.

Regarding the impact of AI on journalistic processes, Tiwari (2024) and Attard et al. (2024) both emphasize the efficiency and speed AI technologies bring to the newsroom. While Tiwari (2024) focuses on Indian media institutions and the ethical challenges in handling complex topics, Attard et al. (2024) explore the new opportunities AI presents for interactive and personalized journalism.

Santos and Cirone (2022) concentrate on specific AI subfields such as machine learning, computer vision, and planning. They argue that the dominance of major tech firms, like Google, in funding development limits the broader use of AI in journalism. In contrast, Simon (2024) addresses the broader implications of AI adoption across the media landscape, highlighting ethical and operational challenges that could fundamentally reshape journalism.

Researcher's Perspective on Trends in International Studies

International studies demonstrate a general consensus on the importance of AI in enhancing journalistic efficiency and productivity. However, they also highlight ethical challenges and the potential erosion of public trust and credibility. These studies reveal both similarities and differences in AI applications across various media contexts, contributing to a holistic understanding of its impact on the future of journalism.

Theme 2: Tracking the Attitudes of Media Elites Toward the Use of AI in Generating News

The studies by Zardaq and Nuno (2023) and Al-Dalou et al. (2022) align in monitoring the attitudes of communication professionals toward the adoption of AI technologies. Both studies indicate that these technologies are widely used in covering breaking news and processing big data. However, Zardaq's study focuses more on digital platforms and their relation to economic and political topics, while Al-Dalou examines the readiness of Palestinian institutions to adopt AI tools.

Similarly, Khattab (2024) and Matawa (2024) assess the impact of AI technologies on media content. Khattab emphasizes the use of augmented reality technologies, while Matawa explores AI's role in fact-checking and content analysis of news stories.

Regarding digital transformations, Fezzi (2024) and Al-Haij (2024) both analyze how technological shifts are reshaping journalistic practices. Both studies show a growing acceptance of AI integration. However, Fezzi focuses on AI's impact on journalists' creative roles, whereas Al-Haij highlights the positive trend toward AI adoption in Egyptian radio broadcasting.

Ayash (2023) shows agreement in identifying the challenges faced by media institutions and communication professionals when using AI technologies. Ayash (2023) concentrates on AI adoption in Palestinian satellite channels to enhance news gathering and editing processes.

Researcher's Perspective on Previous Studies Related to Theme 2

The studies demonstrate consensus on the significant role of AI technologies in enhancing media efficiency and improving news content. At the same time, the variations across the studies reveal the diverse applications and challenges associated with adopting these technologies, offering a comprehensive understanding of AI's role in contemporary news production.

Commentary on Previous Studies

- Most prior studies have focused on analyzing the impact of AI technologies on generating news—whether in news gathering, editing, or verification—as seen with Al-Shibini (2024) and Hajar & Nafisa (2023).
- While many studies have explored the topic in both global and Arab contexts, few have specifically examined the media landscape of the Gulf region. This highlights the need for greater attention to the Gulf context in academic research.
- Some studies, such as those by Abdulrazzaq (2023) and Matawa (2024), examined the attitudes of media professionals, whereas others, like Arguedas (2024), focused on public perceptions and audience trust in AI.
- The reviewed literature includes analysis of various AI technologies such as data journalism, robot-assisted editing, and augmented reality, as discussed by Zaater and Maghrebi (2023) and Al-Harbi (2022).
- Ethical concerns surrounding AI—such as misinformation and algorithmic bias—were addressed in studies like Al-Jadi (2021) and Santos (2022).
- The methodological approaches varied across studies, including field surveys, content analysis, in-depth interviews, and semiotic analysis, as employed in Ba'uthman (2024) and Al-Dalou et al. (2022).
- Studies such as Fezzi (2024) and Za'anouf (2023) confirmed that AI is transforming traditional journalistic roles, necessitating the retraining and upskilling of journalists to adapt to digital transformations.
- Finally, some research, such as that by Simon (2024) and Attard et al. (2024), explored the technical challenges media institutions face when integrating AI into their operations.

Benefits from Previous Studies

- The researcher utilized previous studies to formulate the research problem and develop the study questions, which helped in shaping the theoretical framework and directing the research focus toward analyzing the impact of AI on news content.
- Prior studies guided the researcher in selecting an appropriate methodology, including the use of in-depth interviews and comparative analysis, as demonstrated in Ba'uthman (2024).
- The researcher benefited from the analysis of values influencing news content—particularly the positive values that enhance audience trust—as highlighted in Arguedas (2024).
- Previous studies inspired the researcher to incorporate AI tools, such as algorithm-based fake news detection, as discussed in Al-Jadi (2021).
- These studies provided insights on addressing the ethical challenges associated with AI, contributing to the credibility of news content, as seen in Santos (2022).
- The researcher gained an understanding of media elites' attitudes toward the use of AI in journalism from studies like Al-Dalou et al. (2022).
- Prior research motivated the researcher to explore the impact of AI on traditional journalistic roles and how these roles can be integrated with emerging technologies, as discussed in Fezzi (2024).

Conclusion

A review of previous literature concerning values and various technological advancements reveals that, despite the apparent success of Arabic digital news platforms—such as Shahid—in attracting audiences, this success is more superficial than substantive. The values presented in the content available on these platforms are often framed within Western value systems or lack depth and meaningful impact. This occurs despite the Arab viewer's strong motivation to engage with such platforms. Greater attention should be given to the emotional appeal and persuasive impact of this content and how it fosters dialogue between audiences and the artistic content offered on Arab digital platforms.

Notably, although Arab digital platforms differ in their approaches and orientations, *Netflix* continues to dominate the digital streaming landscape across the Arab world and globally. Therefore, it would be more strategic for Arab news to present its stories and values through a global platform like Netflix. This would not only increase viewership and influence among Arab audiences but also serve to promote Arab values and culture to international viewers.

As audience awareness of the communicative features of digital platforms increases, so does engagement with these platforms. This rising engagement positively correlates with favorable perceptions of platform content and increases the platform's ability to shape viewer habits. Consequently, we recommend that Arab digital platforms adopt the strengths of global platforms in terms of presentation quality, while also focusing on uniqueness and highlighting Arab cultural identity. This should be based on extensive research to understand what the Arab audience seeks from these platforms—what gratifies them, what features attract them, and what values they believe are lacking in society and therefore wish to promote, especially to younger generations and global audiences.

It is essential to understand how digital platforms communicate with viewers, especially when portraying violence, deviant behavior, or glamorized crime. These themes should be examined with specialists to ensure alignment with societal values and cultural norms. While much of the literature analyzes the positive and negative effects of news platforms—often through comparisons—these insights must now inform the creation of artistic content. By leveraging existing findings, content creators can produce works that are not only engaging but also culturally respectful and socially responsible, contributing to a more informed and value-aligned media environment.

Experts point to the fragmentation of Arab media, weak factual reporting, and conflicting stances on Arab issues. They agree that the media plays a limited role in raising public awareness amid growing foreign cultural influence. This reflects a failure to fulfill its societal role. Unifying Arab issues and identifying common ground is essential, given shared challenges and values. Media professionals—especially those on digital platforms, along with writers, directors, and actors—must acknowledge their responsibility in resisting external influences and promoting authentic values. Cultivating greater awareness of this duty is now urgently needed.

References

Arabic Studies

Peer-Reviewed Journal Articles

Abdelhaleem, R. (2024). The reality of Arab journalism in the age of Artificial Intelligence technologies. *Journal of Media Research, Al-Azhar University*, *69*(2023), 1295.

Abdulrazzaq, M. (2022). Artificial intelligence technologies in media: Current reality and future developments. *Egyptian Journal of Media Research, Cairo University*, *81*, 22.

Al-Dalou, J. R., Abu Hashish, Y. Y., & Ismail, A. A. (2022). Media experts' attitudes toward the use of artificial intelligence in Palestinian journalism. *Al-Risalah Journal for Human Studies and Research*, *7*(2022), 59.

Al-Harbi, A. (2022). Utilizing artificial intelligence technology in the television production environment. *Journal of Communication Sciences, Omdurman Islamic University*, *8*(2023), 188.

Al-Jadi, A. (2021). *The use of artificial intelligence in Al Jazeera's newsroom to combat fake news.* Al Jazeera Media Institute, (*2022*), 40.

Al-Sawafi, S., Al-Shaybani, M., & Al-Owaidi, M. (2024). The integrative approach in interpreting the Holy Qur'an. *Journal of Sharia Research*, *4*, 77–95.

Al-Shibini, H. (2024). Uses of generative artificial intelligence in visual media in Egypt: An exploratory study. *Misr University Journal for Human Studies, Misr University*, *4*(2024), 41.

Al-Zahrani, A. (2022). Adoption of AI applications by Arab journalists in media institutions. *Algerian Journal of Media and Public Opinion Research, Algeria* (*5*, 2022, p. 18).

Ayash, A. (2023). Utilizing artificial intelligence technologies in news production at Palestinian satellite channels. *Journal of Political Science and Law, Democratic Arab Center, Germany* (*8*, 2023, p. 266).

Ba'uthman, R. (2023). Designing the homepage of Saudi and American electronic newspapers. *Arab Journal of Media and Communication, Saudi Media and Communication Association, King Saud University, Saudi Arabia*, *38*(2024), 356.

El-Sayed, N. (2024). The impact of digital platform news content on television news production. *Scientific Journal of Radio and Television Research, Cairo University*, *28*, 359.

Fezzi, H. (2024). The impact of technological transformations in the digital media environment on journalism and journalists' role perceptions. *Journal of the Faculty of Arts, Sohag University, Egypt* (*72*, 2024, p. 610).

Khattab, E. (2024). Using augmented reality technologies in content presented on news websites and channels and their impact on content development. *Journal of Media Research and Studies, International High Institute for Media, El Shorouk, Egypt*, *29*(2024), 526.

Matawa, N. (2024). News institutions' journalistic practices in fact-checking in the age of artificial intelligence technologies. *Journal of Media Research, Faculty of Mass Communication, Al-Azhar University, Egypt* (*29*, 2024, p. 501).

Zaater, Z. & Maghrebi, A.. (2023). Artificial intelligence in newsrooms through augmented reality and its impact on news content. *Al-Muqaddimah Journal for Human and Social Studies, University of Constantine*, *8*, 237.

Zardaq, S., & Nuno, F. (2024). Attitudes of media professionals toward the use of AI technologies in digital news platforms. *Egyptian Journal of Media Research, Faculty of Mass Communication, Cairo University*, *86*(2024), 320.

Za'anouf, A. (2023). The future of media in the age of robot journalism. *Al-Risalah Journal for Human Studies and Research, University of Algiers*, *8*, 958.

Unpublished Master's Theses

Hajar, G. N., & Ben, N. (2023). *The use of artificial intelligence technologies in news editing and writing in electronic newspapers.* University of Colonel Ahmed Draia.

Foreign Studies

Attard, M., Davis, M., & Main, L. (2024). *Gen AI and journalism: Exploring the impact of generative AI on news production and the public sphere*. Centre for Media Transition, University of Technology Sydney. https://cmt.uts.edu.au

de-Lima-Santos, M.-F., & Ceron, W. (2022). Artificial intelligence in news media: Current perceptions and future outlook. *Journalism and Media*, *3*(1), 13–26. https://doi.org/10.3390/journalmedia3010002

Ross Arguedas, A. (2024). Public attitudes towards the use of AI in journalism. In *Digital news report 2024*. Reuters Institute for the Study of Journalism. https://reutersinstitute.politics.ox.ac.uk/digital-news-report/2024/public-attitudes-towards-use-ai-and-journalism

Ross Arguedas, A., Fletcher, R., Robertson, C. T., Nielsen, R. K., & Newman, N. (2024). Public attitudes towards the use of AI in journalism. In *Digital news report 2024*. Reuters Institute for the Study of Journalism. https://reutersinstitute.politics.ox.ac.uk/digital-news-report/2024/public-attitudes-towards-use-ai-and-journalism

Simon, F. M. (2024). *Artificial intelligence in the news: How AI retools, rationalizes, and reshapes journalism and the public arena*. Tow Center for Digital Journalism, Columbia University. https://www.cjr.org/tow_center_reports

Tiwari, S. (2024). The role of artificial intelligence in automated journalism: Transforming news production. *International Journal of Creative Research Thoughts (IJCRT)*, *12*(5), 799–838. www.ijcrt.org

Toff, B., & Simon, F. M. (2023).*Or they could just not use it?": The paradox of AI disclosure for audience trust in news*. Pre-print, not peer-reviewed. Hubbard School of Journalism & Mass Communication, University of Minnesota, & Oxford Internet Institute, University of Oxford, Vol. 1, 2–15.

Chapter 20

The Impact of Social Media Use on the Mental Health of Adolescents

Khalid Ali Hadi Ali AlSayyadi

Ahlia University, Bahrain

Abstract

The study aimed to identify the impact of social networking sites on the mental health of adolescents through a review of the theoretical framework and an analysis of previous studies. We examined these studies by reviewing their most important objectives, methodologies, sample populations, and key findings. Furthermore, the results of these studies were compared to identify patterns and differences.

Studies have examined the impact of social media on adolescent mental health, focusing on multiple aspects, including addiction, behavioral deviance, and depression. Studies such as "Ramadan and Abdul Qadir (2023)" and "Abdul Karim and Shukal (2023)" have highlighted the negative effects of addiction, including sleep disorders and anxiety, as well as behavioral deviations like isolation and susceptibility to negative values. Studies such as "Muhammad (2022)" and "Juma and Zainab (2022)" also emphasized the role of apps like "Instagram" and "TikTok" in exacerbating feelings of psychological loneliness and depression.

Conversely, studies such as "Rabab Abd al-Rahman (2022)" and "Naslund et al. (2020)" highlight benefits like enhanced self-expression and psychological support, while cautioning against negative effects like cyberbullying. Studies such as "Bouzette (2022)" and "Al-Hashimi (2020)" emphasized the role of these platforms in shaping adolescents' cultural identity and social values, reinforcing the importance of promoting safe usage.

Keywords: Impact; social media; mental health; adolescents; internet

Digital Dialogues, 191–199

Published under exclusive licence by Emerald Publishing Limited
doi:10.1108/978-1-83708-686-320261020

Introduction

Recent technological developments at the beginning of the millennium of the current century have brought about a qualitative shift in the world of communication, often referred to as the communication revolution. The internet spread rapidly throughout the world, connecting vast geographical regions into what Canadian theorist Marshall McLuhan called a "cosmic village."

The internet and its applications have undergone several developments, with the emergence of websites, personal blogs, and instant messaging services, transforming the form and content of media and communication. These applications have created new modes of communication between administrators and users on the one hand and between users themselves on the other.

Social networking sites have become a critical means of communication, prompting countries to focus on regulating these platforms. Some countries have even amended their laws to address the chaos that can arise from the misuse of these sites. The use of these platforms has also become an integral part of adolescents' lives, as they are among the most affected groups by the increasing reliance on social networking in daily life. This phenomenon is particularly noticeable among university students, leading to both positive and negative effects, especially on their mental health.

With the increasing use of these platforms, individuals often find themselves spending more time on them, eventually struggling to disconnect and becoming increasingly dependent. This dependency affects their social, family, and professional lives. It begins with social withdrawal, reduced direct interactions with others, and an increased reliance on indirect forms of communication. Consequently, users exhibit signs of psychological and social issues, including depression, introversion, and loneliness.

Adolescents are among the most active users of social networking sites, as they adapt to technology more readily. Adolescence is an important stage in human development, representing a critical period for societal progress or stagnation. It is evident that the mental health of young people significantly influences their ability to contribute to societal development. Excessive and improper use of social media adversely affects mental health and exposes adolescents to significant challenges.

The impact of this modern technology has extended to encompass all aspects of economic, social, political, and educational life in modern societies, reaching adolescents, who are considered the fundamental unit of society. The family has played a crucial role in shaping a person's awareness and culture, as well as contributing to the formation of the societal value system they adhere to and the components of social behavior, including those of adolescents. However, today, a significant part of this role has shifted to social media platforms, which have opened up new avenues for communication patterns within the family, used to fulfill needs related to social relationships. The problem of this study revolves around answering the following question: To what extent have social media platforms contributed to influencing the mental health of adolescents?

Theoretical Framework

Concept of Social Networking Sites

Social networking sites are collections of pages and applications on the Web that emerged with the advent of the second generation of the Web. These sites allow the public to communicate with each other, enabling users to share diaries, experiences, information, news, and entertainment. Through these platforms, users become familiar with what other members of the audience are doing (Sameh, 2018, p. 69).

Networking sites are also an interconnected online community that allows the public to create their own accounts, through which they can publish diaries and interact with published content. These sites form a virtual community, bringing the public together based on shared interests, whether spatial, specialized, or hobby-related.

Social media is defined as platforms that allow users to share files, photos, and videos with each other. These platforms also enable users to create blogs, participate in instant conversations, and send messages. The top three major social networks are Facebook, X (formerly Twitter), and Instagram. These platforms have become essential tools for sharing information, news, and diverse content.

Mental Health

Mental health is a state of psychological and emotional well-being that enables an individual to achieve their potential, cope with daily stresses, work effectively, and contribute to their community. It is an integral part of public health, influenced by biological, psychological, and social factors, including the effects of modern technology.

Definition of Mental Health

The World Health Organization (WHO, 2021) defines mental health as "a state of well-being in which an individual is able to fulfill their potential, cope with the stresses of ordinary life, work productively, and contribute to society."

The Impact of Technology on Mental Health

Research suggests that social media use may have **dual effects** on mental health. While social media can foster social support networks and promote interaction, **excessive use** may lead to feelings of isolation, depression, and anxiety. This is often a result of **social comparison** and detachment from real-world interactions (Twenge et al., 2018a).

Adolescents

Adolescence is a transitional stage between childhood and adulthood, characterized by physical, psychological, and social changes that impact an individual's growth and development. **The World Health Organization defines adolescence as the age range of 10 to 19 years.** This stage is critical for identity formation and the development of interpersonal and social skills (World Health Organization [WHO], 2021).

Characteristics of Adolescence

(1) **Physical Changes:** Adolescents experience biological changes such as puberty and rapid body growth.
(2) **Psychological Development:** Abstract thinking emerges, the ability to make complex decisions improves, and the search for personal identity begins.
(3) **Social Changes:** Peer relationships become increasingly significant, and social pressures may influence behaviors (Twenge et al., 2018b).

Previous Studies

Dr Ramadan Lines and Dr. Hannah Abdul Qadir (2023): Addiction to Social Media and Its Impact on the Mental Health of Adolescents

The study aimed to define the concept of social media addiction, examine the role of networking sites in influencing adolescent mental health, identify the direct and indirect causes of addiction, and uncover the psychological effects of addiction on adolescents' mental health. The analytical descriptive approach was employed to collect facts about the phenomenon and analyze its various dimensions. While the text did not provide precise details about the sample size or the number of participants, it focused on adolescents as the primary target group.

The key findings revealed that addiction to social media sites has a significant and negative impact on adolescents' mental health, leading to crises and psychological disorders, sometimes escalating to suicidal tendencies. The most prominent negative effects of addiction include sleep disturbances, depression, anxiety, eating disorders, and a weakened immune system.

Qahariya Abdel Karim and Shukal Mohammed (2023): Abuse of Social Media and Delinquency of Adolescents: A Field Study at Misani Lajal High School, Tibessa

The study aimed to examine the impact of social media misuse on adolescents' behavior, highlight the negative phenomena resulting from such misuse, and explore the relationship between social media addiction and behavioral aberrations. The study employed an analytical descriptive approach to understand and interpret the phenomenon based on field data. The sample consisted of "Hasani" secondary school students in Tibsa State. The findings revealed that the misuse of social media sites leads to significant behavioral deviations among adolescents. The prevalence of negative behaviors, such as social isolation, weakened family relationships, and susceptibility to unethical values was clearly correlated with prolonged time spent on these platforms, which also contributed to increased rates of stress and anxiety among adolescents.

Walid Mohamed (2022): Uses of Social Media and Their Relationship to Depression and Psychological Loneliness Among Egyptian Youth

The study aimed to examine the relationship between young people's use of social media sites and the impact of such use on their levels of depression and psychological loneliness. The survey's descriptive approach was used as the study methodology. The study yielded several key findings. They are as follows:

(1) WhatsApp was ranked as the most frequently used social media platform among the sample group, followed by Facebook and YouTube.
(2) Statistically significant differences were observed between gender and the level of depression, with females showing higher levels of depression compared to males.
(3) The hypothesis that the degree of psychological loneliness varied according to the demographic characteristics of young social media users was partially supported. Statistically significant differences were noted between educational levels and feelings of psychological loneliness.
(4) A significant positive correlation was found between the intensity of TikTok and Instagram use and feelings of depression, indicating that greater use of these platforms was associated with higher levels of depression among young people.

Patti M., Adrian Meier, and Ine Beyens (2022): Social Media Use and Its Impact on Adolescent Mental Health

The study aimed to analyze the impact of social media use on adolescents' mental health through a comprehensive review of studies published between 2019 and mid-2021. Its objectives included identifying the characteristics of previous studies, interpreting their findings, highlighting research gaps, and providing recommendations for future research.

An umbrella review, which involves analyzing published reviews, such as meta-analyses, systematic reviews, and narrative reviews, was employed. The study examined 25 reviews addressing the impact of social media on adolescents' mental health, particularly in relation to outcomes like depression, anxiety, and psychological well-being.

The key findings were as follows:

(1) The relationship between social media use and mental health was described as weak and inconsistent across most reviews.
(2) The impact of social media on mental health was uneven, with some studies reporting slight negative effects, while others identified slight positive effects.

(3) There was a lack of longitudinal studies to establish a causal link between social media use and mental health.
(4) The findings emphasized the importance of focusing on the quality of content and interactions, rather than solely on the duration of use.
(5) The study advocated for the use of more objective measurement methods, such as digital activity recordings, instead of relying solely on self-reported data.

Dr Rabab Abdel Rahman (2022): *Psychological Effects of Social Media*

The study aimed to provide a comprehensive view of the psychological impacts of social media sites on users, monitoring both the positive and negative psychological effects of these sites over the past decade (2011–2020).

The study used a qualitative approach, conducting a second-level analysis based on the review and analysis of 119 Arab and Western studies, including scientific articles, university theses, conference papers, and reports. The studies were divided into 50 Arab and 69 Western sources, addressing both positive and negative psychological effects.

The study found that social media sites contribute to enhanced self-expression, increased self-esteem, reduced loneliness, and depression through interaction, psychosocial support, increased social confidence, and a sense of belonging. However, networking sites were also linked to negative outcomes, such as low self-confidence due to social comparisons, envy, and increased levels of depression and anxiety resulting from addiction to social media use. Additionally, the excessive use of social media contributed to social isolation and family alienation.

Intimate Bosette (2022): The Impact of Social Media on Teen Identity—Facebook as a Model

The study aimed to examine the impact of social media sites, particularly Facebook, on adolescents' identity. It sought to explore patterns of adolescent use of social media sites and highlight new values and behavioral patterns adopted by adolescents as a result of using Facebook.

The descriptive-analytical approach was used for data collection and analysis to understand the relationship between social media sites and adolescents' identity.

A purposive sample was made up of teenagers who are Facebook users.

The study found that the use of Facebook significantly influences adolescents' identity by exposing them to a diverse range of cultural and value-based content. Adolescents adopt new behavior patterns, such as changes in dress and hairstyles, which deviate from traditional customs. This has a noticeable negative impact on their moral and social values, increasing the tendency to identify with Western culture and contributing to a weakening of the adolescent's cultural identity.

Gomaa and Hamoudi Zainab (2022): Impact of the Use of Social Media Sites on the Mental Health of University Students—Instagram as a Model

The study aimed to explore the habits and patterns of university students using the Instagram platform, identify the reasons for their usage, and assess the positive and negative psychological effects resulting from this use. The study relied on a descriptive approach, utilizing a questionnaire tool to collect and analyze data with the help of SPSS software. The study included a purposive sample of 60 students from the Department of Information and Communication Sciences at Kasdi Merbah Ouargla University. The study found that students' use of Instagram was moderate. Motivations for use included following the news, staying informed about individuals, and social interaction. Negative psychological effects emerged, such as addiction to following certain pages and feelings of envy and jealousy.

Conclusion

Various studies on the impact of social media sites on the mental health of adolescents and young people indicate different and multifaceted trends. Many studies have shown the negative effects of addiction to these sites, such as depression, anxiety, social isolation, and sleep disorders. Some studies also highlighted behavioral harms, such as deviance and poor family relationships. On the other hand, other studies have focused on the positive aspects, such as providing social support, promoting self-confidence, and fostering a sense of belonging. However, the results revealed variation in the nature of these effects based on factors such as content quality, duration of use, and demographics, highlighting the importance of developing strategies to raise awareness of the effects of these sites and encourage their positive use, while promoting balanced use to avoid potential harm.

Studies by Ramadan Lines, Hannah Abdel Qader (2023), Walid Mohamed Abdulhadi (2018), and Abdel Karim Ben Mustafa (2019) agree that addiction to social media sites causes significant negative effects on mental health, including anxiety, depression, and sleep disorders. While Ramadan and Hannah's study focused on the impact of addiction on adolescents, highlighting effects such as suicidal ideation, Walid's study showed an association between the use of certain sites, such as TikTok and Instagram, and increased levels of depression. Abdul Karim's study suggested that these sites could provide psychological support in some cases, adding a limited positive dimension.

A study by Qahariya Abdel Karim and Shukal Mohamed (2023) examined the impact of improper use of social media on the emergence of behavioral deviations, such as poor family relationships and social isolation. Hamima Boset's (2022) study focused on the impact of Facebook use on adolescent identity, highlighting the changing values and identification with Western cultures as a result of social media exposure.

The study by Rabab Abdul Rahman Khalifa (2022) provided a comprehensive analysis of the psychological effects of social media, emphasizing both positive aspects, such as enhanced self-confidence and psychological support, and negative ones, such as social comparisons and increased anxiety and depression. Her findings intersect with those of Patti et al. (2022), which also highlighted the weak relationship between media use and mental health, with effects varying based on the quality of the content consumed.

Most studies employed an analytical or descriptive survey approach, highlighting the importance of description and analysis to understand the phenomenon. Studies such as those by Patti et al. (2022) and Rabab Khalifa (2022) relied on extensive reviews of previous studies, offering a broader perspective, while studies like Qahariya and Shukal (2023) focused on collecting direct field data.

In conclusion, studies show a relative consensus that excessive or improper use of social media sites causes clear negative effects on mental health and social behavior, especially in adolescents and young adults. However, the extent of these effects varies based on the quality of the content used, age groups, and cultural conditions. Some studies have also highlighted positive aspects, emphasizing the importance of balance in use and raising awareness of its various dimensions.

References

Arabic References

Abdel Karim, B. M. (2019). The impact of social media use on the mental health of Algerian youth: A relational descriptive study. *Journal of Psychological and Educational Research*, *10*(4), 58–75.

Abdel, K. Q., & Shukal Mohamed, M. (2023). Improper use of social media and deviance in adolescents: A field study at Missani Laajel secondary school, Tebessa. *Journal of Educational and Social Sciences*, *12*(3), 89–105.

Boset, H. (2022). *The impact of social media sites on adolescent identity: Facebook as a model.*

Gomaa, A., & Hamoudi, Z. (2022). The impact of social media use on university students' mental health: A case study of instagram. *Journal of Psychological and Educational Sciences*, *14*(1), 78–92.

Mohamed Abdelhadi. (2018). Characteristics of social media sites. *Journal of Digital Media*, 53–54.

Rabab, A. R. (2022). Psychological effects of social media. *Journal of Mental and Social Health*, *10*(3), 50–66.

Sami, A. (2018). *Audience-communication interaction: A study in communication theories*. Arab Institute for Studies.

Walid, M. (2022). The use of social media and its relationship to levels of depression and psychological loneliness among Egyptian youth. *Journal of Media and Society Studies*, *6*(4), 112–130.

Foreign References

Khalifa, R. A. R. H. (2022). Psychological effects of social networking sites: Towards a theoretical model. *The Egyptian Journal for Media Research*, (*81*), 1–33.

Naslund, J. A., Bondre, A., Torous, J., & Aschbrenner, K. A. (2020). Social media and mental health: Benefits, risks, and opportunities for research and practice. *Journal of Technology in Behavioral Science*, *5*(3), 245–257.

Patti, M., Adrian, M., & Ine, B. (2022). *Social media effects on adolescent mental health.*

Twenge, J. M., Martin, G. N., & Campbell, W. K. (2018a). Decreases in psychological well-being among American adolescents after 2012 and links to screen time during the rise of smartphone technology. *Emotion*, *18*(6), 765–780.

Twenge, J. M., Martin, G. N., & Campbell, W. K. (2018b). The association between screen time and mental health: A meta-analysis. *Psychological Science*, *29*(2), 180–190.

World Health Organization. (2021). *Mental health: Strengthening our response.* https://www.who.int (Accessed on December 18, 2024)

Chapter 21

Educational Values in the Age of Social Media: A Case Study of Instagram

Maznah Khalifa Aldhahrani

Ahlia University, Bahrain

Abstract

Educational values play a pivotal role in shaping individual personalities and fostering societal cohesion. In the digital era, social media platforms, particularly Instagram, have emerged as influential spaces for communication and cultural exchange. This study examines the impact of Instagram on educational values, exploring its potential to both promote and challenge these values. The research begins by defining educational values and their types, such as social, ethical, and cultural values, and discusses their role in personal development. It further delves into the transformative influence of social media on the perceptions and attitudes of youth. Instagram's unique features, including visual content and the celebrity culture it fosters, are analyzed to assess their contribution to disseminating educational values. Case studies of influencers and hashtags promoting positive values, such as empathy and social awareness, are highlighted. However, challenges such as social pressures, jealousy, and negative content are also critically evaluated. Finally, the study emphasizes the role of families and schools in guiding young users toward positive engagement with Instagram to enhance their understanding and appreciation of educational values. The findings underscore the ongoing relevance of educational values amidst the dynamic landscape of social media.

Keywords: Educational values; social media; Instagram; youth; personal development; digital culture

Digital Dialogues, 201–211

Published under exclusive licence by Emerald Publishing Limited
doi:10.1108/978-1-83708-686-320261021

Introduction

In today's digital era, social media platforms have profoundly reshaped human communication and worldview (Thompson, 2020). Among them, Instagram has emerged as a dominant force—particularly among youth—due to its emphasis on visual content, interactive features, and storytelling capabilities (Zillich & Riesmeyer, 2021). Though it began as a photo-sharing app, Instagram has evolved into a dynamic space for personal branding, social interaction, and even advocacy for various causes (Leone & Della Mura, 2020). As it becomes increasingly woven into daily life, its influence on individual and societal values has grown significantly (Caldeira et al., 2020). Educational values—such as empathy, respect, social responsibility, and ethical behavior—have traditionally been instilled by families, schools, and cultural institutions. However, these values are now being shaped, challenged, and reinterpreted within the digital landscape, where platforms like Instagram play a complex dual role (Paul-Mgbeafulike, 2023; Zillich & Riesmeyer, 2021). On the positive side, Instagram enables users to promote and engage with meaningful content through visual storytelling, awareness campaigns, and online communities that reinforce constructive values (Caldeira et al., 2020). Yet, it also presents risks—such as the spread of harmful content, the rise of unhealthy social comparisons, and heightened societal pressures—that may undermine those very values (Thompson, 2020). This research explores the intersection of Instagram and educational values, investigating how the platform shapes user perceptions, attitudes, and behaviors. It highlights the platform's potential to both support and challenge value formation and underscores the need for a balanced digital approach. Ultimately, the study offers insights valuable to educators, parents, and policymakers seeking to foster ethical awareness and social responsibility in an increasingly connected digital world.

Defining Educational Values

Educational values are the foundational principles that shape the way individuals think, behave, and interact with their environment (Davis & Yi, 2022). These values guide moral judgments, influence decision-making, and foster the development of personal and social identity. They encompass a broad spectrum of aspects, including ethical, social, cultural, and intellectual dimensions, and play a crucial role in nurturing responsible and well-rounded individuals (Francisco et al., 2020).

Educational values can be categorized into various types (Caldeira et al., 2020):

- *Social Values:* Principles that encourage collaboration, respect for diversity, and empathy.
- *Ethical Values:* Standards of right and wrong that guide moral behavior, such as honesty, fairness, and integrity.
- *Cultural Values:* Beliefs and practices that preserve heritage and promote a sense of belonging within a community.

In the digital age, educational values are increasingly shaped by the evolution of communication technologies. Instagram, with its visual-centric and interactive environment, represents a prominent space where such values can be both cultivated and contested (Simanjuntak, 2020). These values—integral to personal development, social unity, and continuous learning—provide individuals with the ethical grounding needed to thrive in today's complex world (Paul-Mgbeafulike, 2023). When effectively promoted, they foster a sense of responsibility and awareness, equipping users with the resilience and adaptability essential for navigating an interconnected, fast-paced digital landscape (Leone & Della Mura, 2020).

Social Media and Its Impact on Educational Values

The rapid spread of social media platforms has fundamentally altered how individuals engage with the world around them, particularly shaping the behaviors, attitudes, and value systems of younger generations (Dwivedi et al., 2021). Instagram, as one of the most widely used platforms, facilitates global connections and idea exchange, making it a powerful force not just for communication but also for value formation (Purnama & Asdlori, 2023; Yang et al., 2021).

- *Positive Impacts:* Social media platforms—Instagram in particular—have emerged as valuable tools for promoting educational values. They expose users to a wide range of perspectives and educational content, encouraging engagement in community-based initiatives and social causes (Davis & Yi, 2022). Campaigns focusing on empathy, mental health, and environmental responsibility gain traction on Instagram, enabling users to interact with content that supports personal growth and ethical development (Vautier, 2021). Influencers and educators contribute significantly by sharing motivational messages and fostering spaces for dialogue, collaboration, and learning (Carpenter et al., 2023).
- *Negative impacts:* However, the same platforms can challenge traditional value systems. Instagram's emphasis on curated content and idealized imagery often fuels social comparison, leading to reduced self-esteem and increased materialism (Barrutia et al., 2022). Furthermore, the platform's openness to misinformation and biased narratives can distort ethical frameworks and cultural understanding, particularly for young or impressionable users (Francisco et al., 2020). These risks underscore the platform's dual nature in value transmission.
- *Shifting Value Systems:* Prolonged engagement with digital content tends to reshape both individual and collective value systems (Purnama & Asdlori, 2023). While some users adopt more inclusive and socially conscious views, others may gravitate toward fleeting trends and superficial norms. The way users interpret and interact with content becomes pivotal; the platform's impact depends less on the content itself and more on the depth of user engagement and critical reflection (Leone & Della Mura, 2020).

This dual influence highlights the urgent need for fostering digital literacy and encouraging critical interaction with social media (Thompson, 2020). Understanding Instagram's complex role in shaping educational values provides a necessary foundation for developing strategies that amplify its positive potential while mitigating its negative effects.

Instagram as an Interactive Platform

Instagram has become a leading social media platform, especially among younger generations, thanks to its focus on visual storytelling and interactivity (Arda, 2021; Leone & Della Mura, 2020). Unlike platforms such as Facebook or Twitter, Instagram emphasizes high-quality images and videos, offering creative tools that boost user engagement and content appeal (Rogers, 2021). Interactive features—like likes, comments, polls, and live streaming—deepen user involvement, while hashtags and algorithms help users discover content aligned with their interests, often allowing trends and values to spread widely (Dwivedi et al., 2021). This visual-driven space has been harnessed by influencers, educators, and organizations to promote key social values such as inclusivity, mental health awareness, and environmental responsibility (Barrutia et al., 2022; Bush & Lindsey, 2024; Griffith et al., 2021). Hashtags like #MentalHealthAwareness and #DiversityInclusion amplify these efforts, creating virtual communities around shared ideals (Arda, 2021). Nevertheless, Instagram is not without its drawbacks. Its emphasis on curated aesthetics and follower metrics can lead to superficial engagement and materialistic values (Caldeira et al., 2020). The idealized representations on user profiles may also contribute to distorted views of success and well-being (Davis & Yi, 2022). Ultimately, Instagram serves as a powerful but double-edged tool in the communication of educational and ethical values, with its influence shaped by the ways users interact with and interpret its content (Griffith et al., 2021).

Educational Values Promoted Through Instagram

Instagram serves as a powerful medium for promoting educational values by utilizing its visual appeal, interactivity, and wide reach to encourage positive attitudes and behaviors (Bush & Lindsey, 2024). Below are the key ways in which the platform contributes to spreading these values:

- *Influencers and Thought Leaders:* Many Instagram influencers use their platforms to spotlight essential ethical and social issues such as mental health, environmental responsibility, and civic engagement. For instance, mental health advocates share strategies for emotional well-being and personal stories to foster empathy and normalize self-care. Environmental activists similarly use Instagram to promote sustainable lifestyles, offering practical tips and motivating followers to adopt eco-conscious habits. By connecting with audiences through relatable and authentic content, influencers play a key role in shaping ethical behaviors and awareness (Arda, 2021).

- *Hashtags and Campaigns:* Hashtags like #MentalHealthAwareness, #SocialJustice, and #EcoFriendlyLiving help amplify critical messages across the platform. These digital tags link users to shared causes, sparking community-driven discussions and expanding access to educational content. Campaigns organized around these hashtags not only drive participation and advocacy but also nurture a sense of collective identity rooted in empathy and responsibility (Griffith et al., 2021).
- *Visual Storytelling:* Instagram's visual-first approach—through infographics, short-form videos, and aesthetically engaging posts—makes complex topics easier to understand and more engaging to consume. This method helps organizations and educators deliver important lessons in a way that's memorable and accessible. Whether it's a carousel post on climate change or a reel about inclusivity, visual storytelling encourages active learning while capturing users' attention effectively (Lim & Childs, 2020).
- *Grassroots Movements*: Beyond celebrities and large organizations, smaller creators and local initiatives use Instagram to champion social causes, celebrate diversity, and promote inclusion. These grassroots efforts bring visibility to niche or marginalized issues, helping users connect with global challenges from a local perspective. The authenticity of such campaigns fosters a sense of global citizenship and empowers users to take action within their communities (Rogers, 2021).
- *Youth Engagement:* Instagram's ability to tailor content to resonate with younger demographics makes it a vital tool for instilling values like collaboration, respect, and responsibility. Interactive features such as polls, quizzes, and challenges engage young users creatively, helping them learn and practice positive behaviors in ways that feel both fun and meaningful (Francisco et al., 2020).

Through these mechanisms, Instagram fosters an environment where educational values can thrive, offering a platform for learning, sharing, and inspiring positive change.

Challenges to Educational Values on Instagram

While Instagram holds great promise for promoting educational values, it also presents a range of challenges that may hinder its development and sustainability (Caldeira et al., 2020; Purnama & Asdlori, 2023). These challenges are deeply rooted in the platform's structure, content culture, and user behaviors:

- *Social Pressure and Unrealistic Standards:* The platform's emphasis on curated perfection often sets unattainable benchmarks for beauty, success, and lifestyle. This fosters a culture of comparison and self-doubt, particularly among younger users, undermining core values like self-acceptance, authenticity, and emotional well-being (Verrastro et al., 2020).

- *Negative Content and Misinformation:* Despite the abundance of inspiring content, Instagram remains a space where harmful, misleading, or sensational material spreads easily. Such content can distort ethical perceptions and weaken users' ability to discern credible educational information (Leone & Della Mura, 2020).
- *Addictive Usage Patterns:* Instagram's endless scroll, notifications, and algorithm-driven content are designed to maximize screen time. These patterns often lead to digital overconsumption, detracting from offline educational engagement and weakening values like discipline, focus, and intellectual curiosity (Davis & Yi, 2022).
- *Superficial Interactions:* With its focus on likes, shares, and follower counts, Instagram often promotes quick and shallow exchanges. This undermines deeper values such as empathy, critical dialogue, and collaborative learning, replacing them with validation-seeking behaviors (Thompson, 2020).
- *Cultural Homogenization:* The global nature of Instagram can erode local cultures and educational traditions, as users adopt dominant trends and aesthetics. Influencer marketing further promotes consumerism and external validation, potentially overshadowing intrinsic values like knowledge-seeking, social responsibility, and community involvement (Balogun & Aruoture, 2024).
- *Privacy Concerns and Exposure to Harmful Communities:* Instagram's open and interconnected design exposes users—especially the youth—to harmful communities, inappropriate content, and privacy risks. These exposures can weaken ethical awareness and challenge the safeguarding of users' well-being in a digital environment (Bush & Lindsey, 2024).

Addressing Challenges to Educational Values on Instagram

To ensure that Instagram supports rather than undermines educational values, a comprehensive strategy involving individuals, institutions, platform developers, and policymakers is essential (Thompson, 2020). The following key approaches outline how these challenges can be effectively addressed:

- *Promoting Digital Well-Being:* Encouraging users to adopt healthier online habits—such as limiting screen time and balancing digital with real-life activities—can reduce the negative psychological effects of overuse. Awareness campaigns can help highlight the importance of mindful engagement, especially for younger audiences (Stankov & Gretzel, 2021).
- *Encouraging Critical Media Literacy:* Incorporating media literacy into educational curriculums equips students with the tools to evaluate content critically, detect misinformation, and assess the values being conveyed through social media. This fosters informed and responsible digital behavior (Balogun & Aruoture, 2024).

- *Content Moderation and Platform Accountability:* Instagram must take active steps to regulate harmful content and promote positive value-based content through improved moderation and algorithmic adjustments. Giving users greater control over their feeds can also help shape healthier digital experiences (Purnama & Asdlori, 2023).
- *Empowering Influencers as Role Models:* Influencers should be encouraged to share content that reflects ethical and educational values. Partnerships between influencers and educational organizations can further amplify positive messages and promote responsible online behavior (Caldeira et al., 2020).
- *Fostering Inclusive Online Communities:* Creating spaces on Instagram that celebrate diversity and facilitate respectful dialogue can reinforce values such as empathy, cooperation, and mutual respect. These communities can serve as hubs for meaningful interaction and collective learning (Francisco et al., 2020).
- *Policy Interventions:* Regulatory bodies can support digital well-being by introducing guidelines that promote ethical content and responsible platform use. Policies that focus on digital literacy and mental health can also help mitigate the platform's negative effects (Lim & Childs, 2020).
- *Strengthening Parental Involvement:* Parents play a vital role in guiding their children's social media use. Providing resources and tools for monitoring and engaging in open discussions can help young users navigate Instagram in ways that reinforce positive values (Rogers, 2021).
- *Encouraging Ethical Content Creation:* Users, particularly young creators, should be educated on the ethical implications of the content they share. Workshops and initiatives aimed at teaching responsible content creation can empower users to contribute positively to the digital space, promoting values such as honesty, respect, and social awareness (Kumar et al., 2023).
- *Leveraging Educational Content:* Collaborations between Instagram and educational institutions can lead to the creation of more educational campaigns and features. For example, curated educational accounts, interactive quizzes, and value-driven challenges can engage users while reinforcing core educational principles (Wellman et al., 2020).
- *Promoting Community-Based Initiatives:* Grassroots organizations and local communities can use Instagram to address societal challenges and foster collective action. Initiatives that focus on community service, cultural preservation, and social cohesion can help counteract the platform's potential to promote superficiality and individualism (McNamara et al., 2020).

The Role of Families and Schools in Guiding Instagram Use

To mitigate the challenges associated with Instagram and to harness its potential in promoting educational values, families and schools play a crucial role in shaping how young individuals engage with the platform (Plachynda et al., 2024). This section highlights the responsibilities and strategies that these key stakeholders can adopt to ensure that Instagram use aligns with the reinforcement of positive values.

- *Parental Guidance and Monitoring:* Families can foster constructive Instagram use by actively engaging with their children's online activities. This includes setting boundaries for screen time, discussing the content they consume, and encouraging critical thinking about the values conveyed through the platform. Parents can also model positive online behavior by demonstrating ethical and respectful interactions on social media (Ranzini et al., 2020).
- *Educating on Digital Literacy:* Schools have a significant role in equipping students with the skills needed to navigate Instagram responsibly. Digital literacy programs should focus on teaching students how to critically evaluate content, recognize misinformation, and understand the impact of their digital footprint. These programs can help students develop a balanced perspective on the values promoted on Instagram (Aydin & Erol, 2021).
- *Promoting Value-Based Content Creation:* Both families and schools can encourage young individuals to actively participate in value-based content creation on Instagram. By sharing meaningful stories, promoting social causes, or engaging in community-driven initiatives, students can use the platform as a tool for positive change (Krowinska et al., 2023).
- *Collaboration Between Schools and Families:* A collaborative approach between families and schools is essential for reinforcing educational values. Joint workshops, seminars, and awareness campaigns can help create a consistent message about the importance of responsible Instagram use and the values it should uphold (Zaini, 2023).
- *Encouraging Offline Activities:* To balance the influence of Instagram, families and schools should promote offline activities that strengthen educational values, such as volunteering, participating in cultural events, and engaging in team-based projects. These experiences provide practical applications of values like empathy, teamwork, and respect (Plachynda et al., 2024).

Conclusion

This study has explored the multifaceted relationship between Instagram and educational values, revealing the platform's dual capacity to both reinforce and challenge these values in the digital age. Educational values—such as empathy, ethical responsibility, and social awareness—are increasingly expressed and shaped through platforms like Instagram, which, with its visual and interactive features, acts as a powerful yet ambivalent tool. On the one hand, Instagram facilitates value dissemination through influencers, campaigns, and community-driven hashtags, fostering positive behaviors and global awareness. On the other, it poses significant risks, including the spread of misinformation, the promotion of superficial standards, and the erosion of cultural diversity through homogenized digital trends. The study also emphasized the crucial role of traditional institutions—especially families and educational systems—in equipping young users with the skills to critically navigate the digital landscape. Through media literacy, ethical guidance, and value-centered dialogue, these stakeholders can help users engage with Instagram in ways that promote personal development and societal cohesion. Ultimately, the impact of Instagram on educational values is not fixed but depends heavily on how the platform is approached and utilized. As social media continues to shape human interaction and learning, collective responsibility among individuals, educators, and policymakers becomes vital. Only through intentional, informed, and value-conscious use can Instagram become a sustainable space for nurturing the principles that underpin meaningful education and ethical citizenship in the digital era.

References

Arda, B. (2021). Ephemeral social media visuals and their picturesque design: Interaction and user experience in Instagram stories. *Acta Universitatis Sapientiae, Film and Media Studies*, (19), 156–175.

Aydin, E., & Erol, S. (2021). The views of Turkish language teachers on distance education and digital literacy during Covid-19 pandemic. *International Journal of Education and Literacy Studies*, *9*(1), 60–71.

Balogun, S. K., & Aruoture, E. (2024). Cultural homogenization vs. cultural diversity: Social media's double-edged sword in the age of globalization. *African Journal of Social and Behavioural Sciences*, *14*(4).

Barrutia, L., Vega-Gutiérrez, J., & Santamarina-Albertos, A. (2022). Benefits, drawbacks, and challenges of social media use in dermatology: A systematic review. *Journal of Dermatological Treatment*, *33*(6), 2738–2757.

Bush, L., & Lindsey, K. (2024). *Diversity, equity, and inclusion in strategic communications: Becoming culturally proficient communicators*. Taylor & Francis.

Caldeira, S. P., De Ridder, S., & Van Bauwel, S. (2020). Between the mundane and the political: Women's self-representations on Instagram. *Social Media + Society*, *6*(3). https://doi.org/10.1177/2056305120940802

Carpenter, J. P., Shelton, C. C., & Schroeder, S. E. (2023). The education influencer: A new player in the educator professional landscape. *Journal of Research on Technology in Education*, *55*(5), 749–764.

Davis, S., & Yi, J. (2022). Double tap, double trouble: Instagram, teachers, and profit. *E-Learning and Digital Media*, *19*(3), 320–339.

Dwivedi, Y. K., Ismagilova, E., Hughes, D. L., Carlson, J., Filieri, R., Jacobson, J., Jain, V., Karjaluoto, H., Kefi, H., Krishen, A. S., Kumar, V., Rahman, M. M., Raman, R., Rauschnabel, P. A., Rowley, J., Salo, J., Tran, G. A., & Wang, Y. (2021). Setting the future of digital and social media marketing research: Perspectives and research propositions. *International Journal of Information Management*, *59*, 102168.

Francisco, M. P. B., Hartman, M., & Wang, Y. (2020). Inclusion and special education. *Education Sciences*, *10*(9), 238.

Griffith, F. J., Stein, C. H., Hoag, J. E., & Gay, K. N. (2021). #MentalHealthArt: How Instagram artists promote mental health awareness online. *Public Health*, *194*, 67–74.

Krowinska, A., Backhaus, C., Becker, B., & Bosser, F. (2023). *Digital content marketing: Creating value in practice*. Taylor & Francis.

Kumar, D., Haque, A., Mishra, K., Islam, F., Mishra, B. K., & Ahmad, S. (2023). Exploring the transformative role of artificial intelligence and metaverse in education: A comprehensive review. *Metaverse Basic and Applied Research*, *2*, 55.

Leone, S., & Della Mura, M. (2020). Institutional flows of communication for young people on Instagram and the use of visual images. *Partecipazione e conflitto*, *13*(2), 1085–1109.

Lim, H., & Childs, M. (2020). Visual storytelling on Instagram: Branded photo narrative and the role of telepresence. *Journal of Research in Interactive Marketing*, *14*(1), 33–50.

McNamara, K. E., Clissold, R., Westoby, R., Piggott-McKellar, A. E., Kumar, R., Clarke, T., Namoumou, F., Areki, F., Joseph, E., Warrick, O., & Nunn, P. D. (2020). An assessment of community-based adaptation initiatives in the Pacific Islands. *Nature Climate Change*, *10*(7), 628–639.

Paul-Mgbeafulike, V. S. (2023). Discovering the educational foundations of basic values in society: The pillars of social acceptability. *Nnadiebube Journal of Education in Africa*, *8*(2).

Plachynda, T., Doviga, T., Zavitrenko, D., Snisarenko, I., & Pavlenko, O. (2024). The power of social media: Shaping and reshaping student image. *Diversitas Journal*, *9*(3).

Purnama, Y., & Asdlori, A. (2023). The role of social media in students' social perception and interaction: Implications for learning and education. *Technology and Society Perspectives*, *1*(2), 45–55.

Ranzini, G., Newlands, G., & Lutz, C. (2020). Sharenting, peer influence, and privacy concerns: A study on the Instagram-sharing behaviors of parents in the United Kingdom. *Social Media + Society*, *6*(4). https://doi.org/10.1177/2056305120978376

Rogers, R. (2021). Visual media analysis for Instagram and other online platforms. *Big Data & Society*, *8*(1). https://doi.org/10.1177/20539517211022370

Simanjuntak, M. B. (2020). The educational values of the main character in beautiful mind film. *Journal of Advanced English Studies*, *3*(1), 1–6.

Stankov, U., & Gretzel, U. (2021). Digital well-being in the tourism domain: Mapping new roles and responsibilities. *Information Technology & Tourism*, *23*(1), 5–17.

Thompson, J. B. (2020). Mediated interaction in the digital age. *Theory, Culture & Society*, *37*(1), 3–28.

Vautier, M. (2021). *Doing it for the 'Gram: How Instagram affects values, and what it means for mental and ecological wellbeing*. Doctoral dissertation. Open Access Te Herenga Waka-Victoria University of Wellington.

Verrastro, V., Liga, F., Cuzzocrea, F., & Gugliandolo, M. C. (2020). Fear the Instagram: Beauty stereotypes, body image and Instagram use in a sample of male and female adolescents. *QWERTY-Interdisciplinary Journal of Technology, Culture and Education*, *15*(1), 31–49.

Wellman, M. L., Stoldt, R., Tully, M., & Ekdale, B. (2020). Ethics of authenticity: Social media influencers and the production of sponsored content. *Journal of Media Ethics*, *35*(2), 68–82.

Yang, C. C., Holden, S. M., & Ariati, J. (2021). Social media and psychological well-being among youth: The multidimensional model of social media use. *Clinical Child and Family Psychology Review*, *24*(3), 631–650.

Zaini, A. W. (2023). Social media optimization in school image transformation: Instagram interactive strategies in schools. *Journal of Social Studies and Education*, *1*(1), 01–12.

Zillich, A. F., & Riesmeyer, C. (2021). Be yourself: The relative importance of personal and social norms for adolescents' self-presentation on Instagram. *Social Media + Society*, *7*(3). https://doi.org/10.1177/20563051211033810

Chapter 22

The Impact of Social Media Platforms on Shaping Cultural Identity and Political Awareness in Arab Societies: An Analytical Field Study

Mohamed Naser Louri

Ahlia University, Bahrain

Abstract

This study investigates the transformative impact of social media platforms on shaping cultural identity and political awareness in Arab societies. These platforms have become essential for public engagement and cultural expression. The research highlights both the opportunities and challenges of digital globalization, including misinformation and polarization. Through a review of prior studies and a combination of qualitative and quantitative approaches, the study outlines how social media reshapes cultural and political identities. It offers recommendations for policymakers and civil society to strengthen cultural preservation and political participation in the digital era.

Keywords: Social media; cultural identity; political awareness; Arab societies; field study

Introduction

In recent years, the Arab world has witnessed profound transformations across various spheres, particularly in cultural and political domains. Scholars attribute these changes, in part, to the technological boom and the emergence of social media platforms, which have played a pivotal role in reshaping these dynamics. These digital platforms, born within virtual realms, have become essential tools for opinion expression and participation in public discourse. Consequently, they

Digital Dialogues, 213–221

doi:10.1108/978-1-83708-686-320261022

have contributed to the emergence of new cultural patterns that have redefined the political awareness of the Arab citizen.

The researcher aims, through this study, to analyze the role that social media platforms play in shaping the cultural identity and political awareness of the Arab citizen. The focus will be on how these platforms are utilized as tools for social, political, and cultural interaction. This study will explore the mechanisms through which cultural and political values and meanings are interactively constructed among users and how these processes contribute to the reshaping of cultural and political identities in the era of digital globalization. Furthermore, the study will highlight the challenges facing Arab cultural identity amidst this digital transformation and examine how social media can serve either as a platform for fostering cultural and political dialogue or as a tool for cultural fragmentation.

By employing Cultural Construction Theory and Public Sphere Theory as the primary theoretical frameworks, this study seeks to provide a deeper understanding of the relationship between social media platforms and the formation of cultural and political identities in the Arab world. The researcher aims to offer scientifically grounded practical recommendations for policymakers and civil society organizations on how to leverage these platforms to enhance political participation and preserve cultural identity. Additionally, this study will present an analytical model to comprehend how cultural and political identities are being reshaped through social media. This model is intended to contribute to fostering political and cultural dialogue within Arab societies on social media platforms and in virtual realms.

Literature Review

First Theme: Social Media and Political Engagement

- The study by Barghouth (2024), titled "Social Media Networks and the Dissemination of Popular Movement Culture in Algeria," aimed to analyze the role of social media platforms in spreading the culture of popular movements in Algeria. The research focused on how these platforms serve as tools for political mobilization and engagement during popular movements and public issues. Grounded in Public Sphere Theory, the study examined the role of virtual spaces in promoting political and social awareness. A descriptive methodology was utilized, incorporating surveys and interviews to collect data from 230 social media users who actively participated in discussions about popular movements. The findings revealed that social media platforms, especially Facebook, played a pivotal role in disseminating the culture of popular movements and unifying efforts among participants. Furthermore, these platforms significantly contributed to enhancing political awareness among users.
- The study by Faleh (2024) explored the impact of social media networks in enhancing political awareness among Iraqi university students, focusing on

how these platforms encourage student participation in political activities. The research conducted a field study on a sample of students from Wasit University, employing a purposive sampling survey methodology. Questionnaires were used to collect data, which revealed several key findings. The results highlighted that social media plays an effective role in shaping students' political attitudes and motivating their participation. This includes following political activists' pages and participating in demonstrations and marches as forms of independent engagement. Moreover, the study demonstrated that these platforms increase students' awareness of political issues related to the Iraqi political system, local governmental policies, and global issues.

- The study by Ayad (2024) examined the role of social media influencers in shaping and directing global public opinion regarding the Gaza conflict, emphasizing the significance of digital media in conveying an accurate depiction of events on the ground. The researcher highlighted the efforts of activists and social media influencers in countering Israeli propaganda narratives by utilizing platforms such as Facebook, Twitter, and Instagram to disseminate facts and document violations. Using a descriptive-analytical methodology, the study analyzed audience engagement with digital content, revealing that social media has become a powerful tool for shaping public opinion and rallying international support for the Palestinian cause. However, influencers faced challenges such as content censorship and account restrictions due to the pro-Palestinian nature of their posts, underscoring the importance of strengthening digital advocacy as a potent tool for media resistance.
- The study by Tan (2024) examined the relationship between the use of social media for obtaining political information and its impact on political participation among the internet generation in Malaysia. The researcher applied Political Efficacy Theory to understand the role of social media in empowering youth to acquire political knowledge. The study involved a sample of 379 students aged 18–24 years. The findings revealed a positive correlation between the use of social media to enhance political information and increased political efficacy. This, in turn, was associated with higher levels of political participation both online and offline.
- The study by Wani et al. (2024) explored the profound impact of social media on society, focusing on social behavior, politics, and cultural norms. The research team employed a systematic literature review methodology, analyzing 32 studies and incorporating case studies and real-world examples. The findings highlighted how social media has transformed patterns of communication and human behavior, playing a significant role in shaping cultural and political values within communities. This study underscored the pervasive influence of social media in redefining societal norms and fostering new dynamics in cultural and political engagement.
- The study by *Zbouji (2023)*, titled "Social Media Networks and E-Democracy," analyzed the role of social media platforms as virtual public spaces that enhance political participation and electronic democracy. The research was grounded in Public Sphere Theory to understand how these networks have evolved into

platforms for political and social dialogue and assessed their capacity to foster democratic discourse among citizens. The study employed a descriptive-analytical survey methodology, collecting data through questionnaires and analyzing communicative content on social platforms. The sample consisted of active social media users in Algeria, with a focus on their participation in political discussions. The findings revealed that social media has become a new public sphere that facilitates increased political participation and social debates. This transformation has enabled greater user engagement in public issues compared to traditional media platforms.

- The study by Siyal and Brohi (2023) examined the impact of social media on political awareness among university students in Sindh Province, Pakistan. The researchers employed Social Communication Theory to explore how political discussions on social networks influence students' political knowledge and awareness. Using a descriptive-analytical methodology, the study conducted surveys with a sample of 977 students from the five major universities in Sindh. The findings highlighted that political discussions on social media significantly contribute to enhancing students' political understanding. However, the study noted that the negative use of social media only minimally improves political awareness. Additionally, it was found that personal factors, such as age, gender, and economic status, play a significant role in shaping students' political awareness.
- The study by Adedeji and Nwaoboli (2023) explored the impact of social media on political participation among Nigerian youth, with a specific focus on online election campaigns. The research was grounded in Agenda-Setting Theory, which provided a framework for understanding the role of social media in shaping public discourse among young people and enhancing their political engagement. The study employed a survey methodology, using a sample of 400 young participants from Benin City, the administrative capital of Edo State. The findings underscored the significant influence of social media in driving political discussions and fostering greater involvement in political activities among the youth.

Second Theme: Social Media and Cultural Identity

(1) The study by Tajine and Saleh (2024) examined the role of social media platforms in promoting cultural heritage, focusing on the Facebook page "Algeria: History and Culture" as a case study. The researchers adopted a descriptive methodology to analyze the page's content and its impact on raising awareness of Algerian cultural heritage, including both tangible aspects, such as historical sites, and intangible elements, such as traditional practices and arts. The findings concluded that social media platforms, particularly Facebook, serve as effective tools for introducing a broad audience to cultural heritage. This approach enhances public understanding and fosters a stronger connection to heritage, especially among younger generations. The study recommended increasing engagement on the page

and featuring more content related to intangible heritage, such as customs and traditions that require widespread documentation to preserve and share this legacy with both future generations and a global audience.

(2) The study by *Blaydi (2023)* aimed to explore the impact of Algerian youth's orientation toward social media usage on their cultural identity, particularly in the context of widespread globalization and the diverse digital content these platforms offer. The research highlighted that social media provides alluring options and representations reflective of Western civilization, which, in some cases, encourages youth to consider emigration, posing significant challenges to Algerian cultural identity. This reality has opened avenues for Algerian youth to confront challenges in preserving their cultural identity amidst the influences and temptations presented by these platforms. The findings indicated that social media had a predominantly negative impact on the cultural identity of Algerian youth. However, a segment of the youth remains committed to their cultural values, resisting external influences.

(3) The study conducted by *Al-Kou' et al. (2023)* analyzed the role of Palestinian activists' personal social media pages, particularly that of activist Mona al-Kurd, in resisting displacement and Judaization efforts in the Sheikh Jarrah neighborhood. The researchers employed a descriptive-analytical approach using thematic analysis tools. The study sample included 194 posts published between March and November 2021 on platforms such as Facebook, Instagram, and Twitter. The findings revealed that al-Kurd relied heavily on Facebook (41.2%) to raise awareness about the Sheikh Jarrah case. Her content focused predominantly on calls for solidarity and supporting the resilience of the neighborhood's residents. The study highlighted how activists strategically use different social media platforms to tailor messages for each platform's audience. The study recommended increasing the use of multimedia tools, such as videos and infographics, to enhance awareness of Palestinian issues.

(4) The study by *Ibrahim (2023)* explored the impact of social media in promoting peaceful coexistence among individuals and communities, focusing on the role these platforms play in bridging intellectual and social gaps between different groups. The researcher employed a descriptive-analytical methodology to examine how social media platforms are utilized to disseminate values of coexistence and mutual respect. The findings highlighted that social media effectively contributes to reducing intolerance and fostering social harmony by sharing information and values that promote mutual understanding among diverse communities. The study also emphasized the importance of these platforms in raising awareness about issues of coexistence and social peace. It recommended adopting clear strategies to enhance the positive use of social media for fostering harmony and understanding.

(5) The study by Wu (2023) examined the impact of social media on shaping cultural and political attitudes in contemporary society. The researcher utilized various theories from sociology and cultural studies, alongside

Media Ecology Theory, to understand how social media structures influence public opinion and political culture. The study explained how the architecture of social media platforms shapes cultural and political narratives, altering the way individuals perceive the world around them. By analyzing the interplay between media environments and societal dynamics, the study shed light on social media's role in transforming public discourse and cultural awareness.

(6) The study by Mnemani and Bouragaa (2021), titled "The Impact of Language Used on Social Media Platforms on Shaping Public Opinion," focused on analyzing the influence of language employed on social media, particularly Facebook, in shaping public opinion among users. The researchers applied Uses and Gratifications Theory to understand how language serves as a tool for social communication and its role in shaping and directing public opinion on these platforms. Using a descriptive methodology, the study collected data through questionnaires distributed to 200 university students. The findings revealed several key points, most notably that the random use of colloquial language and symbols on social media has led to a form of linguistic pollution. This, in turn, negatively impacted users' ability to communicate effectively and unify their opinions coherently.

Third Theme: Social Media, Misinformation, and Crisis Management

- The study by Al-Bakri (2024), titled "Hashtags and Crisis Management on Social Media," aimed to explore how hashtags are utilized for crisis management on social media platforms, particularly on the application formerly known as Twitter (now X). The study was based on several media theories, including Media Dependency Theory and Uses and Gratifications Theory, which provided a framework for understanding how users employ hashtags during crises and the impact on their cognitive and emotional behaviors. A quantitative descriptive survey method was employed, incorporating advanced content analysis tools such as Twitter Binder to identify usage patterns. The sample included active Twitter users engaged during crises, and surveys were conducted with a selected group of participants. The findings revealed that most interactions with hashtag content involved retweeting, indicating that users rely on this function as a simple means to engage with events, expand discussions, and support the opinions they adopt or favor. Additionally, the analysis showed statistically significant differences based on gender and levels of technical expertise in how users are influenced by hashtags during crises.
- The study by Bouslimani (2023), titled "The Impact of Political Rumors on Social Media Users," analyzed the effects of political rumors spread via social media, particularly Facebook, on students at Tebessa University. The study was grounded in Media Dependency Theory, examining how users rely on social media as a primary source for political information and the impact of rumors on their emotions and behaviors. A descriptive methodology was

employed, utilizing questionnaires distributed to a sample of 386 university students. The findings revealed that political rumors significantly influence the emotions of social media users, increasing their anxiety levels and diminishing trust in political authorities. Additionally, the study highlighted that such rumors exacerbate political tension and discord within society.

Fourth Theme: Discussion on Literature Review

- *Social Media as a Catalyst for Political Mobilization and Engagement:* The studies within this section collectively underscore the transformative role of social media in fostering political engagement and awareness across different contexts. *Barghouth (2024)* and Faleh (2024) illustrate the utility of social media in mobilizing political movements and encouraging civic participation, particularly in Algeria and Iraq, respectively. Both studies align with Public Sphere Theory, highlighting virtual platforms as spaces for political discourse. While Barghouth emphasizes unifying efforts during popular movements, Faleh focuses on youth engagement in political activities and awareness of both local and global issues. Ayad (2024) expands on this by exploring the global impact of social media influencers in shaping opinions about the Gaza conflict. Ayad's findings parallel those of Barghouth and Faleh but emphasize the role of individual activists in amplifying narratives and overcoming challenges like censorship, a perspective absent from other studies. Similarly, Tan (2024) supports the link between social media use and political participation but through the lens of Political Efficacy Theory, demonstrating the role of platforms in empowering youth with political knowledge in Malaysia. Broader perspectives are offered by Wani et al. (2024) and *Dhiab (2021)*. Wani's systematic review situates social media within societal transformations, linking individual behavior to cultural and political shifts, while Dhiab highlights the risks of polarization and "opinion bubbles." The latter critiques social media for promoting superficial engagement and diminishing critical thinking, providing a counterpoint to studies celebrating its democratic potential. Finally, *Zbouji (2023)* and Siyal and Brohi (2023) reaffirm the importance of social media in enhancing democratic discourse and political awareness, though Siyal & Brohi uniquely emphasize personal factors like gender and socioeconomic status as mediators of this influence.
- *Dual Impact of Social Media on Cultural Preservation and Transformation:* Tajine and Saleh (2024) provide a positive outlook, showcasing how platforms like Facebook foster connections to cultural heritage, particularly among younger generations. However, this optimism is contrasted by *Blaydi (2023)*, who argues that globalization-driven content on social media often challenges traditional cultural identities, encouraging cultural erosion and even emigration among Algerian youth. The study by *Al-Kou' (2023)* offers a case-specific lens, focusing on Palestinian activists like Mona al-Kurd, who leverage social media to resist displacement. This aligns with Tajine and Saleh in emphasizing the role of platforms in preserving cultural and political

identities under threat. Similarly, *Ibrahim (2023)* broadens the scope by discussing social media's role in promoting coexistence, underscoring its potential to bridge cultural and intellectual divides. Wu (2023) provides a theoretical perspective through Media Ecology Theory, analyzing how social media architectures shape both cultural and political narratives. Meanwhile, Mnemani and Bouragaa (2021) critique the random use of colloquial language and symbols, highlighting linguistic fragmentation as a subtle but significant cultural shift facilitated by social media. Together, these studies reveal a nuanced understanding of social media's role as both a preserver and challenger of cultural identity.

- *Multifactorial Role of Social Media in Shaping Political, Cultural, and Crisis-Related Dynamics.* The interplay between political mobilization and cultural transformation is evident in studies like Ayad, Al-Kou', and Wu, which illustrate how political and cultural narratives converge on social media. Similarly, the overlap between cultural transformation and misinformation emerges in studies like Blaydi, which critique social media's role in undermining traditional values through misinformation and unfiltered content. Additionally, political mobilization and misinformation intersect in studies like Dhiab and Siyal & Brohi, which highlight the dangers of polarization and informational fragmentation in political discourse. These connections underscore the dual-edged nature of social media, offering opportunities for empowerment while posing risks to intellectual coherence and societal harmony.

Conclusion

In conclusion, based on this preliminary review of the literature related to the study's topic, it becomes evident that social media has emerged as one of the most influential tools in shaping cultural identity and enhancing political awareness in global societies. Through the theoretical and practical analyses conducted by numerous researchers, it is clear that these platforms are no longer merely channels for communication and entertainment. Instead, they have evolved into interactive spaces that reshape patterns of thought and societal values. Furthermore, these platforms have proven essential in opening new channels for political and cultural dialogue, fostering a dynamic environment for reconfiguring both individual and collective cultural identities. However, the realm of social media is not without its challenges. Issues such as the spread of misinformation, intellectual polarization, and the influence of algorithms in shaping public opinion are pervasive. This underscores the need to develop strategies to address these challenges effectively. By promoting digital literacy, supporting policies that encourage responsible use, and fostering the creation of content that enriches cultural identity and reinforces communal values, the role of social media can be further enhanced. Understanding the relationship between social media and cultural and political identities is not confined to current analysis. It demands continuous research to keep pace with the rapid transformations in this field. By integrating advanced scientific methodologies and fostering collaboration between academics and policymakers, it becomes possible to strike a balance between maximizing the benefits of social media and minimizing its negative impacts. This approach would contribute to building a digital society that promotes a culture of dialogue in the era of digital globalization.

References

المراجع العربية❖

البكري، خ. (2024). الهاشتاغ وإدارة الأزمات عبر مواقع التواصل الاجتماعي (دراسة تحليلية في المحتوى والأثر). رسالة دكتوراه، غير منشورة، جامعة باتنة.

بن, عياد، م (2024). تأثير مواقع التواصل الاجتماعي في بناء الرأي العام: دراسة تحليلية في توجيه القرارات المجتمعية والسياسية. المركز العربي للأبحاث ودراسة السياسات.

بوسليماني، و. (2023). تأثير الشائعات السياسية على مستخدمي مواقع التواصل الاجتماعي (دراسة ميدانية على عينة من الطلبة مستخدمي فايسبوك بجامعة تبسة). رسالة دكتوراه، غير منشورة، جامعة تبسة.

طجين، س.، و صالح، م. (2024). دور مواقع التواصل الاجتماعي في التعريف بالموروث الثقافي (صفحة الجزائر تاريخ وثقافة نموذجًا). مجلة البحوث في الاتصال الثقافي والاجتماعي، *8*(1), 120–105.

فالح، م. (2024). دور شبكات التواصل الاجتماعي في نشر الوعي السياسي لطلبة الجامعات العراقية وعلاقتها بتفعيل المشاركة السياسية. لُبابة، *16*(2), 324–304.

منماني، م.، و بورقعة،س. (2021). تأثير اللغة المستخدمة عبر مواقع التواصل الاجتماعي على تشكيل الرأي العام (دراسة ميدانية على عينة من مستخدمي الفيسبوك). جسور المعرفة، *7*(2), 394–370.

المراجع الإنجليزية❖

Adedeji, A., & Nwaoboli, E. (2023). The impact of social media on political participation amongst Nigerian youths. *International Journal of Multidisciplinary Approach & Studies*, *10*(1), 36–53.

Siyal, N. A., & Brohi, A. M. (2023). Social media and political awareness. *Benazir Research Journal of Humanities and Social Sciences*, *2*(1). https://brjhss.com/index.php/brjhss/article/view/42

Tan, J. J. (2024). Social media political information use and political participation of the Net generation. *Journal of Social Sciences & Humanities*, *21*(1). http://www.rjelal.com/4.2.16C/680-683%20POOJA%20HALYAL.pdf

Wani, Z., Bhat, A., vishnoi, V., Praveen, H., Simon, N., & Hephzibah, D. (2024). Impact of social media on society: A literature review. *Asian Journal of Education and Social Studies*, *50*(4), 320–328. https://doi.org/10.9734/ajess/2024/v50i41334

Wu, W. (2023). The role of social media in shaping cultural and political trends. *International Journal of Business Management and Visuals (IJBMV)*, *6*(1).

Chapter 23

Assessment of Value Systems in Digital Platform Dramas

Sakina Ahmed ALtawash

Ministry of Information, Bahrain

Abstract

Technology has transformed all aspects of modern life, redefining how media content is produced, distributed, and consumed. Television has undergone a significant evolution through digitization, leading to the emergence of paid drama platforms that revolutionize the entertainment industry. These platforms, such as *Shahid* (affiliated with MBC) and *Shasha* (a Kuwaiti-owned platform based in London), offer diverse and contemporary content accessible at any time and free from traditional television constraints such as advertisements, censorship, or fixed broadcast schedules.

Unlike conventional television, these digital platforms operate across smart devices, enabling personalized viewing experiences that transcend geographical and cultural boundaries. By showcasing a wide range of narratives and values, they embody the essence of globalization and contribute to shaping cultural exchange in the digital era. Furthermore, the flexible production models—adopted without restriction by episode length, themes, or audience demographics—have created vast opportunities for creative innovation, investment, and audience engagement.

This study examines the impact of these digital drama platforms on audiences and the values they transmit, focusing on how they influence cultural perception, social behavior, and entertainment consumption patterns in Arab societies. The findings highlight the growing role of digital platforms in redefining drama production, promoting new voices, and reflecting globalized cultural identities.

Keywords: Digital platforms; drama; values; society; audience engagement; media globalization; cultural transformation

Digital Dialogues, 223–231

doi:10.1108/978-1-83708-686-320261023

Introduction

Television was not exempted from this evolution and overlap. As digitization entered the world of television, drama, and movies, an invention overtook the field of drama and the entertainment industry, which is "**Drama Platforms**". Specifically, paid ones provide a diverse and modern group of works. What distinguishes them is that they do not contain advertisements, can be referred to and watched at any time, and are not subject to the same restrictions and censorship that television is—considering television is utilized as a traditional medium that reaches all age groups.

Some of these platforms belong to well-known TV channels, such as the "**Shahid**" platform affiliated with MBC channels, or independent Gulf media institutions, such as the "**Shasha**" platform of a Kuwaiti institution based in the British capital, London. Others, such as the global "**Netflix**", are famous as stand-alone digital platforms. What links all of these platforms is that the subscriber must provide his data, and the subscription is often paid. This is due to the benefits they offer, the feeling of exclusivity provided to the subscriber, or the ease of access via smart devices. As we discussed earlier, these platforms have gained global prominence, showcasing a wide range of ideas, stories, and values that embody the concept of globalization, effectively making the world feel like a small village through their works. They also do not adhere to the standards of television channels that a television producer must adhere to, such as the number of episodes and their content, or people's interests and the emergence of new characters through them. All of this created excellent investment opportunities for success, achieving fame, and the ability to present various ideas, even if some are unfamiliar or diverge from social norms. From this standpoint, it was necessary to study the impact of these dramatic works and the values they present and the extent of their success in achieving the same.

Review of Existing Literature under Two Categories

Literature Targeting Values

Values are of great importance in dramatic or works presented to the public. These values give the most important and supreme merit to those works. Based on what was stated in previous studies that dealt with values, the movement of the camera plays a role in designing the television image and its connotations—which serves the dramatic content—and is gradually reflected in the behavior and values of society and affects its culture, as stated in the study of Al-Sharif and others (2022).

To achieve the societal goal of conveying a specific message to the target audience, it is necessary to identify the value imbued in the media product according to the nature and characteristics of the target audience, which forms a positive mental image and thus affects the behavior of the target group, based on the study of Jamil (2023).

The Negative Message of Arab Media Compared to Foreign Content

Despite the importance and role of these works in promoting societal values, academic experts agree on the slowness of the essential role Arab media plays in supporting the values of Arab culture. Experts agreed on the schism of Arab media toward Arab issues, the weakness of information and the contradiction of media positions of Arab media, and its weakness in consolidating the values of awareness and enlightening the public, considering the spread of values and alien cultures. In turn, this constitutes a functional defect and an obvious deficiency in the role of the media and the tasks assigned to it, just as confirmed by the study of Abu Bakr (2022), and the study of Mohamed (2023).

The main goal of the programs presented by the channels under the study is entertainment and amusement, and the explicit style came at the forefront of the most used artistic styles in presenting social values to the child so that they can understand and absorb them and acquire many social, cognitive, emotional, and behavioral values and behaviors from them. While Al-Nimr's study (2024) confirmed that "electronic blackmail, bullying, crime and violence" were at the forefront of the issues presented by Arab dramas on digital platforms, suggesting a link between the increased intensity of Egyptian university students' viewing of Arab dramas and the increased negative attitude toward the prevailing values of Egyptian society, no significant relationship has been proven between the increased exposure of Egyptian university students to Arab dramas and the increased negative attitude toward the values of their Egyptian society, regardless of the platform.

As for the positive aspects, Trang's study (2024) found that there is a positive impact of using digital drama on developing language skills and intercultural communication skills among students studying English as a second language. The results showed a noticeable development in pronunciation, speaking, listening, reading, and writing skills, with the highest improvement in pronunciation skills. As for intercultural communication skills, students witnessed development in knowledge, cultural sensitivity, teamwork, and cultural thinking, according to Abdelhai's (2023) study.

The Arab audience prefers to adhere to the common dress for men and modest dress for women, which reflects the conservative environment to which the audience belongs as well as its cultural and religious background.

On the other hand, the most negative values presented by Arab movies on the Netflix platform were represented by the values of marital infidelity, distance from religion, and homosexuality, while the positive values were represented by acceptance of others and love of justice. Arab movies relied on using the method of action to express societal values more than words. Most Arab movies on the Netflix platform focus on using direct and clear promotion of values that aim to destroy society. They deliberately promote negative values that affect the moral values of Egyptian society. The percentage of positive societal values decreased compared to negative values, which led to an increase in conviction in those values and their adoption. Arab movies presented negative values within a socially acceptable framework and linked them to factors of success in personal life (Mohamed, 2022).

Literature that Dealt with Drama Platforms

Drama platforms have diversified distinctively, having many followers across the Arab world. Many pieces of literature have dealt with the role of these platforms in spreading culture and presenting different content with a higher ceiling of freedom than what is presented on traditional satellite channels. The study by Sharqawi and Harbi (2024) found that these platforms conveyed ancient Egyptian cultures, heritage, and civilizations, which in turn are reflected in society. These movies relied on the narrative style when discussing events, conveying ideas and information, and focusing on emotions. The study also confirmed the existence of a strong associative effect between the ideological, ethnic, and cognitive background of documentary directors on the nature of the treatment of events presented through the movie and the selection of speakers and angles that are filmed and focused on in the movie.

Studies have indicated the high rates of exposure of the public in most countries and cultures to digital platform dramas and the danger of dramatic content presented through Western platforms that contain a set of messages, such as justified violence, perversion, and crime, in dazzling and attractive forms for the public. Global digital platform dramas attempt to control and dominate culture, to obscure the features of national identities in contrast to the unified global identity, particularly from the American perspective. This impact is noticed in European, Asian, and Arab societies. Additionally, the intensive viewing of platform dramas has dangerous effects on the public's mental and physical health. Meanwhile, the content offered by Arab digital platforms is weaker compared to global platforms, causing the Arab public to turn away and favor subscriptions to global services like **Netflix**. Digital platforms also primarily rely on social media for promotion and marketing.

There are multiple negative impacts of dramatic production in the era of digital platforms on all the pillars and dimensions of Arab identity (in terms of language, religion, customs and traditions, belonging and authenticity, and external appearance), such as cultural penetration, cultural invasion, globalization of thought, and Americanization of minds. As for the dramatic discourse on the Arabic **Shahid** platform, the identity destabilization scale reveals that this discourse has destabilized Arab identity across multiple dimensions. It highlights the belief that Arab platforms focus on preserving an external identity rather than an internal one, influenced by intrusive Western thought. In their efforts to compete with foreign platforms, Arab platforms have followed the same Western trends. Additionally, the noticeable technological advancements in the original series offered by these platforms, such as **Netflix** and **Shahid,** have led to a significant shift in dramatic formats. These series now span genres such as action, crime drama, horror, romance, and comedy, which differ greatly from traditional television formats. The media production of these series has also developed in terms of plot and production, and these platforms have helped revitalize the directorial (in shots—cuts, etc.), and the trend toward promoting short dramatic representations has increased, as the number of episodes of drama series on **Netflix** platform are about six episodes for each series (study sample), while on the **Shahid** platform, it ranged from 10 to 15 episodes. The obstacles facing the Arab cultural identity within the original series were mainly represented in the loss of control over the youth as appeared on the **Shahid** platform and the threat to social institutions and bodies like family or school by the Netflix platform (Hassan, 2023).

Motivations for Watching Digital Platforms

The motive for using digital platforms and mobile applications to follow drama series was the flexibility to choose when and where to watch the dramas. The results showed that the TV-watching platforms that were followed online were **Shahid**, followed by **Netflix**; the high impact of websites and mobile applications on watching TV; and the diversity of services used by the respondents between paid and free (Awida, 2023).

According to studies, an increase in the audience's following of digital platforms, in light of the high level of richness of their technological characteristics as well as the distinction of their content, leads to a high level of positive attitudes toward them and consequently the increase in their ability to shape the communication habits of Emirati youth (Askar, 2023). This means that the higher the motivation of the study sample to follow digital platforms, the more positive the evaluation of the content of these platforms will be. The more followers are aware of the characteristics of digital platforms as a means of communication, the more likely they are to increase their level of intensity in following digital platforms. The higher the intensity of the following digital platforms, the more positive the evaluation or attitude toward the content of these platforms will be.

Netflix, Shahid, and **Watch It** platforms gained the preferences of the respondents, most of whom tended to prefer watching during the evening and night periods. The motives of the respondents to watch Arab and foreign series on drama streaming platforms varied between utilitarian and ritualistic. Social series came at the forefront of the preferred types of respondents, followed by comedy series, then police series, and then historical series. Egyptian series topped the list of favorite series, followed by American and then Turkish series. Economic values came at the forefront of the values adopted by the respondents, followed by social values, then aesthetic and cognitive values. There is a relationship between the intensity of the use of Arab and foreign series on drama streaming platforms and the adoption of the social values included in these series. There is a relationship between the utilitarian motives for following series on these platforms and adopting the aesthetic values implicit in them. There is a relationship between the continuous following of Arab and foreign series on drama streaming platforms and the adoption of the aesthetic values implicit in these series (Abdul Rahman & Al-Hadidi, 2024).

Social networking sites have allowed users to largely express their opinions, unlike what used to happen in traditional media. They have also allowed a great deal of freedom in presenting different points of view without restrictions. In return, this freedom has caused a lot of commotion on these sites, which has contributed to increasing the number of rumors about important issues and figures. It is important to talk here about a very important motive, which is the motive of learning about everything new in life (Juma, 2022).

Costs

In terms of material costs, production companies have come to rely on Netflix to cover these costs, which gives the platform full intellectual property rights. Netflix's investments have contributed to the production of large-budget series and increased diversity in content, such as exploring unconventional drama genres like horror and suspense. The platform provides great creative freedom compared to Korean stations. It has had negative effects, such as **Netflix's** acquisition of broadcast rights, which threatens the financial independence of production companies and local TV stations and increases the industry's dependence on the platform, which weakens local competition (Park, 2023).

Globally, **Netflix** has succeeded in attracting a new global audience that was not accustomed to Korean content, for example, reflecting the platform's role as a cultural mediator. Recommendation technologies and continuous streaming have pushed viewers to consume content in a different way, which has increased the global reach of Korean drama. Korean dramas on Netflix have come to reflect new values such as diversity and inclusion, making them more attractive to global audiences. Korean dramas presented on Netflix have helped break stereotypes about Korean culture and provide new perspectives on social issues (Park, 2023).

Conclusion

Referring to previous literature that dealt with values and dramatic platforms and what they offer of these values, it is noticeable that despite the distinction of Arab digital drama platforms such as the **Shahid** platform in attracting the audience, this distinction is more apparent than essential, as the values presented in the works shown on Arab platforms are either presented in a Western form or they are not deep or not very influential, despite the great motivation of the Arab viewer to follow such platforms. It is also necessary to pay attention to the influence and emotional appeal of these works and focus on them in a dialogue between the audience and the media product presented on the Arab digital platform. It is worth noting that despite the multiplicity of trends and methods of presenting all Arab digital platforms, the "**Netflix**" platform is still at the top of the throne of digital platforms in the Arab world and the world. Therefore, it is more beneficial for Arab drama to present itself and its values through a global platform such as **Netflix**, which ensures a greater following and influence on the

Arab viewer, on the one hand, and the promotion of Arab values and culture on the other hand for the global viewer. The more the viewer is aware of the characteristics of digital platforms as a means of communication, the more this leads to an increase in the level of density of following digital platforms, and the higher the density of followers on digital platforms, the more this leads to an increase in positive evaluations or attitudes toward the content of these platforms. The increase in the study sample's following of digital television platforms leads to an increase in the level of richness of their technological characteristics as well as the distinction of their content, and thus an increase in the level of positive attitudes towards them and consequently an increase in their ability to form habits.

Hence, we recommend that Arab digital platforms use the features of global platforms in display, focusing on excellence and providing Arab privacy after conducting many studies and research to identify what the Arab audience wants from these platforms, what the fulfillments that satisfy them or the features that attract them are, and what are the values that they feel their society lacks and therefore want to promote to the youth in particular and the global viewer in general. All of this falls under the way these platforms address the viewer. Since justified violence, deviant sexual behavior, and crime, in dazzling and attractive forms for the audience, came through digital platforms, it is important to study these behaviors with specialists and how they can be presented through works in a way that serves the values and culture of society. It is noteworthy that most of the literature has focused on identifying the negative and positive effects of dramatic platforms, analyzing them, and comparing them. It is important to invest in these results and build works based on this effect.

Experts agreed on the inconsistency of the Arab media toward Arab issues, the weakness of information, and the contradiction of the media positions of the Arab media, and they agreed on the weakness of its role in establishing the values of awareness and enlightening the public in light of the prevalence of foreign values and cultures, which constitutes a functional defect and a clear deficiency in the role of the media and the tasks assigned to it. Accordingly, we would like to emphasize the necessity of unifying Arab issues and finding common points of understanding between countries due to the similarity of issues, the environment, and the cultural and religious ideology, and the importance of those in charge of the media, specifically those platforms, writers, directors, and artists, realizing their role in defeating foreign cultures and highlighting authentic societal values, and the importance of awareness of the responsibility they undertake.

References

Academic Theses

Abdel-Hay, M. (2023). Cultural values in dubbed Turkish series and their reflection on Egyptian youth. *Scientific Journal of Radio and Television Research*, *25*, 531–580.

Abdulrahman, A., & Al-Hadidi, M. (2024). The relationship between Egyptian youth's exposure to series on drama broadcasting platforms and their awareness of societal values. *Scientific Journal of Radio and Television Research*, *29*, 155–230.
Abu Bakr, H. (2022). The effectiveness of Arab television channels in consolidating the values of cultural identity (Al Arabiya Channel) as a model. *Scientific Journal of Radio and Television Research*, *24*, 413–448.
Al-Nimer, A. (2024). The drama of Arab digital watching platforms and their role in shaping the attitudes of Egyptian university students towards the values of their society. *Scientific Journal of Radio and Television Research*, *29*, 1–123.
Al-Sharif & others. (2022). Semiology of television drama image design and its impact on Egyptian societal values. *Journal of Architecture, Arts and Humanities*, *7*(34), 413–425.
Askar, N. (2023). Emirati youth's evaluation of the richness of digital television platforms and their impact on their communication habits. *Arab Journal of Communication and Digital Media Research*, *2*(3), 23–54. https://doi.org/10.21608/EJSRT.2021.175157
Awida, D. (2023). The Egyptian audience's uses of paid TV viewing applications and the satisfactions achieved from them. *Scientific Journal of Radio and Television Research*, *26*, 375–425. https://doi.org/10.21608/EJSRT.2023.342755
Hassan, N. (2023). The foundations of Arab cultural identity in the drama of original production for digital platforms: An analytical study on the Shahid and Netflix platforms. *Egyptian Journal of Media Research*, *84*, 1327–1397. https://doi.org/10.21608/EJSC.2023.324284
Jamil, N. (2023). The sociology of television advertising and its impact on the societal values of the Egyptian audience. *The Arab Journal of Communication and Digital Media Research*, *4*(2023), 93–114.
Jumaa, N. (2022). Adolescents' exposure to video clips on the TIKTOK application and its relationship to influencing their value system. *Arab Journal of Communication and Digital Media Research*, *1*, 227–254.
Mohamed, O. (2022). Employing digital platforms in promoting societal values "Netflix" platform as a model. *Egyptian Journal of Media Research*, *80*, 917–954.
Mohamed, M. (2023). Social values presented to children on mickey channel and cartoon network. *The Scientific Journal of Radio and Television Research*, *26*(2), 637–656.
Sharqawi, A., & Harbi, M. (2024). The role of documentary films via digital platforms in shaping the image of tourism in Egypt. *Arab Journal of Communication and Digital Media Research*, *5*, 377–380.

Non-Arabic References

Academic theses

Park, S. (2023). Reshaping hallyu: Global reception of South Korean content on Netflix. *International Journal of Communication*, *17*, 6952–6971.

Park, J. (2023). Netflix and platform imperialism: How netflix alters the ecology of the Korean TV drama industry. *International Journal of Communication*, *17*(2023), 72–91.

Trang, L. (2024). The effect of digital drama on EFL students' skills in the intercultural communication course at the university, *European Journal of Foreign Language Teaching*, *8*(2), 1–14.

Chapter 24

The Role of Instagram in Awareness of Women's Health Issues: Evidence From Bahrain

Kaltham Alnamlaiti

Senior Specialist Nurse, Ministry of Health, Bahrain

Abstract

This study examines how Instagram, in partnership with private hospitals, can enhance awareness of women's health issues in Bahrain. Despite growing digital engagement, women's health awareness remains limited due to a lack of targeted, credible information. The researcher did content analysis of Instagram posts of some private hospitals and conducting questionnaires on a random sample of women in Bahrain. Additionally, the researcher will use an interview as a research tool. This descriptive research seeks to determine how hospital-endorsed content influences women's health knowledge and proactive health practices. Through this approach, the study aims to reveal how Instagram and institutional collaborations can foster greater health awareness and engagement. Therefore, based on that, a methodology was used is media survey approach.

Keywords: Instagram; women health awareness; health media and communication; health misinformation; health content governance; multidisciplinary study

The duality of media and health represents the basis on which the health situation is based today, as health is a legitimate humanitarian requirement, and the media is the appropriate container that contributes to promoting this humanitarian demand Gad (2021). Attention to women's health is a top priority,

Digital Dialogues, 233–241

Published under exclusive licence by Emerald Publishing Limited
doi:10.1108/978-1-83708-686-320261024

as women's health means the health of society and future generations. According to the World Health Organization (WHO), women's health is defined as the physical and psychological health of women at different stages of life. Private practice has recently been interested in relying on Instagram to promote their services and raise health awareness in society, as the Internet has increased the speed of dissemination of health awareness messages, which has led to the emergence of a competitive advantage. Kumar and Preetha (2012) have pointed out that health education is a combination of educational experiences that help people to enhance their health by increasing their knowledge, so it is necessary to give health awareness and education.

Literature Reviews

Previous Researches that Reviewed the Role of Traditional Media

Research (Baishi et al., 2021) on the role of health media in health awareness: "Your Health is Your Capital" page in Al-Shaab newspaper as a model. The research targeted media coverage of health issues through the contents of the weekly "Your Health is Your Capital" page. It also examined the role played by health media in raising health awareness among members of society. This research relied on the content analysis method. This research dealt with models of the contribution of health media to spreading health awareness in several aspects, such as the Corona pandemic, mental health, and people with disabilities. As for the results of this research, it was found that the most of the topics were accompanied by pictures at a rate of 68%. It indicates that the image speaks louder than the word.

Study (Khnous & Daghna, 2020): The role of television health programs in developing health awareness among Algerian women. An analytical study of a sample of the "Clinic" program on Numidia News Channel. The study dealt with the weekly television program (the Clinic) that discussed some of the health issues of women, most notably cervical and breast cancer. The researchers used the content analysis method in a quantitative manner, using the content analysis form and the interview as tools for the study, by applying it to a deliberate sample that falls within the nonprobability samples consisting of nine samples. This study is based on the structural functional theory, which contributes to knowing the role of the media as a social structure within society to perform its awareness function. This study explained that health media is one of the branches of specialized media that is interested in studying health issues and raising awareness by presenting facts and statistics, using various effects such as words, pictures, drawings, colors, music, and others. This study confirmed that the relationship between the media and health awareness is a relationship based on two levels: The first is the cooperative level, which means that the media produces health programs and publishes them in the health institution. The second is the functional level, which is that health institutions are open to health media sources, reject rumors, analyze health information and statistics, participate in awareness activities such as World Health Days, perform the duty of advice, and adopt health awareness issues. The study showed that the most important element in health awareness via television is the human element, as it plays a pivotal role in achieving the goal of health discourse. Unfortunately, the professional staff in the health awareness field is not available enough. One of the results of this study is that the television program convinces the viewer more if it presents real stories and cases from patients' experiences. In the content analysis categories, the two methods that most increase health awareness among women are the method of intimidation against neglecting early preventive detection and the method of advice and guidance, followed by relying on famous personalities.

Maghlawi and Nasira (2020) entitled "The Role of Local Radio in Increasing Health Awareness among Women Staying at Home, a Field Study on a Sample of Jijel Local Radio Listeners." This study touched on the contribution of Jijel Radio health programs in achieving health cognitive gratifications among its listeners. The theories explaining the study were the theory of uses and gratifications, the theory of dependence on the media, and prioritization theory (agenda setting). The researcher mentioned the characteristics of radio which are the ease of carrying, reasonable price, preferred by the elderly and those who are not fluent in reading, the budget of productivity is inexpensive, the property of recording radio materials and diversification in the methods of broadcasting. The study talked about the aspects of health awareness, a cognitive side, emotional side and the behavioral side (applied), the study used the descriptive approach and the form research tool, and the methods of analysis were quantitative and qualitative method, the sample was intentional of 50 women staying at home by 64% of the sample married, and for the sample members by educational level 28% secondary and 24% women with university level. This study concluded the following results, most notably that 80% of the respondents benefit from health programs on Radio Jijel. Half of the sample confirmed that the radio contributes to the identification of some diseases where its role is educational, guidance, and awareness. Forty-four percent confirmed that they use other alternatives such as social networking sites and television to get a dose of health awareness. 37.5% equally confirmed the lack of health information presented, the monotony of the content, and the lack of renewal. Thirty-six percent of the sample want to focus more on women's health in radio programs. Last but not least, 84% prefer to listen to radio health programs in the morning because they stay at home.

Previous Researches that Reviewed the Role of Digital Media in Health Awareness

The organizations prefer the digital media rather than traditional media to attract different categories in the society (Esiyok, 2018). The sample was purposive sampling; the Twitter account of the Turkish Ministry of Health was analyzed. Only the public advertisements that are published between July 11, 2018, and October 11, 2018, are chosen. The total number of public advertisements is 59. The results indicated that the use of Twitter by the Turkish Ministry of Health was effective and useful. Eighty percent of males used the internet, while 65.5% of females used the internet. The research indicated that the visual documents and messages were balanced and supportive to each other. The most discussed subjects were healthy pregnancy, breastfeeding, and early diagnosis of breast cancer.

According to Agboola and Ahmed (2020), "Rural Women Perceptions of Digital Media Influence on Awareness Creation about Maternal Health Information in Minna, Nigeria," a questionnaire was the research tool administered to a random sample of 384 women in hospitals. The percentage of married women was 62.4%, while 22.8% were university graduates. The theory used in this research was the uses and gratifications theory. The results showed that 29% of women prefer to receive awareness through WhatsApp groups, while 31.6% prefer SMS messages as remainders about appointments and health instructions. The main challenge is that the internet is weak in those areas. The research emphasized the importance of having a measuring tool to ensure the accuracy of information and to sort out rumors. The research recommended using digital media more effectively to raise awareness about maternal health and introducing video and audio to attract a larger group.

According to Francisco et al. (2022), the mobile phone is an effective communication tool for health awareness among decision-makers. The research compared the impact of traditional media (television and radio) and new media (mobile phones) on health issues such as birth control, birth spacing, contraception, and care during pregnancy, childbirth, and reproductive health. Zimbabwe, Guinea, and Cameroon, respectively, topped the list of countries where women own mobile phones, in addition to television and radio. The study sample consisted of 78,000 women aged 15–49 years who went through at least one pregnancy experience. The individual analysis was based on a cross-section from 11 African countries. The data were analyzed according to the demographic health statistics program, and the data collection tool was the questionnaire. In the recommendations, the study noted the importance of decision-makers' practice of government policies.

Tausa et al. (2022) entitled The potential of social media in health promotion beyond creating awareness, the research talked about developing strategies to change health behaviors, which is one of the biggest challenges in health promotion programming through an electronic research system in which an integrated review and review of literature and studies discussing the role of social media in health promotion campaigns and its effectiveness. Research methodology included both the experimental and nonexperimental approaches. Among the results, it was found that 55.5% of the studies that were reviewed used the quantitative method, while 27.7% of the studies combined the quantitative and qualitative methods, and 16.6% used the qualitative method. Talking about the theory, it was found that 33.3% of the studies adopted the theory of social cognition. For the topics covered by the study, including the subject of cervical cancer, and with regard to the results of the study, it was found that health awareness initiatives attract the public to exposure and participate in health promotion programs on social media. Social media has a role in improving the results of healthy behavior more than treatment and compared to the most social media that affects changing healthy behaviors is Facebook and YouTube, while Twitter and Instagram are used more to observe trends or tendency to change in health behaviors.

Literature Examining the Spread of Health Misinformation on Social Media, Particularly concerning Women's Health Issues

Mohammed, W., Alanzi, T., Alanezi, F., Alhodaib, H., & AlShammari, M. (2021). Usage of social media for health awareness purposes among health educators and students in Saudi Arabia. *Informatics in Medicine Unlocked, 23.*

This study is a cross-sectional study. The questionnaire was initially sent to 450 health educators and students through WhatsApp groups. It indicated that more than half of the participants thought that the use of social networks was very important to increase community health awareness, facilitate access to the public, increase Arabic health content, and correct false information. Forty percent of the respondents did not utilize social media for health awareness because they did not trust online health information. Besides, the amount of information uploaded to these platforms makes it difficult to distinguish between reliable health information and misleading information. Nineteen percent of the cancer information exchanged on Facebook was scientifically inaccurate. As health education spreads more widely on social media, health educators must become more competent in computer-mediated systems. Another challenge is to disprove myths, rumors, and erroneous information circulating on social media about health issues.

Melchior et al. (2022). Health-related fake news on social media platforms: A systematic literature review.

This research aims to (a) investigate the characteristics of both the research community and the published research on health-related fake news on social media platforms, and (b) identify the challenges and provide recommendations for future research on the subject. We reviewed 69 journal articles found in the main academic databases up to April 2021. The studies extracted data mainly from Twitter, YouTube, and Facebook.

Most articles aimed to investigate the public's reaction to fake health information, concluding that health agencies and professionals should increase their online presence.

The articles also suggest that future work should aim to improve the quality of health information on social media platforms, develop new tools and strategies to combat fake news sharing, and study the credibility of health information. Nonetheless, those in control of the platforms are the only ones who can take effective measures to ensure that their users receive reliable information.

- Explaining Health Misinformation Belief through News, Social, and Alternative Health Media Use: The Moderating Roles of Need for Cognition and Faith in Intuition (2023).

  Health misinformation raises important problems for not only individuals but also the society. The rise of the internet, mobile, and social media has complicated and exacerbated the spread and impact of health misinformation. Yet, more people turn to the Internet for health-related information, whether intentionally (by seeking) or incidentally.

- Individuals with polycystic ovary syndrome (PCOS) turn to Instagram influencers as an alternative or complementary PCOS information source to their physicians. Using a directed qualitative content analysis, the authors examined the range of strategies that 10 Instagram PCOS influencers used to signal credibility. They found that influencers utilized a range of pseudo-credibility strategies. Another key contribution of the study is a description of how PCOS influencers reference sources to signal credibility.
- Harm Related to Social Media Misinformation on Pelvic Organ Prolapse in YouTube, Instagram, and Pinterest Posts. Social media can improve patient education but may pose risks due to misinformation. There is no consensus on categorizing types of misinformation and harm. This study aimed to categorize and quantify misinformation and resultant harm from posts on YouTube, Pinterest, and Instagram on pelvic organ prolapse (POP), a prevalent benign condition that impacts quality of life. We conducted a descriptive study of 300 posts presented on these platforms in 2019. Using the Fisher exact test, we show a significant difference in the distribution of misinformation between social media platforms. Harmful posts were most frequently present on Pinterest, leading to harmful inaction and economic harm.
- The study analyzed the clarity of publications on human papillomavirus (HPV) in the Instagram profiles of official Brazilian health agencies. An infodemiological study analyzed publications on HPV in the 81 Instagram profiles selected from the Health Ministry, States' Health Departments, and dental councils and associations.

  The following data were collected: classification of content, type of profiles, type of media, how the content was addressed, number of posts, frequency, likes, comments, views, and hashtags, and how the HPV vaccine was addressed. The clarity of the educational publications was assessed using the Brazilian version of the Clear Communication. Data analysis was performed with Spearman's correlation and the Mann-Whitney test ($p < 0.05$). A total of 504 publications on HPV were found.

  Most publications concerning government actions had low engagement, and the educational information written was of low clarity and quality. However, the effort to reach the population was evident, with an increase in publications over the years.
- Yeung et al. (2022): Social media used for the communication of health-related information and, consequently, for the potential spread of medical misinformation. Conventional systematic reviews have been published on this topic to identify original articles and summarize their methodological approaches and themes. The aim of this study was to perform a bibliometric analysis of the current literature to discover prevalent trends and topics related to medical misinformation on social media. Based on an analysis of 529 papers on medical and health-related misinformation on social

media, we found that the most popularly investigated social media platforms were Twitter.

Investigations on these platforms had different foci. Twitter-based research explored cyberchondria and hypochondriasis, YouTube-based research explored tobacco smoking, and Facebook-based research studied vaccine hesitancy related to autism.

Conclusion

Previous studies were conducted during the time period from 2018 to 2023. Foreign studies have been characterized by the momentum of information in them, and dealt with the subject of health awareness from more than one perspective, specifically with regard to disinformation and in different details, thus opening wider horizons for future research. Various theories, such as the source credibility theory, were used. In Arabic studies they linked health awareness to sustainable development goals (Khnous & Daghna, 2020).

Previous studies have demonstrated the close link between the media, the health field, and other fields and sciences such as multidisciplinary research, psychology, and sociology, confirming the importance of interdisciplinary research.

This was evident within the theoretical framework of previous studies, where the most frequent theories were the theory of uses and gratifications, followed by the theory of functional constructivism, a study (Khnous & Daghna, 2020) whose hypotheses approached the health belief model used by the researcher in the current study, as it considers one of its assumptions to be the use of the method of intimidation and intimidation and the method of advice and guidance in health awareness. Other theories include media dependence theory.

A study showed the differences and comparisons between digital and traditional media, and the studies also stated that women prefer the element of interaction and dialogue when discussing their health issues, and this gives preference to digital media. The content analysis, interviews, and questionnaire tools were adopted. It is noticeable that an analysis of the digital platforms of the Ministry of Health, as in the study, confirms that state-owned entities are a key party in spreading health awareness. The studies included discussions on health awareness in several areas such as Mental Health and Cancers Study (Khnous & Daghna, 2020). The researcher showed the importance of attaching "infographic" images to enhance health awareness, a study (Agbula & Ahmed, 2020), diversification in media arts and presenting realistic stories to patients, which requires qualifying the human element to manage and develop health media and communication in line with the digital revolution. The importance of analyzing posts and followers and classifying misinformation through social media was stressed, and artificial intelligence can be used in this.

Women are the most targeted group for health awareness, regardless of whether a rural woman is married, a housewife, or a university worker. Despite the high percentage of married women being housewives, there is a perception of focusing on other groups. Health education is an urgent need even in developed countries.

Regarding to the study sample, most of them were a deliberate or intentional sample study (Khnous & Daghna, 2020), study (Maghlawi & Nasira, 2020), study (Alali & Zarqouf, 2019) and study (Mohammed et al., 2021), and the samples were objective or related to the target in the study and random in the study (Agbula & Ahmed, 2020).

Future studies should also include social platforms targeting non-English users to provide a wider global perspective.

References

Agbula, & Ahmed (2020). Rural women's perceptions of the impact of digital media on creating health awareness about mothers during pregnancy, childbirth and after governors in Mina Nigeria. *Asian Journal of Social Sciences and Technology Management*.

Alali, & Zarqouf (2019). *The role of the internet in raising awareness of health issues among Algerian women: A field study on a sample of female employees at Jijel University*.

Baishi, et al. (2021). *The role of medical media in health education your health page is your capital in Al-Shaab newspaper as a model* (Unpublished master's thesis). Ahmed and Raya University.

Esiyok, E. (2018). The use of Twitter to increase the awareness on health issues: An analysis through Republic of Turkey Ministry of Health Twitter Account. *International Journal of Health Management and Tourism*, *3*(3), 154–163.

Francesco et al. (2022). *What is the most effective technological means of communication to promote reproductive health? TV, Radio, Mobile*.

Gad, S. (2021). Health awareness campaigns on the pages of the Egyptian Ministry of health on social networking sites. *Egyptian Journal of Media Research*, *2*(77), 1062.

Khnous, & Daghna (2020). *The role of television health programs in developing health awareness among Algerian women: An analytical study of a sample of the "clinic" program, Numidia News Channel* (Unpublished master's thesis). Ibn Khaldun University.

Kumar, S., & Preetha, G. (2012). Health promotion: An effective tool for global health. *Indian Journal of Community Medicine*, *37*(1), 5–12.

Maghlawi, & Nasira (2020). *The role of local radio in increasing health awareness among women staying at home: A field study on a sample of listeners of Jijel Local Radio* (Unpublished master's thesis). University of Mohammed Siddiq bin Yahya.

Melchior et al. (2022). Health-related fake news on social media platforms: A systematic literature review.

Mohammed, W., Alanzi, T., Alanezi, F., Alhodaib, H., & AlShammari, M. (2021). Usage of social media for health awareness purposes among health educators and students in Saudi Arabia. *Informatics in Medicine Unlocked, 23*.

Tausa et al. (2022). The potential of social media in health promotion beyond creating awareness.

Yeung, A. W. K., Tosevska, A., Klager, E., Eibensteiner, F., Tsagkaris, C., Parvanov, E. D., Nawaz, F.A., Völkl-Kernstock, S., Schaden, E., Kletecka-Pulker, M., Willschke, H., & Atanasov, A. G. (2022). Medical and health-related misinformation on social media: Bibliometric study of the scientific literature. *Journal of Medical Internet Research*, *24*(1), e28152. https://pubmed.ncbi.nlm.nih.gov/34951864/

Yuanyuan et al. (2023). Explaining health misinformation belief through news, social, and alternative health media use: The moderating roles of need for cognition and faith in intuition.

Chapter 25

The Role of Instagram in Promoting Sustainable Development Goals: A Study of the Bahraini Context

Menatalla Massod

Ahlia University, Bahrain

Abstract

Social media platforms have become pivotal in advancing sustainable development goals (SDGs), offering innovative avenues for engagement and awareness. This study explores Instagram's role in promoting SDGs within the Bahraini context, emphasizing its capacity to connect individuals, organizations, and communities. With its visual storytelling and interactive features, Instagram transforms abstract development concepts into compelling narratives, inspiring collective action and fostering public understanding. Utilizing a mixed-methods approach, this research combines surveys, content analysis, and interviews with Bahraini stakeholders, including activists, organizations, and digital creators. The findings reveal Instagram's significant contributions to environmental campaigns, educational initiatives, and social equity movements, showcasing its power to mobilize communities and amplify local efforts. Despite these successes, challenges such as the digital divide and the risk of misinformation persist, requiring strategic interventions to maximize Instagram's positive impact. This study highlights the potential of leveraging social media for sustainable change, positioning Instagram as a bridge between awareness and action. By aligning its vast reach with Bahrain's developmental priorities, Instagram emerges as a tool for fostering a shared sense of responsibility and advancing the SDGs, paving the way for a more sustainable and inclusive future.

Keywords: Instagram; sustainable development goals; Bahrain; social media; public awareness; community engagement

---

Digital Dialogues, 243–252

doi:10.1108/978-1-83708-686-320261025

Introduction

In an interconnected world driven by digital innovation, social media has reshaped how individuals and communities perceive and interact with global challenges (Caliandro & Graham, 2020). Platforms such as Instagram have become more than mere spaces for social interaction; they have evolved into dynamic tools for advocacy, storytelling, and collective action. At the heart of this transformation lies the ability to connect people to causes, inspiring change through relatable and visually engaging content (Geraldo & de Souza Pinto, 2020). Among the pressing challenges of our time, sustainable development stands out as an urgent global imperative, calling for creative and inclusive approaches to address environmental, social, and economic disparities. SDGs provide a comprehensive framework for fostering a balanced and equitable future, yet their complexity often renders them distant and abstract to the general public (Pietrzak, 2022). Instagram, with its focus on visual storytelling and interactive features, serves as a bridge between these intricate concepts and everyday human experiences. Through a photograph or a short video, individuals and organizations can narrate compelling stories of change, highlight urgent issues, and mobilize collective action in ways previously unimaginable (Álvarez-Herrero et al., 2021). In Bahrain, a nation actively striving to align its developmental priorities with the United Nations' 2030 Agenda, the integration of digital platforms into sustainability efforts is not just an opportunity but also a necessity (Shrivastava et al., 2021). Instagram has gained prominence as a tool to amplify local efforts, from environmental campaigns to social equity initiatives, uniting communities, fostering understanding, and inspiring action for shared sustainability (AlAmmary, 2022). This study explores Instagram's role in advancing SDGs within the Bahraini context, delving into its ability to engage citizens, support organizations, and highlight local initiatives. This research explores the strengths, limitations, and opportunities of social media to highlight its potential for fostering a sustainable and inclusive future in Bahrain and beyond. In today's digital age, understanding how to effectively use these platforms for sustainable development is essential.

The Role of Social Media in Sustainable Development

Social media platforms have emerged as powerful tools for communication and engagement, transforming the way individuals, organizations, and governments interact. In sustainable development, social media platforms are crucial for spreading information, raising awareness, and encouraging collective action toward the SDGs (De Luca et al., 2022). Their interactive nature and wide reach help connect diverse stakeholders by using engaging visuals, storytelling, and real-time updates. Platforms like Instagram, Twitter, and Facebook can effectively engage users with complex issues (Franco-Riquelme & Rubalcaba, 2021). For example, campaigns on climate change, gender equality, or poverty reduction often gain traction through hashtags, viral videos, and user-generated content, demonstrating how social media can be both informative and transformative (Lozano-Blasco et al., 2023). Social media enables civil society to monitor progress and hold governments and corporations accountable for sustainability commitments. However, challenges like misinformation, digital divides, and algorithmic biases can hinder its effectiveness (Marzouki et al., 2021). Addressing these issues requires a multi-stakeholder approach that includes technological innovation, regulatory frameworks, and digital literacy initiatives to maximize benefits and minimize drawbacks (Bystrov & Panigrahi, 2021). In essence, social media can be pivotal in advancing sustainable development by connecting people and mobilizing action. Their effectiveness in addressing global challenges depends on integration into broader strategies and the collective efforts of users, policymakers, and organizations (De Luca et al., 2022).

The Concept of Sustainable Development and Its Goals

Sustainable development is a multidimensional concept that seeks to balance economic growth, social equity, and environmental preservation (Pietrzak, 2022). This framework, popularized by the 1987 Brundtland Report, emphasizes an integrative approach to addressing global challenges, such as poverty, inequality, and environmental degradation. At the heart of sustainable development are the 17 SDGs, established by the United Nations in 2015 as part of the 2030 Agenda for Sustainable Development (Shrivastava et al., 2021). These goals provide a comprehensive roadmap for addressing critical issues facing humanity, ranging from eradicating extreme poverty (Goal 1) to combating climate change (Goal 13) (Marzouki et al., 2021). The SDGs are interconnected, highlighting the need for holistic strategies that recognize the interdependence of economic, social, and environmental dimensions. For example, achieving quality education (Goal 4) has far-reaching implications for reducing inequalities (Goal 10) and fostering economic growth (Goal 8). Similarly, protecting life below water (Goal 14) contributes to sustainable livelihoods for coastal communities and the broader health of the planet (Alqashar & Sanad, 2024). Sustainable development prioritizes inclusivity and equity, aiming to ensure that marginalized and vulnerable populations are not left behind amidst global challenges (Bystrov & Panigrahi, 2021). This principle encourages targeted interventions to overcome systemic barriers and empower communities. However, challenges such as limited resources and conflicting priorities often hinder progress (Shrivastava et al., 2021). These challenges highlight the importance of innovation, partnerships, and political will for sustainable development. Achieving a more equitable and resilient world requires collective efforts from governments, businesses, civil society, and individuals. By incorporating these principles into policies, societies can move toward a sustainable and inclusive future for all (Pietrzak, 2022).

Instagram as a Tool for Communication and Influence

Instagram has transformed communication and sharing in the digital age. Originally a photo-sharing app, it has become a powerful platform for storytelling, advocacy, and social engagement, thanks to its visually driven format and vast global reach (Caliandro & Graham, 2020). One of Instagram's most defining features is its emphasis on visual content, which allows users to convey complex messages in an accessible and engaging way. Photos, videos, and infographics can communicate ideas and emotions that resonate across diverse audiences, transcending language barriers (Geraldo & de Souza Pinto, 2020). For example, an organization promoting environmental sustainability can use Instagram to showcase compelling images of reforested areas or endangered species, capturing attention and inspiring action more effectively than textual reports (Madonna et al., 2023). Instagram's interactive features, such as hashtags, stories, reels, and live sessions, further enable users to create dynamic content that encourages participation and fosters community engagement (Mittischek & Waldner, 2023). Campaigns that use hashtags, such as #ClimateAction or #ZeroHunger, often gain significant traction by connecting like-minded individuals and amplifying their collective voices (Marzouki et al., 2021). Additionally, Instagram's algorithm-driven interface makes it an ideal tool for targeted communication (Oueiss & El-Khoury, 2023). Brands, nongovernmental organizations (NGOs), and public institutions can leverage data analytics to tailor content to specific audiences, ensuring that their messages reach the right people (Franco-Riquelme & Rubalcaba, 2021). For instance, a campaign promoting gender equality might target young adults and activists who are more likely to engage and advocate for the cause, thereby maximizing impact (AlAmmary, 2022). Moreover, Instagram is a huge platform for influence. Influencers, with their vast followings and trusted voices, play a significant role in promoting sustainable practices and raising awareness of social and environmental issues (Wielki, 2020). Collaborations between influencers and organizations have proven effective in creating relatable content that drives behavior change. For instance, an influencer sharing their journey toward adopting a zero-waste lifestyle can inspire their followers to take similar steps (Soedarsono et al., 2020). Despite its strengths, Instagram's potential is not without limitations. Challenges such as algorithmic biases, the spread of misinformation, and the risk of "slacktivism"—where users engage passively without substantial action—can hinder its effectiveness as a tool for influence (Caliandro & Graham, 2020). Addressing these issues requires strategic content creation and the fostering of genuine engagement.

Instagram's Role in Raising Awareness of the SDGs

Instagram has emerged as a powerful platform for promoting awareness of the SDGs, thanks to its ability to engage users through visually appealing and interactive content (Geraldo & de Souza Pinto, 2020). By combining aesthetics with accessibility, Instagram facilitates the dissemination of critical messages about sustainability and inspires users to contribute to global change (Lozano-Blasco et al., 2023).

- **Showcasing Success Stories and Best Practices:** Organizations and individuals use Instagram to showcase success stories related to the SDGs, such as community-led solar projects and urban farming. These visuals make global goals more relatable by connecting them to tangible local actions, offering scalable models for others to follow (Marzouki et al., 2021).
- **Campaigns and Hashtag Movements:** Instagram has proven to be an effective platform for launching campaigns and hashtag movements. Global initiatives such as #GlobalGoals or #ActForSDGs leverage Instagram's reach to spark widespread conversations and mobilize users (Mittischek & Waldner, 2023). These campaigns encourage individuals to share their contributions, creating a ripple effect of awareness and action. For example, those promoting reduced plastic use often feature user-generated content that showcases alternatives to single-use plastics, fostering collective action (Franco-Riquelme & Rubalcaba, 2021).
- **Collaborations with Influencers:** Influencers can use their connections with followers to communicate messages in a relatable and impactful way. For example, sustainability advocates might collaborate with brands to promote eco-friendly products, while travel influencers might highlight the importance of preserving natural heritage sites (Wielki, 2020).
- **Engaging Youth Audiences:** Instagram's dominance among younger demographics makes it a critical tool for engaging the next generation in sustainability efforts. Youth-focused campaigns often use Instagram to simplify complex SDG topics through infographics, animated videos, and interactive stories. By speaking the language of the digital generation, these initiatives empower young users to take an active role in advancing sustainable development (Hernández-Serrano et al., 2022).
- **Leveraging Storytelling to Drive Emotional Connections:** Instagram's visual storytelling capabilities make it an ideal platform for connecting audiences emotionally with SDG-related issues. For instance, a series of photos documenting the impact of education initiatives in underprivileged areas can evoke empathy and inspire support for Goal 4 (Quality Education). Similarly, videos showing the consequences of climate change can motivate users to take action in line with Goal 13 (Climate Action) (Álvarez-Herrero et al., 2021).
- **Encouraging Behavioral Change:** Through informative posts, reels, and live sessions, Instagram users can learn practical steps to contribute to the SDGs in their daily lives. Content such as "10 Ways to Reduce Your Carbon Footprint" or "How to Support Gender Equality in Your Community" provides actionable insights, making sustainable behavior more accessible and attainable (Soedarsono et al., 2020).

The Bahraini Context: Characteristics and Distinctive Features

Bahrain, as a progressive and dynamic nation, offers a unique context for understanding the role of Instagram in promoting sustainable development. Its distinct blend of modernity, cultural heritage, and digital adoption creates fertile ground for leveraging social media to advance the SDGs (Shrivastava et al., 2021). Below, we explore the specific characteristics of Bahrain and its digital ecosystem, highlighting how Instagram is utilized within this framework:

- **Bahrain's Commitment to Sustainable Development:** Bahrain has demonstrated a strong commitment to sustainable development, aligning its national strategies with the UN's SDGs. Through initiatives like Vision 2030, the country prioritizes economic diversification, environmental protection, and social inclusion (Alqashar & Sanad, 2024).
- **High Internet Penetration and Social Media Usage:** Bahrain boasts one of the highest internet penetration rates in the Middle East, with a digitally savvy population that actively engages with social media platforms (Shrivastava et al., 2021). The widespread use of mobile devices further enhances Instagram's accessibility, allowing users to connect with campaigns and initiatives in real time (AlAmmary, 2022).
- **Cultural Sensitivity and Representation:** In Bahrain, social media campaigns often balance global sustainability themes with local cultural contexts (Aldada et al., 2023). For example, campaigns addressing food security or waste management incorporate traditional Bahraini practices, such as conserving resources or supporting local agriculture (AlGhanem & Mendy, 2024).
- **Engagement of Key Stakeholders:** Government agencies, NGOs, and private enterprises in Bahrain actively use Instagram to promote sustainability. These stakeholders frequently collaborate on campaigns that align with national priorities, such as renewable energy projects, marine conservation, and educational initiatives (Shrivastava et al., 2021).
- **Empowering Youth and Grassroots Movements:** Bahrain's youth play a pivotal role in advancing sustainable development, and Instagram serves as a key platform for their activism (AlGhanem & Mendy, 2024). Young content creators and influencers often use Instagram to share their perspectives on climate change, education, and social equality, inspiring others to take part in the movement (Hernández-Serrano et al., 2022). Grassroots initiatives, such as beach cleanups or recycling drives, gain visibility through Instagram, encouraging broader community participation (Geraldo & de Souza Pinto, 2020).
- **Supporting Local Entrepreneurs and Sustainable Businesses:** Instagram is a vital platform for promoting sustainable businesses and local entrepreneurs in Bahrain (Alqashar & Sanad, 2024). Many small and medium-sized enterprises (SMEs) leverage the platform to market eco-friendly products and services, such as reusable goods, organic produce, or sustainable fashion (Alsridi, 2019). These efforts not only contribute to the economy but also align with

SDGs like responsible consumption and production (Goal 12) (Soedarsono et al., 2020).

Challenges in the Bahraini Context

While Bahrain demonstrates a strong foundation for integrating Instagram into its sustainable development initiatives, several challenges hinder its full potential (Shrivastava et al., 2021). These challenges span technological, social, and structural dimensions, and addressing them is critical for maximizing Instagram's role in advancing sustainable development in the Bahraini context (Bystrov & Panigrahi, 2021).

- **Digital Divides and Accessibility Barriers:** Despite Bahrain's high internet penetration, disparities in digital literacy and access persist among certain demographics (AlAmmary, 2022). Older generations, low-income groups, and marginalized communities may lack the skills, resources, or opportunities to engage meaningfully with Instagram campaigns (Bystrov & Panigrahi, 2021). This digital divide can result in the exclusion of voices that are essential for fostering comprehensive and inclusive sustainable development (Pietrzak, 2022).
- **Overemphasis on Visual Appeal:** The visual nature of Instagram, while highly engaging, may prioritize aesthetic appeal over substantive content (Caliandro & Graham, 2020). Complex issues such as policy development, legislative reforms, or socioeconomic inequalities are often difficult to convey through photos or videos, potentially leading to oversimplified narratives (Marzouki et al., 2021). This limitation can reduce the platform's effectiveness in addressing less visually appealing yet equally important aspects of sustainable development (Wielki, 2020).
- **Risk of Performative Activism:** A significant challenge in using Instagram for sustainability is the prevalence of performative activism, where users engage with content superficially—liking, sharing, or commenting—without taking meaningful action (Franco-Riquelme & Rubalcaba, 2021). This phenomenon may create a false sense of progress, as engagement metrics do not necessarily translate into tangible outcomes or behavioral changes (Ijomah et al., 2024).
- **Misinformation and Lack of Credibility:** Instagram's user-generated content model allows for the rapid dissemination of information, but it also opens the door to misinformation and misleading narratives (Olof Larsson, 2023). In the Bahraini context, inaccurate claims or poorly verified data about sustainability initiatives can undermine trust and dilute the impact of genuine campaigns (AlAmmary, 2022).
- **Limited Reach Among Nondigital Stakeholders:** Although Instagram is popular among younger demographics in Bahrain, its reach may not extend effectively to nondigital stakeholders, such as rural communities or traditional businesses (Bystrov & Panigrahi, 2021). These groups are often key players in sustainable development, yet they may remain disconnected from

Instagram-based campaigns due to a lack of digital integration or cultural preferences for traditional communication channels (Robles-Moral, 2021).

- **Algorithmic Bias and Content Visibility:** Instagram's algorithm prioritizes content that garners high engagement, often favoring entertainment-oriented or sensational posts over educational or advocacy-driven content (Oueiss & El-Khoury, 2023). This bias can limit the visibility of sustainability campaigns, particularly those tackling niche or less mainstream issues, reducing their ability to reach a broad audience (Marzouki et al., 2021).
- **Dependence on Influencers and Branding:** The success of sustainability campaigns on Instagram in Bahrain often relies on influencers and corporate partnerships (Alsaad et al., 2023). While this approach can amplify messages, it risks commodifying sustainability or creating campaigns that prioritize brand image over genuine impact (De Luca et al., 2022). Additionally, over-reliance on influencers may alienate audiences who view such collaborations as insincere or overly commercialized (Madonna et al., 2023).

Addressing the Challenges

To overcome these challenges, a multifaceted approach is necessary (Rashed, 2022). Digital literacy programs can bridge accessibility gaps, while collaboration between stakeholders can enhance the integration of Instagram campaigns with national strategies (Bystrov & Panigrahi, 2021). Promoting high-quality, credible content and diversifying outreach methods can further ensure inclusivity and effectiveness (Shrivastava et al., 2021). Additionally, encouraging meaningful engagement rather than performative actions can foster a culture of genuine commitment to sustainable development in Bahrain (Caliandro & Graham, 2020). By addressing these barriers, Bahrain can unlock the full potential of Instagram as a tool for sustainable development, ensuring that its campaigns are impactful, inclusive, and aligned with long-term national goals (Alqashar & Sanad, 2024).

Conclusion

Instagram has proven to be a transformative platform for promoting sustainable development goals (SDGs), offering unparalleled reach and engagement through its visually driven and interactive features. In the Bahraini context, the platform's widespread popularity, particularly among the youth, makes it an invaluable tool for fostering awareness, driving action, and facilitating collaboration among key stakeholders. By showcasing success stories, amplifying grassroots initiatives, and empowering local entrepreneurs, Instagram leverages its ability to merge storytelling with data analytics, enabling organizations to create targeted campaigns that enhance their impact. However, challenges like digital divides, algorithmic biases, and performative activism highlight the need for inclusive strategies. Effective collaboration among the government, private sector, and civil society is essential to ensure that Instagram campaigns support the attainment of the SDGs. Furthermore, prioritizing digital literacy, credible content, and accessibility is vital for maximizing Instagram's potential. By addressing these limitations and leveraging its strengths, Bahrain can emerge as a leader in using digital media for sustainability, inspiring meaningful change for a better future.

References

AlAmmary, J. (2022). The impact of social media on women's empowerment in the Kingdom of Bahrain. *Gender, Technology and Development, 26*(2), 238–262.

Aldada, A. M., Alrasheed, R., & Khalifa, M. (2023). Sustainable development in light of the Bahraini National Action Charter - an analytical study. *Sustainable Development, 12*, 1–2023.

AlGhanem, N., & Mendy, J. (2024). Sustaining successful organisational change through leadership competence within Bahrain oil and gas: The power of sustainable network leadership approach. *Journal of Organizational Change Management, 37*(3), 524–542. https://doi.org/10.1108/JOCM-07-2023-0268

Alqashar, K., & Sanad, Z. (2024). The role of corporate boards in achieving sustainable development goals: Evidence from Bahrain. In *Business development via AI and digitalization* (Vol. 1, pp. 851–862). Springer Nature Switzerland.

Alsaad, R. I., Hamdan, A., Binsaddig, R., & Kanan, M. A. (2023). Empowerment sustainability perspectives for Bahraini women as entrepreneurs. *International Journal of Innovation Studies, 7*(4), 245–262.

Alsridi, H. (2019). The adoption and use of social media and its impact on mainstream media in Bahrain. *Journalism, 9*(1), 13–25.

Álvarez-Herrero, J. F., Urrea-Solano, M., & Martínez-Roig, R. (2021). Sustainability and education through social networks. Presence and visibility of the school garden on Twitter, Facebook and Instagram. *IJERI: International Journal of Educational Research and Innovation, 16*, 122–141.

Bystrov, I., & Panigrahi, S. K. (2021). Commitment of higher education institutions to sustainability agenda: Evidences from GCC countries. *The Journal of Contemporary Issues in Business and Government, 27*(2), 4182–4189.

Caliandro, A., & Graham, J. (2020). Studying Instagram beyond selfies. *Social Media+ Society, 6*(2), 2056305120924779.

De Luca, F., Iaia, L., Mehmood, A., & Vrontis, D. (2022). Can social media improve stakeholder engagement and communication of sustainable development goals? A cross-country analysis. *Technological Forecasting and Social Change, 177*, 121525.

Franco-Riquelme, J. N., & Rubalcaba, L. (2021). Innovation and sdgs through social media analysis: Messages from fintech firms. *Journal of Open Innovation: Technology, Market, and Complexity, 7*(3), 165.

Geraldo, G., & de Souza Pinto, M. D. (2020). The use of social media Instagram to disseminate sustainable information. *International Journal of Librarianship, 5*(2), 4–12.

Hernández-Serrano, M. J., Jones, B., Renés-Arellano, P., & Ortuño, R. A. C. (2022). Analysis of digital self-presentation practices and profiles of Spanish adolescents on Instagram and TikTok. *Journal of New Approaches in Educational Research, 11*(1), 49–63.

Ijomah, T. I., Idemudia, C., Eyo-Udo, N. L., & Anjorin, K. F. (2024). Innovative digital marketing strategies for SMEs: Driving competitive advantage and sustainable growth. *International Journal of Management & Entrepreneurship Research*, *6*(7), 2173–2188.

Lozano-Blasco, R., Mira-Aladrén, M., & Gil-Lamata, M. (2023). Social media influence on young people and children: Analysis on Instagram, Twitter and YouTube. *Comunicar: Media Education Research Journal*, *31*(74), 117–128.

Madonna, M., Reza, F., & Sovianti, R. (2023). Social media as a platform to increase participation of extension workers and farmers in achieving SDGs. *KnE Social Sciences*, 854–863.

Marzouki, A., Chouikh, A., Mellouli, S., & Haddad, R. (2021). From sustainable development goals to sustainable cities: A social media analysis for policy-making decision. *Sustainability*, *13*(15), 8136.

Mittischek, L., & Waldner, I. (2023). Sustainability aspects and educational relevance on social media influencers for children and adolescents. In *Shaping tomorrow today–SDGs from multiple perspectives* (pp. 281–300). Springer Fachmedien Wiesbaden.

Olof Larsson, A. (2023). The rise of Instagram as a tool for political communication: A longitudinal study of European political parties and their followers. *New Media & Society*, *25*(10), 2744–2762.

Oueiss, E. A., & El-Khoury, J. R. (2023). *Media strategies for promoting sustainable development goals* (Vol. 34, pp. 1–20). Arab Media & Society.

Pietrzak, P. (2022). The involvement of public higher education institutions (HEIs) in Poland in the promotion of the sustainable development goals (SDGs) in the age of social media. *Information*, *13*(10), 473.

Rashed, A. H. (2022). Bahrain's environmental legal tools for giving effect to sustainable development goals: An assessment. *Environmental Policy and Law*, *52*(1), 39–54.

Robles-Moral, F. J. (2021). Learning about sustainability and SDG with future primary education teachers in initial training. *Social Sciences*, *10*(11), 409.

Shrivastava, A., Jain, G., Kamble, S. S., & Belhadi, A. (2021). Sustainability through online renting clothing: Circular fashion fueled by Instagram micro-celebrities. *Journal of Cleaner Production*, *278*, 123772.

Soedarsono, D. K., Mohamad, B., Adamu, A. A., & Pradita, K. A. (2020). Managing digital marketing communication of coffee shop using Instagram. *International Journal of Interactive Mobile Technologies*, *14*(5).

Wielki, J. (2020). Analysis of the role of digital influencers and their impact on the functioning of the contemporary on-line promotional system and its sustainable development. *Sustainability*, *12*(17), 7138.

Chapter 26

Digital Marketing Strategies of the Kingdom of Bahrain Government's Efforts and Their Role in Supporting Sustainable Development Plans

Mona Mohamed Daabis

Ahlia University, Bahrain

Abstract

In the era of digital transformation, governments increasingly rely on technological tools to enhance their efficiency and achieve developmental objectives. Digital marketing strategies represent one of the core pillars that contribute to delivering governmental efforts to various segments of society, thereby fostering awareness and supporting sustainable development plans. These strategies leverage digital media channels and social media platforms to create positive engagement between governments and communities, offering innovative solutions to developmental challenges. Today, sustainable development garners significant attention from nations, international and regional economic organizations, and research centers due to its fundamental role in promoting social justice, protecting the environment, and achieving sustainable growth that ensures the rights of future generations. Sustainable development is considered one of the primary challenges facing the world in the 21st century, necessitating collective efforts to achieve it. This involves enhancing communication methods, raising awareness, exchanging information, stimulating interaction and community participation, and providing solutions to address the challenges faced by various societies. Amid the rapid digital transformations witnessed globally, digital marketing has become a key tool to reinforce governmental efforts and achieve sustainable development goals.

Digital Dialogues, 253–263

Published under exclusive licence by Emerald Publishing Limited
doi:10.1108/978-1-83708-686-320261026

Keywords: Marketing strategies; digital marketing; social marketing; sustainable development; Kingdom of Bahrain's vision for sustainable development

Introduction

In the era of digital transformation and the continuous advancement of communication technologies, governments now possess effective digital tools that enhance their interaction with citizens to achieve developmental objectives. Digital marketing strategies have become a vital means of maximizing the impact of governmental efforts in supporting sustainable development plans. These strategies rely on utilizing social media platforms, smart applications, and websites to raise awareness, enhance transparency, and stimulate community participation. Digital marketing strategies are based on leveraging digital media channels to support sustainable development plans by delivering awareness messages and fostering community interaction (Abu Omar, 2023, p. 427). Digital media is considered an essential tool for achieving sustainable development through its contribution to raising awareness, enhancing community participation, and stimulating social and political change in developing countries. Achieving this requires the integration of media efforts with governmental policies and civil society to ensure the success of sustainable development projects (Jawabra & Mohammed, 2024, p. 355). Sustainable development is a global goal that the international community strives to achieve to ensure the balanced and lasting application of all development sectors. On September 25, 2015, during the United Nations General Assembly, member states adopted an ambitious global development agenda to address the world's major challenges by 2030. This agenda comprises 17 Sustainable Development Goals (SDGs) and 169 sub-targets, covering a wide range of issues such as poverty, gender equality, water and sanitation, energy, sustainable cities, climate change, and peace. The SDGs include social, economic, and environmental reforms and target both developed and developing nations, regardless of their level of development. Achieving these goals requires strong collaboration at international, national, and local levels (Ashiri, 2022, p. 71). With the rapid advancement in digital technology, digital marketing strategies have emerged as one of the primary tools for strengthening governmental efforts to achieve sustainable development. This research paper will address five key areas: marketing strategies, digital marketing, social marketing and governmental policies, sustainable development, and the Kingdom of Bahrain's vision for sustainable development.

First: Marketing Strategies

- **Definition of Strategy:** A strategy is a set of ideas, plans, and principles that an organization relies on to excel in competition and ensure its sustainability by enhancing its performance over a defined period (Al-Jabali, 2016, p. 140). Among the key reasons for failure in strategy implementation are unexpected external conditions, lack of understanding among participants in strategy development, flawed strategy design, misalignment between the strategy and the organization's core competencies, and the absence of accountability or responsibility within the team (Bones et al., 2018, p. 1).

- **Mechanisms and Stages of Strategic Management:** Strategic management is among the highest levels of administrative activities within an organization. The strategic planning process goes through several key stages, including (Al-Jabali, 2016, pp. 138–139):
  - formulating the organization's mission and defining its objectives;
  - identifying the unique characteristics and traits of the organization;
  - analyzing the current external environment;
  - forecasting future environmental conditions;
  - developing alternative strategies along with appropriate tactics and procedures;
  - evaluating strategic options and selecting the most suitable one;
  - preparing contingency plans to align with current developments.
- **The National Sustainability Strategy:** There is an urgent need for every country to adopt a national sustainability strategy. The definition provided by the Organization for Economic Cooperation and Development (OECD) underscores the importance of inclusiveness and integration in sustainability strategies (Sania & Mustafa, 2014, p. 106).

Second: Digital Marketing

- **Definition of Marketing:** Marketing is the process by which companies create value for customers and build strong relationships with them, aiming to obtain reciprocal value from customers (Armstrong et al., 2015, p. 4). The purpose of marketing is to know and understand the customer so well that the product or service fits them perfectly and sells itself (Visser et al., 2019, p. 14).
- **Definition of Digital Marketing:** Digital marketing refers to the process of fulfilling customers' needs and desires using digital means. It is a subset of marketing and can be defined as the process where companies, along with current or potential customers, utilize the internet to create value and exchange products or services (Corcoran, 2023, pp. 3–4).
- **Social Media Marketing:** Social media marketing is defined as the process through which companies and organizations promote their products or services via social media platforms, leveraging the vast community these platforms provide—something traditional media cannot offer. This process involves engaging with the "social media" community and building a relationship with them around the products and services that align with their needs and interests (Alaa El-Din, 2020, p. 137).

Third: Social Marketing and Government Policies

Social marketing emerged as a discipline in the early 1970s and has since made significant progress and profound positive impacts across various fields such as public health, environmental protection, injury prevention, community engagement, and financial well-being. Researchers emphasize the importance of broadening the scope of social marketing to leverage its power not only to change individual behaviors but also to influence environmental and political factors that support positive social change, such as public policies, legislation, curricula, business practices, and local communities (Lee & Kotler, 2019, p. 6). Social marketing has become one of the tools utilized by governments to support development programs and policies in many countries around the world. Although social marketing is not a quick or simple solution compared to commercial marketing, it has proven to be an effective tool in supporting development programs (Mostafa, 2013, p. 207).

- **Social Marketing and Change Programs:** Governments often employ social marketing programs as part of social change initiatives. These programs aim to establish administrative systems that guide change efforts toward improving social structures, thereby influencing individual behaviors and achieving goals in key areas such as healthcare, housing, and education (Mostafa, 2013, pp. 207–208). For instance, educational services include tangible components such as books and tools that support the learning process.
- **Value Creation in Government Social Marketing:** Value creation is a fundamental aspect of marketing; however, there is a clear lack of studies addressing this concept in the context of social marketing. Values are a core element of all marketing activities (Mostafa, 2013, p. 8). The key pillars of social marketing are as follows (Azzam et al., 2018, p. 43):
  - Achieving social well-being
  - Ensuring organizational profitability
  - Meeting consumer needs

Fourth: Sustainable Development

- **Definition of Development:** Development, linguistically, refers to "growth" or gradual increase. Terminologically, it is often used in economic, social, and other contexts (Kafi, 2017, p. 15).
- **Definition of Sustainable Development:** The concept of sustainable development is an updated version of development, tailored to meet the demands of the modern era. It is defined as continuous, equitable, balanced, and integrated development that considers environmental, economic, and social dimensions in all its projects (Abu Al-Nasr & Mohammed, 2017, p. 82).
- **Historical Evolution of Sustainable Development:** In 1972, the Stockholm Conference in Sweden marked a turning point by declaring environmental protection and improvement as central issues impacting the well-being of

nations. It stressed the importance of enhancing the environment for the benefit of citizens (Al-Hayti, 2016, p. 10). Later in 1987, a United Nations report emphasized that development should meet the needs of the present without compromising the ability of future generations to meet their needs, while ensuring equitable wealth distribution and environmental preservation (Mansha, 2019, p. 19). In 1987, a specialized committee reiterated the necessity of pursuing sustainable development without causing environmental harm. The International Labour Conference in 1990 incorporated sustainable development as a fundamental principle for the activities of the International Labour Organization, developing policies that ensure the balanced use of resources. Concurrently, international summits such as the Earth Summit in Rio de Janeiro (1992), the Copenhagen Summit in Denmark (1995), and the Women's Summit in Beijing (1995) collectively underscored the significance of sustainable development (Al-Baridi, 2015, p. 44).

In 2002, the World Summit on Sustainable Development, held in Johannesburg, South Africa, highlighted critical issues such as environmental protection, poverty eradication, and strengthening the capacities of developing countries to tackle global challenges effectively (Kafi, 2013, p. 148). In 2005, Arab ministers adopted the Sustainable Development Strategy as part of the Millennium Development Goals, underlining its regional significance through the Arab League (2010), which emphasized women's pivotal role in sustainable development under the theme "Women: A Key Partner in Sustainable Development" (Abu Al-Nasr & Mohammed, 2017, p. 87). In 2012, the Rio+20 Conference advanced the agenda by introducing the "Higher Education Institutions' Commitment to Sustainable Development Practices" document, urging institutional leaders to sign it and advocate for political endorsement. This initiative emphasized the role of higher education in shaping sustainable futures (Al-Baridi, 2015, p. 45). In 2022, the Stockholm+50 Conference convened to commemorate 50 years of global environmental advocacy under the theme "A Healthy Planet for the Prosperity of All—Our Responsibility, Our Opportunity." The conference addressed the triple planetary crises—climate change, biodiversity loss, and pollution—and emphasized green recovery strategies post-COVID-19 while aligning with the Paris Agreement and the post-2020 Global Biodiversity Framework (United Nations Official Website, 2024).

- **Components of Sustainability:** Sustainability is primarily based on three interconnected and complementary pillars (Maleviti, 2024, pp. 2–4):

  (1) **Environment:** A sustainable environmental system must rely on stable resources and avoid overexploitation of renewable resource systems or depletion of nonrenewable resources without sufficient investment in alternatives.

  (2) **Economy:** A sustainable economic system must be capable of producing goods and services consistently, maintaining manageable levels of public and external debt, and avoiding severe sectoral imbalances that harm agricultural or industrial production.

(3) **Society:** A sustainable social system must ensure equitable distribution of resources and opportunities, provide sufficient social services—including health, education, and gender equality—foster political accountability and democracy, encourage participation, and guarantee human rights.

- **Goals of Sustainable Development:** The goals of sustainable development can be summarized as follows (Shafiqa, 2019, pp. 317–318):
  - **Achieving a better quality of life:** Ensuring access to good health, education, and the inclusion of women and children.
  - **Living with dignity:** Eradicating poverty and striving for justice and equality.
  - **Raising environmental awareness:** Enhancing people's sense of responsibility toward environmental issues and encouraging active participation in finding appropriate solutions.
  - **Partnership:** Promoting global coordination, cooperation, and solidarity for sustainable development.
  - **Respecting the planet:** Protecting ecosystems and fostering inclusive societal practices.
  - **Integrating modern technology with societal goals:** Employing modern technologies to serve societal objectives and educating the population on the importance of embracing various technologies in developmental fields.

The primary objectives of sustainable development include: (Abu Al-Nasr & Mohamed, 2017, p. 88)

- driving economic growth;
- establishing social and economic justice and equality;
- optimizing the use of available resources and minimizing waste;
- protecting the environment and natural resources for future generations;
- enhancing well-being and promoting social development.

The 2030 SDGs, issued in 2015 by the United Nations, consist of 17 objectives that complement the Millennium Development Goals (MDGs). These goals require active governmental roles, particularly in managing and utilizing information effectively (Al-Buaiz, 2019, p. 11):

- eradicating poverty;
- ending hunger;
- ensuring good health and well-being;
- providing quality education;
- promoting gender equality;
- ensuring clean water and sanitation;
- providing affordable and clean energy;
- promoting decent work and economic growth;
- industry, innovation, and infrastructure;
- reducing inequalities;

- sustainable cities and communities;
- responsible consumption and production;
- climate action;
- life below water;
- life on land;
- peace, justice, and strong institutions;
- partnerships (financial cooperation, technology, capacity building, and trade).

In 1996, the United Nations Commission on Sustainable Development published a significant book titled "Indicators of Sustainable Development: Framework and Methodologies." This publication outlined 130 indicators for sustainable development (Mansha, 2019, pp. 29–30):

(1) **Environmental Indicators:** These relate to environmental elements such as the atmosphere, lithosphere, oceans, seas, freshwater, and biodiversity.
(2) **Economic Indicators:** These focus on the economic structure and patterns of consumption and production.
(3) **Social Indicators:** These include aspects such as social justice, health, education, housing, security, and population.
(4) **Institutional Indicators:** These emphasize the institutional framework and organizational capacities.

Fifth: The Kingdom of Bahrain's Vision for Sustainable Development

- **Overview of Bahrain's Vision for Sustainable Development:** In 2008, the Kingdom of Bahrain took a pioneering step by launching its forward-looking initiative, "Bahrain Economic Vision 2030." This vision aims to ensure stability and prosperity for citizens and residents, founded on three main pillars: sustainability, competitiveness, and fairness. It includes clear indicators to measure progress. These goals have been integrated into Bahrain's national priorities as part of its "Bahrain Economic Vision 2030," which represents a transformational shift where economic growth aligns with environmental protection and social justice (Bahrain Government Official Website, 2024). The Bahraini government has prioritized the sustainability of this vision by embedding sustainability principles into its policies and programs. Recently, the government introduced the "From Recovery to Sustainable Growth" program for the 2023–2026 period. This program aligns comprehensively with the SDGs across economic, social, and environmental domains. In addition, the Economic Recovery Plan, launched in 2021, emphasizes a comprehensive, resilient, and sustainable recovery in light of the impacts of the COVID-19 pandemic. These initiatives underscore the government's dedication to achieving balanced and sustainable development (Ministry of Finance and National Economy Official Website, 2024). As part of enhancing Bahrain's efforts to support the SDGs, the Kingdom established a Ministry of

Sustainable Development under the new ministerial formation, as outlined in Royal Decree No. (68) of 2022, issued on November 21, 2022. This ministry ensures effective coordination among relevant entities and monitors the progress made in achieving the SDGs (Ministry of Foreign Affairs Official Website, 2024). In 2023, Bahrain published its Voluntary National Review (VNR), providing a comprehensive report on its progress in implementing the Sustainable Development Agenda. As Vision 2030 approaches, Bahrain participated in the Summit of the Future held in New York in September 2024, where it presented three national voluntary commitments to accelerate SDG implementation (Bahrain Government Official Website, 2024).

- **Principles and Initiatives of Bahrain's Digital Government Strategy:** The Digital Government Strategy in the Kingdom of Bahrain is guided by the following principles (Bahrain Government Official Website, 2024):

    - providing digital services for all individuals, ensuring no one is excluded, with a particular focus on developing strategies that align services with citizens' needs;
    - encouraging more stakeholders to engage with the government through their preferred digital channels;
    - designing new public services based on the principle of "Digital First," focusing on digitizing all activities;
    - restructuring specific public services through digitization;
    - enabling citizens and businesses to submit specific types of data to government entities only once;
    - leveraging advanced technologies to make more accurate predictions and smarter decisions by analyzing massive amounts of data;
    - standardizing government data and making it accessible to the public to enhance transparency and community engagement.

    Following the launch of Bahrain's National Digital Strategy, several initiatives have been implemented to meet the needs of various sectors and communities, including citizens, residents, and visitors. These initiatives have improved services, facilitated business transactions, and increased the efficiency of governmental and societal institutions. Among the most significant initiatives are the following (Bahrain Government Official Website, 2024):

    (1) **Commercial Licensing System:** This system aims to simplify business procedures in line with Bahrain's Economic Vision 2030.
    (2) **National Suggestions and Complaints System "Tawasul":** This system is designed to improve government services by unifying channels for complaints and suggestions.
    (3) **"Qudurat" Program:** This program focuses on enhancing IT skills among citizens and government employees by training them on the latest eGovernment and IT technologies.
    (4) **National Enterprise Architecture for ICT Project:** This initiative aims to improve coordination among government institutions and deliver

integrated services by applying effective governance and technology standards.

(5) **Smart Device Applications:** Responding to the growing demand for smart devices, the government has developed applications for platforms such as iOS and Android.

- Bahrain's Efforts in Achieving SDGs: The government of the Kingdom of Bahrain's efforts to support sustainable development plans include the following (Ministry of Finance and National Economy Official Website, 2024):

  - **Supporting Citizens in the Labor Market:** The Bahraini government aims to make the Bahraini citizen the first choice in the labor market by improving job opportunities, providing training, and developing skills.
  - **Facilitating Business Procedures:** Improving the efficiency and effectiveness of business procedures is a key element in enhancing the business environment in Bahrain.
  - **Major Development Projects:** Major development projects involve strategic investments worth over $30 billion aimed at enhancing Bahrain's economic competitiveness and improving the lives of citizens and residents.
  - **Developing Promising Sectors:** Bahrain has launched strategies to develop six key sectors, including oil and gas, tourism, logistics services, industry, and information and communication technology, to drive economic growth.
  - **Financial Sustainability and Economic Stability:** The updated Fiscal Balance Program includes eight key initiatives focusing on increasing nonoil revenues and controlling expenses to achieve fiscal balance by 2024.

Conclusion

In conclusion, the importance of employing effective digital marketing strategies in supporting sustainable development plans is evident. Digital media plays a vital and impactful role in the lives of individuals and communities in today's world. The significance of digital marketing lies in highlighting initiatives and plans, enriching human knowledge in both cognitive and behavioral awareness, thereby contributing to comprehensive community development. It focuses on the balanced development of natural and human resources, without waste or destruction, based on a collectively planned and cooperative future strategy. The essence of this strategy is to meet the needs of current and future generations, with a focus on cultural and community participation to promote integrated development. The importance of effective marketing strategies lies in building more sustainable and resilient communities. As digital technologies continue to evolve, the need to adopt innovative and integrated marketing policies that ensure the achievement of SDGs on both local and global levels becomes increasingly urgent. Success in this field requires collaboration between different sectors, with the continued development of efficient and innovative strategies to ensure a sustainable and inclusive future for all. The government of the Kingdom of Bahrain has demonstrated its steadfast commitment to achieving sustainable development through innovative digital marketing strategies, enhancing community interaction, raising awareness of development goals, and providing effective digital solutions. With the ongoing evolution of technology, there is an urgent need to strengthen digital efforts, ensuring their inclusivity and sustainability to fulfill the aspirations of future generations.

References

Abu Al-Nasr, M. M., & Mohamed, Y. M. (2017). *Sustainable development: Its concept, dimensions, indicators*. Arab Group for Training and Publishing.

Alaa El-Din, N. (2020). *Managing organizational communication strategies via social media*. Al-Arabi for Publishing and Distribution.

Al-Baiz, I. (2019). *Information and communication technologies in the Gulf states*. Al-Khaleej Publishing.

Al-Baridi, A. A. (2015). *Sustainable development: An integrative approach to the concepts and applications of sustainability with a focus on the Arab world*. Obekan Publishing.

Al-Hayti, S. I. H. (2016). *International responsibility for environmental damage*. Dar Raslan for Printing and Publishing.

Al-Jabali, H. (2016). *Administrative development*. Dar Al-Usra for publishing and distribution. Dar Alam Al-Thaqafa.

Armstrong, G., Adam, S., Denize, S., & Kotler, P. (2015). *Principles of marketing* (6th ed.). Pearson.

Ashiri, M. (2022). *Information technology and human capital: A vision for sustainable development 2030*. Dar Al-Taalim Al-Jami'i.

Azzam, Z. A., Hassouna, A.-B., & Sheikh, M. S. (2018). *Principles of modern marketing between theory and practice* (10th ed.). Dar Al-Masirah for Publishing and Distribution.

Bones, C., Hammersley, J., & Shaw, N. (2018). *Optimizing digital strategy: How to make informed, tactical decisions that deliver growth*. Kogan Page.

Corcoran, A. (2023). *Integrated digital marketing in practice*. Cambridge University Press.

Jawabra, R. Z. A., & Muhammad, A. M. F. K. (2024). The role of digital media in promoting sustainable development goals. *Lark Journal of Philosophy, Linguistics and Social Sciences*, *16*(2), 353–365.

Kafi, M. Y. (2013). *Environmental economics and globalization. Damascus*. Dar and raslan foundation for printing. Publishing and Distribution.

Kafi, M. Y. (2017). *Sustainable development*. Dar Al-Akadmioun Publishing and Distribution Company.

Lee, N. R., & Kotler, P. (2019). *Social marketing: Changing behaviors for good*. SAGE Publications.

Maleviti, E. (2024). *Fundamentals of sustainable aviation*. Routledge.

Manshi, F. A. A. (2019). *Knowledge economy: A vision for sustainability in the Arab world*. Center for Professional Expertise in Management.

Mustafa, S. Al-S. A. A. (2013). *Social and political marketing. Theoretical principles and local and global applications*. Dar Nahdet Misr Publishing House.

Official website of the Government of the Kingdom of Bahrain. https://www.bahrain.bh/wps/portal/ar/BNP/HomeNationalPortal. Accessed on December 1, 2024.

Official website of the Ministry of Finance and National Economy. https://www.mofne.gov.bh/. Accessed on December 1, 2024.

Official website of the Ministry of Foreign Affairs. https://www.mofa.gov.bh/ar/. Accessed on December 1, 2024.

Official website of the United Nations. https://www.un.org/ar/conferences/environment. Accessed on December 1, 2024.

Omar, A., & Hussein, A. M. (2023). The effectiveness of employing E-Marketing in supporting sustainable development programs: An analytical study on some E-Marketing sites. *Scientific Journal of Public Relations and Advertising Research, 25*, 425–466.

Sania, A., & Mustafa, A. L. (2014). *Studies in economic development.* Hassan Al-Asriya library for printing. Publishing and Distribution.

Shafika, M. (2019). *Current research issues and challenges.* Darub for Publishing and Distribution.

Visser, M., Sikkenga, B., & Berry, M. (2019). *Digital marketing fundamentals: From strategy to ROI.* Noordhoff Uitgevers.

Chapter 27

Media Economics on Social Media Toward Achieving Sustainable Development Goals in the Kingdom of Bahrain

Nadia Ismail Moosa

Ahlia University, Bahrain

Abstract

This study focuses on the importance of employing the concept of media economics, especially with the growing international economic crises and the global interest in achieving the 2030 Sustainable Development Goals. There is an urgent need to shed media light on the economy to foster economic community awareness that can adapt to unstable economic conditions. The study also focuses on the importance of media economics as a reliable information interface that supports economic development and encourages attracting international investments in sustainable ways to stimulate initiatives and policies in the Kingdom of Bahrain toward a comprehensive development renaissance.

Keywords: Media economics; digital economy; sustainable economies; digital media; social media; Sustainable Development Goals; mass communication

Introduction

Social media has revolutionized the way we communicate, consume information, and engage with the world. Its rapid growth has profoundly impacted media economics, opening new avenues for content creation, distribution, and consumption. This digital transformation offers immense potential to accelerate progress toward the Sustainable Development Goals (SDGs).

Digital Dialogues, 265–273

Published under exclusive licence by Emerald Publishing Limited
doi:10.1108/978-1-83708-686-320261027

By leveraging social media's ability to connect people across borders and cultures, we can amplify marginalized voices, raise awareness about global challenges, and mobilize collective action. However, the economic dynamics of social media platforms, coupled with issues of digital equity and misinformation, bring new significant challenges to achieving sustainable development.

This research delves into the intricate relationship between media economics and social media, examining how these platforms can be harnessed to address pressing global issues such as poverty, inequality, climate change, and healthcare. We explore innovative strategies to optimize the use of social media for social good, considering factors like monetization models, content curation, and platform governance.

By understanding the economic incentives that drive social media platforms, we can work toward a future where these platforms are used as a force for positive change, empowering communities and promoting sustainable development for all.

Media Economics and SDGs 2030

The intricate relationship between media economics and SDGs has emerged as a critical area of inquiry in contemporary research. Media, as a potent force shaping public opinion and driving social change, plays a crucial role in achieving the SDGs. By examining the economic dynamics of media industries, we can unravel their potential to contribute to global sustainability. For instance, the media's capacity to raise awareness about environmental issues, promote gender equality, and advocate for social justice can significantly impact progress toward these global goals.

Moreover, the rise of digital media and social platforms has further complicated the media landscape. While these platforms offer unprecedented opportunities for citizen journalism, activism, and global connectivity, they also present challenges related to data privacy, algorithmic bias, and the spread of disinformation. To fully harness the potential of media for sustainable development, it is imperative to address these challenges and promote ethical and responsible media practices.

By exploring the intersection of media economics and SDGs, researchers and business organizations can develop innovative strategies to leverage the power of media for positive social change. This may involve examining the role of media ownership and regulation, the impact of advertising and sponsorship on media content, and the potential of public service media to promote sustainable development.

Research Problem

This research aims to contribute to a deeper understanding of the complex relationship between media economics, social media, and SDGs, and to identify strategies for maximizing the positive impact of these platforms on sustainable development. How can media economics on social media platforms be leveraged to effectively address the global challenge of climate change, particularly in terms of raising awareness, mobilizing public opinion, and influencing policy decisions?

Contribution

A notable research gap exists in the integrated study of media economics, its relationship with social media dynamics, and sustainability practices. There is a pressing need for empirical research to facilitate the adoption of sustainable strategies by citizens and businesses, enabling them to align with the opportunities and challenges of the pervasive digitalization era and the concurrent Artificial Intelligence (AI) revolution.

The purpose of the study is to provide and updated literature reviews about media economics to discuss the challenges and to lighten the future competitiveness opportunities for the citizen and the business.

Research Methodology

This chapter is a theoretical study that includes limitations and opportunities and investigates media economies and sustainability.

Literature Review

The related literature on media economics is presented in this chapter. The literature review aims to classify, evaluate, and compare various aspects of the topic. Subsequently, the literature review will provide a summary of different sources and academic references.

Media Economics Overview

Media economics is described as the "study of how people make choices to cope with scarcity". Picard, R. G. (2003) define media economics as "the study of the economic principles and practices applied to the production, distribution, and consumption of media content". On the other hand, Gillian Doyle's book "Understanding Media Economics" provides a comprehensive introduction to the intersection of media and economics. She states, "media economics combines the study of economics with media, focusing on how economic forces influence the decisions of media managers and practitioners. It addresses the informational and entertainment needs of audiences, advertisers, and society using available resources" (Doyle, 2019).

Doyle introduces fundamental economic concepts relevant to media, such as market structures, competition, and the motivations of firms. It emphasizes the importance of understanding these concepts to grasp how media businesses operate and discusses the impact of digitization and the significant changes brought about by the digital revolution, including the challenges and opportunities it presents for media businesses. It highlights the need for new analytical approaches to understand the evolving media landscape. Rather than a sector-specific approach, the book offers a thematic framework that addresses key issues such as innovation, network economics, copyright, and advertising (Doyle, 2019).

"The Media Economy" by Alan B. Albarran analyzes the media industries through the lens of economics, providing a holistic view of how these industries operate within the broader economic framework. The significant changes in the media landscape, particularly in the 21st century, are driven by technological advancements, globalization, and evolving consumer behaviors. According to Albarran, the transformation of media industries since the 1990s highlights the impact of globalization, regulatory reforms, and technological innovations such as mobile devices and broadband networks. It emphasizes the shift from traditional media to digital platforms, including streaming services and social media, and how these changes affect content creation and distribution (Albarran, 2023).

"The Media Economy" serves as an essential resource for understanding the multifaceted relationship between media and economics. It provides a thorough analysis of the current state of media industries, the challenges they face, and the opportunities for growth and innovation. By combining theoretical frameworks with practical case studies, the book offers valuable insights for anyone interested in media management, economics, and the evolving landscape of the media industry.

"Introduction to Media Economics" explores the distinctive economic characteristics and challenges faced by media organizations. A key concept is the dual product market: media firms produce both content (such as television programs, articles, and digital content) and audiences. They then sell access to these audiences to advertisers. The text explains why conventional economic theories often fall short in fully explaining media behavior, as these firms frequently pursue diverse objectives beyond simple profit maximization, including public service, informing the public, and promoting cultural values (Hoskins et al., 2004). The study emphasizes the necessity of government regulation in the media sector. Such regulation aims to balance the pursuit of profit and utility maximization by individual firms with the broader societal welfare, addressing potential market failures and ensuring diverse and accessible information. Media firms are highly sensitive to broader economic fluctuations. Their revenues are strongly correlated with advertising spending, which tends to rise and fall with overall economic activity, and with consumer spending habits. This diversity of objectives complicates the application of traditional economic models, which often assume profit maximization as the primary goal.

"Understanding Media Economics", "The Media Economy", and "Introduction to Media Economics" provide valuable frameworks for understanding the complex interplay between media and economics. They offer critical insights for students, researchers, policymakers, and media professionals seeking to navigate the dynamic and ever-changing media landscape.

Media Economics Impact of Social Media

Social media has profoundly transformed communication, business practices, and economic structures. Several studies and analyses highlight its multifaceted economic impact, focusing on content creation, distribution, consumption, and broader economic development.

"The Economics of Social Media" article analyzes and explores the economics of social media through the lens of content production, distribution, and consumption. User-generated content (UGC) is a cornerstone of social media. Individuals and organizations are incentivized to create content for various reasons, including self-expression, community building, and marketing. Algorithms and social network structures play a critical role in determining content visibility and reach. This raises important issues such as targeted advertising, algorithmic bias, and the formation of echo chambers, where users are primarily exposed to like-minded views, potentially leading to polarization. User interaction with content has significant societal effects. The spread of misinformation and its impact on political discourse and economic decisions are key concerns. Studies also analyze consumer behavior on social media, including how users engage with different platforms and the substitution patterns between them (Aridor et al., 2023).

EconoTimes (2022) discusses the significant impact of social media on the economy, highlighting several key points. First, social media platforms create new opportunities for entrepreneurs to build their businesses, allowing for increased brand awareness and consumer engagement. Second, social media serves as an inexpensive advertising tool, enabling businesses to interact directly with consumers, gather feedback, and respond to their needs without the traditional marketing hype. Third, the rise of social media has lowered barriers for small businesses to reach consumers, allowing them to establish a market presence more easily. Finally, social media platforms like Facebook, Instagram, and LinkedIn control content distribution, disrupting traditional advertising models and significantly influencing market dynamics.

The study titled "The Role of Social Media in Shaping Public Opinion and Its Influence on Economic Decisions" by Abu Muna Almaududi Ausat explores the significant impact of social media on public opinion and economic decision-making. The study aims to understand how social media influences public opinion and the subsequent effects on economic decisions, highlighting the importance of this relationship in contemporary society. Ausat finds that social media serves as a powerful platform for individuals to express their views and share information, which can rapidly shape public sentiment. The information disseminated through these platforms significantly affects individuals' economic choices, as people often rely on social media for insights and opinions (Ausat, 2023).

Zhey Cui studies the impact of social media on economic development, particularly in rural areas. It emphasizes that farmers can benefit significantly from using social media to sell their agricultural products directly to consumers, fostering trust and transparency in the buying process. This direct engagement can lead to increased sales, providing farmers with a stable income and positively influencing regional GDP. The rise of social media usage, especially platforms like TikTok, is noted to create a more interconnected urban environment, enhancing consumer awareness and demand for agricultural products. The document also discusses how social media serves as a cost-effective marketing tool for businesses, facilitating online transactions and improving consumer access to information about products (Cui, 2021).

Media Economics and Sustainability

This section explores the crucial role of media and the digital economy in driving progress toward sustainable development. Several studies highlight different facets of this relationship, emphasizing the importance of independent media, green innovation, and mindful media practices.

According to the MDIF study, the aim is to explore the role of independent media in achieving the SDGs; several sources emphasize the vital role of independent media in achieving the United Nations' SDGs. Independent media acts as an agenda-setter, gatekeeper, and watchdog, fostering transparency, accountability, and informed public participation. This is particularly crucial for SDG 16 (Peace, Justice, and Strong Institutions), which focuses on ensuring public access to information.

The main objective of the study "The Impact of the Digital Economy on Sustainable Development: Evidence from China" is to investigate the impact of the digital economy on sustainable development in China. Research consistently demonstrates the positive impact of the digital economy on sustainable development, with a particular focus on green innovation. Studies examining China's digital economy from 2011 to 2020 and 2015 to 2019 reveal that it significantly enhances sustainable development by promoting green innovation, improving efficiency, reducing operational costs, creating jobs, and contributing to economic sustainability. Government policies like the "Broadband China" initiative play a vital role in optimizing network infrastructure and supporting this growth. The research suggests targeted policy interventions, including increased investment in education and research, enhanced intellectual property rights protection, and policies that encourage green innovation and R&D efficiency. Balanced regional development of the digital economy and regional cooperation are also crucial (An Q et al., 2024).

Bharat Dhiman (2023). discusses in his study "Media Role in Promoting Values and Meditation for Sustainable Development" the significant influence of media in fostering values and mindfulness practices that contribute to sustainable development. The researcher found that the media serves as a powerful tool for raising awareness and understanding of sustainability issues. Ethical storytelling can effectively shape public opinion and promote values aligned with sustainable development. Studies suggest that promoting mindfulness through media can lead to more intentional lifestyle choices and consumption patterns that support sustainability. This encourages a shift toward a culture of mindfulness and ethical living.

The study by Zhang et al. (2021) investigates the impact of the digital economy on high-quality economic development in China, focusing on the period from 2015 to 2019. It identifies a lack of empirical research on this topic and aims to fill this gap by evaluating the development of the digital economy across different regions in China. The research develops an index system to measure the digital economy, selecting core dimensions and indicators to assess overall changes and regional differences in its development. An econometric model is constructed to analyze the effect of the digital economy on high-quality economic development, with technological progress introduced as an intermediary variable. The results indicate that both the digital economy and technological progress significantly enhance total factor productivity. Finally, the paper suggests that the government should improve its governance system and provide precise subsidies to enhance R&D efficiency, rather than relying on inefficient financial subsidies.

Economic Media in the Kingdom of Bahrain

The Kingdom of Bahrain plays a pivotal role in boosting the regional economy, driven by its advanced financial infrastructure and strategic location. To illuminate this role, economic media emerges as a crucial tool for disseminating economic knowledge and fostering transparency within the Kingdom. It represents a cornerstone for achieving sustainable development and solidifying Bahrain's position as a global financial and investment hub.

Bahrain's economic media strives to convey economic news and analysis accurately and objectively, focusing on local, regional, and global issues. This enhances public and investor understanding of economic policies and opportunities within the Bahraini market.

The significance of economic media for the Kingdom of Bahrain lies in its ability to provide a platform that showcases economic successes, such as advancements in the financial sector, infrastructure development, and the prosperity of non-oil sectors like tourism and industry. Economic media also actively supports Bahrain's Economic Vision 2030, which aims to diversify the economy and increase the Kingdom's regional and global competitiveness.

The role of social media in disseminating economic news has become increasingly crucial in the digital age. These platforms offer an effective means of rapidly and widely transmitting economic news and analysis, enabling the public to access information instantly.

Moreover, social media provides a space for public discussions and the exchange of views on economic topics, enhancing community awareness of economic issues and encouraging active participation.

Prominent media institutions shedding light on the Bahraini economy include the Bahrain News Agency (BNA), Al-Ayyam newspaper, Al Watan newspaper, and Akhbar Al Khaleej newspaper. Official websites providing reliable economic information include the Ministry of Finance and National Economy and the Central Bank of Bahrain, which display the latest economic indicators and financial reports. The Economic Development Board and the Ministry of Sustainable Development, meanwhile, review achievements made in the sustainable development plan.

Economic media in Bahrain demonstrates how traditional and digital media can collaborate to support the economy and raise public awareness, contributing to a sustainable economic future.

The economic media has played a prominent role in addressing economic issues, boosting economic confidence, supporting government policies, attracting foreign investment, promoting transparency and accountability, and conveying a positive image.

Examples of media influence in addressing economic issues facing the Kingdom of Bahrain include economic recovery after the Corona pandemic, digital transformation, cybersecurity awareness, and attracting foreign investments.

Economic media significantly impacts the achievement of SDGs, aligned with Bahrain's Economic Vision 2030.

The media highlights the vision's achievements while continuously educating the public about its most important goals and the government's policies to achieve them.

Despite challenges, the Kingdom possesses significant potential to develop this field through investments in technology, leveraging young Bahraini competencies, and supporting the regulatory environment.

Conclusion

Economic media plays a significant role in achieving SDGs through Bahrain's Economic Vision 2030. The media highlights the vision's achievements and educates the public about its goals and progress. Despite challenges, Bahrain has significant potential to develop this field through investment in technology, nurturing young Bahraini talent, and supporting a robust regulatory environment.

This study highlights the significant role of media economics in advancing the SDGs within the Kingdom of Bahrain, particularly in the context of its Economic Vision 2030. Integrating effective media strategies into economic development initiatives is crucial for fostering public awareness and engagement with the SDGs.

Bahrain's diverse media landscape, encompassing both traditional (print, radio, and television) and digital platforms (social media, online news, and websites), plays a vital role in disseminating information about government policies and economic opportunities. By strategically leveraging these channels, the Kingdom can effectively educate its citizens about the importance of sustainable development and encourage active participation in SDG-related initiatives.

In conclusion, this research underscores the significant potential of media economics to support not only Bahrain's economic objectives but also the global agenda of sustainable development. By fostering a collaborative ecosystem involving media organizations, government agencies, the private sector, and the public, Bahrain can strengthen its position as a regional leader in sustainable economic practices.

References

Albarran, A. B. (2023). *The media economy* (3rd ed.). Routledge. https://doi.org/10.4324/9781003392293

An, Q., Wang, R., Wang, Y., & Pavel, K. (2024), *The impact of the digital economy on sustainable development: Evidence from China*. https://doi.org/10.3389/fenvs.2024.1341471

An, Q., Wang, R., Wu, Y., & Pan, K. (2024). The impact of the digital economy on sustainable development: The mediating role of green innovation. *Frontiers in Environmental Science, 10*, Article 1341471. https://doi.org/10.3389/fenvs.2024.1341471

Aridor, G., Jiménez-Durán, R., Levy, R., & Song, L. (2023). *The economics of social media*. https://ssrn.com/abstract=4708840

Ausat, A. M. (2023). The role of social media in shaping public opinion and its influence on economic decisions. *Technology and Society Perspectives (TACIT)*, *1*(1), 35–44.

Cui, Z. (2021). *Analysis of the impact of social media on the economy*. Atlantis Press. https://doi.org/10.2991/assehr.k.211209.500

Dhiman, B. (2023). *Media role in promoting values & meditation for sustainable development*. https://core.ac.uk/download/576856909.pdf

Doyle, G. (2019). *Understanding media economics*. Researchgate. https://doi.org/10.4135/9781446279960

EconoTimes. (2022). *How is social media helping the economy?* How Is Social Media Helping the Economy? - EconoTimes

Hoskins, C., McFadyen, S., & Finn, A. (2004). *Media economics: Applying economics to new and traditional media*. SAGE Publications. https://us.sagepub.com/sites/default/files/upm-binaries/9436_010539Intro.pdf

Picard, R. G. (2003). *Comparative aspects of media economics and - Its development in Europe and in the USA*. https://www.scirp.org/journal/paperinformation?paperid=60170#:~:text=Media%20economics%20consists%20of%20studying,economic%20aspects%20of%20mass%20media

Zhang, W., Zhao, S., Wan, X., & Yao, Y. (2021). Study on the effect of digital economy on high quality economic development in China. *PLoS One*. https://doi.org/10.1371/journal. pone.0257365

Chapter 28

Journalists' Attitudes Toward Media Legislation in the Kingdom of Bahrain

Maha Hameed Alanezi[a], *Hani Hamza Ali Ebrahim*[b], *Maznah Khalifa Aldhahrani*[b], *Mohammed Muflih Mohammad AlQahtani*[c] *and Imad Assali*[b]

[a]Ministry of Education, Bahrain
[b]Ahlia University, Bahrain
[c]Southern Province Cement Company, Saudi Arabia

Abstract

This study examines the significance of media legislation and journalism ethics in addressing contemporary media challenges, such as fake news, misinformation, and rumors, particularly with the rapid growth of digital media. It aims to understand journalists' attitudes toward media laws in the Kingdom of Bahrain, which help balance freedom of expression with social responsibility. By reviewing prior studies, this research highlights the role of media legislation in safeguarding journalism, ensuring transparency, and promoting credibility. Finally, the study advocates for further research on digital journalism ethics to develop innovative solutions for emerging challenges.

Keywords: Journalism legislation; media legislation; journalism ethics; freedom of expression

Introduction

In writing contemporary history, journalists seek to take into account the daily recording of events conducted by the press. Whether through the written word, television images, or radio audio memory, the press provides elements

Digital Dialogues, 275–284

Published under exclusive licence by Emerald Publishing Limited
doi:10.1108/978-1-83708-686-320261028

that—although limited in accuracy, analysis, or focus—contribute to the preservation of collective memory (Muhammad Suleiman, 2017).

The most well-known reason for the importance of journalism is that it leads to changes in history by being a conduit for expressing society. Every piece of information has the potential to change, which, when activated, imprints the dynamic of evolution in social life. The possibility of changing something every day is crucial, and society needs the press as much as the human body needs its sensory organs (Dawadi, 2022).

The press contributes to the development of knowledge of reality. Contextualization, background, and fact projection. By confronting sources and applications of truth, information is transformed into knowledge, which is the foundation of freedom. A society cannot be truly free if it doesn't really know what's going on. When what happens is well known, decisions are freely made, but when there is no such knowledge, society and individuals become manipulative. Ultimately, journalism is important because it contributes to its mission of promoting and exercising freedom (Rumaisah Shahlat, 2022).

Freedom of opinion and expression through the press requires considerable regulation, so that the expression of opinion is in the interest of society, and thus states have drafted media legislation and laws, because media organizations operate as open systems that interact with other regulations in the environment: Economic, political, legal, social and cultural media, therefore, manage information and act responsibly and respect people's rights, and ensure the dissemination of honest, objective and harmless information, through effective regulatory standards and mechanisms, important for promoting a culture of responsibility and ethics among professionals and the media (Amjad, 2020).

The importance of this study is to draw attention to journalists' tendencies toward media legislation in the Kingdom of Bahrain. It is very important because while respecting media legislation, journalists contribute to fulfilling of their high role in the press by playing the high role of journalism, such as transparency and honesty in information provided to society, free from false news, infiltrating citizens' personal lives, or destabilizing society.

The Theoretical Framework of the Study

Study Concepts and Terminology

(1) Journalism: Journalism can be defined as a professional activity to obtain, collect, analyze, create, process, display, and distribute news and information. Moreover, journalism is the product of all these activities together.
(2) Legislation: Legislation is a set of laws that will define and regulate an issue and apply to an area such as an entire state or municipality and can even govern conduct within an institution, such as media legislation on media regulation.

(3) Media Legislation: Laws that regulate media content and practices to ensure ethical standards, protect public interests, and prevent misinformation.
(4) Journalism Ethics: Guidelines for journalists, emphasizing accuracy, fairness, and respect for privacy to promote truthful and responsible reporting.
(5) Freedom of Expression: The right to share opinions freely, essential for democracy, though sometimes limited to prevent harm or incitement.

Previous Studies

Al-Suleiman (2017), in his study titled "Trends of the Egyptian Media Elite Towards Media Legislation Following the January 25, 2011 Revolution," emphasizes that freedom of information is a fundamental human right as it reflects freedom of opinion. The study aimed to explore the legal framework governing the media in Egypt after the 2011 revolution, especially considering the significant shift in the media landscape during that period. Using a qualitative methodology, the study conducted in-depth, semi-structured interviews with a sample of 15 members of the Egyptian media elite. The findings revealed that Egypt's political system continues to have a strong and influential role in shaping the media, whether through ownership or legislation. The study also highlighted ongoing challenges such as self-censorship, driven by fear of legal consequences. Importantly, the study noted that recent media legislation has moved away from vague and ambiguous language, showing some progress. However, it stressed the need for well-defined media laws that can regulate the media sector effectively, as media is an integral part of society and must operate within a clear legal framework.

Dawadi (2022) reviewed a study entitled "Manifestations of the ethics of the media profession in Algerian legislation." The media legislation is based on the 1982 Act No. July 1990 and the Media Amendment Act 2012. After analyzing the legal texts, it was found that ethical obligations and legal texts are complementary. In order to build meaningful information that serves the community, neither of these can be dispensed with as they are complementary. However, corruption can interfere with the media profession, especially in light of significant technological acceleration and the spread of cybercrime, rumors, hate speech, and so on, which have a significant impact on civil society.

The aim of Rumaisah Shahlat (2022) was to present a study entitled "The impact of Algerian media legislation on the professional practice of electronic journalism", which aimed to clarify the status of the electronic press in Algerian media legislation and to draw attention to journalists to respect legislation during the practice of electronic journalism. An electronic questionnaire was distributed to a sample of Algerian journalists in the private sector. (40) The findings of the study suggest that Algerian media legislation has restricted the electronic press to a moderate degree. Therefore, new legislation should be introduced to further regulate the electronic press process. Journalists usually abide by the rules of professional practice and are free to edit on their newspaper websites.

Freedom of the Press and Expression: Survey of Journalists, Writers, and Media Professionals in Bahrain

The 2019 report titled "*Opinion Poll of Bahraini Journalists, Writers, and Media Professionals on Freedom of Opinion and Expression*" provides a comprehensive overview of the state of press freedom in Bahrain. It explores the ability of media professionals to exercise freedom of expression within the local legal framework and highlights the key challenges posed by Bahraini media legislation, including restrictions on both traditional and digital platforms. The report also addresses the effects of censorship, the legal responsibilities tied to media work, and the degree to which national laws align with international standards on freedom of expression. Based on a large-scale survey of Bahraini media professionals, the report reveals varied opinions on the impact of current laws: some see them as obstacles to free speech, while others view them as necessary for balancing freedom with responsibility. Notable findings include that 61% of respondents believe freedom of expression has improved, 22% say the 2002 Press Law has not negatively impacted media freedom, and 42% consider the government's enforcement of the law to be moderate. Additionally, 76% reported not being offered financial incentives that might influence their work, although 81% acknowledged the presence of paid news. A large majority (86%) said they had not faced any legal actions due to their media activities. Furthermore, 61% believe the government is serious about fostering a free media environment, and 62% agree that journalists play a significant role in shaping public opinion.

Awad's study (2020) aimed to explore recent trends in research on the application of ethical controls in digital journalism through a critical analytical vision, and reviewed the significant shifts in digital journalism and their impact on journalistic ethics. While the Internet has removed barriers of time and space and helped access information quickly, new ethical challenges have arisen that require careful consideration.

The study focused on the moral dilemmas facing digital journalism, such as plagiarism, photo and video manipulation, and intellectual property. Problems have arisen regarding the accuracy and integrity of information. The researcher points out that one of the most prominent issues is citizen journalism, where ordinary individuals contribute to the dissemination of news without being subject to traditional journalistic standards, which increases the likelihood of spreading false or misleading news.

Among the issues addressed in the study are automated journalism and artificial intelligence, where algorithms have come to play a key role in determining the news content provided to the public. This technology raises questions about the ethics of algorithms and self-censorship that must be imposed on these technological processes.

The study also highlighted the academic education of ethical controls in digital journalism. The author points out that there is a gap between what is taught at universities and actual practices in digital journalism, which calls for modernizing curricula to cope with new challenges.

The study discussed the concept of self-regulation, with digital journalists requiring internal control systems to ensure that they adhere to the highest ethical standards without the need for state or external intervention. This requires journalists to adhere to the principles of transparency and responsibility for the content they publish.

The study provided an outlook for Arab research into digital journalism ethics, calling for enhanced scientific research on the issue and innovative solutions to emerging challenges, with a focus on how to address ethical responsibility in contemporary digital journalism.

Feedback on Previous Studies

Previous studies have demonstrated many data and information that benefit media professionals and society as a whole. Most studies have relied on the prescriptive approach.

The Role of Media Legislation toward the Media and Society

The role and power of the media in society are undeniable. Its scope and extent facilitate direct communication with the people, and it can be seen that it acts as a kind of fourth power to influence the decisions of today's highest levels of the judiciary.

Freedom of the press is not limited to the mere dissemination of information; it also involves a set of responsibilities alongside the rights it guarantees. Press content must adhere to principles of impartiality, accuracy, and quality, ensuring that information is presented objectively and honestly to prevent distortion or misrepresentation. Since journalistic activity not only reflects public opinion but also plays a role in shaping it, journalists must acknowledge their responsibility for the content they convey. Consequently, media activity requires regulation through appropriate media legislation to ensure accountability and ethical practice (Suleiman, 2017).

The media still play a vital role, for example in the fight against false news and disinformation, and journalists have the task of informing citizens through comprehensive investigation and honest information. Media legislation plays a major role in regulating information and news and preventing the circulation of false ones, especially with the spread of social media and the internet (Kadwani, 2020).

The legal framework governing media activity is primarily rooted in international law and international conventions. Foremost among these is the Universal Declaration of Human Rights (UDHR), which serves as a key reference for interpreting other legal instruments related to media freedom. Article 19 of the UDHR guarantees the fundamental right to freedom of expression, stating that every individual has the right to hold opinions and to seek, receive, and impart information and ideas of all kinds, regardless of frontiers, whether orally, in writing, or in print. This article forms the essential legal basis for defining and framing media freedom at the international level (Awad, 2020).

In addition to regulating freedom of expression for the press, there are other things regulated by media legislation, such as preventing threats to the media and regulating the information broadcast by the media to its audience in order to deceive, lie, and fabricate news that affect public security and prevent the spread of rumors. Therefore, media legislation works in two directions: to preserve the rights of media professionals and their media, and to stimulate the performance of media duties in disseminating information transparently and credibly (Muhammad Suleiman (2017)).

Threats to Journalists and the Media

There are many threats facing journalists in different countries around the world, prompting attention to the development of media legislation to prevent such threats, including (Dawadi, 2022):

- Economic pressures: Many media outlets, especially small ones, suffer from funding difficulties for a variety of reasons. Some do not know how to adapt to the digital age, while others have been victims of arbitrary trials that have exhausted their financial resources or suffered from a reduction in public funds.
- Political pressures: In countries with authoritarian leaders, independent journalism, communication agencies and public broadcasting services are under severe pressure. These attacks range from reducing or revoking public support, withdrawing or denying licenses, and some governments also exert pressure on national authorities to regulate media (responsible for enforcing media laws), even replacing board members with people loyal to them (Maadasi, 2012).
- Confronting violence: Independent media agencies, watchdogs, investigative journalism and their sources have suffered from smear campaigns, harassment, violence, hate speech, and death threats (Allah Faith in God Yasser, 2021).
- Abusive lawsuits: The press is often the target of abusive lawsuits, also known as strategic actions against public participation, and these complaints, usually filed by power holders who fear the appearance of their criminal acts, are solely aimed at intimidating journalists and the press in general, pressuring them to remain silent.
- Concentration of ownership: In a balanced media environment, there are many different media outlets across the political spectrum, each offering unique global perspectives and views on social issues. However, when most of the media sector is in the hands of a few, they can impose their views and thus limit public access to other views. In many countries, even those with a high

rating in the 2022 version of RSF's Global Press Freedom Index, media ownership is concentrated in the hands of a small number of large companies.
- Interference in editorial decisions: Media management must be free to make decisions regardless of the newspaper owner's consent. Otherwise, media coverage may be biased. In some countries, state-controlled public media do not publish opinions critical of the government or news reflecting a poor image of the authorities.

The Importance of Media Legislation for Media and Journalists (Al Tayeb, 2018)

(1) Protect independent media (press, journalists and sources) from public and private interference and ensure editorial independence.
(2) Protect media pluralism to ensure citizens' access to a wide range of information and perspectives.
(3) Increased transparency on governments funds allocated to the media, including the allocation of public announcements.
(4) Increase the transparency of media ownership so that it is clear who really owns every media outlet.
(5) Ensuring the economic sustainability of the media sector.

The role of media legislation in maintaining the transparency of media information:

Transparency serves as an essential mechanism for ensuring accountability and democracy. It increases the media's credibility, legitimacy and confidence indicators. Transparency is synonymous with journalistic quality. The media has developed various tools to be accountable to citizens, especially in the case of public media, where accountability systems must be closely linked to the protection of journalists (Al-Khair, 2016).

But there may be numerous media outlets spreading false and misleading news and rumors to attract more audiences. Fake news is currently of great importance, especially on social networks, and has a remarkable influence on public opinion and the political sphere. This fake news may have a detrimental effect on public opinion and the extraction of security in societies and thus the media and legal legislation had to be enacted to completely curb and prevent this phenomenon (Dawadi, 2022).

The Legislative and Legal Framework Regulating the Work of the Press and Media in the Kingdom of Bahrain

The Kingdom of Bahrain is interested in drafting legislation and court laws to regulate journalistic work through Decree-Law No. 47 of 2002 on the organization of the press, printing, and publishing, which plays a major role in organizing the press and achieving its high role in Bahraini society. These laws include:

Article 1, which affirms freedom of expression of opinion, whether by word, writing, or any other means, but provided that it does not prejudice the Islamic faith or the unity of the people and the security of the country.

Article 27 stipulates that the press must play its role freely and independently, aimed at creating a free climate for the growth and advancement of society with informed knowledge and contributing to better solutions in all matters relating to the interests of the nation and of citizens.

Article 28 clarifies that no newspaper shall be disabled or stopped except through a judicial ruling.

Article 29 further clarifies that journalists are independent in their work and have no authority other than the law.

Article 30 also affirms that a journalist's security is not compromised as a result of an opinion that expresses his or her view and that he or she may not be compelled to disclose his or her sources of information.

Article 32 prohibits any restrictions that impede the flow of information or impede equal access to information between the various newspapers or that may interfere with the citizen's right to advertising and knowledge, without prejudice to the requirements of national security, defense of the homeland, and its supreme interests.

Article 37 affirms that the journalist must abide by the principles and values enshrined in the Constitution and the law in the dissemination of his press information. He must follow honor and honesty and respect public morals during his work, and safeguard citizens' rights and freedoms.

Article 38 emphasizes that it is the duty of the journalist to refrain from disseminating news containing racism and contempt for religions, to disseminate discrimination among others, and to despise the opinion of a range of society's communities.

Article 39 affirms that no journalist has the right to be subjected to the private life of persons and does not conduct public servants or persons in a public representative capacity or in charge of public service, unless the handling is of close relevance to their work and is in the public interest.

Article 42 states: "The newspaper shall be prohibited from publishing any advertisement whose article is incompatible with the values, foundations, principles and public morals of society or with the message and objectives of the press, and the editorial and advertising material shall be completely and prominently separated."

Article 43 affirms that a journalist may not engage in the collection of advertisements or obtain any direct or indirect sums or benefits from the publication of advertisements in any capacity and may not sign advertising material on their behalf.

Article 60 states that the editor-in-chief or the responsible editor shall publish the correction or reply to the facts through the right holder within three days following the newspaper that published the incident or after the newspaper's first publication, whichever is closest, and shall be published in the same place and in the same letters as the article or press material to be corrected.

It is clear from the previous legislative articles that the Kingdom of Bahrain is keen to organize journalism, whether the rights or duties of journalists or the tasks required of them. We affirm that the Kingdom is keen to ensure the regular operation of the press in line with the country's security and the unity of the people and its support for the freedom of expression of opinion to all citizens.

Journalists' Trends toward Media Legislation in Bahrain

A set of values, principles, and methods serves as a template for Bahrain's journalistic work as an advocate of the public interest. During this period, journalists in the Kingdom of Bahrain are keen to practice professional practices within a specific legal and social framework, where the first objective is to promote the homeland and the unity of the people.

The most important practices to be carried out during the Kingdom's press work are as follows:

- Reliable sources: Always cite reliable data and information sources to prevent the spread of rumors.
- Verification: Verification of all data, statement, and all inputs used in the information.
- Fairness: Search for and record statements from sources around which information revolves, especially if they are an accusation.
- Accuracy: Search and register with a reliable and verifiable source independently of all data or data included in the information.
- Completeness: Find and record as many subtopics or angles as possible relevant to the event being investigated.

Conclusion

Finally, the study provides an outlook for Arab research into digital journalism ethics, calling for enhanced scientific research on the issue and innovative solutions to emerging challenges, with a focus on how to address ethical responsibility in contemporary digital journalism.

References

Al-Khair, F. R. (2016). Media legislation in the Libyan press system from 1969 to 2011 and the dilemma of freedom. *The Scientific Journal of Journalism Research*, *8*, 491–542.

Al Tayeb, S. M. (2018). *Media law courses and professional ethics in Saudi universities in light of quality standards*.

Awad, A. A. (2020). UAE media legislation and its role in combating terrorism crimes. *Communication Sciences*, *5*(1), 69–114.

Dawadi, B. D. (2022). Manifestations of media professional ethics in Algerian legislation: An analytical study of Algerian media legislative texts. *Afaq for Sciences*, *7*(1), 96–107.

Faith in God Yasser. (2021). Media freedom of expression in South Sudan - Case study of journalists and journalistic practice. *Media Research Journal*, *59*(3), 1579–1626.

Kadwani, S. M. (2020). Legal controls governing digital media in Egypt: An analytical study. *Arab Journal of Media and Communication Research*, *29*, 380–413.

Maadasi, B. (2012). *The right to information through laws and regulatory texts of media institutions in Algeria: Audiovisual media, print journalism, and news agency* (Unpublished doctoral dissertation). University of Algiers 3, Faculty of Political Science and Media.

Muhammad Suleiman, I. (2017). Trends of the Egyptian media elite towards media legislation following the 25 January 2011 revolution. *Scientific Journal of Public Relations Research and Advertising*, *11*, 417–443.

Rumaisah Shahlat, S. (2022). *The impact of Algerian media legislation on professional practice in the electronic press.*

Chapter 29

The Role of Digital Governance and Artificial Intelligence Technologies in Enhancing Public Confidence in Competitive Justice in the Sports Field: "A Field Study, in the Kingdom of Bahrain"

Layla Abdarasool Hussain

Ministry of Education, Bahrain and Ahlia University, Bahrain

Abstract

This study addresses a pivotal issue by identifying the theoretical foundations of digital governance and artificial intelligence (AI) technologies and their role in enhancing public confidence in sports competitive justice. It also clarifies the role of digital governance and AI technologies in achieving sports competitive justice via the Instagram platform and emphasizes the ability of AI to accurately analyze sports data and better understand performance, contributing to the resolution of complaints or disputes related to competitive justice and accelerating the resolution process in a more accurate and objective manner.

The first axis of the study addresses digital governance, defining its origins, goals, and dimensions. The researcher also examines the challenges specific to the study and discusses the strengths and weaknesses (including both positive and negative aspects) of digital governance. The second axis of the study focuses on AI technologies, providing a definition, discussing their origins, and outlining the types of AI. It further highlights the significance of AI in sports training and concludes by discussing the advantages and disadvantages of AI in this context.

The third axis of the study investigates sports competitive justice, defining the concept and its various aspects while elaborating on its principles and sections. Additionally, the cultural implantation theory is

Digital Dialogues, 285–294

doi:10.1108/978-1-83708-686-320261029

explored, covering its emergence, foundational principles, and assumptions, along with the key criticisms directed at the theory. Lastly, the study explains the relevance of this theory and its application within the research framework.

Keywords: Digital governance; artificial intelligence technologies; sports competitive justice; Instagram platform; Kingdom of Bahrain

This study aimed to identify the challenges facing the application of digital media governance of artificial intelligence (AI) in the sports environment and how this affects achieving competitive justice. It requires exploring how to manage data and modern technologies in a way that maintains the integrity of sports competitions and avoids any bias or manipulation that may arise as a result of using this technology. In the study, we relied on the "correlational relations" approach, which is a form of the descriptive survey approach. It describes the relationship between two variables.

Digital media governance is a contemporary concept that emerged alongside the rapid advancements in information and communication technologies (ICTs) in the modern era, as well as the proliferation of AI applications. Consequently, digital governance has become an urgent necessity to ensure that these technologies are employed in a responsible and ethical manner, safeguarding against violations of moral and ethical principles and preventing conflicts with cultural traditions and customs that shape our societal identity, particularly in sensitive domains such as sports.

With the advent of the third millennium, the widespread use of the Internet and social media has intensified, resulting in a profound transformation in the management and dissemination of information. This evolution has underscored the urgent need for establishing regulations and guidelines to ensure the accuracy, reliability, and ethical dissemination of information and data.

The foundational concepts of governance began to crystallize during the 1940s and 1950s, coinciding with the establishment of international organizations such as the United Nations, which played a pivotal role in fostering global cooperation and formulating governance frameworks. The emergence of digital media governance for AI technologies, coupled with the rise of the Internet as a significant platform for information dissemination between 1990 and 1995, further emphasized the necessity of regulating the flow of information within digital networks. Additionally, governments have increasingly leveraged technology to enhance service delivery and foster greater interaction with citizens.

As we move into 2024 and beyond, discussions surrounding digital media governance and the applications of AI are anticipated to intensify, particularly regarding the development of regulatory frameworks that address the rapid technological, social, and economic changes in this field. Within this context, it is essential to delineate key definitions and terminologies pertinent to the study, with each concept being examined according to the three primary axes.

The First Topic: Theoretical Readings

The First Axis: (Digital Governance)

Digital Governance: Terminology

Digital governance refers to a comprehensive framework of controls and procedures designed to regulate both the internal and external environments impacted by digital transformation. Its primary objective is to develop a strategy in order to facilitate organizational operations in alignment with technological advancements while maintaining a reasonable balance among stakeholders to achieve long-term goals and strategies. Additionally, digital governance plays a crucial role in fostering sustainable growth by supporting investment initiatives and enhancing competitive advantage. Promoting innovation and effective resource allocation enables institutions to adapt to dynamic market conditions and reinforces their ability to remain competitive. According to Rashwan and Abu Rahma (2020), digital governance contributes significantly to achieving targeted strategic objectives, ensuring that institutions are well-positioned to capitalize on emerging growth opportunities while addressing potential risks associated with swift digitalization.

Procedurally. From my perspective as a researcher, I define digital governance as a structured set of systems, regulations, and policies that operate within a regulatory framework and leverage information and communication technologies (ICT) effectively and consistently in institutions or governmental bodies.

The primary objective of governance is to enhance transparency and efficiency through the use of digital tools, such as electronic systems, applications, and data analytics, further decision-making processes, and implement procedures in a practical and timely manner.

The Emergence of Digital Governance. The evolution of digital governance can be traced back to the late 20th century, as governments and institutions sought to enhance administrative performance and improve service delivery to stakeholders through the adoption of modern technologies. This progression can be categorized into distinct phases of digital governance development as follows:

- Late 20th Century (Digital Transformation of Governments): During the 1990s, with the advent of the Internet and information technology, governments and institutions worldwide began implementing electronic systems to facilitate communication with the public and provide services more efficiently. This period marked the initial phase of digital transformation in governance.
- Early Twenty-First Century (E-Government): The early 2000s witnessed the emergence of the "e-government" concept, characterized by enhanced digital interaction and participation between governments and their constituencies. This phase represented a shift toward more structured electronic engagement, aimed at improving accessibility and responsiveness in public service.
- Mid-Twenty-First Century and Beyond (Digital Governance): As technological advancements accelerated, the concept of digital governance evolved,

encompassing a broader spectrum of objectives, such as enhancing transparency, promoting community engagement, and leveraging big data, AI, and Internet-based applications. Digital governance extends beyond service provision, focusing on improved decision-making processes and fostering collaboration between governments, institutions, and the public.

Digital Governance Goals. Here, we can focus on the following objectives: (Hanisch et al., 2023; Manoharan et al., 2023)

(1) Providing services to stakeholders in a profitable and low-cost manner;
(2) Providing information about all transactions between the facility and its customers on the Internet;
(3) Determining the requirements for obtaining services and the required forms in a way that enables them to be completed before going to the place where the service is performed, and thus reducing the time and effort required to perform the service;
(4) Raising the culture and awareness of employees in the various departments of the facility by encouraging them to use modern technology;
(5) Providing an appropriate climate that reduces obstacles and procedures that prevent attracting investors, and that provides an attractive factor for facilities operating in the field of technology;
(6) Improving the efficiency of institutional performance and preparing for integration into the global system to keep pace with the modern information systems used;
(7) Achieving transparency by making information available in an equal manner to all stakeholders." In light of the above, the researcher believes that digital governance contributes significantly to achieving efficiency and effectiveness in providing services to beneficiaries and optimal utilization of resources, and working to ensure the flow of information is accurately, adequately, appropriately, and continuously ready, in addition to creating the appropriate regulatory environment and climate for research and development.

Continuous administration, in addition to creating an educational environment that relies heavily on electronic systems, aims to ensure the provision of effective and supportive mechanisms for decision-making (Dr. Walid Ahmed, 2024, p. 1001).

The Negatives and Positives of Digital Governance. In light of the above dimensions of digital governance, digital governance applies modern digital technologies based on digital transformation to manage government affairs and provide public services. This highlights the positives of governance, which are as follows:

- Improving transparency
- Easy access
- Making and supporting decisions

- Increasing efficiency
- "Digital gap
- Security threats (cybersecurity
- Total reliance on technology
- Fear of surveillance
- Legislation and laws

Second Axis (Artificial Intelligence Technologies)

Artificial Intelligence Technologies (AI): Theoretically

> modern technologies and means of advanced information technology represented by computers and the Internet linked to global databases and information that provide a broad knowledge base that provides its users with the ability to simulate the human mind with superior capabilities to obtain information in real time, store it and retrieve it at the appropriate time with the possibility of predicting future situations (Ahmed, Farouk, & El-Dessouki, 2023, p. 180)

Procedurally. A group of systems and software simulate the human mind in terms of mental abilities such as creative thinking, innovation, discrimination, and decision-making. Examples of these are AI technologies, machine learning, deep learning, neural networks, intelligent robots, computer machines, or computing.

The Importance of Artificial Intelligence (AI). Some important points can be pointed out about the importance of AI, which are as follows:

- It contributes to preserving accumulated human experiences by transferring them to smart machines.
- It helps enable humans to use multiple human languages when interacting with machines instead of computer programming languages. This makes machines and their use accessible to all segments of society, including those with special needs. Previously, dealing with advanced machines was the preserve of specialists and experts.
- AI plays an important role in many sensitive fields such as helping to diagnose diseases, prescribe medications, provide legal and professional consultations, interactive education, and military applications.
- Intelligent systems contribute to the areas in which decisions are made, as these systems enjoy independence, strength, and objectivity, and therefore their decisions are far from error, bias, racism, prejudice, or even external or personal interference.

AI and Its Role in Sports Training. AI plays an important role in training athletes and improving their performance. Here are some ways in which AI contributes to this field:

(1) **Performance analysis:** AI techniques such as machine learning are used to analyze data related to sports performance, such as tracking movement, running speed, muscle strength, and precise technique in performance. This helps coaches provide special feedback to players and improve their performance.
(2) **Customized training**: Training plans can be designed specifically for players and their needs in line with their level of physical fitness, by analyzing historical data of players and their performance in sports training.
(3) **Injury prediction:** This is done by analyzing data related to physical load, sports performance, and predicting possible injuries. Training can be modified to avoid sports injuries for players.
(4) **Assisting in decision-making:** AI helps coaches make strategic decisions during matches by analyzing live data (player movements on the field as in team games).
(5) **Video analysis:** It is used to analyze video clips of matches and training and discover tactics that may not be visible to the human eye, allowing coaches to improve the strategies followed.
(6) **Motivating athletes:** Personal incentives can be provided to players, such as setting short- and long-term goals based on performance analysis and monitoring progress.

Pros and Cons of Artificial Intelligence (AI). Pros of AI:
AI has several advantages, which include the following:

(1) **Increased productivity and efficiency:** AI can perform tasks faster and more accurately than humans, which increases productivity and reduces human errors.
(2) **Improving healthcare:** AI can analyze medical data and diagnose faster and more accurately, which helps provide better and faster treatment for patients.
(3) **Improvement in security:** AI is used to monitor and analyze data to detect suspicious patterns or cyber-attacks, which contributes to enhancing security.
(4) **Development in education:** AI provides innovative approaches to education, such as personalized learning and educational intelligence, which enhance the effectiveness of learning.
(5) **Accelerating innovation:** Used in the fields such as scientific research and engineering.
(6) **Improving user experience:** AI is used the field of e-commerce and services.

Disadvantages of AI

(1) **Job loss:** Heavy reliance on AI could eliminate human jobs, increasing unemployment rates in some industries.
(2) **Biases in algorithms:** If the training data that AI relies on is biased or incomplete.

(3) **Loss of privacy:** AI requires the collection and analysis of massive amounts of data, which can compromise personal privacy and increase the chances of leakage or exploitation.
(4) **Over-reliance on technology:** Heavy reliance on AI could reduce the ability to think critically and make human decisions.
(5) **Challenges in regulation and control:** As AI develops, it becomes more difficult to regulate and monitor it effectively, which could create problems in determining responsibility in the event of errors or problems.
(6) **Security threats:** AI could be used to develop technological weapons or cyber-attacks, posing a threat to public security.
(7) **Impact on social interaction:** AI may negatively affect human interaction.

Third Axis: (Competitive Justice)

Competitive Justice: Technically

"The value perceived by employees of the results they obtain as material or moral outputs in exchange for what they provide to the institution, in light of clear objective procedures and policies, and good and appropriate treatment of the information and explanations provided to them regarding the results of the outputs, procedures and decisions related to them" (Zaid, 2023, p. 397).

Procedurally. Ensuring that all participants in sports competitions have equitable and equal opportunities through the application of fair and standardized rules and regulations within the competitive environment.

Principles of Sports Competitive Justice

- Equality of opportunity to participate and compete (gender, race, religion, or any other factors);
- Integrity and transparency in terms of organization, arbitration, and evaluation;
- Fair and impartial arbitration in terms of equal conditions for all players and participants (laws, equipment) and without any type of fraud, such as manipulation of results or doping;
- Equal facilities, that is, providing the same capabilities and training facilities, equipment, health resources, etc.;
- Applying clear and equal rules that should not be exceptional or distortive in favor of any party;
- Protecting the rights of athletes, such as the right to participate;
- Responsibility and transparency in sports management.

Sections of Competitive Justice. Competitive justice can be divided and discussed in this context as follows:

First: Legal justice
Second: Social justice
Third: Economic justice
Fourth: Distributive Justice

Fifth: Procedural Justice
Sixth: Arbitral justice
Seventh: Preventive Justice
Eighth: Justice in Penalties

Section Two: Scientific Theories

First: The Theory of Cultural Implantation

The Origin of the Theory. The origins of this theory go back to the American scientist "George Gerlrener", who researched the impact of mass communication on the cultural environment within the framework of his project on cultural indicators on three interrelated issues:

(1) Studying the messages, values, and mental images reflected by the media;
(2) Studying the structures, pressures, and processes that affect the production of media messages;
(3) Studying the independent participation of mass messages on the public's perception of social reality.

The cultural horse theory is an applied conception of the ideas related to the processes of constructing meaning and shaping social facts, learning through observation, and the roles played by the media in these mechanisms, as it confirms the general idea around which the previous theories agree, which is the ability of the media to influence the knowledge of individuals who are exposed to these media in large quantities. This theory arose in the face of social conditions, especially in the United States of America, represented by the emergence of waves of corruption, crimes, and assassinations in American society in the late 1960s, and people linked these waves to the widespread use of television, which prompted researchers and the research institution in America to conduct many studies on the relationship between watching television and high crime rates and aggressive behavior. From the results of that research (Kafi, 2015, p. 222.221).

The Foundations and Principles the Theory Based on

> Television is a distinct medium from other media: Television is the medium that enters homes for more than seven hours a day and is distinguished by its ability to attract adults and children around it, which makes it an environment for learning. It is a basic distributor of the mental image, and it also constitutes the prevailing trend of our personal culture on the other hand. What also distinguishes television is its ability to unify cultural patterns, simplify them, and make them common among all members of society. Hence, the process of understanding only interacts with television (Bousbat Laouira, 2015, p. 28)

Theoretical Assumptions. Media of communication today and the theory of cultural inculcation are considered an applied conception of the ideas related to the processes of constructing meaning and forming social facts and learning through observation and the roles played by the media of communication (Forshid, 2011, p. 151).

> It also assumes that those who watch television infrequently are exposed to various and many other sources other than television, some of which are personal and some of which are public, while those who watch in a qualitative manner depend on television more than others to access information (Ahmed & Mahmoud, 2008, p. 117).

The Most Prominent Criticisms Directed at the Theory of Cultural Inculcation

> 1. The theory did not take into account other variables through the intensity of viewing that enter into the process of television influence, such as demographic factors.
>
> 2. Both (Hawkter and Pingry) believe that the relationship between watching television and the cultural horse when watching it can be attributed to some of the content of television materials or programs, and does not apply to some other programs, and also that this relationship does not apply to watching the content of all television materials or programs in general, but it has transcended as a result of specific programs.
>
> 3. The material presented through television may be subject to distortion and falsification by viewers, and viewers' responses may be variable, and thus the foundations on which the concepts of the dimensions of the relationship between viewing and influence are built according to the perspective of the cultural horse in inaccurate concepts and dimensions. (Kafi, 2015, p. 222).

Employing the Theory in the Current Study

(1) Using the theory helps in understanding how digital governance and AI can contribute to enhancing competitive justice by framing sports practices and interactions and promoting values with transparency and equality.
(2) The theory of cultural implantation can be applied by integrating the theory with digital governance to study how Instagram algorithms and AI contribute to shaping cultural perceptions related to competitive justice in sports. By affirming values such as transparency and distraction through algorithms or displayed content, which thus affects followers' perceptions of justice in sports competitions.
(3) Using the cultural implantation theory in analyzing the role of digital governance and AI technologies on the Instagram platform, which helps in

understanding the effects of these technologies in enhancing competitive justice and influencing the cultural perceptions and expectations of the sports community.

(4) The cultural implantation theory has its impact on Instagram and its relationship in enhancing justice and spreading sports content through videos, photos, and comments that create certain images.

References

Ahmed, A., Farouk, S., & El-Dessouki, M. (2023). Employing artificial intelligence applications in health awareness among sports leaders in light of the national standards for a clinic. *Scientific Journal of Sports Sciences and Arts*, *0073*(3), 180 (Helwan University).

Ahmed, F. M. (2008). *Television and children* (p. 117). Scientific House for Publishing and Distribution.

Al-Tarbisha, M. A.-S., & Aziz, A. (2006). *Communication theories* (1st ed., pp. 282–283). Dar Al-Nahda Al-Arabiya.

Bousbat, L. (2015). *The role of new media in developing cultural awareness among university youth* (p. 28). University of Mohamed Seddik Ben Yahia.

Forshid. (2011). *Mass communication and media, development, characteristics and theories* (1st ed., p. 151). Amman.

Kafi. (2015). *Public opinion and communication theories* (1st ed., p. 222). Dar Al-Hamed for Publishing and Distribution.

Rashwan, A. R., & Abu, R. (2020). Digital transformation and its implications for the practice of the accounting and auditing profession. In *The first international conference on information technology and business*.

Walid, R. (2023). A proposed model for using artificial intelligence applications to raise the efficiency of administrative systems in sports clubs in Upper Egypt. *Assiut Journal of Physical Education Sciences and Arts*, *68*(3), 885. (Faculty of Physical Education, Aswan University).

Walid, A. (2024). Measuring the impact of the professional suitability of the internal auditor on the quality of cybersecurity in light of digital governance: An applied study. *Scientific Journal of Financial and Commercial Studies and Research*, (2), 1001. (Faculty of Commerce, Damietta University).

Zaid, J. (2023). The impact of organizational justice on job burnout, a field study in pharmaceutical companies in the capital, Sana'a. *The Academic Journal of Scientific Research and Publishing*, (34).

Foreign References

Hanisch, M., Goldsby, C. M., Fabian, N. E., & Oehmichen, J. (2023). Digital governance: A conceptual framework and research agenda. *Journal of Business Research*, *162*.

Idzi, F. M., & Gornes, R. (2022). Digital governance: Government strategies that impact public services. *GPPG*, *2*.

Manoharan, A. P., Melitski, J., & Holzer, M. (2023). Digital governance: An assessment of performance and best practices. *Public Organization Review*, *23*(1).

Chapter 30

Media Framing for Processing Visual Content on Digital Platforms and Its Role in Tourism Promotion

Afaf Ayesh Ali Al-Muhaysin

Saudi Broadcasting Corporation, Bahrain and Ahlia University, Bahrain

Abstract

This study aimed to uncover the themes, content, issues, and media forms framed on the YouTube channels "Visit Saudi" and "Ministry of Tourism" to promote tourism in Saudi Arabia. It sought to identify the framing mechanisms and appeals present in the media messages directed at the audience, examine the temporal and spatial frameworks of each message, and analyze the language used in the videos published on the YouTube channels of the two official entities: "Visit Saudi" and the Ministry of Tourism.

Keywords: Tourism promotion; digital platforms; YouTube channel; Visit Saudi; Saudi Ministry of Tourism

Introduction

Tourism is a vital economic pillar for many nations, with some heavily relying on it as a primary source of income. The World Tourism Organization has played a key role in enhancing tourism's impact and driving economic transformation, making it an essential resource for impoverished countries with limited alternatives.

Since the media plays a vital role in attracting tourists through tourism promotion and marketing activities, it highlights a range of benefits using a promotional mix. This activity continues to thrive and strengthen day by day,

Digital Dialogues, 295–305

doi:10.1108/978-1-83708-686-320261030

thanks to various tools employed to disseminate advertisements, publicity, and promotional content.

Undoubtedly, the digital revolution has significantly expanded opportunities for promotion and marketing, playing an active role in boosting tourism among a broad audience of social media platform users. These platforms have become essential tools for delivering messages to the public, thanks to their unique features and advantages.

As Saudi Arabia's development and economic transformation plans target tourism services as an additional source of income, the Kingdom designated 2023 as a year for promoting tourism and fostering openness to others. Consequently, Saudi Arabia intensified its focus on tourism-related media in various forms and engaged several government entities in tourism promotion through their official platforms.

YouTube enables global audiences to access content, explore tourism-related themes through live or recorded broadcasts, and share links widely. This platform plays a key role in promoting Saudi tourism, a task managed by the Ministry of Tourism and Visit Saudi Arabia. Both entities use their YouTube channels to showcase tourism events and activities, encouraging audience interactions.

Recognizing the significance of these platforms in disseminating tourism content, this study seeks to answer the following question: What media framing strategies are employed for visual content on digital platforms related to Saudi tourism, as presented on the YouTube channels of the Ministry of Tourism and Visit Saudi? Additionally, how do these channels contribute to promoting tourism in Saudi Arabia and delivering targeted messages to audiences through these digital platforms?

Literature Review

First Theme: Studies on Tourism Promotion on Digital Platforms

(1) The study by Hamdi and Abdelrahman (2024) examined the effectiveness of Facebook in promoting tourism by showcasing heritage landmarks and focusing on tours, visits, and exhibitions. The research highlighted the use of both Modern Standard Arabic and colloquial Arabic, as well as foreign languages, in promotional content. It also emphasized the integration of customs and traditions into tourism-related topics. Additionally, the study revealed significant audience engagement on the Facebook platform.

(2) The study by Mahfouz (2024) examined the role of Facebook in promoting tourism diversity, highlighting various elements such as tours, short videos, recreational activities, and heritage displays. The platform provided comprehensive information, including hotel offers and service locations, and achieved a notably high viewership rate.

(3) The study by Ben Zabiya (2024) demonstrated that Libyan content creators on Facebook played a significant role in promoting and providing

information about tourist attractions, attracting tourists, offering discounts and promotions, and contributing substantially to the activation and promotion of Libyan tourism.

(4) The study by Jadin et al. (2024) emphasized the use of the (X) platform by the audience to access information, updates, and tourism events. It highlighted a variation in the dissemination of information related to heritage sites. The audience primarily relied on official accounts to learn about events.

(5) The study by Mohammed (2024) highlighted that text accompanied by images is one of the most effective tools for tourism promotion. It also found that digital media platforms (Facebook, Instagram, YouTube, and Twitter) contributed to tourism development through official accounts and that comments played a significant role in advancing tourism.

(6) The study by Hussein et al. (2024) concluded that social media platforms facilitated tourism promotion and attraction through photos and videos published on Facebook. It also revealed that the audience used social media to learn about tourism resources and obtain promotional offers.

(7) The study by Aziz and Sabti (2024) demonstrated the role of news reports in promoting tourism topics related to training courses, scientific seminars, and inspection tours. It also found that the audience targeted recreational tourism activities on the platform.

(8) The study by Ammar (2024) showed a high concentration of YouTube users seeking tourism information, learning about customs and traditions, and engaging with content related to tourism information.

(9) The study by Helmy (2024) highlighted a significant increase in audience engagement on social media platforms regarding tourism and promotional content. It emphasized the interest of both government and private institutions in promoting tourism through official platforms.

Second Theme: Studies on Digital Promotion Strategies

(1) The study by Ibrahim and Oqeili (2024) highlighted the diverse results of employing digital technology in attracting and promoting tourism and raising awareness of tourist landmarks. It emphasized the role of visual effects in reinforcing content and enhancing cultural awareness among recipients and visitors.

(2) The study by Al-Kutbi and Abu Shouq (2024) emphasized that using a historical approach in tourism promotion significantly encouraged visitors to revisit targeted sites. Heritage-rich tourist areas were key attractions, supported by tourism services as effective promotional tools.

(3) The study by Atef and Ghandour (2024) highlighted the role of digital technology and artificial intelligence (AI) in promoting Egyptian tourism, particularly in South Sinai destinations like Sharm El-Sheikh and Ras Sedr. AI enhanced tourists' experiences and identified preferences, while video content offered precise information, saving time and effort. The study also

found cultural heritage, historical sites, and museums to be among the most favored destinations.

(4) The study by Al-Shiha (2024) showed a statistically significant effect of goal-setting when applying digital marketing strategies to enhance tourism appeal and promote digital tourism. It found a modest correlation between digital marketing and selecting marketing channels but a strong correlation between digital marketing and audience attraction.

(5) The study by Al-Ghazawi (2024) revealed that technological advancements and the availability of communication tools and digital platforms contributed to delivering information to tourists.

(6) The study by Salem (2024) indicated a statistically significant positive relationship between the regulations of smart tourist cities and tourism promotion. Smart cities employed various effective promotional methods to enhance tourism, with audiences possessing substantial knowledge about smart cities' tourism offerings due to their diverse attractions. Digital advancements in smart cities also significantly contributed to tourism promotion efforts.

(7) The study by Ibrahim (2024) revealed that the Northern Channel significantly boosted tourism in the Northern State by providing new information, enhancing tourism knowledge, and showcasing archeological and historical activities. Its promotional efforts fostered emotional and historical connections and patriotism, and encouraged site visits.

Third Theme: Studies on Digital Tourism Marketing Platforms

(1) The study by Raji et al. (2024) highlighted differences in tourism promotion between the United States and Africa due to the diversity of geographical features. The United States employs varied promotional mechanisms across digital platforms, focusing on storytelling and catering to audience preferences on digital platforms.

(2) The study by Vioralba and Durjana (2024) found that the most frequent users of digital platforms are aged between 20 and 40 years, with Facebook being the most popular among audiences. Women were identified as the most active demographic on these platforms. The research also highlighted the role of digital platforms in facilitating access to tourism information, offering virtual experiences for visitors, and integrating text, audio, and visuals to create engaging promotions for tourist landmarks.

(3) Singh (2024) found collaborative initiatives between professionals and academics to attract tourists, with tourism curricula focusing on customer service in the tourism sector, such as hotels and restaurants. The study also noted that professionals' awareness of technologies contributed to tourism education through digital platforms, and the Indian government encourages using online platforms for tourism education.

(4) The study by Fedeli et al. (2024) highlighted that increased public sector investment in tourism promotion boosts institutional revenue and fosters a

positive exchange between public and private sectors. It emphasized the importance of sectoral cooperation in sharing tourism information and the impact of positive messaging on destination choices.

(5) The study by Oka and Subedra (2024) highlighted that promotion is crucial for gaining a competitive edge, especially in the economic domain. Digital platforms were instrumental in spreading Balinese culture in Indonesia and attracting tourists to villages through digital tourism promotion. The study found that promotional dimensions such as online media, social media, search engines, email marketing, and online advertising contribute to sustainable tourism in Indonesian rural villages.

(6) The study by Shahzad et al. (2024) showed that promotions by official entities are more trusted by the public than those by private entities. It also revealed a positive relationship between promotion and the spread of technology and innovations, such as social media and digital tools in Pakistan. The study emphasized the importance of promotional offers, images, videos, and tourism planning.

(7) The study by Tajin and Mubarak (2024) highlighted the role of YouTube tourism channels created by influencers in promoting domestic tourism in Algeria, raising awareness about tourism, and attracting tourists.

(8) The study by Jinqhuan and He (2024) found that Macau's interactive online platform achieved significant success in attracting tourists. The digital platform simplified travel options and provided travelers with easy access to information. Social media played a pivotal role in promoting Macau through engaging content and the strategic use of promotional dimensions.

(9) The study by Alonso et al. (2024) concluded that digital transformation enhances tourism and increases demand for rural tourist destinations. There was a significant rise in using digital platforms for booking accommodations, with a strong correlation between tourists and quick transactions, as well as promotional offers available through digital tourism platforms in rural European villages.

(10) The study by Savitri et al. (2024) revealed that Telaga Saat in Indonesia relied on advertising, direct sales, and branding for tourism promotion. The promotion focused on nature attractions, with paid digital media and social media playing a substantial role in promotional activities and attracting tourists.

Digital Platforms

Digital platforms on the internet have become one of the most significant contributions of contemporary technology to humanity. Their importance stems from being essential hubs that facilitate various roles and activities, easing people's daily lives across different domains. These platforms enable the interactive exchange of goods, services, ideas, and information among users.

Digital platforms serve as the backbone for many organizations, whether official or unofficial, as they contribute to managing and distributing products to the end consumer in a scientifically accurate and organized manner, helping organizations achieve their objectives effectively.

With technological advancements and the proliferation of big data on the internet, these platforms have brought about a significant leap in simplifying people's lives. This is attributed to the diversity of digital systems and the accelerated pace of innovation and development. As a result, these platforms have emerged as an inevitable outcome of this evolution, offering diverse methods for accessing services, goods, ideas, and information.

Definition of Digital Platforms

The Digital Government Authority (DGA) defines digital platforms as technological solutions that underpin digital products and services, delivering enhanced experiences to users through digital portals or smart device applications. These platforms facilitate seamless connectivity and integration among various channels and enable the incorporation of external services, exemplified by Saudi Arabia's "Absher" platform.

The Most Used Platforms Worldwide

When exploring the most popular and widely used platforms globally, personal and organizational experiences often overlap, encompassing relationships, objectives, and purposes. To achieve clarity, proper classification is essential in the digital realm. These platforms are variably referred to as social networks, social platforms, new media, alternative media, social media, communication tools, or new mediums, reflecting their multifaceted roles and evolving definitions.

First: Social Media Platforms

According to the United Nations Educational, Scientific, and Cultural Organization (UNESCO, 2022), the term "social networks," in the context of digital technology, refers to a service that brings people together to exchange opinions on specific topics. The origins of this service can be traced back to the forums that emerged in the early days of the internet, such as discussion groups and chatrooms.

Second: Alternative Media Platforms

This type of platform facilitates publishing, interaction, and content sharing among users. These platforms have emerged as tools of new media, such as social networking sites like Facebook, Twitter, MySpace, and other social networks. These platforms have successfully created a form of media distinct from traditional media, differing in presentation, interaction, speed of dissemination, and the ability to support content with documents and live images (Al-Abdullah & Sheen, 2014).

Third: New Media or Communication Media

Given the advanced capabilities of platforms categorized as part of social media and alternative media, Al-Abdullah and Sheen (2014) suggested preferring the term "new media" or "communication media" to describe and define them. These platforms have gained extensive traction among users and encompass numerous platforms worldwide.

(1) Facebook Platform: Launched in 2004, Facebook rapidly gained global popularity, becoming a significant platform for users worldwide. It enables individuals and organizations to create networks based on shared interests and affiliations, serving as a prominent hub for advertising and media. This environment has allowed companies and tech enthusiasts to establish competitive online social networks. Additionally, Facebook has evolved into a fundamental tool for public relations, facilitating the expression of opinions, organization of meetings, and documentation of news through images and videos.
(2) Twitter (X) Platform: Launched in 2006 under the name Twitter, the platform was rebranded as X in 2023. It has achieved widespread global recognition and exerts significant influence due to its massive user base.

The platform provides microblogging services, allowing users to post updates called "tweets." Other users can retweet or like these posts. Despite the character limit of 280 per tweet, the platform enables users to share content directly through the platform, via SMS, or through instant messaging programs.

(3) YouTube Platform: YouTube, launched in 2005, is one of the world's most prominent websites, renowned for its widespread popularity. The platform enables users to upload, download, share, and stream audio and video content free of charge.

According to Amira Sayed Ahmed (2019), YouTube quickly established itself as one of the most visited social media platforms, offering media services that no other medium could provide by combining synchronous and asynchronous communication features.

Rady and Al-Tamimi (2017) emphasized YouTube's role as an indispensable social media platform, offering numerous features that cater to diverse user needs. For instance, parents and educators benefit from tools that tailor video content to specific age groups, restrict viewing access, and manage options like search and viewing duration. These features enable parents to regulate content exposure, ensuring age-appropriate usage for younger audiences.

Tourism Promotion Through Digital Platforms

As a result of the transformations brought about by the internet and the digital revolution, numerous platforms have emerged, including digital stores for goods and services. These platforms and stores have attracted a wide range of audiences locally and globally.

Given the critical role of advertising, promotion, and marketing in promoting goods, services, ideas, and information, numerous entities have emerged to provide these services, often supported by specialized platforms. Hatimi (2015, p. 30) noted that the cost-effectiveness of online marketing compared to traditional methods, coupled with its capacity to expand markets and boost sales, has driven its rapid global growth

Social Media Platforms in Advertising and Promotion

As social media platforms offer diverse services for delivering messages to a broad audience, they have become the primary medium for disseminating such messages. These platforms now serve as advertising and media tools, carrying various promotional, marketing, and publicity messages to users.

For any entity planning to publish, advertise, promote, market, or engage in public communication with the audience, social media platforms are undoubtedly the go-to solution to achieve all these objectives simultaneously.

Marketing, promotion, publicity, and advertising through social media platforms can be defined as "The utilization of social media networks for the purpose of promotion, sales, or customer service" (Hatimi, 2015, p. 49).

YouTube as a Platform for Audio-Visual Promotion

Since its inception, YouTube has established itself as a prominent platform for publishing audio-visual materials, essentially serving as a television channel for every user with an account. It has also become a vast archive for all audio-visual content uploaded to the platform. According to Digital Orcs, YouTube is the second most popular search engine after Google and one of the most widely used social media platforms. It represents a dynamic platform suitable for businesses of all types and sizes, enabling them to connect with audiences worldwide ("Professional Advertising on YouTube with Digital Orcs").

According to the Saudi Ministry of Tourism (2022), 44% of travelers prefer receiving travel advice from family and friends, while 39% rely on websites for updates. Additionally, 25% obtain travel advice from social media travel information providers, and 16% turn to bloggers and vloggers for guidance.

Conclusion

The findings from previous studies revealed that utilizing digital technologies in tourism promotion through texts, images, and videos played an effective role in boosting tourism. Digital platforms such as Facebook, YouTube, and Twitter contributed significantly to tourism development. Additionally, feedback and comments were found to be crucial for enhancing tourism, raising awareness of tourist landmarks, and attracting audiences to explore destinations, activities, events, and tourism programs. Texts supported by images and audio-visual materials emerged as among the most effective tools for tourism promotion.

The results also highlighted the substantial role of documentary films produced for tourism promotion, which were published on YouTube, in supporting and advancing tourism. Audience engagement with this content was significant, reflecting the extensive use of digital platforms. Furthermore, the findings emphasized that content shared by influencers greatly contributes to tourism promotion and effectively attracts tourists.

References

Abdelfattah, I. A. (2024). The role of Al-Shamal channel in promoting tourism in the Northern state. *Ibn Khaldun Journal of Studies and Research*, *4*(7), 341–371.

Al-Abdullah, M., & Sheen, A. K. (2014). *Dictionary of modern concepts in media and communication*. Dar Al-Nahda Al-Arabia.

Al-Ghazawi, R. M. J. (2024). Technological development and its impact on the growth of tourism in the Kurdistan region of Iraq for the year 2023. *Journal of College of Education*, *2*(56), 1–423.

Alonso, N., Vicente, L., & Trillo, D. (2024). Digital transformation and rural tourism development in Europe. *Journal of Tourism Studies and Management*, *20*(1), 33–44.

Al-Shiha, A. A. A. (2024).The impact of digital marketing strategies on enhancing the attractiveness of cultural and heritage tourism in the Kingdom of Saudi Arabia. *Journal of the College of Tourism and Hotels*, *8*(1), 131–138.

Ammar, M. R. S. I. (2024). Motivations behind the Egyptian audience's exposure to tourism documentaries on YouTube. *Scientific Journal for Radio and Television Research*, *27*, 377–404.

Atef, H., & Ghandour, M. H. (2024). Employing artificial intelligence applications in promoting international tourism in Egypt. *Arab Journal for Research in Digital Communication and Media*, *5*, 27–375.

Aziz, S. S., & Sabti, M. K. (2024). Media promotion of tourism topics on social media platforms. *Journal of Management and Economics*, *49*(143), 177–182.

Ben Zabiya, N. K. (2024). The role of Libyan content creators on Facebook in promoting domestic tourism. *Journal of Humanities*, *28*, 492–525.

Digital Government Authority. (2024). *Glossary of digital government terms*. King Salman Global Academy for Arabic Language.

Fedeli, G., Tavares, J. M., & Kumail, T. (2024). Bridging the information gap: Public sector intervention in tourism promotion during crises. *Journal of Tourism Science*, *16*(1), 1–200.

Ghadin, N. H. R., Tayeb, M. S. O. H., & Atia Allah, Z. A. A. (2024). Utilizing social media applications in tourism promotion in Saudi Arabia: A case study on X (formerly Twitter). *Arab Journal for Digital Communication and Media Research*, *5*, 1–28.

Hamdi, A., & Abdelrahman, E. (2024). The role of social media in tourism promotion in Egypt: Facebook as a model. *Arab Journal for Research in Digital Communication and Media*, *6*, 1–225.

Hatimi, H. M. (2015). *Public relations and social media networks*. Osama Publishing and Distribution House.

Hatimi, R. M. J. (2024). Technological development and its impact on tourism growth in the Kurdistan region of Iraq in 2023. *Journal of the College of Education*, University of Wasit, *2*(56), 1–424.

Helmy, D. H. G. (2024). Government use of social media platforms and their impact on Egyptian citizens' tourism behavior. *Arab Journal for Digital Communication and Media Research*, *6*, 51–86.

Hoover, K. C. (2018). Sensory disruption in modern living and the emergence of sensory inequities. *Yale Journal of Biology & Medicine*, *91*, 53–62.

Hussein, B. S., Sadiq, K. H., & Ramadan, B. S. (2024). The actual use of social media platforms for promoting recreational tourism in the Kurdistan region of Iraq. *Journal of Physical Education and Sports Research Studies*, *3*(34), 130–147.

Ibrahim, B. S. (2024). The impact of tourism promotion policies on improving domestic tourism. *Journal of the University of Kasdi Merbah Ouargla – Faculty of Economic and Administrative Sciences*, 1–171.

Ibrahim, G. A. M., & Oqeili, M. M. A. (2024). The effect of hologram technology as a visual stimulus in enhancing tourism in Southern Saudi Arabia. *Arab Journal of Literature and Humanities*, *8*(33), 1–228.

Invest in YouTube Advertising Services. (2024, November 17). *Digital orcs. Professional YouTube advertising with digital orcs.*

Jadin, N. H. R., Al-Tayeb, M. S. O. H., & Atiyah Allah, Z. A. A. (2024). Employing social media applications in promoting tourism in the Kingdom of Saudi Arabia: The (X) application (formerly Twitter) as a model. *Arab Journal of Communication and Digital Media Research*, (5), 1–28.

Jinqhuan, Z., & He, W. (2024). Local government media promotion of city image and travel intentions: The moderating effect of tourism experience. *International Journal of Tourism Policy*, *14*(1), 70–90.

Kutbi, A. M. A. G., & Abu Shouq, M. (2024). Sharjah's efforts in promoting the tourism sector. *Journal of Literature*, *150*, 355–372.

Mahfouz, I. H. A. (2024). The role of the official "ECO EGYPT" campaign Facebook page in promoting environmental tourism in Egypt. *Egyptian Journal of Media Research*, *1*(89), 695–741.

Ministry of Tourism Saudi Arabia. (2022). *Digital marketing for tourist destinations*.

Mohamed, N. N. (2024). The role of official websites of the Ministry of Tourism in Tourism Development and heritage protection. *Arab Journal for Research in Digital Communication and Media*, *5*, 30–64.

Oka, M. D., & Subedra, N. (2024). Digital marketing of sustainable tourism village in Bali: A mixed methods study. *Journal of Infrastructure, Policy and Development*, *8*(7), 1–3726.

Rady, W. F., & Al-Tamimi, M. H. (2017). *New media: Communicative transformations and contemporary perspectives*. University Book Publishing House.

Raji, M. A., Olodo, H. B., Oke, T. T., Afua Addy, W., Ofodile, O. C., & Oyewole, A. T. (2024). Digital marketing in tourism: A review of practices in the United States

and Africa. *International Journal of Applied Research in Social Sciences*, (6), 26–408.
Salem, M. M. B. (2024). The role of smart cities in promoting Egypt as a tourist destination. *Journal of the Higher Institute for Specialized Studies*, *4*(12), 634–669.
Savitri, D., Nugraha, R. N., Aquila, T., & Nurmantu, F. C. (2024). The role of promotion in increasing the number of tourist visits to Telaga Sat Puncak, Bogor, West Java. *Western Journal of Social Sciences and Humanities*, *2*(1), 218–226.
Sayed, A., & Amira, M. M. (2019). *Digital media*. Al-Mutanabbi Library.
Shahzad, S., Zaib, F., & Tariq, N. (2024). Use of social media in tourism promotion and tourists' intentions: An innovation diffusion approach. *Journal of Media Studies and Entrepreneurship*, *14*, 228–473.
Singh, G. K. (2024). The role of tourism education and awareness in tourism promotion: A critical review of the strategies of the government of India. *International Journal of Research Publications and Seminars*, *15*(1), 1–97.
Tajin, S., & Mubarak, S. (2024). Digital influencers as a mechanism for tourism promotion in Algeria: An analytical study of a selected group of tourism channels on YouTube. *Journal of Financial Transactions Review*, *9*(2), 44950–44973.
UNESCO. (2022). *Index of UNESCO IT terminology guide*. King Salman Humanitarian Aid and Relief Center.
Vioralba, V., & Durjana, V. (2024). Digital marketing and its importance in tourism promotion "The case of Southern Albania". *Mediterranean Journal of Social Sciences*, *15*(2), 2039–2117.

Chapter 31

Social Responsibility of Saudi Energy Companies and Its Relationship to Achieving Electronic Reputation Goals: An Applied Study

Mohammed I. Al-Zahrani

Equestrian Authority, Saudi Arabia

Abstract

This study examines the role of corporate social responsibility (CSR) in enhancing the digital reputation of Saudi energy companies, focusing on how various CSR dimensions contribute to building trust, engagement, and a positive organizational image across digital platforms. It also explores the relationship between CSR initiatives and digital audience perceptions, emphasizing their contribution to achieving strategic communication objectives.

Adopting a descriptive–analytical approach, the study analyzed data from previous research, corporate reports, and field surveys. The sample included leading Saudi energy corporations such as Aramco and SABIC, providing insights into CSR strategies and their impact on digital reputation indicators.

Findings reveal that CSR initiatives significantly strengthen corporate digital reputation by fostering community loyalty and promoting positive engagement on digital platforms. Transparent, sustainable CSR practices were found to improve public trust and satisfaction, while investments in digital CSR programs—such as environmental sustainability and e-learning initiatives—enhanced alignment between social responsibility and organizational strategy.

The study recommends developing integrated CSR strategies that reflect evolving digital audience expectations and employing modern communication tools to increase public awareness of CSR activities. It also highlights

Digital Dialogues, 307–316

doi:10.1108/978-1-83708-686-320261031

the importance of periodically assessing the digital impact of CSR efforts to identify areas for continuous improvement and sustain long-term reputational growth.

Keywords: Corporate social responsibility; digital reputation; energy companies; Saudi Arabia; sustainability; digital engagement

Introduction

In the modern world, institutions have undergone radical transformations that have pushed them to reconsider their methods and objectives, leading to the establishment of corporate social responsibility (CSR) as a vital artery for the sustainability of companies and their positive impact on communities. Today, companies are competing to adopt innovative strategies that go beyond merely achieving financial profits, aiming instead to become pillars in promoting sustainable development, protecting the environment, and achieving social balance. This shift is a direct result of the growing global awareness of the environmental and social challenges facing societies, and the crucial role of the private sector in effectively and responsibly addressing these challenges.

CSR supports a comprehensive vision that seeks to improve the quality of life, not only by providing outstanding products and services but also by contributing to building a better future. Socially responsible companies are based on a deep understanding of the needs of their surrounding communities, responding to these needs through practical initiatives that range from supporting education, improving healthcare, and protecting natural resources to empowering marginalized groups. This commitment is a fundamental element in strengthening the relationship between companies and communities, as it establishes trust and enhances the companies' position as forces supporting human development.

CSR interacts with the rapid technological advancement that has reshaped the concept of corporate reputation. Companies are now required to communicate directly with a wide digital audience that can assess their performance and contributions in real time. This digital audience does not simply observe the outcomes of CSR but also helps shape new expectations that push companies toward transparency and innovation. These transformations are reflected in how companies manage their digital reputation, which has become a key criterion for assessing the success of organizations in fulfilling their social commitments.

Leading companies today recognize that CSR is no longer merely an ethical choice or a means to enhance their public image but has become a strategic investment that enhances their long-term competitiveness. By committing to CSR, companies create a sustainable work environment that encourages innovation, attracts talent, and enhances customer loyalty. They also contribute to stimulating innovation by providing practical solutions to social issues, which strengthens their ability to compete in markets characterized by rapid changes and growing demands.

This shift toward CSR is a direct response to the profound changes taking place in societies, whether in addressing environmental challenges such as climate change or social issues like inequality in opportunities and resources. These challenges oblige companies to take bold steps and comprehensive initiatives that contribute to achieving sustainable development, where success is no longer measured only by revenue but by the positive and lasting impact on the communities in which they operate.

Within this framework, partnerships between various sectors play a central role in strengthening CSR. Companies collaborate with governments, non-profit organizations, and local communities to develop comprehensive initiatives that effectively address complex issues. This cooperation reflects the companies' commitment to working as an integral part of the social fabric, striving for real and sustainable change that goes beyond individual achievements to reach a level of collective impact.

CSR motivates companies to adopt innovative practices based on human values and integrates economic objectives with social and environmental dimensions. This integrated approach makes CSR an integral part of the business strategy, where it is translated into tangible actions that make a real difference in people's lives and promote environmental sustainability. As global challenges escalate, companies' commitment to CSR becomes a necessity rather than an option, positioning them at the forefront of global efforts to balance economic growth with sustainable development.

Concept of CSR

The concept of CSR dates back to 1953 and has gained significant attention from academic researchers and international organizations due to the impact that institutions can have on their internal and external environments through influencing the behavior of various stakeholders. CSR has established recognized principles at the international level, emphasizing that a company's responsibility is defined by its social performance and the benefits it brings to society. The corporate charter encourages the adoption, activation, and support of a set of principles and values, including human rights, labor standards, environmental protection, and anti-corruption.

This is also supported by the World Business Council for Sustainable Development, which emphasizes that CSR involves a continuous commitment by business institutions to ethical behavior, as well as contributions to economic development and improving the quality of life for employees, local communities, and society at large. The theory of CSR refers to the obligation of an enterprise to the society in which it operates through the contribution of a wide range of social activities that society needs, leading to the strengthening of state pillars and achieving sustainable economic development. In this context, the media plays a supportive role for the government rather than criticizing it. Despite the clear differences between the various definitions of CSR, it can be defined as the voluntary commitment of the business sector to its employees, the community in which it operates, and the surrounding environment, by contributing to a wide array of social activities of a human and social nature. The scope and importance of this sector have expanded due to the crucial role it plays, especially given the limited capacities of the government in some developing countries (Salah, 2022).

Digital Reputation Concept

Digital reputation is defined as the general impression or mental image that the public forms about an organization, company, or individual through the information available online and on social media platforms. It is considered an extension of traditional reputation, but with added dynamism and speed due to the continuous and immediate interaction between organizations and the public through digital media (Dijkmans et al., 2015).

Digital reputation is built through several factors, including the quality of digital content provided by the company, the level of transparency in dealings with the public, and the ability to respond quickly to crises. Moreover, the company's tangible actions, such as social and environmental initiatives, play a significant role in forming a positive image with the public, especially if documented and shared in innovative and engaging ways (Kaplan & Haenlein, 2010).

One important aspect of digital reputation is its direct impact on a company's success. Studies show that companies with a positive digital reputation attract customers easily, maintain their loyalty, and enhance investor confidence. Additionally, digital reputation is considered a vital tool in improving market competitiveness, as it presents the company as a leader committed to human values and social responsibility (Jones et al., 2018).

In the energy sector, digital reputation emerges as a critical factor in building public trust, especially with the environmental and social challenges associated with this sector. Companies can use social media platforms to showcase their social and environmental responsibility initiatives, contributing to improving their public image and reinforcing their commitment to sustainable development. Studies indicate that customers have become more aware of corporate practices, evaluating them based on available online information, making digital reputation an indispensable tool (Aula, 2010).

Challenges Faced by Companies in Building Digital Reputation

In the digital age, companies face a range of complex challenges when striving to build a strong digital reputation. These challenges arise from technological advancements, the rapid dissemination of information, and changing customer expectations, making digital reputation building a dynamic process that requires well-thought-out and sustainable strategies.

One of the most significant challenges is managing information and rumors. In the digital environment, information can spread rapidly, whether it is true or false. Negative news or rumors about a company can significantly impact its digital image, as correcting misconceptions after they have spread is often difficult. Such situations require a quick and effective response across social media channels and digital platforms, but managing this type of crisis demands an experienced team and clear strategies.

Another challenge is the diversity and variation in audience expectations. Customers and target audiences come from different cultural and social backgrounds, which means that what is considered positive or acceptable for one group may not be so for others. Building a digital reputation requires taking this diversity into account, ensuring that the messages and values the company reflects align with the expectations of both the general and local audiences (Kaplan & Haenlein, 2010).

Cybersecurity breaches and security threats also pose a significant challenge. If a company experiences a cyberattack that leads to the leakage of customer data or sensitive information, it can severely affect its digital reputation. Customers become less trusting of the company if they feel their data are not secure, requiring companies to invest in information security systems and strengthen their cybersecurity infrastructure (Aula, 2010).

Challenges Faced by Companies in Implementing CSR

Companies face numerous challenges when implementing CSR initiatives, especially in the complex and diverse demands of today's market. Despite the significant importance of CSR in enhancing a company's reputation and promoting sustainable development, its implementation is not without obstacles. These challenges can be categorized into several main areas, including financial, administrative, cultural, and regulatory aspects.

Financial Challenges

The costs associated with CSR programs are among the most prominent obstacles faced by companies, especially small and medium-sized businesses. These programs often require significant financial resources for long-term projects, such as environmental conservation, supporting education, improving working conditions, and providing humanitarian aid. For some companies, balancing the allocation of these resources with achieving adequate profits to sustain operational activities can be difficult (Carroll & Shabana, 2010). Additionally, the lack of immediate financial returns from these programs creates a further barrier, prompting many companies to reconsider their prioritization of CSR efforts.

Administrative and Organizational Challenges

Many companies suffer from weak administrative structures dedicated to CSR management. The absence of a clear and integrated strategy for implementing CSR leads to fragmented efforts and a lack of desired results. Additionally, executives often face difficulty convincing all levels of management about the necessity of integrating CSR into the company's overall strategy. This requires a shift in corporate culture and a redefinition of goals and priorities (Waddock, 2004).

Lack of Awareness and Knowledge

A major challenge faced by companies is the lack of awareness regarding the importance of CSR and how to effectively implement it. In some cases, CSR is viewed merely as a promotional activity rather than a strategic commitment. This narrow understanding leads to CSR initiatives being limited to short-term marketing campaigns, reducing their impact on the community and the environment (Visser, 2010).

Resistance to Cultural Change

Companies face cultural resistance, both internally and externally. Employees, for example, may resist the shift toward a CSR culture unless there are awareness and training programs that emphasize its role and significance. On a societal level, CSR initiatives may encounter cultural or social barriers that hinder their acceptance or support, particularly in environments that lack awareness of CSR concepts (Kotler & Lee, 2005).

Legal and Regulatory Challenges

Some companies struggle due to the absence of a clear legal and regulatory framework outlining CSR standards and requirements. This lack of clarity results in inconsistencies in CSR commitment levels among companies and makes it difficult for regulatory bodies to monitor their social performance. On the other hand, stringent regulations may impose additional costs on companies and limit their flexibility in designing CSR programs that align with their business objectives (Porter & Kramer, 2011).

The Importance of CSR

CSR is one of the key pillars for enhancing the role of companies in society, providing a model that demonstrates organizations' commitment to achieving goals that go beyond financial profit to include positive impacts on the environment, community, and economy. The importance of CSR has increased in the modern era due to social and economic changes that have forced companies to play a larger role in addressing societal and environmental challenges.

Achieving Sustainable Development

CSR contributes to sustainable development through initiatives aimed at improving quality of life and promoting environmental sustainability. For instance, by reducing carbon emissions, using renewable energy sources, and supporting environmental projects, companies help preserve natural resources for future generations, which is a crucial part of balancing economic growth with environmental protection (Carroll & Shabana, 2010).

Enhancing Company Image and Reputation

CSR initiatives reflect companies' commitment to human values, which enhances their positive image and increases their reputation among customers, investors, and society at large. Companies that show strong commitment to social and environmental issues are often seen as more credible and attractive, helping them stand out in competitive markets (Bhattacharya et al., 2008).

Increasing Customer Loyalty

Today's customers tend to support companies that demonstrate a genuine commitment to social and environmental issues. By implementing CSR programs, companies can build stronger relationships with their customers, as they feel proud to associate with companies that support humanitarian and community causes (Kotler & Lee, 2005).

Motivating Employees and Increasing Productivity

CSR not only influences external relationships but also impacts internal relationships. Employees feel more satisfied and loyal when working in an environment that supports human values and demonstrates a commitment to CSR. This enhances their job satisfaction and motivates them to work more efficiently (Glavas & Piderit, 2009).

Attracting Investment and Strengthening Partnerships

Companies that show a genuine commitment to CSR become more attractive to investors looking for investment opportunities in businesses that balance financial goals with social responsibility. Strategic partnerships between companies with a shared focus on CSR contribute to innovation and achieving shared goals (Porter & Kramer, 2011).

Regulatory Compliance and Risk Mitigation

CSR helps companies comply with international standards and regulations related to human rights, environmental practices, and decent work. By adhering to these standards, companies can reduce potential legal and financial risks associated with irresponsible practices (Waddock, 2004).

The Integration of Digital Reputation and CSR for Achieving Sustainable Development

The integration of digital reputation and CSR is one of the essential pillars that organizations rely on to achieve sustainable development in the modern era. Amid rapid digital transformations, digital reputation has become a pivotal tool for influencing public perceptions and building trust between organizations and communities. This integration is not merely a strategic option but a necessity to ensure a comprehensive balance between economic, social, and environmental goals, which are the core of sustainable development (Porter & Kramer, 2011).

Digital reputation depends on the mental image that is created from the information shared about an organization through digital platforms. In this context, CSR plays a key role in shaping this reputation, as community and environmental initiatives reflect the organization's commitment to societal issues, thereby enhancing its credibility and attractiveness. When CSR is integrated with digital means, these initiatives become clearer and more effective, enabling organizations to communicate directly and transparently with their audience, which leads to increased trust among customers and investors (Dijkmans et al., 2015).

The integration between digital reputation and CSR is not limited to promoting initiatives but also extends to effectively managing crises. If an organization faces criticism or challenges that affect its reputation, it can use its digital channels to provide quick and transparent responses, demonstrating its commitment to resolving issues and addressing problems in a way that reflects respect for the community. This immediate response is a crucial element in building and maintaining digital reputation, enhancing the organization's standing as a responsible entity capable of tackling challenges (Gorry & Westbrook, 2009).

The integration of digital reputation and CSR represents a strategic pathway that can effectively achieve sustainable development. Organizations that adopt this approach are not only able to improve their financial performance and enhance their competitiveness but also contribute to creating a sustainable environment that meets the needs of the present without compromising the opportunities of future generations. This integration allows organizations to become true partners in building a better future for both society and the environment.

Leveraging CSR to Enhance Digital Reputation

CSR represents an effective strategic tool for enhancing digital reputation, playing a central role in building a positive image for organizations on digital platforms and strengthening their alignment with societal values and expectations. In the current digital age, digital reputation is one of the most important intangible assets for any organization, reflecting public perceptions of its performance, behavior, and values. This makes enhancing it through CSR essential for achieving sustainable success (Porter & Kramer, 2011).

The benefit of CSR in enhancing digital reputation begins with the organization adopting a transparent and solid approach that focuses on meeting community needs, protecting the environment, while ensuring profitability. When companies announce their social initiatives, such as supporting education, improving community infrastructure, or reducing carbon emissions through their digital channels, they enhance their ability to communicate their messages directly and effectively to their audience. This direct communication demonstrates the organization's commitment to the values that matter to society, leading to the building of a strong digital reputation that can withstand challenges (Dijkmans et al., 2015).

Conclusion

CSR highlights a fundamental value of increasing commitment to environmental, social, and economic issues, as a responsibility that is inseparable from the role of companies in achieving sustainable development. This commitment obligates organizations to shift from traditional thinking, which is focused solely on maximizing profits, to a more inclusive perspective that integrates the achievement of economic goals with contributions to societal well-being.

Leading companies enhance their role through innovative strategies aimed at utilizing available resources in ways that promote long-term development. CSR is translated into tangible initiatives that contribute to achieving a sustainable positive impact. Additionally, the growing awareness among the public of the importance of this responsibility acts as a driving force, pushing organizations to adopt more transparent and innovative practices to meet societal expectations and strengthen mutual trust.

Digital reputation plays a central role in framing corporate efforts and endeavors within the scope of CSR, as digital platforms have become a vital window that allows companies to communicate with their audience and enhance their transparency. This reality requires organizations to adapt to technological developments and invest in building a positive image based on sustainability and responsibility, which in turn positively impacts their competitive position in the market.

In light of global challenges such as climate change, increasing population growth, and economic pressures, the role of companies in leading the transition toward sustainable and inclusive solutions becomes even more significant. Responsible organizations embrace business models that focus on innovation, adaptation, and multi-sector partnerships to ensure the achievement of tangible impacts that reflect their role as strategic partners in community development.

References

Aula, P. (2010). Social media, reputation risk, and ambient publicity management. *Strategy & Leadership*, *38*(6), 43–49.

Bhattacharya, C. B., Sen, S., & Korschun, D. (2008). Using corporate social responsibility to win the war for talent. *MIT Sloan Management Review*, *49*(2), 37.

Carroll, A. B., & Shabana, K. M. (2010). The business case for corporate social responsibility: A review of concepts, research, and practice. *International Journal of Management Reviews*, *12*(1), 85–105.

Dijkmans, C., Kerkhof, P., & Beukeboom, C. J. (2015). A stage to engage: Social media use and corporate reputation. *Tourism Management*, *47*, 58–67.

Elkington, J. (1997). *Cannibals with forks: The triple bottom line of 21st century business*. Capstone Publishing.

Glavas, A., & Piderit, S. K. (2009). How does doing good matter? Effects of corporate citizenship on employees. *The Journal of Corporate Citizenship*, *36*, 51–70.

Gorry, G. A., & Westbrook, R. A. (2009). Winning the internet confidence game. *Corporate Reputation Review*, *12*(3), 195–203.

Jones, B., Temperley, J., & Lima, A. (2018). Corporate reputation in the era of Web 2.0: The case of Primark. *Journal of Marketing Management*, *35*(9–10), 1–20.

Kaplan, A. M., & Haenlein, M. (2010). Users of the world, unite! The challenges and opportunities of social media. *Business Horizons*, *53*(1), 59–68.

Kotler, P., & Lee, N. (2005). *Corporate social responsibility: Doing the most good for your company and your cause*. Wiley.

Porter, M. E., & Kramer, M. R. (2011). Creating shared value. *Harvard Business Review*, *89*(1/2), 62–77.

Salah, W. (2022). Communication ways in digital platforms for corporate social responsibility and their role in managing social dialogue and achieving sustainable development goals. *The Egyptian Journal of Media Research*, *2022*(80), 1685–1714.

Visser, W. (2010). CSR 2.0: The evolution and revolution of corporate social responsibility. In *Responsible business* (pp. 311–328). Wiley.

Waddock, S. (2004). Parallel universes: Companies, academics, and the progress of corporate citizenship. *Business and Society Review*, *109*(1), 5–42.

Chapter 32

Members of the Legislative Authority and the Public in the Kingdom of Bahrain Rely on Social Media as a Source of Information on Legislative Issues

Khalid Ali Hadi Ali AlSayyadi[a] *and Maha Hameed Alanezi*[b]

[a]Ahlia University, Bahrain
[b]Ministry of Education, Bahrain

Abstract

This study examines the role of social networks as sources of information on legislative issues in the Kingdom of Bahrain, focusing on their impact on both members of the legislature and the general public. The research highlights that platforms such as Instagram have become key channels for exchanging opinions and legislative information, fostering dialogue between the National Council and citizens. Social networks facilitate public engagement in decision-making, enhance transparency, and promote community participation.

However, these platforms face challenges, including the spread of disinformation, difficulty in verifying sources, and public pressures that may influence legislative decisions. Prior studies indicate an increasing reliance on social media as a major information source across health, social, and political domains. These studies demonstrate the positive role of social media in raising awareness, promoting engagement, and supporting informed participation during crises, such as the COVID-19 pandemic. They also reveal a complex relationship between social media dependence and trust, noting variations in the perceived credibility of content.

The findings underscore the dual nature of social networks: while they enhance civic participation and dialogue, they also require careful navigation to prevent misinformation and enhance content validation. The study emphasizes the importance of guiding users toward conscious,

Digital Dialogues, 317–324

doi:10.1108/978-1-83708-686-320261032

systematic, and responsible use of social media to maximize its benefits in legislative and political communication.

Keywords: Social media sites; members of the legislature; public; source of information; legislative issues; civic engagement; information credibility

Introduction

Social networking is a form of media that has seen increased use in the last 10 years and has become one of the basics essential for young people in particular and other groups in general. Social networks are pages and platforms that allow interaction and sharing with others, creating a virtual community composed of individuals chosen by the user.

The legislative authority is the authority that carries out the tasks of legislation, enacting laws, and imposing control and accountability over the rest of the authorities, such as the executive authority and the judiciary. In the Kingdom of Bahrain, the legislative authority consists of the National Assembly, which includes the Shura Council (comprising 40 members appointed by the King of the country) and the House of Representatives, which consists of 40 members freely elected by the people.

With the continuous development of technology and the widespread use of social networks, these networks play an important role in shaping public opinion and disseminating information. In the Kingdom of Bahrain, members of the legislature and the public increasingly rely on social media as a primary source of information on legislative issues. This shift has profound implications for decision-making processes and democracy itself.

There is a significant amount of political activity on social networks in general and on the Instagram platform in particular, where pages specializing in legislative affairs share updates on this subject. Different topics related to legislative issues are presented and discussed by the public and by some members of the legislative authority.

Social networks are increasingly important as a means of conveying information and exchanging views in the Kingdom of Bahrain, and they help to expand public dialogue on legislative issues and monitor different perspectives. At the same time, however, the phenomenon poses many challenges, including identifying sources of correct and reliable information, and addressing the spread of false and misleading information along with its impact on decision-making and democracy.

Social media has a huge impact on all aspects of life, including politics and legislation. Among the parties that have been significantly affected by this development are members of the legislative body in the Kingdom of Bahrain and the public. The 80 members of the National Assembly (Shura Council and House of Representatives) rely on social media as an additional source of information on legislative issues, while the public uses these networks to communicate and exchange opinions and information on legal and political issues.

The study's problem arises from the following question: To what extent do members of the legislature and the public in the Kingdom of Bahrain rely on social media as a source of information on legislative issues, and how does this dependence affect the decision-making process?

Theoretical Framework

Social Networks

The main idea of a social network is to collect data from members who subscribe to a website and publish these data publicly, so that members with common interests, who are looking for files, photos, etc., can connect. It can be said that it is an effective network of sites dedicated to promoting social life among a group of acquaintances and friends. It also enables old friends to reconnect, and, years later, communicate visually and vocally, share photos, and perform other functions. This strengthens the social relationships between them.

Social networks, also known as online networking systems, allow subscribers to create their own sites and then connect with other members who share similar interests and hobbies through electronic social media systems (Abdul Moneim, 2013, p. 291).

Types of Social Networks

Social media networks can be classified into several types, based on the primary purpose of their use:

- Public social networks, such as Facebook and Twitter, are used for public social communication and the sharing of ideas, images, and news among users.
- Professional networks, such as LinkedIn, aim to build professional relationships, share experiences, and search for employment opportunities.
- Visual networks and visual content, such as Instagram and YouTube, are used to share photos and videos, making them ideal for businesses that rely on visual content.
- Specialized networks, such as Goodreads and discussion forums, focus on specific topics or interests, such as literature or technology.
- Local community networks are used to coordinate local activities and events.

Members of the Legislative Authority

It is a body composed of a group of persons who draft legislative laws in order to achieve democracy among the people. The members of the legislature shall be representatives of the people as a whole and shall be vested with unique powers not granted to others, as part of their responsibilities. These responsibilities include:

- They enact laws, develop government budgets.
- Approving executive appointments (in some countries), each according to the relevant constitutional provisions,
- Ratifying treaties.
- Investigating the conduct of administrative bodies.
- Prosecuting members of the executive and judicial bodies, and dismissing them if necessary.
- Addressing complaints and constituent issues.
- Reviewing financial allocations.
- Levying and collecting taxes.

Types of Legislative Powers

Elected bodies: The House of Representatives' members are elected by the people in free elections. **Appointed bodies**: Advisory Council members are appointed by His Majesty the King.

Powers of Members of the Legislative Authority

- Drafting and amending laws that regulate the lives of citizens.
- Oversight and accountability: Monitoring the performance of the executive branch and ensuring transparency and accountability.
- Approving budgets: Reviewing and approving government budgets.
- Ratification of conventions and treaties: Ensuring that foreign policies are in line with the interests of the state.
- Discussing public complaints, considering citizens' issues, and finding effective solutions to them.

Definition of Legislative Issues

Legislative issues refer to topics and questions that require the intervention of the legislature to formulate laws or make decisions that affect society. These issues are often related to public policies, human rights, and economic and social laws.

The Relationship Between Social Networks and the Legislative Authority

The Positive Effects

- **Enhancing transparency**: Social networks contribute to improving the transparency of legislative work by disseminating information about laws and parliamentary deliberations.
- **Interaction with the public**: Enables members to communicate directly with citizens and listen to their opinions.
- **Awareness raising**: Contributes to raising public awareness of legislative issues and public policies.

Audience

An audience is defined as a group of individuals who influence and understand each other because of common characteristics and goals, and as a group with a particular psychological and emotional state. They are those who **see themselves** as a group of individuals who temporarily share common values, unite, and feel similar emotions.

The audience can be classified based on several criteria, including interests, geographic location, interaction, or the means used to reach it.

- **General audience**: Includes all individuals in the community without specifying an age or social group, such as the audience of national media channels.
- **Target audience**: Determined based on specific characteristics such as age, interests, or geographic location. It is usually used in advertising or awareness campaigns.
- **Specialist audience**: Consists of individuals with an interest in or in-depth knowledge of a particular field, such as engineers or doctors.
- **Virtual audience**: An audience made up of Internet users and social media sites. It is a dynamic and constantly changing audience.
- **Local Audience**: Refers to individuals who live in a specific geographical area and are interested in local issues.
- **International Audience**: It consists of individuals or groups from different countries around the world and is influenced by global or local issues that are gaining international attention.

Previous Studies

Tahat and Al-Samadi, 2022: "The Jordanian Public's Reliance on Citizen Journalism as a Source of Information on Issues of Social Violence."

The study aimed to identify the dependence of the Jordanian public on citizen journalism as a source of information on issues of social violence. This descriptive study, which was based on the survey methodology, involved 400 individuals from the study community, represented by the Jordanian public. To achieve the objectives of the study, the researchers adopted the questionnaire as a tool for data collection.

The study found that the Jordanian public follows citizen journalism at a low rate of 59.8% and relies on it as a source of information on issues of social violence with an average score of 53.7%. The study showed that the most prominent forms of citizen journalism to which the Jordanian public is exposed are social media sites (Facebook, Instagram, Snapchat, TikTok). The study found that the most important reasons for the Jordanian public's dependence on citizen journalism are the ease of using it, followed by the speed at which it transmits news, information, and various issues related to social violence.

The results revealed that the most important challenges facing the researchers in relying on citizen journalism are the lack of training on its use and the lack of follow-up to the technical developments related to it. The study showed the existence of cognitive, emotional, and behavioral effects resulting from relying on citizen journalism as a source of information on issues of social violence, to an average degree. The results revealed a strong and statistically significant relationship between the degree of Jordanian public reliance on citizen journalism and their confidence in it as a source of information on issues of social violence.

Arab Study and Murabati (2022): "The Adoption of University Students on Social Media as a Source of Information."

The study aimed to reveal the extent of university students' reliance on the Facebook site as a source of information by monitoring the interest and follow-up of university students on the content presented on Facebook. It also sought to determine the type of topics students follow and how they engage with them in the research sample.

This study was conducted at the University of Kasdi Merbah Ouargla through a field study of a purposive and specific male and female sample consisting of 50 participants. It focused on students from the Department of Information and Communication and the second cohort. The study was based on a descriptive approach and used a questionnaire as a tool for data collection.

The study reached a number of conclusions, the most important of which are:

- Students at the University of Kasdi Merbah rely on Facebook as a source of information.
- Facebook provides content and information for college students.
- Students at the University of Kasdi Merbah Ouargla rely on Facebook as a source of information because of its ease of access and the speed at which information is transmitted.
- There is a relationship between the degree of the university students' reliance on Facebook and their trust in this network to transmit information.

Dabba Study (2022): "Saudi Youth's Reliance on Social Media to Get Information about the Latest Health Situation".

The study aimed to identify the extent of Saudi youth's dependence on social media as a source of information about the latest health situation. The survey methodology was used, employing a questionnaire tool applied to a purposive sample of 215 Saudi youth in Jeddah. The study reached many results, most notably:

- Saudi youth rely heavily on social media as a source of information about the latest health situation, with 62.79% of respondents indicating reliance.
- Twitter was the leading social media site that respondents relied on to get updates about health status.
- More than 54.88% of respondents use social media to get information about their health status, followed by 25.11% of those using it to protect themselves and their families from viruses and epidemics.

Jiang et al. (2022): "The Reliance on Social Media and Its Correlation with People's Space-Time Mappings".

The study aimed to find out the causal relationship between the experience of using social media and its link to time and space in the audience. It is necessary to discuss this relationship from other cultural aspects. Social media dependence has become an integral part of culture nowadays. The relationship between social media dependence and the connection to time and space was measured using a questionnaire as a research tool. Studies have shown that an intense focus on social media or thoughts directed toward the past leads to more severe negative moods. Over time, as outlined earlier in this study, in the public's tendency to have more future-oriented ideas during the *pregnancy* experience.

Neely et al. (2021): "Health Information Seeking Behaviors on Social Media During the COVID-19 Pandemic Among American Social Networking Site Users: Survey Study."

The study of 1,003 US.-based adults aimed to better understand how healthy consumers use social media to learn and stay informed about the COVID-19 pandemic, how they rely on reliable scientific sources of information, and how they did verify information about the epidemic?

A web-based survey was conducted using a sample purchased through an industry-leading market research provider. The results were reported with a confidence level of 95% and a margin of error of 3%. Among the participants were 1,003 adults residing in the United States (whose ages total 218 years). Participants were selected through a class quota sampling approach to ensure that the sample represented the US population. Balanced quotas (by region of the country) were determined by gender, age, and race.

The results showed significant social media dependency during the COVID-19 pandemic. More than three-quarters of respondents reported having relied on social media at least "slightly," and 59.2% of respondents indicated that they had read information about the corona virus on social media at least once a week. According to the findings, most social media users are unlikely to validate what they see online with a health professional, despite high levels of distrust of the accuracy of corona virus-related information on social media.

Conclusion

Most studies have relied on media dependency theory as the theoretical framework for previous research. Most of the previous studies were based on quantitative surveys and descriptive methods. Previous studies have relied on the questionnaire as a data collection tool.

Previous studies have also shown that there is a rise in the rates of exposure to social media in relation to what is discussed on social media networks regarding legislative issues and the ways members of the legislative authority can benefit from the content presented on these platforms.

Study (Tahat & Al-Samadi, 2022): This study sheds light on the Jordanian public's reliance on citizen journalism to obtain information on issues of social violence. It reveals challenges such as the lack of training in using these tools and the failure to follow technological developments.

Study (Arabic & Murabati, 2022): This study highlights the adoption of Facebook by university students in Algeria as a source of information, emphasizing faster access to information.

Study (Denba, 2022): This study highlights the importance of social networking sites for Saudi youth in obtaining information about the health situation. It also illustrates the preference for using Twitter as the main source of information.

Saleh Study (2016): This study highlights the use of social media by university youth in Jordan and its impact on political and social awareness.

Jiang et al. (2022): This study focuses on the relationship between social media use and its connection to time and space. The study shows that excessive focus on social media and thoughts directed toward the past may lead to more severe negative moods, highlighting the importance of balancing the use of these platforms.

Neely et al. (2021): This study shows the importance of social media in conveying information about important events, such as the COVID-19 pandemic. However, it also points to the challenges related to users' confidence in the authenticity of this information.

Social media is used for political information but also emphasizes the need to consider the credibility of information circulating through these platforms.

References

Arabic References

Arabi, S., & Merabti, H. (2022). *University students' reliance on social media as a source of information*. Kasdi Merbah University.

Denba, F. (2022). The reliance of Saudi youth on social media to obtain information about health developments. *Al-Hikma Journal for Media and Communication Studies*, *10*(3).

Tahat, Z., & Al-Samadi, Y. (2022). The Jordanian public's reliance on citizen journalism as a source of information on issues of social violence. *The Scientific Journal of Journalism Research*, *24*(2).

Foreign References

Jiang, H., Wang, X., & Li, X. (2022). The reliance on social media and its correlation with people's space-time mappings. In *Proceedings of the 2022 international conference on social sciences and humanities and arts (SSHA 2022)*. https://www.atlantis-press.com/proceedings/ssha-22/125972510

Neely, S., Eldredge, C., & Sanders, R. (2021). Health information seeking behaviors on social media during the COVID-19 pandemic among American social networking site users: Survey study. *Journal of Medical Internet Research*, *23*(6). https://www.jmir.org/2021/6/e29802/